P9-BIH-983

Us versus Them

DOUGLAS LITTLE

Us versus Them

The United States, Radical Islam,
and the Rise of the Green Threat

The University of North Carolina Press *Chapel Hill*

© 2016 The University of North Carolina Press
All rights reserved

Set in Arno by codeMantra
Manufactured in the United States of America

The University of North Carolina Press has been a member of the
Green Press Initiative since 2003.

Jacket illustrations: "Osama Meets a B-52," Air Force leaflet ADF03a,
from Operation Enduring Freedom, October 2001, U.S. Department
of Defense; translation from Dari (top), "It is not possible to escape
or hide." Earth image, © antartis/123RF Stock Photo.

Library of Congress Cataloging-in-Publication Data
Little, Douglas, 1950–
Us versus them : the United States, radical Islam, and the rise of the green threat /
Douglas Little.
    pages cm
Includes bibliographical references and index.
ISBN 978-1-4696-2680-2 (cloth : alk. paper) — ISBN 978-1-4696-2681-9 (ebook)
1. Cold War. 2. Islamophobia—United States. 3. United States—Relations—Middle East.
4. Middle East—Relations—United States. I. Title.
DS63.2.U5L59 2016
327.73056—dc23
2015031953

This book is for all the Clarkies I have taught since 1978.

There have been few dull moments.

Fiat Lux!

When I was coming up, it was a dangerous world, and you knew exactly what they were. It was us versus them, and it was clear who them was. Today, we are not so sure who the they are, but we know they're there.

—George W. Bush, campaign speech, 21 January 2000

We are the sole superpower in the world. We remain the one indispensable nation. There's no issue in which our leadership is not critical. . . . The biggest impediment to American leadership is not external. The thing that's gonna hold us back is gonna be us. And if we make good decisions then we will continue to be not only the dominant power but a benevolent force around the world.

—Barack Obama, interview, 8 August 2014

Contents

Maps

Acknowledgments

Writing a book is solitary work, but making a book is a group effort. This project actually began five years ago in my seminar on America and the Middle East, when three undergraduates ignored my warning that there were too few primary sources to do real research on the U.S. response to radical Islam since 1989 and proceeded to write excellent papers on the Clinton and Bush administrations. Not only was I impressed, I was inspired. When I taught the seminar again in 2014, I had the class read the first draft of *Us versus Them*. Everyone liked everything except the chapter on the Bush Doctrine, which most found overly harsh on America's forty-third president (a rare sentiment here at Clark). I took their advice and toned it down. Two graduate students, Austin Alexander and Mike Bocco, unearthed important documents from the 1970s during their research at the Carter Library in Atlanta. A third, Erin Redihan, nodded when I drew parallels between the Red and Green Threats, while a fourth, Lauren Cyr, helped with fact-checking and the index. These undergraduate and graduate students are just the latest in a long line of Clarkies—almost all of them square pegs in round holes—who have kept me on my toes for nearly forty years and to whom this book is dedicated.

As my interest in the Muslim world deepened over the years, I have benefited from conversations with John Esposito, Bob Vitalis, Jim Goode, and, more recently, Juan Cole, all of whom know the region far better than I and all of whom will cringe at some of the oversimplifications I have made in the introduction. Believe me, guys, I really was listening. Four historians doing pathbreaking work on U.S. foreign policy in the Middle East—Roham Alvandi, Paul Chamberlin, Ann Heiss, and Salim Yaqub—traded ideas with me and compared research notes. Clea Hupp and Margaret Manchester invited me to share my preliminary findings in Little Rock and Providence. George Billias, who published a prize-winning book not long after his ninetieth birthday, urged me not to let my relative youth stand in the way of *Us versus Them*. Anne Gibson not only made the maps but came up with a cartographic way to visualize the surge of radical Islam after 1989. Steve Rabe, my SHAFR roommate and frequent partner in crime, pointed out similarities between the Red Threat in Latin America and the Green Threat in the Middle East and teased me mercilessly when his Giants knocked my Packers out of the Super Bowl not once but twice.

And then there were those who actually read the manuscript. Drew McCoy gave chapter 1 the once-over and pointed out that monarchism was the ur-ideology that gave U.S. policy makers nightmares long before Josef Stalin or Osama Bin Laden arrived on the scene. Paul Ropp read the chapters on Dubya and Obama, sharpening my analysis of the war on terror, but also suggesting that I keep my inner Lewis Black in check and dial back my criticism of both administrations. Walt LaFeber gave chapters 5 and 6 remarkably careful scrutiny, pressing me for greater clarity and precision, reminding me always to remember my audience, and reassuring me that "contagement," although neither pretty nor alliterative, was a useful way to describe Obama's approach to the Middle East. Frank Costigliola and Peter Hahn read the entire manuscript and suggested where to smooth out the rough patches, how best to highlight the trajectory of America's evolving post–Cold War national security strategy, and when to trim the purple prose.

We historians could not do what we do without help from librarians and archivists. Here at Clark, I was supported by Goddard Library's splendid reference staff—Rachael Shea, Ed McDermott, Holly Hawes, and Anthony Penny. At the Reagan Library in Simi Valley, Jennifer Mandel kept the NSC files coming and saved the day by overnighting the hard-copy key to 1,500 digital images that I had inadvertently left behind in the research room. Rachael Altman at the Bush Library in College Station guided me through stacks of declassified materials and gallantly retrieved my laptop and digital camera from the research room after a bomb threat shut down the entire Texas A&M campus on short notice a few hours before my scheduled departure. David Langbart, an old friend and archivist extraordinaire, filled my in-box with hard-to-find documents, tutored me on the CIA's amazing CREST declassified database at College Park, and led me to the best Burmese food inside the Beltway.

I am also grateful for those who helped with little things along the way that have made a big difference on this project. Nehama and Yigal Ne'eman ensured that my stay in Israel in 2001 was pleasant and productive. Allison Hodgkins and Arafat Karoute made sure that my visit to Jordan eleven years later was memorable. Herb Friedman provided the high-resolution copy of the U.S. air force propaganda leaflet on the present book's cover, and the University of Massachusetts Translation Center in Amherst deciphered the caption. Diane Fenner, our departmental administrative assistant, got me the photocopies I needed, made sure that nothing was ever lost in the mail, and kept me abreast of the latest rumors on the Clark grapevine.

This is my second book with the University of North Carolina Press. Chuck Grench is truly a writer's editor, providing just enough guidance to keep me from going totally off the rails while giving me the freedom to try out unconventional ideas. The rest of the UNC crew—especially Heidi Perov, Kim Bryant, Jay Mazzocchi, and Iza Wojciechowska—kept the project on schedule and made my job much easier, while Petra Dreiser handled the copyediting with a careful eye and a light touch. I'm delighted that *Us versus Them* will be part of North Carolina's outstanding list of monographs on diplomatic history. It is customary, of course, for authors to absolve their friends, colleagues, and editors from any errors. I'm happy to do that here, and readers who stumble across the inevitable mistakes that mar these pages should realize that somebody somewhere along the way almost certainly tried to prevent me from screwing up.

It is also customary for authors to thank their families. Colin, Lydia, and their two sons, Henry and Raymond, have initiated me into the wonders of grandparenthood. Alison has proven once again that daughters are usually much smarter and always much sassier than their fathers. And forty years on, Pat continues to keep me centered, working her summer magic with the hydrangeas and black-eyed Susans while charming me with her radiant smile. I could not be more grateful.

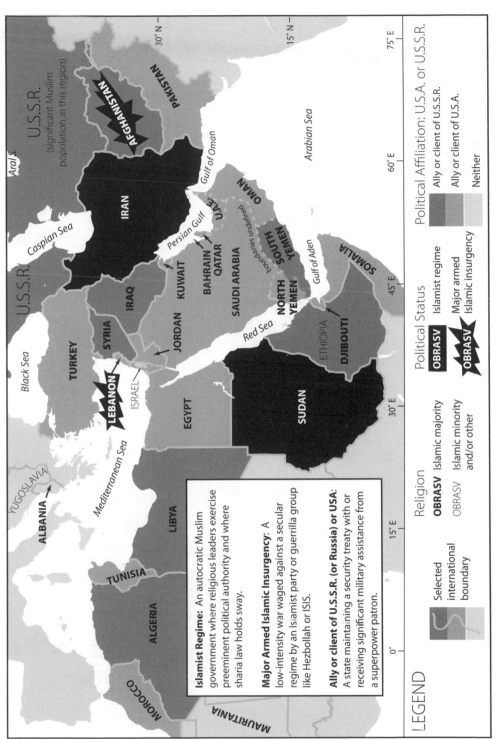

LEGEND

Selected
international
boundary

Religion

OBRASV Islamic majority

OBRASV Islamic minority
and/or other

Political Status

OBRASV Islamist regime

OBRASV Major armed
Islamic insurgency

Political Affiliation: U.S.A. or U.S.S.R.

Ally or client of U.S.S.R.

Ally or client of U.S.A.

Neither

Islamist Regime: An autocratic Muslim government where religious leaders exercise preeminent political authority and where sharia law holds sway.

Major Armed Islamic Insurgency: A low-intensity war waged against a secular regime by an Islamist party or guerrilla group like Hezbollah or ISIS.

Ally or client of U.S.S.R. (or Russia) or USA: A state maintaining a security treaty with or receiving significant military assistance from a superpower patron.

1989: Radical Islam in the Middle East at the End of the Cold War (Map by Anne Gibson)

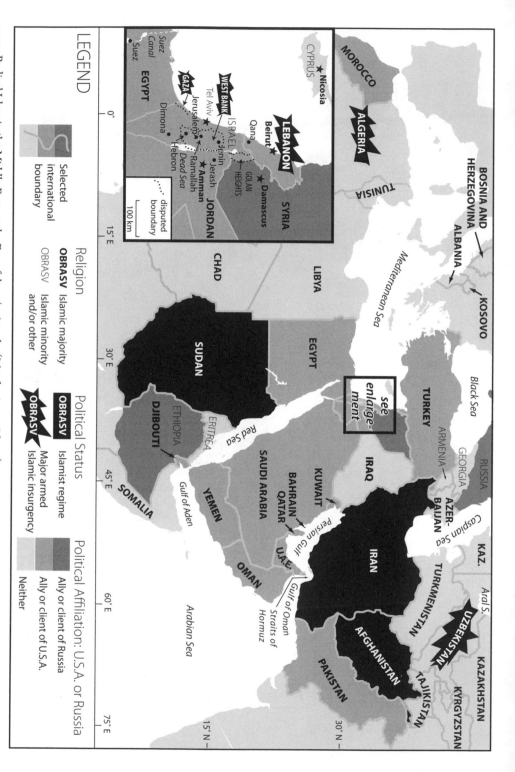

2000: Radical Islam in the Middle East on the Eve of the 9/11 Attacks (Map by Anne Gibson)

LEGEND

Selected international boundary

Religion

OBRASV Islamic majority

OBRASV Islamic minority and/or other

Political Status

OBRASV Islamist regime

OBRASV Major armed Islamic insurgency

Political Affiliation: U.S.A. or Russia

Ally or client of Russia

Ally or client of U.S.A.

Neither

MOROCCO

ALGERIA

TUNISIA

LIBYA

EGYPT

CHAD

SUDAN

DJIBOUTI

ETHIOPIA

ERITREA

SOMALIA

YEMEN

SAUDI ARABIA

OMAN

U.A.E.

QATAR

BAHRAIN

KUWAIT

IRAQ

IRAN

AFGHANISTAN

PAKISTAN

TURKEY

ARMENIA

GEORGIA

AZER-BAIJAN

RUSSIA

KAZAKHSTAN

KAZ.

TURKMENISTAN

UZBEKISTAN

TAJIKISTAN

KYRGYZSTAN

BOSNIA AND HERZEGOVINA

ALBANIA

KOSOVO

Mediterranean Sea

Black Sea

Caspian Sea

Aral S.

Red Sea

Gulf of Aden

Arabian Sea

Gulf of Oman

Straits of Hormuz

Persian Gulf

see enlarge-ment

0°

15° E

30° E

45° E

60° E

75° E

15° N

30° N

CYPRUS
★ Nicosia

EGYPT

Suez
Suez Canal

GAZA

WEST BANK

Tel Aviv
Jerusalem

ISRAEL

Dimona

Hebron

Dead Sea

Ramallah

Amman ★

Jerash ★

Jenin

Qana

Beirut ★

LEBANON

GOLAN HEIGHTS

Damascus ★

SYRIA

JORDAN

disputed boundary

100 km

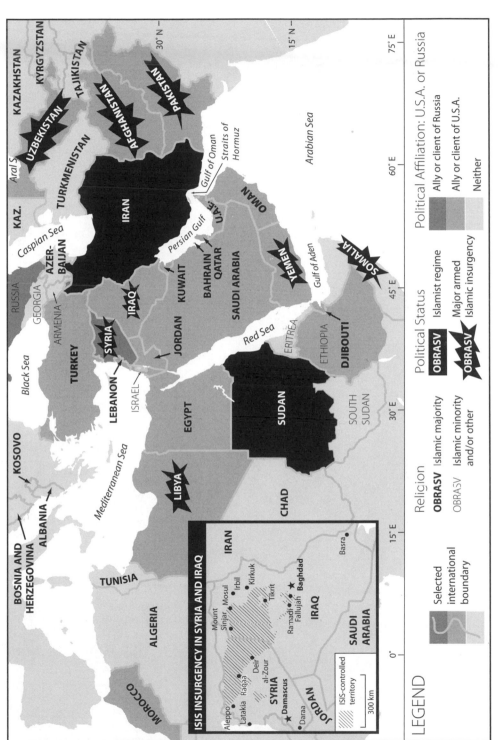

LEGEND

Religion

OBRASV Islamic majority

OBRASV Islamic minority and/or other

Political Status

OBRASV Islamist regime

OBRASV Major armed Islamic insurgency

Political Affiliation: U.S.A. or Russia

Ally or client of Russia

Ally or client of U.S.A.

Neither

Selected international boundary

2015: Radical Islam in the Middle East in the Age of ISIS (Map by Anne Gibson)

The Middle East in 2015 (Map by Anne Gibson)

LEGEND

selected international boundaries, 2015

selected national capitals

100 km

international boundary
disputed boundary

see enlarge-ment

30° E   45° E   60° E   75° E

15° N —

30° N —

Introduction

Us versus Them: America and Islam in the Age of Terror

In March 2012, I found myself on the road in Jordan. Route 35, the King's Highway, snakes north out of Amman through rolling hills and verdant meadows that reminded me a little of Minnesota and Wisconsin, where I grew up. Before long, my Jordanian driver, Arafat, who was named after someone most Americans regarded as a terrorist, pointed out Baqa'a, the Palestinian refugee camp to which his parents had fled following Israel's victory in the June 1967 war. A few minutes later we pulled into Jerash, where Farid, a charming schemer in a keffiyeh who had once worked for a U.S. oil company, gave me a guided tour of the ancient ruins of one of the most important Roman trading centers along the Silk Road to China. Arafat and I briefly toyed with driving another fifty miles up Route 35 to the border with Syria, where a brutal civil war was raging, but we decided to head back to the Jordanian capital instead. Later that afternoon, I sat down for tea with Jawad and Rana, a Muslim couple who were hosting two Clark University undergraduates studying abroad in Amman.

As I checked my e-mail late that night in the lobby of the Hotel Geneva at the end of a long day, I glanced up at the obligatory portrait of Jordan's King Abdullah, a man who preferred Savile Row suits and whose English was reportedly better than his Arabic, and reckoned that at least in this part of the Middle East, people did not seem all that different from Middle Westerners like me. To be sure, Arafat, Farid, Jawad, and Rana were all Muslims, but they had made their peace with America's consumer culture, they hoped for secular democracy, and they were deeply worried by the surge of Islamic extremism enveloping the region. How was it, then, that so many of "us" had come to regard so many of "them" as a menace to our own security and well-being? This book seeks to provide some tentative answers.

Anthropologists and social psychologists analyzing the development of collective identity have long recognized that defining a "negative reference group" often makes for a crucial first step in building solidarity among one's own kin, clan, or tribe. Throughout history, religion has proven an especially powerful marker for distinguishing ourselves from others and for separating us from them. The recent collision between United States and the Muslim world is no exception to this rule. In July 2014, the Pew Research

Center, a nonpartisan think tank specializing in public opinion polling, released "How Americans Feel about Religious Groups." Using survey data collected from more than three thousand adults from every faith and creed, Pew researchers developed a "feeling thermometer" with a hundred-degree scale, where the higher the temperature, the warmer and more positive the attitude toward the group in question. While Protestants, Catholics, and Jews all received temperate scores in the low sixties, Muslims came in dead last at forty, one degree behind atheists. The feeling thermometer for Muslims dipped even lower among Evangelical Christians, where the temperature stood at a frosty thirty, two degrees below freezing.[1] A year earlier, the Pew Center's biennial survey of "Global Attitudes and Trends" had revealed that the Muslims of the Middle East and South Asia reciprocated these negative feelings. The "favorable rating" for the United States ranged from a high of 47 percent in Lebanon to 16 percent in Egypt and the Palestinian Territories to 14 percent in Jordan to just 11 percent in Pakistan. Moreover, when asked whether they viewed America as an enemy, one-third of Jordanians, two-thirds of Pakistanis, and three-quarters of Palestinians replied "yes."[2]

Although religious differences certainly explain some of this mutual animosity, more is at work here than the belief that my God is better than yours. For half a century after 1945, the United States and the Soviet Union were locked in a Cold War, a ferocious ideological struggle for power and influence between capitalist democracy and communist autocracy that reached every corner of the globe. Sometimes that struggle took on quasi-religious overtones, with both American and Russian leaders depicting themselves as noble crusaders in a battle pitting good against evil and us against them. When Gallup pollsters developed what amounted to a primitive version of the Pew Center's feeling thermometer during the late 1940s to assess attitudes toward the Soviet Union, 77 percent of Americans responded that the Kremlin "wants to rule the world," and 73 percent believed that the United States was being "too soft in its policy toward Russia."[3] With the country obsessed with the burgeoning Red Scare, U.S. Cold Warriors pursued a policy of containment to deter Soviet aggression and prevent communist subversion. With increasing frequency during the 1950s and 1960s, Washington resorted to covert action and military intervention in "the Third World," that portion of the globe that lay outside both "the Free World" and "the Soviet Bloc," to shore up pro-American regimes, protect U.S. interests, and keep Moscow off balance. Chapter 1 of *Us versus Them* examines the history of containment in the Middle East, where, as the Cold War wound down during the 1980s, the United States would channel arms and dollars to Muslim guerrillas resisting the Russian invasion of Afghanistan.

Because they were preoccupied with combatting international communism, few U.S. policy makers paid much attention to the Islamic revival percolating throughout much of the region. Most Americans knew next to nothing about Islam, and what they did know derived from the religious upheaval that had rocked Iran during the late 1970s and opened the door for the Ayatollah Ruhollah Khomeini, who quickly branded America as "the Great Satan" and embraced the binary logic of "us versus them." Living in a society where the secular had trumped the sacred and where modernity had triumphed over tradition, the American public and American leaders greatly underestimated the appeal of religion in the Muslim world, where for centuries Islam had served as a potent catalyst for political and social change. As a result, when the Cold War finally ended following the collapse of the Berlin Wall in November 1989, U.S. policy makers had given little thought to what role the planet's second-largest religion might play in the "New World Order" they were busily planning.

The last of the three great monotheistic faiths, Islam had emerged in the Arabian Peninsula during a time of religious turmoil and tribal warfare early in the seventh century. After receiving spiritual revelations in 610 C.E., Mohammed ibn Abdullah, a forty-year-old merchant born in Mecca, spent the following two decades preaching what he called Islam, an Arabic word meaning "submission to God's will." The Prophet Mohammed collected the sacred revelations into a book of scripture known as the Koran and claimed that his new religion was the ultimate fulfillment of two older Abrahamic faiths, Judaism and Christianity. Thanks to his military prowess, his personal charisma, and his commitment to social justice, Mohammed won thousands of converts, or Muslims, and by the time he died in 632, Islam held sway throughout most of southwestern Arabia, where pilgrims trekked to the holy cities of Mecca and Medina.

Who should succeed Mohammed? This question would bedevil his followers for a generation. Most Muslim elders argued that they should select the caliph, or deputy of the Prophet, relying on *sunna,* an Arabic word meaning "custom," to identify the best candidate. Others rallied around Mohammed's cousin and son-in-law Ali, insisting that the next imam, or supreme leader, must be a blood descendant of the Prophet. Following a series of brutal coups and countercoups that culminated in Ali's assassination in 661, the Sunnis emerged triumphant and Caliph Umar founded the Umayyad dynasty in Damascus. Meanwhile, Muslim dissidents calling themselves

Shias, or "followers of Ali," bided their time and waited for the Hidden Imam, or Mahdi, Mohammed's legitimate heir, to reveal himself on the day of judgment.

With the Sunnis firmly in control in Damascus, Islam expanded with breathtaking speed, and by the first years of the eighth century, Muslim rule had extended as far west as Spain and Morocco and as far east as Persia and Afghanistan. Although some Europeans attributed the rapid expansion of the Umayyad Caliphate to bloodthirsty Islamic zeal that forced Christians to convert at sword point, there was a far more prosaic motive—plunder pure and simple. Before long, greed, corruption, and imperial overstretch undermined the legitimacy of the Umayyads, enabling the Abbasids, another group of Sunnis, to seize control in 750 and move the capital to Baghdad. The Abbasid Caliphate endured for five centuries, preserving ancient learning and perfecting modern mathematics during the Dark Ages and resisting Christian Crusaders who sought to liberate the Holy Land from Muslim "infidels," before finally succumbing to Mongol invaders in 1258.

Out of the ensuing chaos, smaller gunpowder empires would eventually emerge in Persia, India, and Turkey, all three of which were held together by the spiritual glue of Islam. In Persia, for example, Shah Ismail founded the Safavid dynasty in 1501 and forced his people to convert to Shiism, hoping thereby to shore up his realm by demonizing the Sunnis next door in Damascus and Baghdad. Across the Arabian Sea on the Indian subcontinent, the Mogul warlord Babur established a Muslim empire in 1526 and secured support from the Hindu majority by embracing religious pluralism. Three thousand miles to the northwest in Turkey, Sultan Suleiman the Magnificent and his successors rejuvenated the truncated caliphate, asserting Turkish control from Egypt to Morocco and sending Muslim armies to the gates of Vienna in 1583. When the first English settlers arrived in North America a quarter of a century later, the Ottoman Empire was the most extensive in the world, stretching from the Persian Gulf to the Western Mediterranean and relying on Sunni Islam to defend its legitimacy.

The Muslim world would look very different by the dawn of the nineteenth century, however, when Islam began its slow-motion retreat, with the Safavids and the Moguls in rapid decline and the Ottomans on the defensive against European expansion. Between 1830 and 1882, Turkey lost control of Algeria to the French, Bosnia to the Austrians, and Egypt to the British. Nicknamed "the Sick Man of Europe," the shrunken Ottoman Empire was swiftly becoming an ethnographic crazy quilt, with Syrian Arabs, Armenian Christians, and mountain-dwelling Kurds, the non-Arab Muslim people who inhabited eastern

Anatolia, seeking independence. Meanwhile, the theological authority of the Muslim elite in Istanbul was called into question by Sunni rivals in Cairo and Mecca, by Shia dissidents in Baghdad and Basra, and by mystical sects like the Alawites, who practiced a syncretistic religion combining elements of Islam and Christianity in their villages northwest of Damascus.

Hoping to defuse an explosive situation, the Young Turks, a band of military officers bent on secular reform, seized power in 1908 and placed the sultan under house arrest. In short order, the Young Turks established a constitutional monarchy and cracked down on nationalist groups and religious dissenters. They made a huge blunder, however, by aligning Turkey with Germany when the First World War erupted in August 1914, and then horrified the world in March 1915 by launching a campaign of genocide against Armenian "subversives" that ultimately claimed more than one million lives. Appalled by what they regarded as an Islamic atrocity perpetrated against Christendom, the victorious British and French, with a nod from the United States, dismantled the Ottoman Empire in 1920, dissolved the caliphate, and carved out so-called mandates for themselves. Under the auspices of the new League of Nations, Britain gained control of Palestine and Iraq, while France subjugated Lebanon and Syria. Thirteen hundred years after the Prophet Mohammed's triumph, Islam was in eclipse.

For the following fifty years, secular nationalists in the Muslim world would challenge the foreign intruders, frequently with support from the Soviet Union, but as the twentieth century drew to a close, the most potent weapon against Western imperialism seemed to be radical Islam, whose proponents resorted to increasingly violent tactics to resist European and American domination. Among the earliest advocates for religious resistance to foreign encroachment was Jamal al-Din al-Afghani, a Persian-born and British-educated activist who traveled the Muslim world at the end of the nineteenth century promoting pan-Islamic unity, theological reform, and economic modernization. Following the carve-up of the Ottoman Empire and the imposition of European control over the Middle East after the First World War, Islam would emerge as a favorite Muslim antidote. In 1928, Hassan al-Banna, an Egyptian school teacher and part-time preacher, founded the Muslim Brotherhood, a secret society that helped the poor and the sick while pressing Britain to relinquish its empire on the Nile. Thirteen years later Abul Ala Maududi, a South Asian journalist who opposed British rule in India, founded Jamaat e-Islami (the Islamic Group), which embraced a much more extreme strategy for achieving independence than the nonviolent approach favored by the Hindu leader Mahatma Gandhi.

The man who provided the theoretical underpinnings for what we recognize today as radical Islam, however, was Sayid Qutb, an Egyptian philosopher who was influenced by both al-Banna and Maududi. Condemning liberal values as a potentially fatal source of corruption for Islamic society, Qutb called for a return to sharia law, a Koranic system of jurisprudence dating from the time of the Prophet Mohammed. In his masterwork, *Milestones*, published just two years before the Egyptian government hanged him for treason in 1966, Qutb dismissed secular Arab nationalism as a dead end, denounced modernization and westernization as antithetical to Islam, and urged all Muslims to wage violent jihad (an Arabic word meaning "struggle") against the enemies of the faith. Among those who would later answer Qutb's call for jihad were al-Qaeda, the Taliban, and ISIS (the Islamic State in Iraq and Syria).

While Sunni radicals like al-Banna, Maududi, and Qutb were refining their extremist ideology, elsewhere in the region Shia clerics were developing a similar cure for what ailed Islam. Perpetual underdogs versus the Sunnis for thirteen centuries, Shias comprised less than 15 percent of the world's Muslim population and were concentrated mainly in Lebanon, Iraq, and Iran, as Persia was now known. In the Shia slums of Beirut, Musa al-Sadr, an Iranian-born imam committed to social justice and political reform, employed his religion as a counterweight to Lebanon's Christian minority, who had held power for thirty years thanks to support from Israel and the United States. Meanwhile in Baghdad, the Ayatollah Ali al-Sistani, another Iranian-born Shia activist, hedged his bets, deferred to his country's Sunni minority, and bore silent witness against the secular tyrant Saddam Hussein, whose patrons in Moscow were no friends of Islam. The most strident champion of the Shia brand of radicalism, however, was "the Other Ayatollah"—Khomeini—whose shrill indictment of the Shah of Iran and his patrons in Washington for crimes against Islam during the late 1970s provoked charismatic disorder, violent confrontation, and eventually regime change in Tehran.

With his black turban, his white beard, and his heart-stopping scowl, the Ayatollah Khomeini would soon become synonymous with radical Islam for most Americans. Intolerant of any practice that deviated from the Koran and unwilling to permit any dissent, Khomeini implied that he was the incarnation of the Mahdi, the Shia messiah, prompting Western critics to compare him to Christian fundamentalists. After Khomeini's supporters occupied the U.S. embassy in Tehran in November 1979 and held fifty-two Americans hostage for 444 days, it became easy to equate radical Islam with terrorism. Yet although the media depicted the Ayatollah as a reactionary ogre, certain aspects of his theology were truly revolutionary, especially his doctrine of *velayet e faqih* (the guardianship of the jurist), which paved the way for a religious dictatorship in Tehran unprecedented in the annals of Shia Islam. Khomeini's death on 3 June 1989 was overshadowed by the notorious massacre in Beijing's Tiananmen Square the next day and by the fall of the Berlin Wall the following November, but twenty-five years later, the Ayatollah remains an avatar of radical Islam in the United States and an inspiration for both Shia and Sunni extremists eager to cleanse the Muslim world of Western contamination.

Us versus Them traces the evolution of U.S. national security policy across four administrations from the end of the Cold War through high noon in the war on terror and shows how the "Green Threat" of radical Islam gradually replaced the "Red Threat" of international communism in the mind of America. President George H. W. Bush was a classic Cold Warrior, ever mistrustful of the Kremlin and deeply wedded to the doctrine of containment. Once Bush and his advisers were certain that Mikhail Gorbachev's reforms would endure and that the communist menace truly was a thing of the past, however, they began moving beyond containment and announced that the United States would take the lead in creating a New World Order. Although no one saw any reason to reconsider U.S. objectives in the Middle East, where ensuring access to Persian Gulf oil and promoting Israeli security remained top priorities, the Bush administration did try to pry open the door to peace between Israel and the Arabs. Prospects for a new Middle East grew darker in August 1990, however, when Iraq invaded Kuwait, prompting Bush to unleash Operation Desert Storm in early 1991. Yet while the president savored his victory over Saddam Hussein, his critics felt increasingly alarmed by the wave of Muslim extremism that was surging from Afghanistan to Algeria and that seemed more and more likely to supplant communism as America's chief nemesis abroad.

Bush's successor, Bill Clinton, was a baby boomer critical of the "us versus them" mind-set that had sent Cold Warriors on a fool's errand in Southeast Asia. Clinton expected the end of the Cold War to yield a "peace dividend" that would facilitate reform at home. Overseas, he envisioned a world in which watchwords like "globalization," "free trade," and "high technology" held sway, and where America's overwhelming military superiority and financial power would contain outlaw regimes and curb ethnic violence. After the Israelis and Palestinians revealed a tentative framework for peace in Oslo, Norway, in August 1993, Clinton sought to broker a comprehensive settlement between Arabs and Jews that might also improve U.S. relations with the Muslim world. A key part of his ambitious plan for the Middle East was a policy of "dual containment" directed at Iraq and Iran, two "backlash states" capable of destabilizing the entire region. In the end, however, the Oslo peace process deadlocked at Camp David in July 2000, and Clinton's efforts to isolate Baghdad and Tehran did little to stem a rising tide of anti-Americanism from South Asia to North Africa, where Islamic radicals and non-state actors like al-Qaeda were taking up arms against the United States and its friends. By the late 1990s, the idea that radical Islam might soon become an existential threat similar to what bolshevism had been eight decades earlier did not seem so farfetched after all.

George W. Bush rejected Bill Clinton's formula of economic globalization and dual containment as a prescription for failure in the Middle East and vowed instead to flex more military muscle to show the world that America could still protect us from them. According to Dubya, as his friends liked to call him, "rogue states"—some great powers in their own right, like Russia and China, and others regional troublemakers like Iraq—posed the biggest threat to U.S. security. While containment might constitute the best way to restrain Moscow or Beijing, the Bush administration was loaded with Cold Warriors who preferred to handle rogues like Saddam Hussein with a strategy straight out of the 1950s—rollback. Rolling back rogue states would require a big increase in the Pentagon's budget and a bold commitment to unilateral American action. When al-Qaeda terrorists attacked the U.S. homeland nine months into his first term, Dubya relied on "us versus them" rhetoric to build support for a "global war on terror" whose trademarks were greater government surveillance at home and preventive war abroad. The first application of the Bush Doctrine came in Baghdad, where the White House imposed regime change in April 2003 and then stood by helplessly as Iraq descended into a bloody quagmire that blackened America's reputation in the Muslim world and strengthened the hand of Islamic extremists loyal to Osama Bin Laden and al-Qaeda. Although Dubya would make what he called "exporting freedom" a central objective of his second term, he left office well aware that rogue-state rollback had backfired and that his policies in the Middle East had inadvertently enabled the new Green Threat of radical Islam to replace the old Red Threat of international communism.

Although repairing the economic damage caused by the Great Recession of 2008 presented a huge challenge for Barack Obama, reversing the diplomatic fallout from his predecessor's foreign policy in some ways proved even more daunting. By shooting first and asking questions later in Iraq, the

Bush administration had squandered a unique opportunity to exert U.S. moral leadership in the post- 9/11 world and stoked the fires of anti-Americanism in the Middle East. Rather than resorting to a fresh round of unilateral rogue-state rollback, Obama unveiled a more complex approach that combined the engagement of Muslim moderates with the containment of Muslim radicals. The Chinese, who got a firsthand look at a similar U.S. policy directed toward Asia in early 2009, labeled the new approach "contagement." In the Middle East, contagement meant withdrawing from Iraq and Afghanistan, jump-starting the Israeli-Palestinian peace process, and persuading friendly Arab tyrants that the best way to inoculate their societies against radical Islam was to hold elections and halt political repression. Contagement proved to be a non-starter, however, because combining engagement with containment confused U.S. clients in Baghdad and Kabul and generated little traction in breaking the Arab-Israeli deadlock. After a series of upheavals rocked Arab capitals from Tunis and Tripoli to Cairo and Damascus in early 2011, Obama relied more and more on Navy SEALs and CIA drones to combat Islamic radicals. Despite working hard to reshape America's relations with the Middle East, as Obama started his second term, he confronted a world still governed by the iron law of us versus them.

Indeed, early in the new millennium, the United States found itself swamped by a wave of Islamophobia that had deep historical roots. Fourteen years after the 9/11 attacks, the media crawled with reports of Muslim plots to destroy America that echoed xenophobic tales from the distant and not-so-distant past exaggerating the malevolent intentions and diabolical powers of Native Americans, African slaves, Nazi spies, and Bolshevik revolutionaries eager to do "us" harm. The Internet and the air waves were saturated with right-wing bloggers and talk radio "shock jocks" who shrieked that sharia law was coming to Main Street and who hinted that President Obama himself was a closet Muslim—not one of "us" but rather one of "them." Pulp fiction, cable television, and video games presented radical Islam as an existential menace unparalleled since the height of the Cold War. And when ISIS guerrillas donned their black balaclavas, climbed into their white Toyota pickup trucks, and rode off to conquer much of northern Iraq, beheading several American hostages along the way, critics of Obama's foreign policy were heard to say, "We told you so." Despite repeated assurances from the White House that the homeland remained secure, rumors flew that foreign foes were conspiring with an "enemy within" to achieve the "Islamization of America." With the 2016 election just eighteen months away, the field of Republican presidential hopefuls swelled to more than a dozen, every one of whom accused the Obama administration of being soft on radical Islam. "Us versus them" was back with a vengeance.

I have purposely written this book from the perspective of "us" rather than "them," not because I believe that what Muslims think is irrelevant or unimportant, but rather because the Green Threat that dominates so much of the discourse about radical Islam in the United States has been generated by American policy, popular culture, and public opinion. The average American has had little if any direct contact with Arabs or Iranians, and what most of us know about the Muslim world has resulted from racial or religious stereotypes reinforced by our own government officials. Were I able to read Arabic or Farsi or Pashto or Dari, of course, I could have created a much richer context for my narrative. There are other ways, however, to capture the human dimension of the story I tell here. At the end of my stay in Jordan, Arafat drove me to Queen Alia International Airport on the outskirts of Amman. As we hustled through the arrivals hall toward my departure gate, I noticed a long line of passengers who had just cleared customs but were placing their luggage on a conveyor belt that led to a huge X-ray machine. I gave Arafat a quizzical look. "Here in Jordan we screen baggage not only on the way out but also on the way in," he explained. "It's the most effective way to prevent Islamic radicals from smuggling weapons." I nodded and murmured to myself: "Just another day in the grim world of us versus them."

CHAPTER ONE

Genesis

Containment and Cold War in the Muslim World

"Why do they hate us?" When George W. Bush posed this question during a televised address just nine days after the 9/11 attacks, most Americans thought they already knew the answer. Muslim extremists had destroyed the World Trade Center and attacked the Pentagon on 11 September 2001 because they despised America's Judeo-Christian religious tradition, because they envied America's economic prosperity and political liberty, and because they resented America's unmatched military power. Not only do "they hate our freedoms," Bush intoned, "they want to overthrow existing governments in many Muslim countries" and "drive Israel out of the Middle East." Simply put, Bush told his listeners, "they stand against us, because we stand in their way."[1] This was a truth that millions of Americans held to be self-evident at the dawn of the new millennium, when their country's good intentions and its desire to make the world a better place seemed only to evoke bitter recriminations and acts of unspeakable evil.

Yet although the source of the 9/11 attacks was quite novel and although both the scale and the location of the harm "they" inflicted on "us" were unprecedented, the notion of a virtuous America endangered by wicked and violent enemies was not new at all. Indeed, from the moment that John Winthrop and the Puritans dropped anchor in Massachusetts Bay in 1630 and vowed to build a "City Upon a Hill," Americans have tended to view the world in terms of "us versus them." In the beginning, it was Native Americans who mounted the most sinister challenge to Winthrop's utopian experiment, with Wampanoags and Algonquians and later Seminoles and Sioux defending their turf and terrorizing white settlers. Then, during the nineteenth century, the anxiety generated by the Native American "red threat" would be exacerbated, first by a "black threat" triggered by bloody African slave revolts from the Caribbean to the U.S. South, and later by a "yellow peril" that materialized as hundreds of thousands of Asian immigrants headed east across the Pacific to the United States.

Beyond these racial anxieties, Americans also recognized that foreign ideologies could pose grave existential perils. For decades after 1776, the Founding Fathers were haunted by the specter of European monarchism, whose proponents hoped to strangle the infant American republic. Before

long, Europe would spawn even more dangerous "isms." Fascism, symbol-
ized by the brown-shirted Nazi thugs who began bullying German Jews during the 1920s, would metastasize into a genocidal "brown threat" after Adolf
Hitler seized power in 1933. Meanwhile, the Bolshevik takeover in Russia in
1917 sparked fears of an irrepressible global communist revolution, a new
"red threat" quite different from the one that Winthrop had encountered.
After 1945, the United States would find itself locked in a Cold War with the
Soviet Union and wedded to the doctrine of containment to protect "us"
from "them." Ideological and racial anxieties soon intersected in frightening ways. Marxism-Leninism plus oriental despotism, for example, would
transform Russia from a vital ally to a mortal threat. Likewise, the Chinese
communist revolution would combine the worst aspects of the yellow peril
with that of the red menace to make the People's Republic of China the geopolitical bogeyman of the 1960s.

The us-versus-them dynamic that prolonged the Cold War confrontation with Moscow and Beijing would also influence Washington's policies
in the Middle East. Eager to preserve Western access to Persian Gulf oil,
protect Israel, and prevent Soviet subversion, American policy makers
embraced containment and placed themselves at odds with Arab nationalists like Egypt's Gamal Abdel Nasser and Iraq's Saddam Hussein, both of
whom evoked unflattering comparisons with Hitler and Attila the Hun. To
protect us and contain them, Washington resorted again and again to CIA
covert action while bankrolling pro-American autocrats from North Africa
to Central Asia. When Kremlin-backed Arab radicals like the Palestine
Liberation Organization (PLO) unleashed brutal violence against Israeli
"pioneers," U.S. policy makers quickly equated revolutionary nationalism
with terrorism, in effect fusing two red threats—one Native American and
the other Bolshevik—into a monstrous and barbarian new them eager figu-
ratively to lift Uncle Sam's scalp.

With the waning of the Cold War, most observers expected race and
ideology to become much less important, undermining the traditional
us-versus-them dichotomy and ushering in a less dangerous era marked
by peace, stability, and globalization. Yet after Muslim radicals overthrew
the Shah of Iran in 1979 and denounced his chief patron, the United States,
as "the Great Satan," resurgent Islam emerged inexorably as the new them,
a green-colored reincarnation of the red, black, and yellow bogeymen of
yesteryear. Until the glowering visage of the Ayatollah Khomeini became
a staple feature of the nightly news, Islam had remained largely invisible to
the average American, who was saturated in secularism. For their part, Cold

Warriors from Dwight Eisenhower to Ronald Reagan typically assumed that Islam could serve as a highly effective religious antidote to the atheism preached by the godless Kremlin. Prior to 1989, few in Washington possessed the expertise necessary to decipher the explosive mixture of religion and politics brewing throughout the Muslim world, and fewer still recognized that Islamic radicalism might eventually present a bigger challenge to American interests in the Middle East than Soviet subversion. Although communism had largely disappeared from America's threat matrix by the twilight of the twentieth century, radical Islam would take its place early in the new millennium, evoking not-so-distant memories of other thems who had threatened us and our security.

Like Rome versus Carthage:
The Red Threat and the Rise of Containment

Although the primordial battle between us and them had started not long after 1630 as a bloody race war between white and red, by the time John Winthrop's City Upon a Hill emerged as a world power three centuries later, the greatest threat to American security appeared to be ideological, not racial. President Woodrow Wilson felt deeply troubled by the rise of revolutionary nationalism early in the twentieth century, first next door in Mexico, then in China, and finally in Russia, where V. I. Lenin and the Bolsheviks seized power in an anticapitalist coup in late 1917 and vowed to export communism far and wide. To that end, two years later the Kremlin established the Communist International, or Comintern, to coordinate Lenin's global offensive against Western imperialism. During the two decades following World War I, Wilson and his successors combatted this new Red Threat by jailing left-wing dissidents at home and supporting anticommunist dictators from Nicaragua and El Salvador to Greece and Spain.

The most dangerous and lethal "ism" to appear prior to 1945, however, actually came in a brown wrapper, not a red one. Nazism, the German variant of fascism, a movement that first emerged in Benito Mussolini's Italy during the 1920s, was the brainchild of Adolf Hitler, a xenophobic nationalist and violent anti-Semite who relied on a fanatical band of brown-shirted, swastika-bearing storm troopers to strike fear in the hearts of European socialists and American liberals. Because Hitler demanded total submission to the state, his opponents labeled Nazism a totalitarian ideology whose goals included the destruction of democracy and the elimination of Jews and other so-called inferior races, as well as the establishment of a global dictatorship. Hitler's megalomania made many American officials very nervous. The House of Representatives, for example, established a Special Committee on Un-American Activities (HUAC) in 1934 to combat Nazi propaganda and monitor pro-fascist groups like the German American Bund. Six years later, President Franklin D. Roosevelt ordered the FBI to wiretap Charles Lindbergh and other leaders of America First, a mass movement sympathetic to Hitler's Germany.

Roosevelt died three weeks before V-E Day, but as the brown threat of fascism receded in May 1945, FDR's successor, Harry S. Truman, became preoccupied with another threat colored red—communism. While Hitler and the Russian dictator Josef Stalin had been blood enemies during World War II, many Americans regarded their two regimes as the same under the skin. Like Nazism, communism was a totalitarian ideology based on ruthless one-party rule, and even though America had aligned itself with the Soviet Union to defeat German aggression, U.S. policy makers expected the Kremlin to make trouble once the shooting stopped. Truman's own anti-Soviet inclinations were on display as early as the summer of 1941, shortly after Hitler's forces had attacked Stalin's realm. "If we see that Germany is winning we ought to help Russia and if Russia is winning we ought to help Germany," the junior senator from Missouri told a reporter as Nazi tanks clanked toward Moscow, "and that way let them kill as many as possible, although I don't want to see Hitler victorious under any circumstances."[2] President Truman saw no reason to reconsider this harsh assessment after 1945. Indeed, relations between Moscow and Washington had become so frosty that by early 1947, Walter Lippmann, one of America's leading public intellectuals, christened the conflict between the two former allies "the Cold War." J. Edgar Hoover, the FBI director who had spent the war hunting Nazis, now became obsessed with hunting communists, issuing shrill postwar warnings about a new and more virulent strain of totalitarianism and insisting on aggressive surveillance tactics. "The mad march of Red fascism is a cause for concern in America," he told HUAC in March 1947, not only because communists were "far better organized than were the Nazis in occupied countries prior to their capitulation" but also because "their goal is the overthrow of our government."[3]

Even as Hoover sounded the alarm on Capitol Hill, Truman and his advisers were already developing a strategy to combat what they regarded as a mortal threat to U.S. security posed by the Soviet Union. The political and economic chaos that afflicted most of Europe and Asia after World War II would have made these areas ideal spawning grounds for communist revolution, even if the Kremlin had chosen not to fish in troubled waters. The way American experts on Soviet Russia like George F. Kennan saw it, however, Stalin already had a rod and reel and lots of bait. A brilliant and ambitious foreign service officer who had spent the 1930s at the U.S. embassy in Moscow watching Stalin execute thousands of Russian communists suspected of disloyalty, Kennan expected more of the same from the Soviet dictator after 1945. Explaining the Kremlin's foreign policy as a noxious blend of traditional Russian expansionism and Marxist-Leninist ideological dogma fueled by Stalin's own paranoia, Kennan insisted that the most effective way to combat the Red Threat was to use America's political influence, its wealth, and, if necessary, its military power to "contain" the Soviet Union.

Within two years, Kennan would offer up a blueprint for winning the Cold War. The first draft came in a remarkable eight-thousand-word telegram that he sent to the State Department from Moscow in early 1946. "Soviet power, unlike that of Hitlerite Germany, is neither schematic nor adventuristic," Kennan cabled Secretary of State James Byrnes on 22 February. "It does not work by fixed plans. It does not take unnecessary risks." This should make combatting the Kremlin less dangerous than defeating the Nazis. "Impervious to [the] logic of reason" but "highly sensitive to [the] logic of force," the Soviet Union "can easily withdraw—and usually does—when strong resistance is encountered at any point." According to Kennan, "if the adversary has sufficient force and makes clear his readiness to use it, he rarely has to do so."[4] The "long telegram" not only set off alarm bells at the State Department but also caught the attention of Secretary of the Navy James Forrestal who helped Kennan craft a shorter version that appeared under the pseudonym "X" in the high-profile journal *Foreign Affairs* in July 1947. The logic of us versus them had never been presented with greater force or clarity. "Soviet power as we know it today is the product of ideology and circumstances: ideology inherited by the present Soviet leaders from the movement in which they had their political origin, and circumstances of power which they now have exercised for nearly three decades in Russia," Mr. X intoned. Although the Kremlin was ruthless and relentless in pursuing its agenda, it was also clever and patient, relying on ideological subversion rather than brute force. "In the light of the above," Kennan concluded, "it will be clearly seen that the Soviet pressure against the free institutions of the western world is something that can be contained by the adroit and vigilant application of counter-force at a series of constantly shifting geographical and political points, corresponding to the shifts and maneuvers of Soviet policy."[5]

The challenge facing Truman, Forrestal, and Kennan by the late 1940s was to determine just how much "counter-force" to employ at just which shifting points. One of the earliest hot spots was Greece, where the communist-led resistance had taken up arms against a right-wing regime that Britain had installed in Athens following the end of the Nazi occupation. When the British could no longer afford to bankroll the Greek anticommunists, the Americans stepped into the breach in early 1947. The leading advocate for what would soon become known as the Truman Doctrine was the under-secretary of state, Dean Acheson, who claimed that a communist triumph in Greece would "open three continents to Soviet penetration" and slam the door shut on American-style democracy. "Like apples in a barrel infected by one rotten one, the corruption of Greece would infect Iran and all to the east," he recalled later. "It would also carry infection to Africa through Asia Minor and Egypt, and to Europe through Italy and France, already threatened by the strongest domestic Communist parties in Western Europe."[6] Armageddon was at hand, he told congressional leaders during a White House meeting about the Greek crisis on 27 February 1947. "We have arrived at a situation which has not been paralleled since ancient history," Acheson explained while President Truman nodded in agreement. "Not since Athens and Sparta, not since Rome and Carthage have we had such a polarization of power." Unless "we" acted fast, Acheson warned, "they" would rule the globe. "It is a question of whether two-thirds of the area of the world and three-fourths of the world's territory is to be controlled by Communists."[7]

After a brief moment of stunned silence, Arthur Vandenberg, the Michigan Republican who chaired the Senate Foreign Relations Com-mittee, offered Truman some blunt advice about foreign aid for Greece. "Mr. President, if that's what you want, there's only one way to get it," he observed grimly. "That is to make a personal appearance before Congress and scare hell out of the country."[8] That was just what Truman did on 12 March 1947 during a speech that was broadcast live to a national radio audi-ence. Greece, Truman explained, "is today threatened by the terrorist activi-ties of several thousand armed men, led by Communists" backed by Russia. "If Greece should fall under the control of an armed minority, the effect upon its neighbor, Turkey, would be immediate and serious," he continued. "Confusion and disorder might well spread throughout the entire Middle East." Therefore, "it must be the policy of the United States to support free peoples who are resisting attempted subjugation by armed minorities or by outside pressures."[9] Two months later, as Vandenberg had predicted, bipartisan majorities in both houses of Congress approved $400 million in economic assistance, half of which would go to Greece as a down payment for Truman's crusade to contain international communism.

The Truman administration attended to the remaining balance in short order. Secretary of State George Marshall unveiled a multi-billion dollar recovery plan in June 1947 designed to prevent political and economic chaos from breeding communist revolution in postwar Western Europe. Later that summer, Truman secured passage of the National Security Act, which established the Central Intelligence Agency (CIA) and gave the White House broad new powers to protect the homeland. A year later, he welcomed the division of Germany into two states, the westernmost of which served as a barrier to Soviet expansion. The capstone for containment came in July 1949, when the United States joined the North Atlantic Treaty Organization (NATO), America's first entangling alliance in nearly two hundred years. Vandenberg, who helped secure the necessary two-thirds majority in the Senate, called joining NATO "the most important step in American foreign policy since the promulgation of the Monroe Doctrine."[10] Truman did not disagree. Indeed, the Truman Doctrine, the Marshall Plan, and NATO struck him as a winning combination that would guarantee victory in the Cold War.

America's thirty-third president was soon forced to reconsider that verdict. In August 1949, the Soviets exploded their first atomic bomb, two months later Mao Zedong and the Chinese Communists seized power in Beijing, and in June 1950 the North Koreans launched a surprise attack on the U.S.-backed regime south of the thirty-eighth parallel. This series of setbacks ushered in an ugly era of "red baiting" spearheaded by Senator Joseph McCarthy, a Wisconsin Republican who charged that Truman was soft on communism, not only abroad but also at home. The Truman administration responded by reexamining its entire approach to national security. In January 1950, the banker-turned-diplomat Paul Nitze replaced George Kennan as the director of policy planning at Foggy Bottom, the nickname for the State Department's new home a mile southwest of the White House. Later that spring, Nitze would convene an informal steering group of the National Security Council (NSC), Truman's de facto war cabinet, which began drafting a more aggressive plan to contain international communism in light of recent Kremlin gains.

On 14 April, NSC-68, a new blueprint for winning the Cold War, landed on Truman's desk. Drafted largely by Nitze, the report described the Red Threat in apocalyptic terms. "The Soviet Union, unlike previous aspirants to hegemony, is animated by a new fanatic faith, antithetical to our own."

Simply put, Stalin sought the "destruction not only of this Republic but of civilization itself" in order to impose "slavery under the grim oligarchy of the Kremlin." The stakes had never been higher. "In a shrinking world, which now faces the threat of atomic warfare, it is not an adequate objective merely to seek to check the Kremlin design." Instead, NSC-68 recommended "a rapid build-up of political, economic, and military strength in the free world," including a massive increase in defense spending, the development of a hydrogen bomb, the creation of more regional security organizations like NATO, the expansion of CIA covert operations, and a more muscular surveillance program at home to keep America safe from spies, saboteurs, and subversives. "In other words," the report concluded, "it would be the current Soviet Cold War technique used against the Soviet Union."[11]

Although Truman agreed that the United States faced an unprecedented ideological threat, he was initially reluctant to sign off on NSC-68, partly because of the cost, estimated at $80 billion per year, but mainly because of the scope, which implied greater government regimentation of everyday life. All that changed on 25 June 1950, however, when the Cold War suddenly turned hot in Korea. Confronted with what he regarded as the opening move in a Soviet plan for world conquest, Truman decided to send U.S. troops to help the South Koreans repel the northern invasion the next morning. Confessing that "he was more worried about other parts of the world," Truman walked over to a globe in the Oval Office, "put his finger on Iran," and warned George Elsey, a top White House adviser, that "here is where they will start trouble if we aren't careful." The distance between Seoul and Tehran was shorter than it seemed. "Korea was the Greece of the Far East. If we are tough enough now, if we stand up to them like we did in Greece three years ago, they won't take any next steps," Truman explained. "But if we just stand by, they'll move into Iran and they'll take over the whole Middle East. There's no telling what they'll do, if we don't put up a fight."[12]

Containment Comes to the Middle East

The "if we, then they" framework that Elsey's boss endorsed in the Oval Office on 26 June 1950 became the lodestar that guided the Truman administration and its successors for more than three decades, not merely in Asia and Europe but also in the Middle East. Truman worried that his decision to recognize Israel in May 1948, which signaled the birth of a special relationship between America and the new Jewish state, would enhance Soviet influence and encourage communist subversion in the Arab world. As a result, when an anti-American regime in Syria stirred up trouble along the Israeli frontier and blocked construction of a pipeline bringing Saudi oil to the Mediterranean in early 1949, Truman's CIA helped plan a military coup that brought a more pliable leader to power in Damascus.[13] A few months later, the Council on Foreign Relations, the elite organization that published *Foreign Affairs*, invited a dozen professors and policy makers to New York City to examine recent trends in the Middle East. The group's findings were troubling but predictable: "Change has been too rapid to be healthy," the Arabs were drifting toward "violent nationalism," and there was evidence of "exceedingly active Communist agitation."[14] Meanwhile, Dean Acheson, who had recently succeeded George Marshall as Truman's secretary of state, detected eerie parallels between medieval Islam and modern Marxism-Leninism as he helped Paul Nitze put the finishing touches on NSC-68. "The threat to Western Europe [in 1950] seemed to me singularly like that which Islam had posed centuries before, with its combination of ideological zeal and fighting power," Acheson recalled many years later. In the first instance, "Germanic" and "Frankish" power had repelled the Muslim menace, but "this time it would need the added power and energy of America" to save Western Europe and the world from communist subversion.[15]

By the twilight of the Truman administration, an Islamo-Bolshevik crusade or an Arab nationalist assault on Western influence in the Middle East did not seem all that far-fetched. After political turmoil engulfed Iran, for example, Truman confidant Adolf Berle blamed "fanatic Mohammedan nationalism" abetted by the Kremlin.[16] In Egypt, by contrast, the chief source of instability was the secular pan-Arabism of Gamal Abdel Nasser, who deposed the British-backed King Farouk in July 1952 and refused to join the Middle East Defense Organization, a proposed anti-Soviet alliance modeled on NATO. Before long, a debate erupted among the academic experts. Some, like Princeton University's Bernard Lewis, a founding father of Middle Eastern studies in the United States, insisted that Islam was inherently autocratic and xenophobic, which made Muslims particularly vulnerable to Soviet-style totalitarianism. Others, like the University of Chicago's Marshall Hodgson, disagreed and argued instead that Muslims in general and Arabs in particular were actually quite interested in democracy and open to modernization, provided outsiders ceased meddling in their affairs.[17]

No more certain than the experts inside and outside the Truman administration about how best to implement containment in the Middle East or anywhere else, President Eisenhower ordered a review of his predecessor's foreign policy from top to bottom in 1953. In early May, he established a

panel of former government officials, code-named Project Solarium after
the rooftop White House hideaway where the group met, and broke them
up into three task forces, each of which was instructed to evaluate a single
strategy for winning the Cold War—containment, massive retaliation, or
rollback.[18] Two months later during a day-long session in the Solarium,
Eisenhower listened to each group's presentation. Task Force A, chaired by
George Kennan, the father of containment, reaffirmed Truman's approach
as outlined in NSC-68—a long twilight struggle against the Kremlin. Task
Force B, by contrast, plumped for massive retaliation and presented a
breathtaking list of military options, including a nuclear attack on the Soviet
Union. Task Force C aimed to split the difference with a strategy of roll-
back. Arguing that "the U.S. cannot continue to live with the Soviet threat"
and that the Kremlin's empire "will not fall apart, but must be taken apart,"
Task Force C aimed "to create the maximum disruption and popular resistance throughout the Soviet Bloc" by relying on covert action rather than
overt military force, thereby "ending the Iron Curtain" peaceably.[19] General
Andrew Goodpaster, a White House insider who participated in Project
Solarium, recalled long afterward that "President Eisenhower had put me
on Task Force C" because "he wanted the 'rollback' option thoroughly eval-
uated." In the end, however, Eisenhower sided with Kennan's group and
embraced containment, though he also decided to rely more heavily than
Truman on the CIA to keep the Kremlin and left-leaning regimes around
the world off balance.[20]

On 19 August 1953, just four weeks after Project Solarium drew to a
close, the CIA orchestrated one of its earliest and most controversial covert
actions—a coup d'état in Iran that overthrew Mohammed Mossadegh, a left-
wing secular nationalist. After becoming prime minister two years earlier, the
charismatic Mossadegh had persuaded Iran's parliament to nationalize the
Anglo-Iranian Oil Company, pushing pro-Western Shah Reza Mohammed
Pahlavi aside and welcoming the pro-Soviet Tudeh party into his cabinet.
The Truman administration briefly considered supporting a British-backed
military takeover in Tehran before backing out at the eleventh hour.
Truman's successor had no such qualms. Having just updated containment
with a pinch of rollback in the White House Solarium, Eisenhower secretly
approved Operation Ajax, the CIA scheme that deposed Mossadegh and
restored the Shah to power. The president was pleased by the results, but he
was also worried about possible long-term consequences. "The things we
did were 'covert,'" he confided in his diary on 8 October 1953. "If knowledge
of them became public, we would not only be embarrassed in that region,

but our chances to do anything of like nature in the future would almost totally disappear."[21]

Handling the volatile Nasser regime in Cairo would prove much more problematic than deposing Mossadegh. Eisenhower and his secretary of state, John Foster Dulles, had originally thought they could to do business with Nasser, especially after he had cracked down on anti-Western extremists in Egypt's Muslim Brotherhood in 1954. A year later, however, Nasser signed a $200 million arms agreement with Moscow, prompting Washington to rescind its own $100 million offer to finance the Aswan Dam, a massive hydroelectric project designed to transform life in the land of the Pharaohs. Nasser retaliated in July 1956 by seizing the British-owned Suez Canal Company and using the tolls to replace the missing U.S. dollars. The U.K.'s prime minister, Anthony Eden, was furious, branding Nasser as "Hitler on the Nile" and preparing for armed intervention. Eisenhower and Dulles urged the British not to resort to military force, but rather to rely on covert action modeled on Operation Ajax. "The Americans' main contention," Eden remarked privately in mid-September, "is that we can bring Nasser down by degrees rather on the Mossadeg[h] lines."[22] Nevertheless, Eden ignored the advice and secretly approved an elaborate, tripartite scheme in late October calling for Israel to invade Egypt and for British and French troops to move into the isthmus of Suez to "protect" the canal from damage. Livid over what he regarded as a reckless display of old-fashioned imperialism that seemed likely to drive Egypt and other Muslim nations into the Kremlin's orbit, Eisenhower employed economic leverage and diplomatic pressure to force Britain, France, and eventually Israel to withdraw from Egyptian territory.

Having thwarted both European imperialism and Israeli expansionism, Eisenhower returned to the conundrum that had triggered the Suez Crisis in the first place—how best to cope with radical political change in the Muslim world. Convinced that Nasser was fast becoming a Soviet stooge, he sought to contain pan-Arab nationalism in January 1957 by promulgating the Eisenhower Doctrine. Moving quickly, he secured congressional authorization to deploy U.S. dollars and U.S. troops to defend any Middle Eastern nation threatened by international communism. The most memorable example of the Eisenhower Doctrine in action would come in July 1958, when fourteen thousand GIs waded ashore at Beirut to bolster the anti-Nasser regime in Lebanon. The most intriguing aspect of this new initiative, however, involved Saudi Arabia's King Saud, whose role as the keeper of the Islamic holy places in Mecca made him, at least in Eisenhower's eyes, the ideal counterweight to Nasser. Because bolshevism was synonymous with atheism, Eisenhower believed that Islam could serve as a bulwark against Soviet subversion, and he saw King Saud as "the natural choice" to prevent further "Communist penetration" in the region. "If we could build him up as the individual to capture the imagination of the Arab World," Eisenhower had told Dulles on 12 December 1956, "Nasser would not last long."[23] Yet the Saudi monarch had a reputation for being extravagant, lecherous, and weak, most of which was confirmed when he paid a call to the White House in February 1957. Saud proved quite interested in the Eisenhower Doctrine and seemed "more than anxious to be decent and honest," but he also struck the U.S. president as "strictly medieval," politically naive, and no match for Nasser.[24]

As King Saud's star waned, the Eisenhower administration scrapped the idea of using Islam as an antidote to Soviet-backed pan-Arabism and sought other options for stabilizing the Middle East. By the late 1950s, the best bet appeared to be modernization theory, popularized by a smug band of so-called "action intellectuals" like MIT's Walt Rostow, who argued that rapid economic growth combined with gradual political reform was the best prescription for warding off communism among the newly emerging nations of the Third World. Daniel Lerner, one of Rostow's colleagues at MIT, spelled out the implications for the Middle East in *The Passing of Traditional Society*, a widely praised primer on modernization published in 1958. Depicting Islam as a retrograde social force that impeded economic progress, Lerner believed that the Muslim world was ripe for westernization and that oil-rich traditional societies like Iran possessed the resources necessary to modernize, provided they invested wisely and pursued a secular agenda.[25] Five years later, Manfred Halpern, a Princeton University political scientist, updated Lerner's theory for the 1960s. Although communism remained a major worry, Halpern was even more troubled by the growth of "neo-Islamic totalitarianism" in Pakistan, Saudi Arabia, and especially Egypt, where the Muslim Brotherhood still commanded widespread support. Yet he was also heartened by the growth of a new Muslim middle class more interested in economic development than religious tradition, a middle class that might, with American encouragement, serve as the vanguard for reform from North Africa to the Persian Gulf.[26]

For political scientists and policy makers alike, the acid test for modernization in the Middle East would come in Iran. In the wake of Operation Ajax, Shah Mohammed Reza Pahlavi had used his oil revenues to upgrade his country's economic infrastructure, investing heavily in education and industry, encouraging rapid urbanization, and marginalizing mullahs like

Ruhollah Khomeini, who condemned modernization as an affront to traditional Islam. Because the Shah had no interest in reforms that might curb his
absolute power, however, he refused to hold elections and banned political
parties. He also spent lavishly on internal security and military hardware.
As a result, by the time John F. Kennedy entered the White House, Iran
was a virtual police state, where the SAVAK, the Shah's CIA-trained intelligence service, silenced all opposition with ruthless efficiency. Meanwhile,
the oversized Iranian army protected the Pahlavi dynasty from any external
threat. After Tehran and other Iranian cities were rocked by strikes and riots
in early 1961, the Kennedy administration concluded that economic modernization without political liberalization was a recipe for disaster. "Crudely
stated, our goal in Iran is enough stability to avoid violent revolution," which
required "rapid enough progress to satisfy growing popular frustrations,"
Robert Komer, the chief Middle East expert on JFK's NSC staff, explained
in the autumn of 1962. "We need a 'controlled revolution' in Iran," because
"just bottling up" the pressure for change would merely mean "postponing
the inevitable."[27]

The Shah obliged early in the new year by launching a "revolution from
the top," which Kennedy's national security team regarded as a big step in the
right direction. "We got the Shah onto the wicket of running a white revolution instead of a red one," Komer recalled several years later.[28] Yet although
land reform and anticlerical decrees broadened the regime's base of support
among peasants and the urban middle class, the White Revolution also
triggered a violent backlash from landlords and mullahs, who found their
wealth and power diminished. Iran was the heartland of Shiism, a branch
of Islam with a thousand-year tradition of challenging the region's Sunni
majority and a more recent history of resisting Iranian leaders who deviated
from religious orthodoxy. When the SAVAK arrested Khomeini and other
Shia clerics, their supporters launched the most serious disturbances since
the Mossadegh era. American officials were shocked when Iranian troops
fired into "mullah-led crowds" in Tehran on 5 June 1963, killing two hundred
people. "The Shia hierarchy has in essence declared a civil war against the
regime in reaction to the Shah's reform program, particularly land reform
and women's rights," Assistant Secretary of State Phillips Talbot reported
the next day. "Should the regime be toppled," religious figures like Khomeini
would see to it that "any successor government would be neutralist or
reactionary." Therefore, the United States must back the Shah to the hilt.
"Should the disorders be repressed," Talbot explained, "religion as an active
political force in Iran will have been dealt a mortal wound."[29] With help from

an American "counterinsurgency mobile training team" the Shah restored order by the end of the month and sent Khomeini into exile next door in Iraq. Now that the "reactionary landlords and clergy" were on the run, the Iranian monarch assured U.S. diplomats on 24 June, "nothing can stop the 'White Revolution.'"[30]

Even more welcome in Washington than the Shah's White Revolution was his increasingly pro-American foreign policy, which made him a fierce opponent of pan-Arab nationalism and a strong supporter of Israel when it attacked Nasser's Egypt in June 1967. Lyndon B. Johnson, the Texas Democrat who became president after JFK was assassinated in late 1963, had long maintained close ties with the American Jewish community, which led him to adopt a pro-Israel outlook. Yet he also quickly developed an intense dislike for Nasser, who supported Arab radicals from Algeria to Iraq and denounced U.S. intervention in Vietnam as imperialism pure and simple. For his part, the Shah expressed "genuine worries about an eventual threat from radical Arab forces in the Persian Gulf," where he detected Egyptian meddling, and he let Washington know during the spring of 1967 that it was time to cut Nasser down to size.[31] That is precisely what the Israelis would do on 5 June, with LBJ's tacit blessing. Thrilled by Egypt's defeat in the Six-Day War, the Shah "ordered the Iranian press to eliminate its criticism of Israel and to renew 'as strongly as possible' its attacks on Nasir."[32] All this delighted Johnson, who invited the Iranian monarch to the White House for a pair of one-on-one meetings in late August. Although there is no record of either conversation in the archives, LBJ evidently assured that Shah that the "U.S. regard[ed] him as [a] true friend," encouraged him to work closely with Israel and Arab conservatives to keep Nasser in check, and drew "parallels between our 'Great Society' effort and Iran's 'White Revolution.'"[33] In short, by the time Johnson left the Oval Office in January 1969, containment seemed to be working well in the Middle East, keeping us and our friends safe from them.

The Nixon Doctrine

Richard Nixon and his national security adviser, Henry Kissinger, were as determined to contain the Kremlin as Kennedy and Johnson had been, but the new administration preferred slightly different tactics. Nixon and Kissinger preached détente between the superpowers predicated on the "relaxation of tensions" between Washington and Moscow, but they also pursued ruthless anticommunist policies in Southeast Asia, Latin America, and elsewhere in the Third World, relying on regional proxies to counteract Soviet influence. As late as the spring of 1970, the Middle East provided a good example of the Nixon Doctrine in action. With help from two partners—Iran and Israel—U.S. policy makers appeared to have put both Islamic radicalism and pan-Arab nationalism on the defensive, making the Muslim world relatively safe from communist subversion. Ironically, however, the Shah's relentless pursuit of a White Revolution in Tehran and the recent Israeli victory over Egypt would eventually help destabilize the region. In particular, Nasser's inability to prevent Israel from conquering the Sinai and Syria's Golan Heights, seizing East Jerusalem, and occupying Gaza and the West Bank in June 1967 convinced Yasser Arafat and Palestinian radicals that Arab leaders were neither willing nor able to establish an independent Palestine. Arafat and the PLO soon took matters into their own hands, staging hit-and-run raids against targets in Israel and the Occupied Territories, threatening the pro-American regime in Jordan and hijacking several airliners loaded with Western passengers. In September 1972, Palestinian terrorists shocked the United States and the world by murdering eleven Israeli athletes at the Olympic Games in Munich, Germany.

Because the Kremlin refused to condemn the Munich massacre and supported the PLO's "war of national liberation" against Israel, the Nixon administration regarded terrorism as merely a virulent mutation of the communist menace that had threatened America for half a century and took bold steps to defend us from them. Two weeks after the Olympic tragedy, Nixon approved Operation Boulder, a secret surveillance program designed to defeat the PLO and protect America from "Arab terrorist groups based in the Middle East."[34] During the next two and a half years, the State Department prevented hundreds of travelers with PLO connections from obtaining visas, while the FBI wiretapped ninety-four U.S. citizens allegedly linked to Palestinian extremists and burglarized the Arab Information Center in Dallas, Texas. In April 1974, the FBI director Clarence Kelley claimed that the new program had foiled several deadly plots. Even after news of Operation Boulder leaked out following Nixon's resignation four months later, the FBI insisted that it remained "one of the primary means of keeping terrorists out of the United States."[35] Nixon's successor, Gerald Ford, thought otherwise, however, and discontinued the program in March 1975. Focusing on the threat posed by secular radical groups like the PLO, many of which were backed by Moscow, made a certain amount of sense during the early 1970s, when the Nixon and Ford administrations pursued détente with the Kremlin at the strategic level while seeking to curb

Soviet influence in the Middle East. Terrorism was not an imaginary danger. Sirhan Sirhan, the man who shot Robert F. Kennedy in a Los Angeles hotel in June 1968, was a Palestinian refugee, and the gunmen who killed two U.S. diplomats in Khartoum, the capital of Sudan, in March 1973 were quite real and definitely Palestinian.

Nevertheless, Washington's preoccupation with the PLO blinded U.S. policy makers to another unintended consequence of the decline of pan-Arab nationalism in the wake of the Six-Day War—the emergence of radical Islam as a catalyst for political change. After much soul-searching, many Muslims concluded that Nasserism had proved a dead end and insisted that the Egyptian strongman, who died of a heart attack in September 1970, had inadvertently placed the Arabs on the road to defeat and humiliation by abandoning Islam and embracing secularism and nationalism. Sayyid Qutb, the chief theorist for the Muslim Brotherhood, had castigated Egyptian leaders again and again for succumbing to the siren song of westernization until Nasser had him executed in August 1966. After Israel seized the Sinai and Gaza ten months later, another Islamic activist, Muhammad Jalal Kishk, loudly insisted that only a religious revival could restore Egypt's dignity. In Beirut, Shia activists like Imam Musa al-Sadr echoed Kishk's critique of secular Arab nationalism, while from their well-appointed mosques in Riyadh and Jidda, Sunni clerics chided Saudi leaders for ignoring God in favor of Mammon.[36]

Before long, these rumblings began to concern U.S. officials, including George Denney, the director of the State Department's Bureau of Intelligence and Research. Worried that from Cairo to Riyadh, fallout from the Six-Day War would spark an ugly confrontation "not only with the West, but also with peoples of a modernized Near Eastern background such as the Israelis," Denney prepared a think piece titled "The Roots of Arab Resistance to Modernization" in September 1969. He did not mince words. Islam, whose hallmarks were "authoritarianism" and "atomism," lay at the heart of the Arab world's "ambivalent" relationship with the West. According to Denney, "authoritarianism" led to "dogmatism, egocentricism, subjectivity, and lack of empathy" among the Arabs, who "find their outlet against out-group members such as minorities, foreigners, 'imperialism,' and Israel." This was compounded by "atomism," the Arab tendency to identify with tribe and clan rather than with the broader community. "The individual cannot give loyalty or cooperation to any larger social or political entity that might conflict with the interests of his family," Denney explained. Moreover, because "Islam is not merely a religion in the Western sense, but an all-encompassing undifferentiated religious, social, economic, and intellectual system," prospects for an accommodation between America and the Arab world were bleak. "What modernization requires of the Arabs, in effect, is their de-Arabization," Denney concluded, but they clung to "their religiously sanctioned pre-modern tradition, because in collective conflicts, such as the one with Israel," it was Islam that "provided the only underpinning of their collective identity."[37]

The revolution already unfolding in Libya, where Colonel Muammar Qaddafi had seized power on 1 September 1969, seemed to confirm Denney's prediction that Arabs would serve as the vanguard in the coming clash of civilizations between Islam and the West. Although Qaddafi idolized Nasser and embraced pan-Arab nationalism, he was also a devout Muslim who vowed to resist westernization. Libya's oil wealth not only enabled Qaddafi to bankroll the PLO and stock his own arsenal with Soviet military hardware but also helped him finance Islamic radicals in Chad, Nigeria, and the Philippines. Even more disturbing, Qaddafi endorsed America's own Black Muslims, who ranked near the top of Nixon's infamous "enemies list," and offered to lend Herbert Muhammad, the leader of the Nation of Islam, $3 million to combat religious and racial intolerance in the United States.[38] In May 1973, CIA experts warned that "Qadhafi's fanatical commitment to Islam and his aversion to non-Arab values" virtually guaranteed that he would become "more extreme in both his foreign and domestic policies."[39]

Despite Qaddafi's antics in Libya, however, by the mid-1970s U.S. officials worried that even bigger trouble was looming in Iran, where the White House had been grooming the Shah to replace Britain, which was ending its long run as the guardian of the Persian Gulf. "That vacuum is going to be filled," President Nixon told Douglas MacArthur III, the U.S. ambassador in Tehran, in April 1971, and "Iran is going to have to play the major part in doing it." MacArthur, the nephew of the architect of victory in the Pacific during World War II, agreed that Iran was "the only building block we've got that is strong, that is sound, [and] that is aggressive" between Western Europe and Japan. This made the Shah a veritable poster boy for the new Nixon Doctrine, which was designed to avoid future U.S. military intervention in the Third World by relying on right-wing autocrats to maintain order and prevent communist subversion from Southeast Asia to Latin America. Nixon had seen the Shah's handiwork before and liked what he saw. "I just wish there were a few more leaders around the world with his foresight," Nixon sighed, "and his ability to run, basically, let's face it a virtual dictatorship in a benign way."[40]

The Shah was quite eager to serve as America's partner in the Persian Gulf, as Nixon would learn when he visited Tehran in May 1972. Claiming that the Kremlin was making giant inroads in Oman, Iraq, and Syria, the Shah said he could repel the Red Threat, but only if he received the latest U.S. military hardware. It was an offer that Nixon could not refuse. He agreed to let the Shah purchase any non-nuclear weapon in the American arsenal, then looked him in the eye and said: "Protect me."[41] The Shah did just that sixteen months later when Egypt and Syria attacked Israel in a futile bid to regain territory they had lost in 1967. Angered by Nixon's decision to replace Israeli military hardware destroyed in battle, Arab members of the Organization of Petroleum Exporting Countries (OPEC) imposed an embargo on America in October 1973 that sent the price of crude oil through the roof. Not only did the Shah refuse to take part in the embargo but he used the ensuing surge of petro-dollars into Iran to finance a $12 billion military spending spree. The Shah was showing that he could "play [a] constructive leadership role in regional affairs," Ambassador Richard Helms, MacArthur's successor in Tehran, reported on 26 June 1974. "Iranian actions seem almost [a] classic case of [the] Nixon Doctrine in action."[42] Shortly after replacing Nixon in the Oval Office the following August, Gerald Ford let it be known that, like his predecessor, he regarded "a strong and stable Iran as a key to the stability of the oil-rich Persian Gulf region."[43] Meanwhile, Kissinger, who stayed on as secretary of state in the new administration, took to calling the Shah "a world statesman."[44]

The Shah looked far more benign and statesmanlike, however, when viewed from Washington than from Tehran, where a broad cross-section of the Iranian public denounced his conspicuous consumption of U.S. military hardware and insisted that their country's resources could be better spent on domestic projects. By the spring of 1975, complaints had multiplied that the oil boom served only to enrich a small elite who catered to the whims of the Pahlavi dynasty and that, under the Nixon Doctrine, the Shah had become little more than an American puppet. "Even though superficially everything appears normal on the surface," CIA operatives in Tehran reported on 8 May, dissent among Iranian students, civil servants, and labor groups had "reached an alarming degree," largely because "the prosperity promised to everyone is being enjoyed by [only] a few." According to the CIA, one important spark for the deepening political turmoil was "a new manifesto issued in March 1975 by exiled Iranian religious leader Ayatollah Ruhollah Khomeini," who commanded strong support not only among the mullahs at home but also among "dissident Iranian students abroad."[45] President Ford was far too busy that spring dealing with the collapse of the pro-American regime in Saigon to devote much attention to the trouble brewing in Tehran, but the Georgia Democrat who succeeded him on 20 January 1977 would have his hands full dealing with radical Islam in Iran, Libya, and elsewhere.

Iran, Afghanistan, and the Carter Doctrine

Jimmy Carter arrived at 1600 Pennsylvania Avenue having promised to move beyond the us-versus-them mentality that had propelled the United States into Vietnam and other military quagmires abroad and paved the way for a Cold War national security state at home that culminated in the Watergate scandal. Although Carter made almost no mention of foreign policy in his inaugural address, he laid out the ground rules for a new approach to the world during a commencement speech at the University of Notre Dame on 22 May 1977. Americans had learned some hard lessons about the arrogance of power from the Tonkin Gulf to the Mekong Delta, but "we are now free of that inordinate fear of communism which once led us to embrace any dictator who joined us in that fear." Noting that all three of his fellow Notre Dame honorary degree recipients were human rights activists—one from Rhodesia, one from Brazil, and one from South Korea—Carter vowed to put some distance between America and repressive regimes everywhere. "The world is still divided by ideological disputes, dominated by regional conflicts, and threatened by danger," Carter said, insisting nonetheless that "we can no longer separate the traditional issues of war and peace from the new global questions of justice, equity, and human rights."[46]

Back in Washington, the White House national security team was trying to piece together a foreign policy that reflected both the old dangers and the new realities. Despite all the talk about social justice and human rights in the Third World, Zbigniew Brzezinski, the Polish-born action intellectual who served as Carter's NSC adviser, remained fixated on the threat posed by the Soviet Union, as did Samuel P. Huntington, a Harvard political scientist who signed on as the new administration's chief military strategist. As a result, Presidential Review Memorandum (PRM) 10, the three-hundred-page grand strategy paper that landed on Carter's desk in July 1977, provided a detailed analysis of the nuclear arms race, the nasty rivalry between Moscow and Beijing, and the need to deploy U.S. forces rapidly to regional hot spots, but it said very little about new global questions. According to William Odom, who served on Carter's NSC staff for four years, this triumph of traditional Cold War thinking was quite predictable, because with Brzezinski's blessing, "Huntington consciously sought to make [the] PRM-10 Net Assessment the lineal descendant of NSC 68." To that end, Huntington included "a clear-eyed assessment of U.S.-Soviet competition in the Persian Gulf region," where "he began to speculate about the implications of internal disorders and how Moscow would react to them."[47]

When Carter turned his attention to the Middle East that summer, however, he devoted far less time to the Persian Gulf than to the Arab-Israeli dispute. The peace process remained deadlocked, thanks mainly to the stubbornness of Israel's new prime minister, Menachem Begin, who showed no interest in a peace-for-land settlement with Anwar Sadat, Nasser's successor as president of Egypt. Having publicly endorsed the idea of a Palestinian homeland during a town-hall meeting just outside Boston in April 1977, Carter quickly became frustrated with Begin's intransigence. "The Israelis for a number of years have never intended to withdraw from the West Bank," the president growled to his diary on 7 June, "and their major commitment regardless of party, is to maintain the status quo and basically let us pay for it."[48] Despite all this, Begin's first visit to the Oval Office in mid-July proved "quite congenial," but after Israel used American cluster bombs against PLO commandos operating in southern Lebanon later that summer, relations between Washington and Tel Aviv once again turned frosty. "Last night we sent a very strong message to Begin," Carter noted on 24 September 1977, "that unless they withdraw troops and weapons they acquired from us immediately from Lebanon, then we will go to the Congress and demand that all shipment of military supplies cease."[49]

Much to Carter's relief, Begin pulled out of Lebanon in early October, clearing the way for Sadat to make a surprise visit to Jerusalem, where he delivered a passionate appeal for peace on 20 November. Nine months later, Carter invited Begin and Sadat to Camp David, the presidential retreat in Maryland's Catoctin Mountains, to discuss peace. The briefing book that Secretary of State Cyrus Vance handed the president on the eve of the summit spelled out a comprehensive settlement based on UN Security Council Resolution 242, an ambiguously worded proposal adopted shortly after the Six-Day War whose central premise was that Israel would withdraw from the Sinai, the West Bank, Gaza, and the Golan Heights in exchange for peace with its Arab neighbors. "The problem at Camp David," Vance explained, "is to find ways to apply the principles of 242 like withdrawal and security in the 1978 world," so that Arab moderates like Sadat could "keep at arm's length the Soviets and other radical forces." Given Israel's "common security interests with other moderate Arab states" like Saudi Arabia, Vance hoped Begin would realize that "the real guarantee against terrorism is the collaboration of governments at peace with each other in suppressing terrorist movements."[50] The best way to combat Palestinian radicalism, Brzezinski argued in a separate background paper, was for Israel to accept "a moratorium on organized settlement activities" on the West Bank. Begin, however, would likely be "very resistant to pressures for substantive concessions," because he *"probably believes that a failure at Camp David will hurt you and Sadat, but not him."*[51]

For thirteen days, Carter nudged Sadat and badgered Begin toward a comprehensive peace agreement at Camp David. As Vance and Brzezinski had predicted, Begin's desire to keep the West Bank threatened to derail the negotiations from the very start. Late one night during a one-on-one session with Carter, Egypt's president laid out his dilemma. "Begin wants the West Bank; originally he was prepared to turn over Sinai to me in return for the West Bank," Sadat explained. "I must have also resolution of Gaza/West Bank. I cannot do Sinai alone."[52] Committed to "a just and lasting peace" for all the peoples of the Middle East, including the Palestinians, Carter adopted a hard line with the Israelis and came close to a historic breakthrough. "Begin agrees for the first time to accept 242 in all its parts applicable to all its neighbors," Carter boasted in his diary on 16 September, "including the West Bank and Gaza." When he followed up by pressing the Israelis "to focus on settlements," however, "Begin was shouting words like 'ultimatum,' 'excessive demands,' and 'political suicide,'" and the breakthrough quickly broke down.[53]

Rather than return from the mountaintop empty-handed, Carter swallowed hard and settled for a bilateral Israeli-Egyptian deal on the Sinai that was contingent on Israel freezing construction of settlements on the West Bank and commencing Palestinian autonomy talks within ninety days. When Begin stopped by the Oval Office to say farewell on 19 September, the Georgia Democrat presented him with a plaque that read "SHALOM Y'ALL" and urged him privately "to restrain himself" when talking about the Palestinians. "A flap developed between us on the West Bank settlements," Carter grumbled afterward. "He's trying to welsh on the deal."[54] Neither the president nor his national security team held out much hope that Palestinian autonomy talks would bear fruit any time soon. "The issues are too deeply rooted in history and psychology to be resolved by patient negotiations," Brzezinski advised Carter on 9 November 1978, and "can be used by the parties to delay any outcome and simply stall," which "is clearly Begin's intention in regard to the West Bank."[55]

Later that same day and halfway around the world in Tehran, U.S. ambassador William B. Sullivan took a long, hard look at Iranian history and psychology before firing off a top-secret cable entitled "Thinking the Unthinkable," which hinted that time was running out for Shah Mohammed Reza Pahlavi. For almost two years, Carter had maintained an ambivalent relationship with the Shah, publicly pressing him throughout 1977 to show greater respect for human rights and yet endorsing him privately in one of the most ill-timed New Year's Eve toasts on record. "Iran, because of the great leadership of the Shah," the president declared on 31 December 1977 during a visit to Tehran, "is an island of stability in one of the more troubled areas of the world."[56] While Carter was closeted with Begin and Sadat at Camp David nine months later, the island of stability was swept by a political tsunami, with huge crowds of Iranian merchants, students, and workers inspired by the Ayatollah Khomeini in the streets demanding regime change. On 8 September, Iranian troops opened fire on a big demonstration in Tehran's central square, killing more than four hundred protestors and wounding nearly four thousand. As he had during his showdown with Mossadegh, the Shah blamed the Soviet Union and claimed that Khomeini, who had recently fled from Baghdad to Paris, was doing Moscow's bidding.

Yet U.S. officials knew better. To be sure, Carter would warn Russia's Leonid Brezhnev not to meddle in Iran. "Soviet interference in Iranian affairs," Carter emphasized, "would be a matter of utmost gravity."[57] Yet by the autumn of 1978, the White House national security team recognized that the escalating turmoil in Tehran was not the product of communist subversion but rather the result of an Islamic backlash against the White Revolution, which Khomeini angrily dismissed as "Westoxification." As the crisis deepened, the Shah invited Ambassador Sullivan and his British counterpart, Sir Anthony Parsons, to the Niavaran Palace on 31 October to discuss an exit strategy. "We are melting away daily like snow in water," he told the two diplomats. "The oil fields were paralysed, demonstrations and riots were continuing throughout the country, and the universities and schools were totally out of control." Should the "melting process" accelerate, the Shah "would be faced with a clear choice of total surrender (he implied that this meant his own departure) or a total clamp down which would be bloody and would solve nothing."[58] Nine days later, Sullivan informed Foggy Bottom that the time had come to think the unthinkable. "If the Shah should abdicate," the best-case scenario was that Khomeini would assume "some sort of Gandhi-like position in the political constellation" while a reformist coalition ran the government. Yet Sullivan suspected that "a Nasser-Qadhafi type" with an anti-Western agenda "might be the Ayatollah's preferred candidate," and he urged Washington on 9 November to prepare for just such a contingency.[59]

Neither the Gandhi nor the Qaddafi scenario appeared particularly attractive to the man in the Oval Office, who decided to stand by the devil he knew. "We're walking a tightrope in Iran," Carter admitted two days before Christmas, "giving the shah every assurance but encouraging him to be decisive." Over the holidays, however, the situation in Iran went "from bad to terrible," and on 4 January 1979 the White House learned that senior Iranian military officers were planning "a coup to take over the government" should the Shah depart. Carter briefly considered covert action. "We are sticking with the shah until we see some clear alternative," he explained, "since we can't force the shah to leave and the military must be kept cohesive."[60] According to Gary Sick, the chief Iranian expert on the NSC staff, "Carter made it clear that he shared the view that the *threat* of a military coup was the most effective leverage available to forestall a revolutionary power grab" by Islamic radicals.[61] Rumors flew that a military takeover was imminent after the Shah stepped down and fled the country in mid-January, but it all became academic when an Air France 747 touched down at Tehran's Mehrabad International Airport on 1 February carrying the Ayatollah Khomeini, whose vow to reject the West and embrace Islam evoked a thunderous ovation from a crowd estimated at 5 million.

During his daily briefing session with Carter the next morning, Brzezinski downplayed the broader significance of Khomeini's triumph. "We should be careful not to overgeneralize from the Iranian case," Brzezinski advised his boss. "Islamic revivalist movements are not sweeping the Middle East and are not likely to be the wave of the future." To be sure, Shia Islam was "particularly suited to attacking corruption, social injustice, and foreign intervention," but the Carter administration's "commitment to social justice should place us in a strong position to deepen our dialogue with the Muslim world." The real danger, Brzezinski insisted, was "communist influence" in the "arc of instability" that stretched from the Persian Gulf to North Africa. "As Qadhafi has shown, there is nothing preventing a pro-Soviet foreign policy from being followed by an anti-Communist Muslim leader," he pointed out, and "the not-so-encouraging news [from Iran] is that the Tudeh Party—which was suppressed nearly 30 years ago—has become an active participant in the present crisis." Having spent his entire career sounding the alarm against Soviet subversion, Brzezinski remained trapped in the Cold War us- versus-them paradigm in which the Red Threat loomed large.[62]

Yet as Khomeini consolidated his power in Tehran and invoked his own version of us versus them by branding America as the Great Satan, U.S. officials became increasingly concerned about the Green Threat posed by radical Islam. In late February, the State Department's Bureau of Intelligence and Research (INR) circulated a report titled "The New Islamic Fundamentalism" that challenged Brzezinski's assumptions. Modernization had touched off a revolution of rising expectations throughout the Muslim world, where "Western forms of radicalism (such as communism and fascism) will be rejected in favor of more indigenous forces of extremism based either on religion or ethnicity." Although there would almost certainly be "attempts by communist elements to use to their own political advantage the anti-Western manifestations of Islamic revival movements," the INR experts regarded homegrown extremism, especially among the Sunni majority in the Arabian Peninsula and South Asia, as a greater menace. The pro-American regime in Saudi Arabia, for example, believed that it could escape the Shah's fate by pursuing "modernization without Westernization," but the House of Saud was suspect "among the young, educated military and civilian elites who have espoused the new Islamic fundamentalism." The situation was more ominous in Pakistan, where "the devout and Islamically orthodox" General Mohammed Zia al-Haq had seized power eighteen months earlier. A sinister opportunist, Zia had forged an unlikely coalition of army officers, peasants, and mullahs by vowing "to legitimize the state of Pakistan in Islamic terms."[63]

Before the year was out, the State Department's worst fears would come to pass. By late summer, an Islamic Republic was taking shape in Iran, where Khomeini continued to demonize America. Bruce Laingen, the U.S. chief of mission in Tehran, complained bitterly in August that the peculiar traits of "the Persian psyche"—paranoia, narcissism, and "the so-called bazaar mentality"—made negotiating with the new revolutionary regime impossible. He saw Islam as a principle part of the problem, because by emphasizing the omnipotence of God, it produced "a general incomprehension of causality" and left "little room for understanding points of view other than one's own."[64] On 4 November 1979, two weeks after the exiled Shah arrived in New York City for medical treatment, several hundred Iranian radicals stormed the U.S. embassy, took Laingen and fifty-one other Americans hostage, and demanded that the Carter administration extradite Mohammed Reza Pahlavi to Tehran, where he would stand trial for crimes against Islam. Carter refused to turn over the Shah and held Khomeini personally responsible for the hostage crisis. "It's almost impossible to deal with a crazy man," America's thirty-ninth president remarked privately, "except that he does have religious beliefs and the world of Islam will be damaged if a fanatic like him should commit murder in the name of religion against sixty innocent people."[65] While Laingen and the other hostages settled in for what would eventually be 444 days of captivity, heavily armed Islamic fundamentalists seized control of the Grand Mosque in Mecca on 20 November in an abortive attempt to destroy the House of Saud, whose close ties with the United States were anathema for Sunni extremists. The following day, thousands of protestors swarmed into the American embassy compound in Islamabad, Pakistan, killing two U.S. Marine guards, terrorizing one hundred diplomats, and burning most of the complex to the ground before President Zia al-Haq belatedly dispatched troops to quell the rioting.

Preoccupied with freeing the hostages in Iran, reassuring jittery friends in Saudi Arabia, and pursuing diplomatic damage control in Pakistan, Carter and his advisers were blindsided on 26 December when the Kremlin sent the Red Army into Afghanistan. Historians would learn long afterward that Moscow's action was almost certainly defensive—shoring up a communist regime in Kabul besieged by Islamic insurgents and preventing radical Islam from spreading to the Muslim population of Soviet Central Asia— and definitely not the first move in a red offensive against the oil fields of the Persian Gulf. Carter, however, regarded Russia's bold move as "a radical departure from the reticence the Soviets have shown since they overthrew the government in Czechoslovakia" three decades earlier. On 28 December, he activated the Washington-to-Moscow Hot Line and fired off "the sharpest message I have ever sent to Brezhnev," warning him that unless the Russians pulled out of Afghanistan, it would be impossible to sustain détente.[66] A week later, Brzezinski spelled out the implications of the situation in the us-versus-them language of the Cold War he knew best. "Afghanistan is the *seventh* state since 1975 in which communist parties have come to power with Soviet guns and tanks, with Soviet military power and assistance," from Angola and Ethiopia to South Yemen and Vietnam. "We have to move deliberately to fashion a wider security arrangement for the region," he advised Carter, "lest the Soviet influence spread rapidly from Afghanistan to Pakistan and Iran" and "place in direct jeopardy our most vital interests in the Middle East." There was no need to remind his boss that 1980 was an election year, but Brzezinski could not resist: "You have the opportunity to do what President Truman did in Greece and Turkey, and I believe that this is desirable both for domestic and international reasons."[67]

A few hours after Brzezinski had made his pitch, Carter resurrected Truman's Cold War rhetoric on national television. Calling the Kremlin's

intervention in Kabul "a callous violation of international law" and "a deliberate effort of a powerful atheistic government to subjugate an independent
Islamic people," Carter told the American public on 4 January 1980 that "a
Soviet-occupied Afghanistan threatens both Iran and Pakistan and is a step-
pingstone to possible control over much of the world's oil supplies." Given the
gravity of the crisis in Southwest Asia, it would be both unconscionable and
unwise "to do business as usual with the Soviet Union." Declaring détente
dead, Carter withdrew the recently concluded Strategic Arms Limitation
Treaty (SALT) from consideration by the U.S. Senate, banned high technology and grain exports to the Soviet Union, and prohibited American participation in the upcoming summer Olympic Games in Moscow.[68] What
the president chose not to announce, however, was that earlier that same
day he had also authorized the CIA to work with Pakistan's Inter-Services
Intelligence Agency (ISI) to funnel arms to the mujahedin, the Muslim guerrillas fighting the Red Army in Afghanistan. "We discussed aid that might go
to Pakistan and therefore to the Afghan rebels," Carter confided in his diary.
"My preference is to send them weapons they could use in the mountains,
primarily against tanks and armored personnel carriers." A little nervous
about running guns to Islamic militants, Carter hoped that the Saudis and
other Muslim moderates would help finance the covert arms pipeline, "so
that the Paks won't be seen as dependent on or subservient to us."[69]

Brzezinski and the NSC staff, by contrast, had fewer qualms about arming Muslim radicals because they had convinced themselves that, at least in
Afghanistan, the enemy of my enemy is my friend. "Our response has to be a
sustained one and a regional one," Carter's NSC adviser explained on 9 January,
including more military assistance for Pakistan and greater U.S. access to
forward bases in the Horn of Africa and the Arabian Peninsula. Noting that
"we need to generate a wider domestic consensus behind legislative and
budgetary matters," Brzezinski suggested that the president "might want to
think of a 'Carter Doctrine.'" Carter liked the concept and instructed the
Special Coordination Committee (SCC), a new inter-agency group chaired
by Brzezinski, to move forward. On 14 January, the SCC reviewed the deteriorating situation in Southwest Asia, which Thomas Thornton, a veteran
Cold Warrior who had succeeded Samuel P. Huntington as the NSC's chief
global strategist, described as "a prime target of Soviet expansion" and a place
where "instability is inevitable." On the plus side of the geopolitical ledger,
Thornton noted, "Islam and independent nationalism can be strong blocks
to Soviet expansion," but there were also some big minuses. "Strong ties
between the radical Arab states and the USSR" had created a "deep aversion

by most countries in the region, flowing from a mix of anti-colonialist, Third World, Arab, and Islamic ideologies, to close political and security ties to Western Powers." The SCC quickly accepted Thornton's most important recommendation, "that a clear, simple policy statement is needed comparable to the Truman Doctrine of the 1940s and the Eisenhower Doctrine of the 1950s."[70] Later that same evening, Carter accepted the SCC's bleak diagnosis and its robust prescription, observing that "to a remarkable degree [the] Afghanistan, Iran, and Palestinian problems are interrelated."[71]

Carter confirmed just how interrelated those problems were on 22 January during his annual State of the Union address, which he devoted almost entirely to the unstable situation in Southwest Asia. Depicting the hostage crisis in Iran and the Soviet invasion of Afghanistan as the geopolitical equivalent of a perfect storm that threatened to derail the Middle East peace process, destroy pro-American Muslim regimes, and disrupt Western access to Persian Gulf oil, the president vowed to batten down the hatches and weather the ideological whirlwind sweeping the region. "An attempt by any outside force to gain control of the Persian Gulf region will be regarded as an assault on the vital interests of the United States of America," Carter declared, "and such an assault will be repelled by any means necessary, including military force."[72]

In a desperate attempt to win reelection in 1980, Carter branded the Kremlin as a pariah at the United Nations, created a Rapid Deployment Force to defend the Middle East, and sent more weapons to the Islamic insurgents battling the Red Army in Afghanistan. Yet this long-shot bid to duplicate Truman's stunning come-from-behind victory in 1948 would come up short, largely because voters regarded Carter as a far less convincing Cold Warrior than his Republican opponent, Ronald Reagan. Despite Carter's bold claim at Notre Dame in May 1977 that America had moved beyond the Cold War mantra of us versus them, containment was alive and well when he left office four years later. Indeed, Reagan's foreign policy did not look much different from what Carter would likely have delivered in a second term: crisis and confrontation with the Kremlin accompanied by chaos and confusion in the Muslim world.

To the Reagan Doctrine

For those Americans who believed that the Soviet Union had surpassed the United States as the world's leading superpower during the Carter years, Reagan was the right man with the right line at the right time. Ridiculed by Hollywood's A list as the "King of the B movies," Reagan was elected president of the Screen Actors Guild after World War II and spent the late 1940s helping the FBI purge communists and fellow travelers from the film industry. He soon became one of the country's most visible anticommunists, preaching the gospel of free enterprise as a pitchman for General Electric and leading a choir of conservative Republicans whose favorite hymns chided liberal Democrats for being socialist sinners. After two terms as governor of California, Reagan emerged as the GOP front-runner during the 1980 primaries, where voters cheered his critique of the Carter administration as a bunch of "tax and spend" do-gooders who were addicted to "big government" at home and who preferred a much smaller U.S. footprint abroad. Charging that Carter's weak-kneed foreign policy had enabled Iranian radicals to take all of America hostage, Reagan won in a landslide on 4 November.

Iran would release all the real hostages on 20 January 1981, literally moments before the White House changed hands, which Reagan took as a sign that getting tough with Muslim and Soviet totalitarians was the surest way to protect us from them. He filled his administration with Cold War hard-liners. Chief among them was Secretary of State Alexander Haig, a West Point martinet and Nixon administration insider whose five-year appointment as supreme allied commander in Europe was nearly cut short in June 1979 when left-wing terrorists tried to blow up his armored limousine as it left NATO headquarters in Brussels. Secretary of Defense Caspar Weinberger, another anti-Soviet "hawk" with ties to Nixon, would spend the early 1980s helping Reagan beef up the Pentagon budget, reversing Carter-era cuts, restoring America's nuclear superiority, and restructuring U.S. conventional forces for rapid deployment to the Persian Gulf. To lead the CIA, Reagan tapped William J. Casey, a Wall Street big shot whose obsession with communism and fascination with covert action dated from his stint as a U.S. intelligence officer during the final days of World War II, when he had watched the Red Army sweep into Central Europe. Elsewhere in the Reagan administration, a cadre of neoconservative intellectuals who equated détente with appeasement and who favored closer relations with Israel moved into key posts. Richard Perle, a former Senate staffer who liked to blast the Kremlin for mistreating Russian Jews and supporting Third World revolutionaries, became the assistant secretary of defense. Paul Wolfowitz, a fiercely anti-Soviet arms-control specialist fond of issuing dire warnings about Moscow's aggressive agenda, received George Kennan's old position as director of policy planning at Foggy Bottom. And Douglas

Feith, a twenty-seven-year-old graduate of Georgetown law school, joined the NSC staff, where he monitored developments in the Middle East for Richard V. Allen, the Reagan campaign's chief foreign policy expert, who became White House national security adviser in January 1981.

In short order, the new president revealed the muscular anti-Soviet thrust of his foreign policy. "So far détente's been a one-way street," Reagan told reporters during his first press conference on 29 January, because Kremlin leaders remained committed to "the promotion of world revolution and a one-world Socialist or Communist state" and "reserve[d] unto themselves the right to commit any crime, to lie, to cheat, in order to attain that."[73] In early 1981, Reagan and his national security team regarded Central America as the place where the Kremlin was working hardest to promote world revolution. Secretary of State Haig took the lead in securing support on Capitol Hill for more military assistance for El Salvador, where U.S. officials viewed the landless peasants battling the tiny country's right-wing oligarchy as communist subversives. Next door in Nicaragua, where the Sandinistas, a left-wing guerrilla movement with ties to Fidel Castro's Cuba, had toppled an American-backed dictator eighteen months earlier, Casey and the CIA recruited and armed a small band of counterrevolutionaries, or *contras,* to turn back the clock in Managua.

The Reagan administration also held the Soviets responsible for violent political unrest far beyond Central America. Here they were influenced by the journalist Claire Sterling, whose best-selling exposé *The Terror Network* alleged that the German Baader-Meinhof gang, which had nearly killed Haig in Brussels, the Italian Red Brigades, who did murder Italy's former prime minister, Aldo Moro, in Rome, and the flamboyant Venezuelan terrorist Ilich Ramírez Sánchez, better known by his nom de guerre Carlos the Jackal, all formed part of a worldwide communist conspiracy headquartered in Moscow. According to Sterling, the principal battleground for the Kremlin's global terror network was the Middle East, with the Palestinians at the front lines. Because most terrorists started "without experience, skills, money, weapons, or international connections," they turned to Moscow for help. Yasser Arafat and his fedayeen guerrillas were a case in point. "Wholly armed by the Soviet Union," the PLO was able not only to "mount its own multinational terrorist hits abroad" but also to "provide training and shelter for the most lethal terrorist bands in the world." Although Leonid Brezhnev and his comrades denied any responsibility, Sterling insisted that "in effect, the Soviet Union had simply laid a loaded gun on the table, leaving others to get on with it."[74]

Not everyone in Washington was persuaded. Indeed, John McMahon, the CIA's deputy director of operations during the Reagan administration, recalled long afterward that Sterling's book frequently relied on evidence drawn from a disinformation campaign that the agency had run during the late 1970s and early 1980s to blacken the Kremlin's reputation. "Our analysis showed that what she claimed often didn't stand up," he told a reporter. "It just was not true." Nevertheless, Casey remained a huge Sterling fan and rejected reports that she had "insufficient evidence" to sustain her thesis. "Of course, Mr. President," the CIA director told Reagan in late 1981, "you and I know better."[75]

By linking the Kremlin to Palestinian terrorism, Reagan and his advisers hoped to create an informal anticommunist alliance that would bring Israel together with Arab moderates and, perhaps, redirect the rage of Islamic radicals away from America and toward Soviet Russia. When Secretary of State Haig stopped off in London on the return leg of a tour of Middle Eastern capitals on 10 April 1981, he told Lord Carrington, Britain's foreign secretary, that both the Israelis and the Jordanians liked the idea of a "strategic consensus," which would "create external security for the Middle East within which the peace process could go forward." Haig was even more pleased by the favorable reception he got in Saudi Arabia, where King Fahd was clearly alarmed by Soviet support for left-wing radicals next door in South Yemen. Yet Haig was "worried about the fragility of the Saudi regime," which seemed to function in "something of an Alice in Wonderland atmosphere." In short, big trouble might lie ahead. "There was no real stability behind the façade of new buildings and expensive military equipment" in Riyadh, Haig concluded darkly, and "there was an obvious parallel with the Shah's Iran."[76]

The atmosphere in Tel Aviv, on the other hand, was something straight out of *Raiders of the Lost Ark*, with Prime Minister Begin casting his minister of defense, Ariel Sharon, as an Israeli Indiana Jones in the war against the Arab bad guys. While Haig flew home across the Atlantic, Begin assured President Reagan that Israel was "in complete agreement" regarding "the dangers of Soviet expansionism" in the Middle East. Noting that Syrian president Hafez al-Assad, one of Moscow's chief Arab clients, was deploying tanks and surface-to-air missiles in southern Lebanon to support PLO commandos operating in the area, Begin informed the White House on 13 April 1981 that he was considering preemptive air strikes.[77] Following a personal appeal from Reagan himself, Begin agreed not to bomb Syrian forces, but in mid-May Israeli warplanes attacked Palestinian targets nearby. When U.S. officials complained on 3 June that the air raids had "made it a great deal more difficult" to maintain good relations with Arab moderates, Begin retorted that "we never asked for any green lights," that "we are absolutely and totally responsible for the decisions we must take to defend our people," and that "when, where, or in what form we will carry out our action we will of course consider among ourselves."[78]

When and where became clear four days later in the skies southeast of Baghdad as Israeli F-16s destroyed the soon-to-be-operational Osirak nuclear reactor, which could have provided the Iraqi dictator Saddam Hussein, yet another Soviet client, with weapons-grade plutonium. Although the State Department condemned the air strike and the Pentagon briefly delayed a new shipment of F-16s bound for Tel Aviv, the American Israel Public Affairs Committee (AIPAC), one of the most powerful and best connected advocacy groups in Washington, defended the raid on Osirak and worked with its friends on Capitol Hill to ensure that the White House did not overreact. The NSC adviser Richard Allen and his staff proved quite receptive and recommended proceeding with caution. "The raid's historical context deserves emphasis," Feith pointed out on 9 June, and in light of Saddam's recent saber rattling, the Reagan administration should do nothing "to embolden the anti-Israel (and largely anti-US) chorus at the UN which revels in denunciations of Israel's 'criminality.'" Feith's boss agreed that America must not "unduly antagonize Israel" and persuaded the president to veto a UN Security Council resolution declaring the attack on Iraq a violation of international law.[79] Despite the hubbub at the United Nations, Ronald Reagan took his cues from Allen, Feith, and AIPAC, telling reporters on 16 June that there was no point in punishing the Israelis for their attack on Iraq, because they "might have sincerely believed it was a defensive move."[80]

Israel's elastic concept of self-defense came into even sharper focus six months later, when Sharon proposed teaching the Arab radicals a lesson by destroying the PLO infrastructure in Lebanon with a swift and massive application of military force. According to the U.S. diplomat Morris Draper, in December 1981 Sharon said that the Israelis intended to "cause such heavy casualties to the terrorists that they will not stay there as a political or military factor," and he "made it quite clear that he would be marching up to the outskirts of Beirut at least, and that he would bring all kinds of firepower to bear."[81] Alarmed by this scenario, which would destroy any remaining hope for a "strategic consensus" between Israel and Arab moderates, Secretary of State Haig warned Prime Minister Begin two months later that military intervention in Lebanon was "a Soviet trap and we must not fall into it."[82] Yet when Sharon arrived at the State Department on 28 May 1982, Haig realized that there was no stopping the Israelis. In a presentation that would have made Claire Sterling proud, Sharon insisted that "virtually all terrorist operations originate from Beirut" and unveiled a "small and efficient" operation to "clean out" the PLO, "turn Lebanon toward the free world," and outfox the Syrians and the Soviets. "Like a lobotomy?" Haig asked. Sharon nodded. Noting that "the U.S., as an ally, cannot tell Israel not to defend its interests," Haig warned his visitor that before performing any geopolitical brain surgery, "there must be a recognizable provocation."[83]

Six days later, gunmen loyal to Abu Nidal, one of Yasser Arafat's leading Palestinian rivals, ambushed an Israeli diplomat in London, leaving him critically wounded and giving Sharon the provocation he needed. On 5 June, Israeli tanks rolled into southern Lebanon and Israeli warplanes pounded PLO targets as far north as Beirut. With Palestinian casualties mounting and with the Lebanese capital surrounded by Israeli soldiers, Menachem Begin arrived at the White House on 21 June for a postmortem on Sharon's botched lobotomy. "Your actions in Lebanon have seriously undermined our relationships with those Arab governments whose cooperation is essential to protect the Middle East from external threats and to counter forces of Soviet-sponsored radicalism and Islamic fundamentalism now growing within the region," President Reagan complained. "Our ultimate purpose is to create 'more Egypts' ready to make peace with Israel," but the war in Lebanon seemed likely to create more Syrias and Iraqs. Begin bristled at Reagan's lecture and retorted that Israel was merely acting in self-defense. "For God's sake, we did not invade Lebanon; we were being attacked by bands operating across our border and we decided we had to defend ourselves against them," he insisted. "What would you have done if Russia were still occupying Alaska and was permitting armed bands to operate across your border?" Then Begin drew a parallel from an episode in the American past. "Didn't the United States on at least two occasions do exactly the same thing to defend itself across the Mexican border," first during the 1840s and then again "in Woodrow Wilson's day when armed bands were crossing into Texas and you sent General Pershing after them?"[84] Because Reagan had majored in economics, not history, he may not have realized that the Mexican incursions that prompted Pershing's foray south of the border had come into Arizona and New Mexico, not Texas, but he found it hard to refute Begin's us-versus-them logic.

The longer Israel's war in Lebanon lasted, the bloodier it became. In mid-August, the Reagan administration managed to broker a cease-fire that called for Arafat and several thousand PLO fighters to head into exile in Tunis while a multinational peacekeeping force including 2,500 U.S. Marines arrived in Beirut to protect the thousands of Palestinian refugees, most of them women and children, who remained behind. Shortly after the PLO evacuation was complete, however, Secretary of Defense Weinberger moved the American peacekeepers out of harm's way and onto vessels of the U.S. Sixth Fleet hovering just offshore, leaving the Sabra and Shatila refugee camps in West Beirut unguarded when heavily armed Christian Lebanese militiamen with close ties to Israel arrived at dusk on 16 September. The next morning, at least eight hundred Palestinian civilians, most of them Muslims, had been brutally slaughtered, shocking the world and shaming the Reagan administration, which sent U.S. troops back ashore to help restore order. There they would remain for another thirteen months, until a Muslim suicide bomber drove a truckload of explosives into their barracks at the Beirut airport on 20 October 1983. When the smoke cleared, 242 Marines were dead, the largest number of casualties that "the Proud and the Few" had suffered in a single day since World War II. The attack should not have come as a surprise. The previous April, a huge car bomb had destroyed the U.S. embassy in downtown Beirut, killing seventeen Americans, including several of the CIA's leading experts on the Arab world. A shadowy Lebanese Shia group calling itself Islamic Jihad, which within a few years would become notorious as Hezbollah, claimed responsibility for both attacks.

Nevertheless, throughout his first term, the man in the Oval Office remained convinced that the Kremlin and its Arab clients posed a greater danger to the United States than Islamic radicalism. On 17 January 1983, Reagan signed off on National Security Decision Directive (NSDD) 75, his version of NSC-68, which spelled out a plan "to contain and over time reverse Soviet expansionism." To this end, NSDD-75 called for "active efforts to encourage democratic movements and forces to bring about political change" inside "Soviet Third World allies and clients."[85] The president revealed the rationale for what would become the Reagan Doctrine six weeks later when he assured a group of evangelical Christians that the Soviets and their communist allies were indeed "the focus of evil in the modern world" and vowed to repel "the aggressive impulses of an evil empire."[86] In practice, this meant stepping up covert assistance for anticommunist "freedom fighters" like the Nicaraguan *contras* and confronting Soviet-backed radicals like Libya's Muammar Qaddafi, who was "public enemy number one" for U.S. policy makers like Paul Wolfowitz. It also meant stepping up pressure on the frail gerontocracy who ruled the evil empire in Moscow, where excessive military spending was eroding the Russian standard of living. After seventy-five-year-old Brezhnev suffered a fatal stroke in November 1982, he was succeeded by KGB chief Yuri Andropov, who in turn succumbed to kidney disease fifteen months later and was replaced by Konstantin Chernenko, an invalid slowly dying of hepatitis. When asked by reporters why there had been no Soviet-American summit meeting during his first term, Reagan quipped that Kremlin leaders kept dying on him. At times during his reelection campaign, the president indulged in some black humor. "My fellow Americans, I'm pleased to tell you today that I've signed legislation that will outlaw Russia forever," Reagan inadvertently joked into a live microphone during a sound check before his regular weekly radio broadcast on 11 August 1984. "We begin bombing in five minutes."[87]

After winning a second term in another political landslide, however, Reagan eschewed bombing and turned instead to radical Islam to help "outlaw" Soviet Russia. U.S. officials realized that reliance on Muslim extremists to help defeat the Kremlin meant playing with fire. As early as March 1981, for example, CIA Middle East experts warned that the United States not only had "become identified as the cause of frustrations arising from the modernization process" from North Africa to the Persian Gulf but also had "come to serve as the scapegoat for national ills" in places like Egypt and Saudi Arabia. To make matters worse, "continued US support for Israel—a constant reminder of Muslim military defeat and Western imperialism—also resonates negatively through Islamic lands."[88] Three years later, the agency confirmed that Hezbollah, with support from revolutionary Iran, "was determined to eliminate the US presence in Lebanon," clearing the way for the creation of "an Islamic state" in Beirut modeled on the one in Tehran. As a result, the CIA predicted that "attacks by extremist Shia against US interests in the Middle East—particularly Lebanon—will continue," a prophecy that Hezbollah fulfilled during the autumn of 1985 by taking several Americans in Beirut hostage.[89]

The Reagan administration responded with a harebrained plan that soon became known as "the Iran-Contra Affair." To curry favor with Hezbollah's Iranian patrons, who were locked in a gruesome war with Saddam Hussein's Iraq that would eventually claim half a million lives, the White House secretly agreed to ship hundreds of U.S. antitank missiles to Iran through Israeli intermediaries. In return, the Iranians were to persuade Hezbollah to free the American hostages in Lebanon. In an even more bizarre twist, the NSC staffer Oliver North laundered the profits from the arms-for-hostages deal through a Swiss bank account and then sent the proceeds to the Nicaraguan *contras*, circumventing a congressional ban on all official U.S. aid.

Although the *contras* got their dollars, the hostages stayed put. When the details leaked out in late 1986, Reagan's critics wondered which part of the scheme—violating the law to assist anticommunist "freedom fighters" in Central America or trusting Islamic radicals in Tehran and Beirut to free the hostages—was more foolhardy.

While the American public focused on the fallout from one of the most embarrassing clandestine episodes on record, the Reagan administration was running one of the most successful covert operations ever in the mountains of Southwest Asia, where the CIA provided the Afghan mujahedin with $3 billion worth of weapons and logistical support to defeat the Red Army. The arms pipeline had originated during Carter's final months in office, but it was not until William Casey became director of central intelligence in 1981 that Afghanistan emerged as the principal battleground in America's covert Cold War against the Soviet Union. The blueprint for the Reagan Doctrine that the White House approved in January 1983, NSDD-75, described the Afghan war as a spoiling operation designed to drag the Kremlin into a Vietnam-like quagmire: "The U.S. objective is to keep maximum pressure on Moscow for withdrawal and to ensure that the Soviets' political, military, and other costs remain high while the occupation continues."[90] By late April, it was clear that the Kremlin's costs were already high and were likely to grow even higher. "The casualties over the past two years have been over fifteen thousand killed and three to four times that many wounded," an NSC staff memo pointed out. "There is no way they can win the war militarily unless they triple or quadruple the size of the forces which Andropov is unlikely to do at this time."[91]

Two years later, Russia had a new supreme leader. Mikhail Gorbachev, a fifty-four-year-old lawyer with a reputation as a reformer, took over the Kremlin in March 1985 and quickly proved to be far more pragmatic than aging ideologues like Andropov. Among Gorbachev's biggest worries was the escalating military stalemate in Afghanistan, where 115,000 Soviet troops were battling 150,000 mujahedin guerrillas and where Red Army casualties were still running 500 per month. The CIA did not expect Gorbachev to change course, however, partly because he would not want to appear weak but mainly because he regarded Afghanistan as "important to the security of Soviet Central Asian border regions."[92] The guerrilla forces arrayed against the Red Army were an ideological and ethnic hodgepodge. Some of the Afghan-born mujahedin were secular radicals, like Ahmed Shah Massoud, a Tajik bankrolled directly by the CIA, while others were Islamic extremists, like Gulbuddin Hekmatyar, a Pashtun who maintained close ties with

Pakistani intelligence. All of them were ferocious warriors whose knowledge of the local terrain gave them an advantage over the better-armed Soviet troops.

What made the resistance movement most distinctive, however, was the presence of thousands of non-Afghan guerrillas who hailed from forty-three countries in the Muslim world, including Egypt, Saudi Arabia, and the Palestinian territories. Ayman al-Zawahiri, an Egyptian pediatrician who founded Gamaat Islamiyya, the terrorist group responsible for assassinating Anwar Sadat in October 1981, fought in Afghanistan, as did Osama Bin Laden, a lanky thirty-something engineering student from a wealthy Saudi family. According to Ahmed Rashid, a Pakistani journalist who spent time with the mujahedin during the 1980s, the guerrillas also included hundreds of Uzbek and Tajik exiles from Soviet Central Asia who, armed and encouraged by the CIA, made occasional forays into their homelands, where they hoped to spark Islamic wars of national liberation against Moscow's empire.[93] Trapped in a costly and open-ended quagmire in Afghanistan that threatened to infect the Soviet Union with the virus of radical Islam, Gorbachev moved to cut his losses. Insisting that his predecessors "had made a mistake and it should be rectified, the sooner the better," Gorbachev informed a group of high-ranking Soviet officials on 17 October 1985 that they must now take steps that would "lead to our withdrawal from Afghanistan" within three years.[94]

While Gorbachev and his comrades secretly prepared to pull out, Reagan and his national security team upped the ante in September 1986 by equipping the Afghan mujahedin with shoulder-launched Stinger surface-to-air missiles capable of bringing down Soviet helicopter gunships. Before long, the guerrillas were using the Stingers to disrupt tactical air support for the Red Army, whose soldiers hunkered down in Kabul and other Afghan cities while the Kremlin put the finishing touches on its withdrawal plan. "We must and will continue to give aid to the freedom fighters," Reagan concluded on 6 March 1987 following a White House meeting on Afghanistan.[95] When Gorbachev confirmed in May 1988 that all Soviet troops would return home within nine months, America's fortieth president pinched himself and wondered whether Uncle Sam might have won the Cold War. Seventy years after Woodrow Wilson had sounded the first alarm about the Bolshevik menace, the Red Threat seemed to be fading away. Four decades after George Kennan sent his "long telegram" and Harry Truman signed off on NSC-68, containment seemed to have worked. Having spent most of his political career preaching the importance of protecting us from them, the

California Republican was tempted to take a victory lap as his second term drew to a close.

On 11 August 1988, just three days before Reagan passed the torch to his vice president, George H. W. Bush, at the Republican National Convention in New Orleans, a small group of Islamic extremists including Osama Bin Laden sat down together in Peshawar, a Pakistani city just across the border with Afghanistan where the CIA had established the intake valve for its arms pipeline to the mujahedin. First among equals that day was Mullah Abdullah Azzam, a founding father of Hamas, the Palestinian offshoot of the Muslim Brotherhood, who was splitting his time between Afghanistan and the West Bank, where he had helped organize the intifada, a grassroots uprising against the Israeli occupation that had erupted independent of PLO control in December 1987. Back in Peshawar, Azzam joined Bin Laden and the other Arab Afghans in celebrating the successful jihad against the Soviet invasion. Now that the Red Army was on the run, they began to consider new tasks that might lie ahead. According to handwritten notes takes by one of the participants, the group agreed "to start a new project from scratch" to be overseen by a new organization called al-Qaeda, Arabic for "the base." Bin Laden described the two years that he and Azzam had spent fighting alongside the mujahedin as "a period of proving ourselves to the Islamic world" during which "we made huge gains." Now, however, al-Qaeda must prepare itself for a much more ambitious undertaking—a new jihad to protect Muslims from Palestine to the Persian Gulf from the corrosive impact of the West.[96]

Ronald Reagan had never heard of Osama Bin Laden or al-Qaeda, of course, and the CIA was only dimly aware of the Arab Afghans, who evidently never received any U.S. arms through the Peshawar pipeline. Yet even if Bin Laden had appeared on the Reagan administration's geopolitical radar screen, he would have been only a tiny blip overshadowed by many much larger threats, almost all of which emanated from Moscow. For most of the twentieth century, American policy makers had preoccupied themselves with combatting communist subversion, frequently embracing brutal right-wing dictators like the Shah of Iran and propping up modern-day "oriental despots" like Saudi Arabia's King Saud. Then during the 1980s, U.S. officials went a step further and snuggled up with Islamic radicals like the Afghan mujahedin, failing to notice that opposition to communism was merely one aspect of a much broader antagonism toward westernization that was coursing through the Muslim world. General Anthony Zinni, who headed the U.S. Central Command responsible for the defense of the Persian Gulf during the late 1990s, may have put it best in a memoir that appeared early in the new millennium. "During the final decades of the Cold War, we missed the emerging turmoil in Islam," Zinni recalled, "a historical event with political and religious consequences that will likely surpass those of the Protestant Reformation."[97]

Like John Winthrop, the Puritan pioneer who had brought the Protestant Reformation to the New World four centuries earlier, Ronald Reagan liked to call America "a shining city upon a hill." From the dawn of the republic through the twilight of the Cold War, none of Reagan's predecessors had ever taken exception to American exceptionalism. Indeed, they all agreed that America's bright and lofty perch should make it a model for the rest of the world to emulate. Most of them also recognized, however, that America's wealth and power, and the way in which Americans had gone about acquiring that wealth and power, could easily inspire envy and resentment, eventually making us a target for them to destroy. For more than two hundred years, nervous U.S. leaders had managed to keep Native Americans, African Americans, and Asian immigrants at bay, sometimes through punitive legislation and at other times through brute force. More recently, they had defeated the brown shirts in Europe and contained the Red Threat around the world. Once the Cold War ended, American policy makers would begin to ask themselves: Was there a way to move beyond containment and transcend the us-versus-them paradigm to seize new opportunities and build a new world order while avoiding new dangers? As Reagan's successors would learn during their struggle to cope with radical Islam after 1989, there was no easy answer.

CHAPTER TWO

George H. W. Bush and the End of the Cold War
"Beyond Containment" in the Middle East

When George H. W. Bush took the oath of office on 20 January 1989, he became the first sitting vice president to move into the White House since Martin Van Buren had succeeded Andrew Jackson 150 years earlier. Like Old Hickory, Ronald Reagan was a tough act to follow. Bush lacked the Great Communicator's charisma and harbored private doubts about Reaganomics, but he had been a key figure on Reagan's national security team and anticipated that the end of the Cold War would bring big dividends for America from Central Europe to the Middle East. A charter member of the Greatest Generation who had come of age during the 1940s in the shadow of totalitarianism, George H. W. Bush based his view of the world on the "us-versus-them" paradigm and regarded the Red Threat as a grave existential danger to the American way of life. Having learned the hard way that appeasing dictators like Adolf Hitler did not pay but reluctant to risk nuclear war by rolling back the Iron Curtain, Bush had embraced the doctrine of containment and aligned himself against right-wing proponents of more aggressive policies toward the Soviet Union during the Nixon, Ford, and Reagan administrations.

After settling into the Oval Office, President Bush adopted a cautiously optimistic approach to the Kremlin. To be sure, Reagan's successor never wavered in his conviction that containment was much safer and far more effective than rollback in combatting the Red Threat, but Bush did worry that Mikhail Gorbachev's political reforms and innovative diplomacy might spark a backlash among Soviet hard-liners who regarded military confrontation with the United States as a convenient way to reassert the superiority of communism over capitalism. As a result, when it came to the Soviet Union, the Bush administration's mantra during the first months of 1989 was "status quo plus," which, when translated into the vernacular of Russian-American relations, meant to wait and see whether the Cold War was really over. Once the fall of the Berlin Wall confirmed later that year that the Red Threat was truly a thing of the past, Bush and his advisers turned their attention to the future, where they imagined an era beyond containment in which America, the planet's sole remaining superpower, would lead Eastern Europeans, South Africans, Arabs, and everyone else into a brave New World Order.

The triumph of containment did not alter long-standing U.S. assumptions about the Middle East, where oil and Israel remained top priorities, but the end of the Cold War did quell fears that the Soviets might sweep into the Persian Gulf and raised hopes that they might help promote peace between their radical Arab clients and Israel. After moving from 1 Observatory Circle to 1600 Pennsylvania Avenue, President Bush tried to cajole the Israelis into talking with the PLO as part of a peace process bankrolled by Saudi Arabia, but he succeeded only in straining relations between Washington and Tel Aviv. Meanwhile, his plans for a New World Order took a grim turn in August 1990, when Saddam Hussein sent the Iraqi army into Kuwait and converted the region's third-largest oil producer into Iraq's nineteenth province. Convinced that the crisis was the handiwork of Hitler on the Euphrates and fearful that the conquest of Kuwait would transform Saddam Hussein into Nasser with oil wells, President Bush sent half a million U.S. troops to the Persian Gulf and mobilized a broad coalition that included NATO allies and Arab moderates. Dismissing a negotiated settlement as appeasement, the White House launched Operation Desert Storm in January 1991 and liberated Kuwait in a splendid little war that stopped short of regime change in Baghdad.

After the guns fell silent in late February, U.S. policy makers shifted their focus from Baghdad to Madrid, where they convened an Arab-Israeli peace conference designed to drain the reservoir of anti-Americanism that fueled the poisonous game of us versus them in the Middle East and to create a new regional balance of power based on free markets and free elections. With the collapse of the Soviet Union during the autumn of 1991, the Arab radicals lost their most important patron and arms supplier, forcing them to become more flexible at the bargaining table. The Israelis, on the other hand, grew more inflexible after the meltdown in Moscow and sought to outflank the orphaned Palestinians by building more Jewish settlements on the West Bank. When the Bush administration declared these new settlements "obstacles to peace," the peace process ground to a halt in early 1992.

Bush built his case for reelection on his foreign policy successes—his masterful handling of the Cold War endgame that enabled America to move beyond containment and his bold stand against Saddam Hussein's threat to the New World Order in the Persian Gulf. Bush's critics usually retorted that his diplomatic accomplishments were far outweighed by his domestic failures, but they could also point to some unresolved problems abroad. Many American Jews and AIPAC complained that the Bush administration's peace-for-land formula was pro-Arab and anti-Israel, while human rights activists insisted that the White House ought to have done more to halt the vicious ethnic violence that erupted from the Balkans to Iraq, where Saddam's Sunni-dominated regime slaughtered thousands of Kurds and Shias. By election day in November 1992, however, some observers wondered whether Bush's biggest foreign policy blunder was to have paid too little attention to a rising tide of Muslim extremism that seemed poised to replace communism as the gravest danger America faced overseas. From Kabul to Sarajevo and from Gaza to Algiers, Islamic radicals rejected Washington's blueprint for the post–Cold War world and projected their own alternative vision of a future free from secularism and Western domination. No one had foreseen this on election day four years earlier.

Containment and the Connecticut Yankee

George H. W. Bush was the last American president born prior to the Second World War. The son of Prescott Bush, an investment banker and U.S. senator, young George grew up in Greenwich, Connecticut, where he learned how high finance intersected with party politics and how technology and ideology were making it impossible for America to isolate itself from the world. He enlisted in the U.S. Navy a few months after Pearl Harbor and became a pilot, flying fifty-eight combat missions in the Pacific before his torpedo bomber was shot down over the Bonin Islands in September 1944. Rescued by an American submarine, Bush returned home after the war and enrolled at Yale University, where he majored in economics and played first base for the Elis before heading to Midland, Texas, after graduation. Having made a small fortune in the postwar oil boom, Bush moved to Houston, America's petroleum capital, and quickly emerged as the favorite son of the Lone Star State's small Republican Party. Elected to Congress in 1964, he became a reliable member of the GOP's moderate wing, his firm anti-communism tempered by an internationalism that reflected lessons learned from his own wartime experience.

Bush would become known as "the man with the résumé" as he ascended through a series of increasingly influential diplomatic posts during the 1970s. Richard Nixon appointed him U.S. ambassador to the United Nations in 1971, and three years later Gerald Ford tapped him to direct America's newly opened liaison office in Beijing. Then in 1976, Ford named Bush director of central intelligence in an effort to restore public faith in an agency whose reputation had been badly damaged by domestic surveillance schemes and foreign assassination plots. George H. W. Bush would spend the Carter years angling awkwardly for the GOP presidential nomination, only to be outmaneuvered by Ronald Reagan, who surprised many conservatives by inviting the man with the résumé to take the second slot on the Republican ticket in 1980. A model vice president, Bush not only attended state funerals and presided over the U.S. Senate but also chaired the Special Security Group, Reagan's elite NSC crisis management team, and served as a diplomatic troubleshooter in Central America and the Arab world.

Although Reagan depicted the Soviet Union as an evil empire and a mortal threat to the United States during his first term, Vice President Bush privately regarded the ferocious anticommunist rhetoric emanating from the White House as "excessive" and supported the doctrine of containment, not rollback. He applauded when the Kremlin anointed Mikhail Gorbachev as its new alpha male in March 1985, and during the following three years, Bush welcomed glasnost and perestroika as signs that real changes might be afoot in Moscow. Gorbachev's announcement in February 1988 that he would withdraw Soviet forces from Afghanistan within a year and his recommendation shortly thereafter that the PLO accept Israel's right to exist suggested that the Kremlin intended to make less trouble in the Muslim world than at the height of the Cold War. Bush regarded all this as good news while he worked relentlessly to secure the Republican presidential nomination later that spring, but he sounded a note of caution a few weeks before the GOP convention in New Orleans. Gorbachev's ongoing reforms might be "truly revolutionary and [could] mean historic change," candidate Bush told the Northern California Council for World Affairs on 29 June, but "the Cold War is not over." He reminded his listeners that the momentous changes inside the Soviet Union "didn't take place in a vacuum but in the context of reinvigorated American strength," and that whatever the future held, "we must be bold enough to seize the opportunity of change, but at the same time be prepared for what one pundit [has] called 'the protracted conflict.'"[1]

When the ballots were counted on 8 November, Bush defeated his Democratic rival by seven percentage points and wasted little time putting together his own foreign policy team. First among equals was James Baker, a longtime friend and confidant, whom the new president selected as secretary of state. A Houston-born and Princeton-educated lawyer, Baker was a shrewd and pragmatic dealmaker who shared Bush's internationalism and anticommunism. Bush's first choice as secretary of defense was former Senator John Tower, another Texan whose hard-drinking and skirt-chasing ways eventually derailed the nomination, forcing the White House to

choose Dick Cheney, a conservative Wyoming congressman who had earlier served as Gerald Ford's chief of staff, to take over at the Pentagon. For
the post of NSC adviser, Bush turned to Brent Scowcroft, another friend
from the 1970s who had held the same post during the final two years of the
Ford administration. A retired Air Force general and onetime professor of
Russian history at West Point, Scowcroft was even more skeptical than his
new boss about Gorbachev's staying power. "As we began our own planning
about new approaches, I felt that the stakes were far too high for us to operate on the basis of wishful thinking," Bush's NSC adviser recalled ten years
later. "The real question was: were we once again mistaking a tactical shift
in the Soviet Union for a fundamental transformation of the relationship?"[2]

To answer that question, President Bush asked Scowcroft and the NSC
staff to review U.S. relations with the Kremlin. "Containment is being
vindicated, as the peoples of the world reject the outmoded dogma of
Marxism-Leninism in search of prosperity and freedom," Bush explained
on 15 February 1989, yet despite Gorbachev's reforms, "the Soviet challenge
may be even greater than before because it is more varied."[3] In early March,
the new president requested a second broader examination of America's
grand strategy. "Changes in Soviet domestic and foreign policies," Bush confessed, "are hopeful signs. But it would be reckless to dismantle our military
strength and the policies that have helped make the world less dangerous,
and foolish to assume that all dangers have disappeared."[4] Predictably, the
NSC report that landed on Bush's desk on 14 March remained quite ambivalent and very cautious. "It was disappointing," Scowcroft observed long
afterward, "mainly a 'big picture' document short on detail and substance,
without the kind of specific and imaginative initiatives needed to set US-
Soviet relations on a productive path."[5] Parts of the report, now dubbed by
State Department Soviet experts "status quo plus," leaked to the press in
early April, prompting one journalist to dismiss it as "pedestrian at best" and
to ask: "Is Bush building toward something, or just playing horseshoes?"[6]

Anticipating such criticism, Scowcroft had already asked the Soviet
specialist on his NSC staff, a thirty-four-year-old political scientist from
Stanford named Condoleezza Rice, to reassess America's options. Rice
delivered a series of think pieces insisting that the changes in Moscow were
real, not some devious Marxist-Leninist tactical shift, and that the time was
ripe to move "beyond containment."[7] Scowcroft relayed her assessment
to Bush's entire foreign policy team and warned that by being overly cautious, the United States risked "losing that battle with Gorbachev over influ-
encing the direction of Europe."[8] The man in the Oval Office agreed and

asked Rice to incorporate her ideas into the commencement address that he delivered at Texas A & M University on 12 May 1989. Bush began his remarks with a bow to "wise men" like Dean Acheson and George Kennan, who had "crafted the strategy of containment" forty years earlier, gradually forcing the Kremlin to "turn inward and address the contradictions of its inefficient, repressive, and inhumane system." Declaring that "containment worked," Bush was ready "to move beyond containment." No longer was it necessary to view Russia through the lens of us versus them. "The United States now has as its goal much more than containing the Soviet expansionism," Bush declared. "We seek the integration of the Soviet Union into the community of nations."[9] Three weeks later, he reiterated that "our doctrine need no longer be containing a militarily aggressive Soviet Union." Moving "beyond containment" reflected "a significant shift in the Soviet Union," which meant that "what we've got to do is through cautious contact and hopefully some other bold proposals, challenge the reality of all this [and] encourage change."[10]

Before the year was out, political upheavals from Berlin to Budapest would encourage momentous changes in Soviet-American relations. Ever since armed workers had revolted against the communist regime in East Germany in 1953, the Kremlin had dealt with any serious challenge to its Eastern European satellites by sending in the Red Army, in Hungary in 1956 and again in Czechoslovakia twelve years later. After Russian tanks crushed the Prague Spring in 1968, the Soviet leader Leonid Brezhnev promulgated the doctrine that bore his name and vowed that Moscow would never permit non-communist rule within its sphere of influence. By the late 1980s, however, Gorbachev's reforms inside the Soviet Union had led Kremlin watchers on both sides of the Iron Curtain to wonder whether the Brezhnev Doctrine still applied. Throughout the first nine months of 1989, opposition movements sprang into action against Moscow's puppets, first in Poland and Hungary and then in Bulgaria and East Germany. On 22 September, George H. W. Bush signed off on National Security Directive 23 (NSD-23), which spelled out U.S. expectations during the twilight of the Cold War. "Containment was never an end in itself," the drafters of NSD-23 pointed out; "it was a strategy born of the conditions of the postwar world." Glasnost and perestroika constituted most welcome developments, but they were not in themselves sufficient to transform relations between the superpowers. For that to happen, "Moscow must authoritatively renounce the 'Brezhnev Doctrine'" and "permit self-determination of the countries of East-Central Europe."[11]

That is precisely what the Kremlin did shortly afterward when the East Germans tore down the Berlin Wall. With the dissident Solidarity movement already in control of the Polish parliament and with reformers running the Hungarian Politburo, peaceful demonstrators took to the streets of Leipzig and Dresden in September calling for Erich Honecker, Moscow's man in East Berlin, to embrace perestroika, German style. Honecker stepped down on 18 October after Soviet officials warned him not to expect the Red Army to come to his rescue. A week later, Gorbachev himself gave a speech in Helsinki, Finland, disavowing Moscow's right to intervene militarily in Eastern Europe, prompting Gennady Gerasimov, the Soviet Foreign Ministry spokesman, to tell Western reporters that "the Brezhnev doctrine is dead" and would soon be replaced by "the Sinatra doctrine," if all went as planned. "You know the Frank Sinatra song, 'I Did It My Way?'" he explained. "Hungary and Poland are doing it their way."[12]

Gerasimov might well have added: "And so is East Germany." On 9 November 1989, a few hours after Egon Krenz, Honecker's successor, announced that East Germans were free to leave the country if they wished, thousands of young men and women armed with picks, shovels, and sledgehammers gathered at the Brandenburg Gate and began dismantling the ugly concrete barrier that had separated East from West Berlin for nearly thirty years. "If the Soviets are going to let the Communists fall in East Germany," George H. W. Bush told his NSC team after watching the fall of the Berlin Wall on live television courtesy of CNN, "they've got to be really serious— more serious than I realized."[13] During a telephone conversation the following afternoon, Bush and the West German chancellor Helmut Kohl agreed that there must be no gloating, either in Washington or in Bonn. American officials would "continue to avoid especially hot rhetoric that might by mistake cause a problem," Bush assured Kohl, adding that that "my meeting with Gorbachev in early December has become even more important."[14]

Bush and Gorbachev's two-day mini summit on the Mediterranean island of Malta began inauspiciously on 2 December, when high seas and gale force winds trapped the two delegations aboard a Soviet cruise ship anchored in Valetta harbor. In a "scene-setter" laying out the agenda for Bush's first meeting with the Soviet leader since moving into the Oval Office, Secretary of State Baker had reminded his boss that the stakes could not be higher. "While democratization is moving forward in the USSR, it has unleashed some dynamic forces that are beyond Gorbachev's ability to control," not only in Eastern Europe but also inside the Soviet Union itself, where "ethnic ferment" was rumbling from the Baltics to the Caucasus. As a result, Bush should reassure his Russian counterpart that "we are not out to destabilize the USSR" and should consider offering U.S. economic and technological support, provided that the Kremlin continued to show restraint in handling political unrest.[15]

In spite of the stormy weather, the mini summit went extremely well. Bush praised Gorbachev's handling of recent turmoil, not only in East Germany but also in Czechoslovakia and Bulgaria, where Moscow had not lifted a finger to prevent non-communist revolutions from toppling loyal Soviet clients. "I hope you've noticed that as change has accelerated in Eastern Europe," Bush pointed out, "we haven't responded with flamboyance or arrogance so as to make your situation difficult."[16] Although the two sides reached no meeting of the minds regarding the size of their nuclear and conventional arsenals, the Americans were amazed to hear Gorbachev embrace "democratic values" as the cornerstone of an emerging post–Cold War world order. They were even more amazed when the Soviet leader declared that "we don't consider you an enemy anymore" and that the bad old days of us versus them were over. "Things have changed. We want you in Europe," Gorbachev told Bush. "It's important for the future of the continent that you're here."[17] In the Third World, by contrast, some things seemed relatively unchanged. Bush complained that the Kremlin was too wedded to Fidel Castro's regime in Cuba and claimed that the Soviets were still doing too much to assist the Sandinistas in Nicaragua and too little to prevent Libya's Muammar Qaddafi from developing the "poor man's atom bomb"—chemical weapons. Gorbachev retorted that the United States had been too quick to intervene in places like Panama and the Philippines and that America was playing with fire in Afghanistan, where the CIA continued to funnel guns and dollars to Islamic guerrillas ten months after Soviet troops had departed Kabul.[18]

Despite Moscow's meddling in Central America and Washington's meddling in Central Asia, however, the two sides left Malta basically on the same page regarding Central Europe, where the Cold War had started four decades earlier. To be sure, the superpowers might still butt heads from the Caribbean to the Hindu Kush and they might still haggle over nuclear throw weights and space-based defense systems, but Gorbachev's promulgation of the Sinatra Doctrine and Bush's refusal to "dance on the Berlin Wall" heralded an amicable resolution of the age-old German question at the heart of their rivalry. In just nine months, the Bush administration had moved from status quo plus to beyond containment. Gone was the saber rattling and mutual demonization that had poisoned Soviet-American relations since

1945. Indeed, when Gorbachev called Bush in late January 1990 to discuss reciprocal troop reductions in Central Europe, he assured the Connecticut Yankee: "You can expect our cooperation—our constructive cooperation."[19] Whether such cooperation would extend to Third World hot spots, where Soviet and American leaders had seldom seen eye to eye, remained unclear.

An Old Israel in a New Middle East?

During their time together at Malta, neither Bush nor Gorbachev had said much about the Middle East, but some U.S. policy makers were already speculating that the end of the Cold War might create opportunities to resolve the Arab-Israeli conflict and promote greater stability in the Persian Gulf. George H. W. Bush had taken the oath of office on 20 January 1989 fresh on the heels of some very positive developments in the Muslim world—the Soviet withdrawal from Afghanistan, the end of the Iran-Iraq War, and the PLO's recognition of Israel's right to exist—that, under the right circumstances, might transform the geopolitics of the region. "The Soviets have ceased to see the Third World as ripe for leftist revolution or adding to the socialist camp," CIA analysts pointed out in early April, and "in the Middle East, the policy of 'neither peace nor war' no longer suits Soviet interests."[20] Worried that the charismatic Gorbachev might launch his own unilateral diplomatic initiative, the Bush national security team scrambled throughout the summer and into the fall to "breathe new life into the Arab-Israeli peace process," much to the irritation of the Kremlin.[21] "We are working with Gorbachev in regional and global questions," a satisfied Bush told Yemeni president Ali Abdullah Saleh six weeks after the mini summit at Malta. "We still have some differences on the Middle East," but "there is a declining Soviet role in the region," Bush explained, and "this is good."[22]

As the Cold War wound down, the White House discovered that it also had some differences with Israel, a longtime American client and partner that some Bush administration insiders no longer regarded as a strategic asset, but rather as a diplomatic liability. Washington's relations with Tel Aviv had been strained for more than a year, partly because of fallout from the Palestinian intifada that erupted in December 1987, but mainly because Israel continued to expand its presence on the West Bank, where during the two decades since the 1967 Six-Day War, ninety thousand Israeli Jews had settled among 2 million Arabs. Prime Minister Yitzhak Shamir was a feisty veteran of Israel's War for Independence who insisted that God had intended the Jews to have all the land west of the Jordan River ever since biblical times and that creating new settlements in the Occupied Territories—"facts on the ground"—constituted the surest way to fulfill His intention. "The United States is our best friend," Shamir informed a reporter three months before Bush won the 1988 presidential election, and he predicted that "our relations will be strengthened even more, despite our differences in views."[23]

When Shamir arrived at the White House on 6 April 1989, however, sparks flew. Bush began by urging Israel to consider opening a dialogue with the PLO, but he succeeded only in evoking Shamir's "categorical opposition to a Palestinian state." According to the Israeli prime minister, the core issue was really quite simple: "Israel thought Palestine belonged to it, [while] Palestinians believed it was theirs." The gloves came off after the two men turned to the fate of the Occupied Territories. Saying that he was "greatly upset" that "Israel went ahead and started up new settlements," Bush warned that if the Jewish state did not cease and desist, "the United States could well have no alternative but to support a critical resolution in the UN." A little startled, Shamir reassured his host "that settlements ought not to be such a problem." Yet shortly after returning to Tel Aviv, he unveiled plans for still more housing on the West Bank to accommodate thousands of Jewish immigrants pouring into Israel from the Soviet Union. Angered by what seemed like an Israeli double-cross, Secretary of State Baker made it clear six weeks later during a speech at AIPAC's national conference that he was not amused. "For Israel, now is the time to lay aside, once and for all, the unrealistic vision of a greater Israel," he declared. "Forswear annexation; stop settlement activity; allow schools to reopen; reach out to the Palestinians as neighbors who deserve political rights."[24]

Baker's remarks did not sit well with Shamir, AIPAC, or their friends on Capitol Hill and Main Street, but the White House was unfazed. Noting that "the Israelis were upset," President Bush assured the British prime minister Margaret Thatcher in mid-July that "they would not dictate American policy."[25] After Israeli commandos snatched Sheikh Abdel Karim Obeid, Hezbollah's leader in South Lebanon, later that month, Bush called Shamir to complain that the kidnapping would complicate U.S. efforts to free seven American hostages seized by Iranian-backed Islamic radicals during the Reagan administration. Shamir asked Bush to please remember that the Jewish state existed in a dangerous neighborhood and remained "a small nation that must struggle all the time." There should be "no doubt regarding the strength of US support for Israel," Bush retorted, but "the relationship should be a two-way street."[26] Yet Israel's doubts grew stronger as Washington moved closer to Arab moderates like the Egyptian president

Hosni Mubarak. In September 1989, Richard Haass, one of the NSC's Middle East experts, escorted Mubarak to a Baltimore Orioles baseball game at Camden Yards. "You hug Mubarak like your bubalah [sweetheart]," Israeli cabinet secretary Eli Rubinstein told Haass afterward, "and you treat us like shit."[27] On 16 October, Prime Minister Shamir informed reporters that peace talks with the Palestinians were out of the question and implied that Israel's presence on the West Bank would continue to grow, whether Washington liked it or not. "I've just read the wire story quoting you about a confrontation with the United States," Bush replied angrily the next day. "If you want that—fine." Shamir insisted he did not want that, but neither the White House chief of staff John Sununu nor his boss trusted "that little shit," as they liked to refer to the five-foot-tall Israeli leader.[28]

Mutual mistrust escalated when Bush sat down with Shamir in the Oval Office to discuss how to jumpstart the Middle East peace process on 15 November, just six days after the fall of the Berlin Wall. Brushing aside his visitor's congratulations for America's smooth handling of recent events in Central Europe, the president focused instead on surprising news of still more Israeli expansion in the Occupied Territories. Reminding Shamir that "settlements are unacceptable to us," Bush asked: "Why just before you coming here would you confront me with this embarrassment?" Claiming that there were no new settlements, Shamir explained that Israel had merely altered earlier plans and redirected Jewish settlers to different sites on the West Bank. Bush refused to acquiesce in such semantic sophistry. "The world will see it as your staking a flag, creating a fait accompli," he warned Shamir. "A strong relationship with Israel is in our interest," Bush continued, "but the relationship has gotten off track." Ironically, the end of the Cold War might actually make a bad situation worse. "If any of these settlements are used for Soviet Jews," Bush pointed out as the meeting broke up, "it will put us in an extremely difficult position and limit sharply our ability to facilitate their resettlement."[29]

Determined to make a bad situation better, the Israeli minister of defense Yitzhak Rabin flew to Washington early in the new year to call on the NSC adviser Brent Scowcroft. A warrior turned politician with a reputation for moderation and flexibility, Rabin was already a favorite inside the Bush administration. The two old military men reviewed some sensitive topics—the recent Israeli crackdown on West Bank Palestinians and the recent American intervention to depose the Panamanian dictator Manuel Noriega—before turning to the State of Israel's special relationship with the United States. "Strategic cooperation in general terms may be a less critical area in view of the changes in the Soviet Union," Scowcroft explained. "I hope you understand how serious our situation is—I just came from a meeting where we discussed how to find several hundred million dollars for Panama." Rabin responded with his own pitch for mutual understanding. "We supported your action in Panama," he told Scowcroft. "When you do it 500 miles from the US, we hope you will see how we are justified in doing it three miles from Jerusalem." As for changes in the Soviet Union, Rabin quipped that the Kremlin's two largest exports to the Middle East would likely remain Russian arms for the Arabs and Russian Jews for Israel.[30] The latter half of Rabin's quip proved to be quite true, and before long the Bush administration worried that the fresh influx of Russian Jews would require the Israelis to build still more new housing in the Occupied Territories. "They were not going to stop settlement activity," Bush growled to Scowcroft and the rest of his national security team in June 1990, "because this Israeli government has an ideological belief in it."[31] By the end of the summer, however, Bush's mounting frustration with Israel would prove the least of his problems in the region thanks to the smash-and-grab tactics that Saddam Hussein employed in the Persian Gulf, where a very different kind of New Middle East loomed after the Cold War.

Iraq: The Enemy of Our Enemy?

George H. W. Bush inherited a checkered relationship with Saddam Hussein from his predecessor. The Reagan administration had originally tilted toward Iraq in its long and bloody war with Iran because, as the U.S. ambassador David Newton bluntly pointed out in late 1985, an Iranian victory would have been "catastrophic" for American interests in the Persian Gulf. "The longer the war drags on, the more likely an Iraqi collapse becomes," Newton reported from his perch in Baghdad. "Few doubt that [Ayatollah] Khomeini wants his interpretation of Islam to dominate Iraq," and "even now the Iranians are seeking to undermine several Gulf regimes, most notably in Bahrain and Kuwait." In short, a victorious Iran would "dominate oil policy in the region" and would probably deepen its commitment to "Iranian-supported groups in Lebanon such as Hizbollah and Islamic Amal," which were escalating their guerrilla war against Israel. To avert this catastrophe, Newton concluded, "Iraq needs bolstering."[32] U.S. policy makers were quick to oblige during the mid-1980s, providing Saddam Hussein with agricultural credits, satellite photos of the Iranian order of battle, and dual-use equipment like trucks and helicopters that were quickly converted to military purposes. Yet at the same moment that Ambassador Newton was making the case for bolstering Iraq, the White House secretly approved a controversial scheme to free seven Americans held hostage by pro-Iranian Islamists in Lebanon by selling hundreds of antitank missiles to Iran via Israel for use against the Iraqi army.

Saddam Hussein was angered by "Irangate," but he was hardly surprised. The secret U.S. arms deal with Iran, he informed President Reagan on 18 November 1986, would "bolster the Iranian war machine, prolong the war and threaten the security and safety of Iraq and all the countries of the region."[33] Saddam privately branded the Americans "conspiring bastards," and after the shooting in the Persian Gulf stopped two years later, he suspected that the Reagan administration would cut a deal with Iran to "deprive Iraq of its victory."[34] He need not have worried, however, because by the autumn of 1988, U.S. policy makers believed that "in many respects our political and economic interests run parallel with those of Iraq." Saddam Hussein was "clever, ruthless, and extremely ambitious," the State Department's Iraq experts acknowledged on 9 September, but "the regime he heads is disciplined and relatively free from corruption: an Arab East Germany." Having eked out a narrow victory over Iran, "Iraq emerges from the war as the dominant military power in the Persian Gulf," which meant that "it is in our interest to see Iraqi influence in the Arab world used constructively, as part of the grouping of conservative Arab states which includes close friends of the US: Egypt, Jordan, [and] Saudi Arabia."[35] In early January 1989, George H. W. Bush's transition team received some proposed "Guidelines for U.S.-Iraq Policy" from Foggy Bottom making the case that Saddam Hussein had become "a wavering Soviet quasi-client" whose regime served as "a bulwark against expansion of the Islamic Revolution" that Iran sought to export to its Arab neighbors. "It is up to the new Administration," State Department officials concluded, " to decide whether to treat Iraq as a distasteful dictatorship to be shunned" or to recognize its potential as "a more responsible, status-quo state working within the system, promoting stability in the region."[36]

The Bush administration agreed that Iraq was a potential partner in a very unstable part of the world and spent nine months crafting a policy designed to make that partnership a reality. With most eyes riveted on the momentous events unfolding in Eastern Europe, on 2 October 1989 President Bush approved NSD-26, which spelled out a new approach to the Persian Gulf. The end of the Cold War might alter the geopolitical balance in the Middle East, but the decline of Soviet power would not reduce the importance of the region's oil, which the United States was prepared to defend through military force, if necessary. By cultivating "normal relations" with Saddam Hussein's regime and by providing "economic and political incentives for Iraq to moderate its behavior," the drafters of NSD-26 hoped to "promote stability in both the Gulf and the Middle East," create "opportunities for U.S. firms to participate in the reconstruction of the Iraqi economy, particularly in the energy area," and make military American intervention less likely. To be sure, the Iraqi strongman's record on human rights left much to be desired, and his use of poison gas against the Kurds during the war with Iran had been deeply disturbing. Moreover, Iraq's on-again, off-again efforts to develop nuclear weapons gave Israelis and Arab moderates alike the jitters. Yet the lure of low-interest loans, high-tech oil equipment, and "non-lethal forms of military assistance" seemed likely to make Saddam more cooperative on matters of great importance to the United States, such as helping halt the "subversive activities" undertaken by his archenemy, the Islamic Republic of Iran.[37]

American policy makers had few illusions that implementing NSD-26 would prove easy. "It was a classic case of constructive engagement" that was supposed to "build bridges with a country that was an adversary," NSC Middle East expert Richard Haass recalled long afterward. "But it was also an example of conditional engagement, since it emphasized that normalization would not go ahead if Iraq acted in ways contrary to U.S. interests."[38] Four days after Bush signed NSD-26, Tariq Aziz, Iraq's minister of foreign affairs, sat down with Secretary of State Baker to review the ground rules for normalization. Aziz evinced a "strong desire for the very best possible relationship with the United States," prompting Baker to seek assurances that the Iraqis would tone down their incendiary rhetoric and avoid making trouble for their neighbors. "Iraq has said clearly that it wants to maintain the whole region intact—including the individual countries," Aziz replied, adding that "Iraq's objective was and is good relations with them all, particularly Saudi Arabia and Kuwait." Neither man fully trusted the other, of course, and they traded barbs about reports that Baghdad was stepping up its efforts to acquire weapons of mass destruction (WMD) and rumors that Washington was running covert operations inside Iraq. After Baker secured Department of Agriculture approval for a $1 billion credit line to expand Iraqi grain imports from the United States on 31 October, however, Aziz assured Saddam Hussein that the Bush administration really wanted to do business with them.[39]

Before long, U.S. officials were having second thoughts. Kenneth Pollack, a young CIA analyst who worked closely with Haass, remembered that by

January 1990, "my colleagues and I were deeply suspicious of Saddam's WMD programs and his designs on the rest of the region," because "the devastation of Iranian military power meant that, for the first time, Iraq was effectively unrestrained in how it could pursue its regional ambitions."[40] Secretary of Defense Dick Cheney was likewise quite skeptical about the Iraqi leader's intentions and made sure early in the new year that the Pentagon's long-range planners understood that "the Arabian Peninsula had high priority and that we should plan for a crisis in the [Persian] Gulf."[41] Before long, Saddam Hussein resumed his fiery anti-Israel rhetoric and ratcheted up his pressure on Kuwait to forgive more than $15 billion in loans that the sheikdom had made to Baghdad during the Iran-Iraq War. In mid-March, Haass and the NSC staff were asking themselves: "Should we shut down (as some in Congress argued) what little there was of the U.S.-Iraqi relationship, or was it smarter to keep at least something in play (call it constructive engagement lite)?"[42]

Ambassador April Glaspie, an Arabic-speaker who was completing her second year in Baghdad, opposed shutting things down. "Historically, the Iraqis do not take kindly to being told what to do," she cabled Washington on 9 April. They still faced a very real threat just across the Shatt al-Arab in Iran, and they bridled at what they saw as an American double standard when it came to Israel. "Saddam is dwelling more and more on the theme that Arabs are seen from abroad as second-class human beings," Glaspie explained, and was asking himself why Uncle Sam believed that "the Israelis can be trusted with chemical and nuclear weapons and space technology, while Arabs cannot."[43] During a visit to Baghdad in late May, Haass reminded Foreign Minister Aziz that the Bush administration had already upgraded Iraq to first class and that time was running out on constructive engagement. "The meeting was in Aziz's office at the ministry," Haass recalled many years later. "The coffee was strong, the Havana cigars we each smoked top-of-the-line, and the conversation combative, almost debatelike." He assured Aziz "that we had not written off Iraq nor made up our minds that it was a threat or adversary." Nevertheless, Haass warned his host that "what Iraq was saying and doing was a source of growing concern, and that it was Iraq that would determine how things would evolve between us by what they said and, more important, did."[44]

What Saddam Hussein did after Haass returned to Washington was not at all reassuring. On 15 July 1990, Baghdad delivered what amounted to an ultimatum to Kuwait and the United Arab Emirates (UAE), both of which had repeatedly exceeded their monthly OPEC production quotas, driving down the price of Persian Gulf crude and eroding Iraq's own oil revenues. "We guess Saddam has finally understood that without rapid, massive doses of cash, he will have to cut back drastically on major civilian and perhaps even military projects," Ambassador Glaspie reported three days later. Saddam "does not quite rattle sabers at Kuwait (and the UAE)," but he "will unabashedly threaten [his] neighbors" until he got what he really wanted—"a Marshall Plan for Iraq."[45] Alarmed by Saddam's bullying tactics, State Department officials summoned the Iraqi ambassador to Foggy Bottom and warned him that the United States was determined "to ensure the free flow of oil from the [Persian] Gulf" and stood ready "to support the sovereignty and integrity" of all members of the Gulf Cooperation Council (GCC).[46]

April Glaspie tried to deliver the same message in Baghdad on 25 July, but as it turned out, Saddam Hussein did most of the talking. Adopting a "cordial, reasonable, and even warm" manner, Saddam confirmed that he was "worried" about his relationship with Washington. That said, he was also furious with Kuwait for exceeding its OPEC production quota and pumping more than its fair share of black gold from the Rumaila oil fields straddling the border between the two countries, and he was angry about the sheikdom's refusal to forgive Iraq's war debts. "Iraq wants friendship, but does the USG [U.S. government]?" he asked Glaspie. "Iraq suffered 100,000's of casualties and is now so poor that war orphan pensions will soon be cut; yet rich Kuwait will not even accept OPEC discipline." Saddam recalled "the many 'blows' our relations have been subjected to since 1984, chief among them Irangate," and accused the Bush administration of using Kuwait and the UAE as "spearheads" to wage "economic warfare" against Iraq by forcing down oil prices. Indeed, by having the U.S. Fifth Fleet based in Bahrain conduct joint naval maneuvers with the two sheikdoms earlier that summer, Washington had "encouraged them in their ungenerous policies" toward Baghdad. Saddam insisted that Iraq did not want war, but he warned Ambassador Glaspie: "Do not push us to it; do not make it the only option left with which we can protect our dignity." A little taken aback by all this, she replied that the United States would not take sides in the disagreement between Iraq and Kuwait, but she also reminded her host that "we can never excuse settlement of disputes by other than peaceful means."[47]

Back in Washington, U.S. policy makers held their breath. "Saddam was engaging in a modern-day form of gunboat diplomacy" by bullying his neighbors, the NSC's Haass remembered thinking, yet surely he would stop short of an invasion.[48] On 28 July, Glaspie received instructions to inform the Iraqi leader that the United States "continued to desire better relations," but that his dispute with Kuwait was "best resolved by peaceful means and not by threats involving military force."[49] Saddam, however, was then in Jidda, where the Saudis were desperately attempting to broker a compromise, and by the time he returned to Baghdad, Iraqi troops were massing along the border with Kuwait. Once U.S. surveillance satellites confirmed on the evening of 1 August that Iraq's army was poised to attack on short notice, Haass and Scowcroft rushed to the White House "sick bay," where they found the president getting a rubdown, "the result of having hit a bucket's worth of golf balls earlier in the day." The two men were urging their boss to warn Saddam personally not to do anything rash when word arrived from Foggy Bottom that Iraqi tanks had crossed the frontier in the wee hours of 2 August, Baghdad time, and were rolling toward Kuwait City. "Our plan to phone Saddam had just become OBE," Haass recalled grimly, "overtaken by events."[50]

Hitler on the Euphrates?

The Bush administration reacted swiftly. At 5:00 A.M. on 2 August, the president ordered American warships based at Diego Garcia in the Indian Ocean to head north toward the Persian Gulf and froze all Kuwaiti and Iraqi financial assets in the United States. "Saudis are concerned, and in my view, all of the GCC countries must be quaking in their boots," Bush confided in his diary. "This is radical Saddam Hussein moving."[51] Later that morning, Bush convened an emergency meeting of the National Security Council to discuss further action. Secretary of State Baker was visiting Mongolia, but three other key policy makers—Dick Cheney from the Pentagon, CIA director William Webster, and General Colin Powell, the new chairman of the Joint Chiefs of Staff—joined the president and Scowcroft in the Cabinet Room. Everyone agreed that Saddam must not be permitted to make Saudi Arabia his next conquest, but there was some debate about whether protecting the House of Saud would be sufficient or whether expelling Iraqi forces from Kuwait would also become necessary. Acknowledging that the threat to Saudi Arabia was quite real, Powell reported that General Norman Schwartzkopf, who headed the U.S. Central Command (CENTCOM), was already developing plans to deploy the Eighty-Second Airborne to the kingdom. Liberating Kuwait, on the other hand, would be far riskier, much more complicated, and extremely expensive. Therefore, why not have CENTCOM "draw a firm line with Saudi Arabia," Powell suggested, and rely on economic sanctions to punish Iraq for gobbling up its smaller neighbor?[52] Convinced that America's Arab friends would interpret acquiescence as appeasement, Bush insisted that "the aggression had to be stopped, and Kuwait's sovereignty restored." Before boarding Air Force One for a whirlwind flight to Aspen, Colorado, for a long-scheduled meeting with the British prime minister Margaret Thatcher, he requested a more thorough assessment of the situation.[53]

Most U.S. policy makers saw the crisis in the Persian Gulf as a double-barreled threat to American interests. If Iraq's takeover of Kuwait was not reversed, Bush's New World Order would be dead on arrival and Saddam Hussein would become the arbiter of the world's oil. Brent Scowcroft, for example, remembered being "frankly appalled" on 2 August that anyone would even suggest "resignation to the invasion," which he regarded "as the major crisis of our time," one that had profound implications for U.S. foreign policy far beyond the Middle East.[54] Secretary of Defense Cheney likewise recalled stewing "about the enormous economic clout that Saddam would gain from Kuwait, how its wealth would enable him to acquire increasingly sophisticated capabilities, chemical weapons, nuclear weapons, and ballistic missiles," and then racing back to the Pentagon, where he scribbled himself the following note: "No non-military option is likely to produce any positive result," because "U.S. military power [was] the only thing Hussein fears."[55] The NSC's Haass spelled out just how high the stakes were later that afternoon in a background memo he prepared for Scowcroft. "Accepting this new status quo . . . would be setting a terrible precedent—one that would only accelerate violent centrifugal tendencies—in this emerging 'post–Cold War' era," Haass reminded his boss. "We would be encouraging a dangerous adversary in the Gulf at a time when the United States has provided a de facto commitment to Gulf stability . . . that also raises the issue of U.S. reliability in a most serious way." Although "we don't need to draw any lines just yet," Haass believed that the Bush administration must be prepared to act forcefully, sooner rather than later.[56]

The president would prove far more willing to draw that line much sooner than Haass or Cheney could ever have imagined. Energized by his rapid-fire skull session with Thatcher in the foothills of the Rocky Mountains, Bush returned to the White House on 3 August and informed his NSC team that "the status quo is intolerable." Despite the "hand wringing" of moderates like Egypt's Hosni Mubarak and Jordan's King Hussein, who still hoped to arrange an "Arab solution," Bush and Thatcher had agreed that there was no room in the New World Order for someone as "ruthless and powerful" as Saddam Hussein. Nodding, Scowcroft added that permitting the Iraqi dictator to hang on to Kuwait virtually guaranteed that he "would dominate OPEC politics, Palestinian politics and the PLO, and lead the Arab world to the detriment of the United States." Undersecretary of State Lawrence Eagleburger, who was pinch-hitting while Jim Baker completed his Mongolian odyssey, termed the assault on Kuwait "the first test of the post [Cold] war system."[57] Ironically, turmoil in Moscow was actually giving Baghdad greater flexibility. "Pipsqueaks like Saddam Hussein can do more rather than less because they aren't constrained by their Big Brother," Eagleburger growled. "If he succeeds, others may try the same thing." All in all, "it would be a bad lesson."[58] Insisting that "the problem will get worse, not better," Cheney predicted that "with his new wealth" stolen from Kuwait, Saddam "will be able to acquire new weapons, including nuclear weapons." As he had the previous morning, Colin Powell sounded a lonely note of caution. Arguing that Kuwait was the wrong place to draw a line in the sand and reminding everyone that armed intervention in Iraq would be very different from regime change in Panama, he warned that "this would be the NFL, not a scrimmage. It would mean a major confrontation." Not only was Saddam Hussein "a professional and megalomaniac," but the military balance was "weighted in his favor."[59]

Hoping to avoid a major confrontation but also determined to protect Saudi Arabia and liberate Kuwait, Bush settled on a policy that combined elements of firmness and caution during his third NSC meeting in three days on 4 August. The State Department would seek UN economic sanctions against Baghdad and would mobilize a broad coalition of NATO allies and friendly Arabs to prevent further Iraqi aggression. William Webster, the CIA's director, would explore covert ways to topple Saddam Hussein with help from dissidents inside the Iraqi army. Generals Powell and Schwartzkopf would revise CENTCOM's contingency plans to incorporate up to 250,000 GIs as part of an operation soon to be known as Desert Shield. And Secretary of Defense Cheney would fly to Riyadh to secure King Fahd's personal approval for the deployment of American forces inside Saudi Arabia. As the meeting broke up, a jetlagged Secretary of State Baker, fresh off a red-eye flight from Ulan Bator, summed things up this way: "Our strategy is three-fold: to keep Saddam out [of Saudi Arabia], to make him a pariah, and to topple him through sanctions and covert actions." President Bush reckoned that this was a good start, but he saw trouble looming not too far down the road. "We have a problem if Saddam does not invade Saudi Arabia but holds on to Kuwait," he reminded his NSC team. The Iraqi strongman might be "underestimating world opposition" to his power play in the Persian Gulf, however. "Lots of people are calling him Hitler."[60]

Half a century earlier, George H. W. Bush had flown his torpedo-laden TBF Avenger against the Japanese navy in the South Pacific, not against German warships in the North Atlantic, but in his mind's eye, the Nazis remained the ultimate manifestation of them and the threat they posed to us Americans. "In the first weeks of the [Persian Gulf] crisis, I happened to be reading a book on World War II by the British historian Martin Gilbert," Bush recalled eight years later. "I saw a direct analogy between what was occurring in Kuwait and what the Nazis had done, especially in Poland." Simply put, "it was a matter of good versus evil," and "Saddam had become the epitome of evil."[61] Bush was hardly surprised when other world leaders drew similar lessons from the past. Appeasement, Thatcher had reminded him during their meeting in Aspen, was no better an option in 1990 than in 1938. After the Iraqi blitzkrieg in Kuwait, Saudi Arabia's King Fahd informed Bush that "Saddam Hussein [is] like Hitler" and "called him a liar."[62] And the Turkish president Turgut Ozal warned Bush in early August that even if Saddam could be persuaded to withdraw from Kuwait in exchange for the sheikdom forgiving Iraqi war debts, there would still be a problem: "If the solution is that Iraq pulls back and Kuwait pays, that is not a solution but would be another Munich." The old Avenger pilot in the Oval Office did not disagree. "What worries me is that Iraq may go further down the Gulf," Bush told Ozal. "We should not repeat the mistakes made at the beginning of World War II."[63]

One leader who saw things differently was Jordan's King Hussein. Wedged between Iraq in the east and Israel in the west, the king's hatchet-shaped realm was home to 3 million Palestinians, who comprised 60 percent of the population and whose sympathies lay clearly with Saddam Hussein. Moreover, Jordan had no oil reserves of its own and relied on imports from Iraq to meet most of its energy needs. In the immediate aftermath of Iraq's invasion of Kuwait, King Hussein tried to arrange an Arab solution to the crisis, but King Fahd's decision to permit U.S. troops to enter Saudi Arabia under the auspices of Operation Desert Shield on 6 August dashed those hopes. Ten days later, the Jordanian monarch and his foreign minister, Zaid bin Shaker, arrived at the summer White House in Kennebunkport, Maine, for a postmortem with Bush and Scowcroft. The procedure did not begin well. At bottom, King Hussein insisted, the dispute between Kuwait and Iraq was a classic case of "have & have not," with Saddam cast as a tribune of hungry, homeless, and hopeless Arabs everywhere. "Irony here," Bush retorted, "the 'have-nots' benefit from lower oil prices—yet [Saddam] argues he needs ↑ price . . . He's a have—he'd be rich if he'd reorder his priorities."[64] Maybe so, the king replied, but the "danger of getting all our friends involved, because of fundamentalism, holy places, [and] left-[wing] radicalism" would still have made it much less risky "to settle w/in [an] Arab framework."[65]

For Bush, however, the danger of doing nothing was far greater than the danger of doing something. "People are watching" how the United States responded to Iraqi aggression. "Will we stand firm by principle or turn away?" Whether the king wanted to admit it or not, Saddam Hussein was "not a good man & not well motivated," and "the world is outraged by what he has done." Of course there were strategic and economic interests at stake, but Bush claimed that America's most important concern was the sanctity of international law, not the security of Persian Gulf oil. "There is a historical lesson here—esp[ecially] for little countries," he pointed out. Some self-styled Hitler on the Euphrates "can't just come into K[uwait], seize it & brush away [the] govt because he didn't get his way."[66] When the two Jordanians persisted in pressing for a negotiated settlement, Bush had had enough. "I will not let that little dictator control 25 percent of the civilized world's oil," he exploded.[67] "I am not J. C. [Jimmy Carter] & I will do whatever is necessary" to force Saddam Hussein to withdraw from Kuwait. "I don't have [a] brilliant idea—except that he has to get out."[68]

Offended by Bush's snide remark implying that Arabs were uncivilized, King Hussein and Zaid bin Shaker skipped their dessert, said their good-byes, and cleared the deck for two Saudi princes—Foreign Minister Saud bin Faisal and Bandar bin Sultan, Riyadh's ambassador in Washington—whose afternoon appointment went far more smoothly than the luncheon meeting with the Jordanians. "We're delighted you're here," Bush told his Saudi guests. Relieved that the first GIs had begun arriving in Saudi Arabia to deter a possible Iraqi attack, he and Secretary of State Baker turned to their larger objective: "[We] want SH [Saddam Hussein] OUT" of Kuwait. To this end, U.S. officials had "tried to mobilize int[ernational] support" and intended "to make sure the eco[nomic] noose is tight" around Iraq's neck. Bush, however, was worried that Saddam might retaliate by taking some or all of the 3,800 American civilians currently working in Iraq and Kuwait hostage. "What would be the reaction if the US retaliated by bombing Iraq?" Baker wondered. "Public reaction in SA [Saudi Arabia] would not oppose any action vs. Iraq," Foreign Minister Saud bin Faisal replied. "But you should go all the way or nothing." What about "KH's [King Hussein's] line that the whole Arab world is against us," Bush asked. "Not true—espec[ially] in Jordan," Bandar bin Sultan assured the president. "Also, lots of Egyptians favor us. SA too." With the House of Saud serving as a bellwether, then, moderate Arabs seemed likely to welcome U.S. military intervention. Although the official account of this conversation remains classified, one can easily imagine the four men celebrating their "meeting of the minds" over Bandar's beverage of choice, Johnnie Walker Black.[69]

By late August, a sober Bush administration realized that stopping Saddam Hussein might well mean going all the way and bombing Iraq. Leaving "all that Kuwaiti wealth" in the hands of the Iraqi equivalent of Adolf Hitler was simply not an option, Cheney recalled thinking, even if Saddam kept his hands off Saudi Arabia. "He will dominate the Gulf. He will dominate OPEC," Bush's secretary of defense observed grimly, and "he will acquire more, deadlier armaments."[70] Scowcroft and his staff echoed Cheney's assessment, but drew an analogy from the history of the Middle East rather than from Central Europe. "Saddam seeks to become the next Nasser," an NSC briefing paper pointed out, "but unlike the original he would have all sorts of conventional and unconventional military means at his disposal."[71] Back in Kennebunkport at summer's end, Scowcroft warned his boss that if America appeased this Nasser on the Euphrates, "we'll look like a paper tiger." Angling for bluefish just off the Maine coast aboard the presidential speedboat *Fidelity* on 23 August, Bush ruminated over the threat that old-fashioned villains like Saddam Hussein posed to the emerging New World Order. Returning to the historical analogy he liked best, "the first fisherman" reiterated that it was high time for the "civilized nations" to stop "another Hitler."[72] To this end, Secretary of State Jim Baker resumed his diplomatic globetrotting to assemble the broadest possible "coalition of the civilized" committed to doing whatever was necessary—everything from tighter economic sanctions to armed intervention—to liberate Kuwait under the auspices of the United Nations.

While Baker piled up the frequent flyer miles, the president put the finishing touches on a formal statement of U.S. policy in the Persian Gulf that he would unveil just after Labor Day. "Vital issues of principle are at stake. Saddam Hussein is trying to wipe a country off the face of the Earth," Bush told a joint session of Congress on 11 September 1990. "Vital economic interests are at stake as well. Iraq itself controls some 10 percent of the world's proven oil reserves. Iraq plus Kuwait controls twice that." Without mentioning either Nasser or Hitler, the president emphasized the broader implications of the crisis. "An Iraq permitted to swallow Kuwait would have the economic and military power, as well as the arrogance, to intimidate and coerce its neighbors—neighbors who control the lion's share of the world's remaining oil reserves." Not only was Saddam's aggression anathema under existing international law; it was also antithetical to the emerging post–Cold War world order. "We cannot permit a resource so vital to be dominated by one so ruthless," Bush vowed. "And we won't."[73]

During the following four months, the Bush administration left no doubt that it would make good on that vow. At the United Nations, U.S. diplomats steered five resolutions condemning Iraq through the Security Council in just six weeks. Across the Atlantic, Britain, Turkey, and other NATO allies agreed to deploy combat units as Desert Shield morphed into Desert Storm, while Syria and Egypt promised to provide logistical support. And inside the White House, Bush and his national security team decided to double the size of the American expeditionary force in the Persian Gulf from 250,000 to 500,000 troops. Inside the Kremlin, however, Gorbachev and his advisers were deeply ambivalent about impending military intervention against Moscow's former client in Baghdad. On 19 October, Yevgeny Primakov, a leading Russian expert on the Middle East who was well acquainted with the Iraqi dictator, paid a visit to the Oval Office, where he proposed linking the liberation of Kuwait to the resurrection of the stalemated Arab-Israeli peace process. "Don't push Saddam into a corner," Primakov told President Bush. Instead, why not permit him to save face through a diplomatic quid pro quo? Bush was having none of it. Saddam Hussein was "like Hitler & the Nazis," Bush informed the Soviet diplomat. "You give a face-saver to someone who's part of the civilized world, but he's not part of the civilized world."[74]

When Jim Baker arrived in Moscow in early November seeking support for a UN ultimatum demanding that Iraq withdraw from Kuwait, he was pleased to learn that Kremlin decision makers were actually much less sympathetic to Saddam Hussein than Primakov had led Bush to believe. "What's really important is that we stick together," Gorbachev declared on 8 November. "We can't let a thug like this get away with what he's done."[75] Otherwise, "there'll be no hope for the new kind of international reality we'd like to see."[76] Did this mean, Baker wondered, that the Soviet Union would support military intervention if Iraq defied the United Nations? Gorbachev nodded, but was quick to point out: "You understand, now, that if we pass a resolution authorizing the use of force, and Saddam does not move, you will actually have to use force. . . . Are you really ready to do that right now?"[77] Yes we are, came the reply. Then, speaking as one child of the 1930s to another, Baker made an oblique but unmistakable reference to a painful lesson from the past: "We can't have the UN go the way of the League of Nations."[78] On the way back to Washington, Baker stopped briefly in London and Paris, where he received wholehearted support for a hard-line approach toward Iraq from two of America's oldest allies, both of whom, like Uncle Sam's new friend in Moscow, remembered their history all too well. "If Saddam Hussein does not feel threatened," President François Mitterrand, himself a veteran of the French Resistance during World War II, told Baker on 10 November, "he will not give up anything."[79]

Three weeks later, France, Britain, the Soviet Union, and eight other members of the UN Security Council approved Resolution 678, an American-sponsored ultimatum calling for the use of "all means necessary," including armed force, against Iraq if Saddam Hussein did not withdraw his troops from Kuwait by 15 January 1991. Secretary of State Baker, who flew to New York City to introduce the ultimatum personally, likened the 1990 crisis in the Persian Gulf to yet another episode from the 1930s, Italy's invasion of Ethiopia, whose leader Haile Selassie had, like the Emir of Kuwait, immediately sought outside help. "Sadly, his appeal to the League of Nations fell upon deaf ears," Baker reminded his colleagues on the UN Security Council, "and international disorder and war ensued."[80] Having obtained passage of Security Council Resolution 678, the Bush administration sought congressional approval early in the new year to expel Iraq forcibly from Kuwait. Following three days of ferocious debate, Congress passed a joint resolution on 12 January authorizing U.S. armed intervention to enforce the UN ultimatum, assuming that "all appropriate diplomatic and other peaceful means to obtain compliance by Iraq" had been exhausted. Bush's margin of victory in the Senate was just 52 to 47, with a half-dozen Democrats, including Tennessee's Albert Gore Jr., providing the decisive votes. Thirty-six hours after the UN deadline expired, hundreds of Tomahawk cruise missiles and F-117 Stealth fighters struck high-value military targets in Baghdad. As of 17 January 1991, America was at war.

Despite Saddam Hussein's bombastic vow to wage "the mother of all battles" and despite dire warnings from the war's critics on Capitol Hill that Operation Desert Storm would become a Middle Eastern Vietnam, the outcome was never really in doubt. For more than a month, the U.S. Air Force and its coalition partners pounded Iraqi positions in Kuwait and disrupted Iraqi supply lines stretching south from Baghdad into the tiny oil sheikdom. Then at 4:00 A.M. on 24 February, General Norman Schwartzkopf unleashed a blitzkrieg that saw American armored columns sweep into Kuwait City and southern Iraq. Just one hundred hours later, "Stormin' Norman" and his desert warriors had liberated Kuwait, leaving a "Highway of Death" that ran north toward Baghdad littered with burned-out Iraqi tanks and bloated Iraqi corpses. When the shooting stopped on 28 February, Iraq counted 20,000 war dead and another 60,000 wounded. U.S. casualties, by contrast, totaled just 148 killed in action. Schwartzkopf was eager to march on the Iraqi capital and impose regime change, but the White House worried that an assault on Baghdad would fracture the anti-Saddam coalition and create a power vacuum in the Persian Gulf that would only benefit Iran. As a result, Saddam Hussein clung to power, wounded yet still dangerous. To be sure, U.S. forces had destroyed the world's fourth-largest army in just four days. Saddam's paramilitary Republican Guard, however, remained largely intact, and he used it ruthlessly to crush the Shia and Kurdish separatists whom Bush and the CIA had encouraged to take up arms against Hitler on the Euphrates after the First Gulf War ended.

Lessons from the 1930s remained an essential element of the post–Cold War operational code for a chief executive who continued to view the world as a struggle between us and them. On 22 January 1991, President Bush explained his rationale for war in a letter to Boston's Cardinal Bernard Law, a leading opponent of Operation Desert Storm. "I must confess my mind always went back to the questions: What if Hitler's aggression had been checked earlier on? How many lives would have been saved?" Saddam Hussein "has been the bully in the neighborhood for a long time," Bush reminded Cardinal Law. "For me, this is good versus evil. It is right versus wrong. It is the world versus Iraq's brutal dictator, with his cruelty, his international arrogance, his thumbing his nose at the rest of the world."[81] Nearly two decades later, Richard Haass confirmed that "the key to understanding George Herbert Walker Bush and what made him tick was his sense of decorum." America's forty-first president "was genuinely offended by the Iraqi invasion," Haass recalled, because "it was simply not how civilized countries behaved." For someone who regarded appeasement as a dirty word, Saddam Hussein's barbarism "harkened back to a crude era of international relations when might made right."[82] Secretary of State Jim Baker likewise interpreted events in the Persian Gulf through the lens of Hitler's earlier aggression. "Kuwait was just a down payment on Saddam's regional, and perhaps even global, ambitions," Baker insisted in his memoirs. The demise of Iraq's Soviet patron and the ascension of America as the world's sole remaining superpower had created a "unipolar moment" filled with both opportunity and danger for Baghdad. "The greatest threat Saddam saw to his grandiose plans to become the new Nasser lay far to his northwest: America." He intended to present Baker and Bush with a fait accompli in Kuwait while they had their hands full with Russia. Like Hitler and Nasser, however, Saddam Hussein had gambled and lost. Might his defeat pave the way for peace between the Arabs and the Israelis?[83]

From Bagdad to Madrid: Jumpstarting the Peace Process

One of the Bush administration's most remarkable accomplishments during the run-up to Operation Desert Storm was preventing the Persian Gulf crisis from morphing into round five of the nonstop Arab-Israeli battle royal. Based on Saddam Hussein's nasty rhetoric and aggressive behavior, Israel's leaders saw him as Hitler on the Euphrates, and having watched him swallow Kuwait, they were more convinced than ever that the best defense was a good offense. For his part, Saddam tried to pressure Syria, Egypt, and other Arab states into leaving the American-led coalition, first by promising to pull out of Kuwait in exchange for Israeli withdrawal from the Occupied Territories and then, when all else failed, by lobbing a few Scud missiles at Tel Aviv and Haifa with an eye to provoking Prime Minister Yitzhak Shamir to retaliate. Keeping Israel on the sidelines was a high priority for the Bush administration from the start of the crisis. As early as 17 August 1990, Secretary of Defense Cheney thanked his Israeli counterpart, Moshe Arens, for having adopted a "wisely-chosen low profile policy" at "an extremely delicate time for us." Noting that "thousands of American troops are already in Saudi Arabia" to protect "enormous economic and geopolitical interests," Cheney praised the Israelis for "not making any statements or more important taking action that would remove the focus from where it properly is, on Iraq's invasion and occupation of Kuwait."[84] Two months later, when the Soviet Union's Yevgeny Primakov tried to change that focus by proposing a "compromise" whereby Iraq would withdraw from Kuwait and Israel would turn the West Bank over to the Palestinians, Dennis Ross, Jim Baker's chief peace processor, retorted that such an arrangement would merely "pave the way for a much bigger war" between Arabs and Israelis. "You'll make [Saddam] a hero of unprecedented scale, especially among Arab masses, if you let him get away with what he's doing," Ross warned Primakov. "He'll be the arbiter of what happens in the future."[85]

No one in Washington was interested in making Saddam Hussein the arbiter of anything, but Ross and his boss believed that once Iraq was expelled from Kuwait, they could jumpstart the stalled Middle East peace process, provided that Israel steered clear of the conflict in the Persian Gulf.

To this end, President Bush assured Yitzhak Shamir on 11 December 1990 that if Saddam attacked Israel, or even "if an attack becomes apparent," U.S. forces "have the capacity to obliterate his military structure," and they would do so. "A preemptive strike by Israel would be very bad," Bush explained, because it would rally Arab support for Iraq. Although Shamir promised to consult Washington before taking any military action, he emphasized that "we will be obliged to defend ourselves," because despite America's best efforts to obliterate Saddam's Scud missiles, "you may miss some."[86] A few days later, the Pentagon installed a special hotline to the Israeli Ministry of Defense codenamed "Hammer Rick" to ensure that Cheney and Arens remained on the same page once Operation Desert Storm got under way. After a dozen Scuds landed in Tel Aviv and Haifa during the wee hours of 19 January 1991, Hammer Rick lit up for the first time, with Arens barking that "Israeli commandos were loaded into helicopters ready to fly into Iraq" and demanding that Cheney provide him with the transponder identification codes necessary to distinguish friendly American aircraft from hostile Iraqi warplanes.[87] When Cheney refused, Arens contacted the State Department with some ominous news. "They've hit us. We have to hit them back," he told Secretary of State Baker. "Israel can't sit here and be hit with missiles and do nothing." Because the Scuds were not very accurate and did only minimal damage, however, in late January the Bush administration was able to persuade Arens and Shamir not to retaliate by agreeing to provide Israel with Patriot antimissile missiles, the technicians necessary to operate them, and real-time satellite surveillance confirming successful U.S. air raids against military targets inside Iraq.[88]

Having barely managed to keep Israel out of the Persian Gulf War, U.S. officials turned to the more daunting task of getting Shamir to the peace table. America's triumph over Iraq had done nothing to soften Shamir's long-standing opposition to trading peace for land. Why should he start talking with Yasser Arafat, who had been foolish enough to support Saddam Hussein's invasion of Kuwait? And how could he stop building settlements on the West Bank when what had once been a trickle of Russian Jews into Israel was becoming a torrent? For Jim Baker, the answer to both questions was obvious: Because peace with the Palestinians was the only way the Israelis could ever achieve the security they craved. Two weeks after the shooting stopped in the Persian Gulf, he arrived in Riyadh, the first stop on a five-day trip to "test the waters" for a Middle East peace conference. Adopting as his motto "Don't let the dead cat die on your doorstep," Baker cajoled Saudi Arabia's King Fahd and Egypt's Hosni Mubarak into supporting the idea. When Bush's secretary of state landed in Tel Aviv on 11 March, however, Shamir informed him that Israel would never sit down with the PLO. Two days later, while Baker was en route back to Washington empty-handed, Ariel Sharon, Shamir's minister of housing, unveiled plans to construct thirteen thousand new residential units on the West Bank.[89]

Hoping to turn the Israelis around, Baker flew back to Tel Aviv in early April with an ingenious proposal to create a Palestinian negotiating team whose ranks would not include any PLO members and a request that Shamir shelve plans for new housing in the Occupied Territories. His return engagement, however, went no better than his original visit. Shamir haggled over the composition of the Palestinian delegation and refused to repudiate Sharon's statement regarding the expansion of West Bank settlements. Baker was livid on both counts, accusing the Israelis of "a deliberate effort to sabotage peace" and hinting that the peace conference was going to go forward, regardless of Israel's foot-dragging.[90] "I'm working my ass off, and I'm not getting cooperation from you," Baker snapped. On the way to the airport, he turned to one of his Middle East advisers and said: "I'm going to leave the dead cat on Shamir's doorstep."[91]

More convinced than ever that Israeli expansion on the West Bank was the most serious "obstacle to peace," President Bush tried a more indirect approach in late July, asking one of his old friends, Jacob Stein, the former chairman of the Conference of Presidents of Major Jewish Organizations, to deliver a personal note to the Israeli prime minister: "Mr. Shamir, it would be very much in our mutual interest if you would put a halt to settlements," went the message from the White House. After all, the population of the West Bank had been overwhelmingly Arab under both Ottoman and British rule. "The territory belongs to Israel," came the reply from Shamir. "It doesn't belong to the Turks. It doesn't belong to the British Mandate."[92]

Frustrated and fearful that Israel's intransigence would thwart plans to convene a Middle East peace conference in Madrid later that fall, on 12 September 1991 Bush revealed that he was deferring until New Year's Day a decision on $10 billion in U.S. loan guarantees earmarked for Israel to ensure that Tel Aviv stopped building settlements and started talking with the Palestinians.[93] Shocked and angered by such explicit use of economic leverage, Shamir announced a "pause" in construction on the West Bank and flew to Madrid on 30 October, where just moments before the opening session of the peace conference, he informed Bush that Israel would not accept an American diktat. "We are not trying to impose a settlement," Bush retorted. "We want to be a catalyst." Shamir saw it very differently and implied that the United States was tilting toward the Arabs at Israel's expense. "The other parties are not risking anything," he complained. "We are the ones taking risks."[94]

Memorable mainly for marking the first time that Israelis and Palestinians actually sat down together at the same negotiating table, the Madrid Conference succeeded only in raising hopes in Arab capitals that a long-awaited breakthrough might be at hand. When Shamir met Bush and Baker again on 22 November, however, there were more angry words. Rejecting an American offer to host multilateral peace talks in Washington, the Israeli prime minister said that any further negotiations must be bilateral and must take place in the Middle East. "The Arab perception is that the U.S. President and government support their position," Shamir explained, "so they like Washington, not to negotiate with us but to work on you and the American people." This surprised Bush, who thought that "the Arabs don't like Washington" because they worried that "the traditional U.S.-Israeli relationship" would put them at a disadvantage. "Not so," Shamir replied. "They think the U.S. has decided to change its policy towards Israel and support the Arabs." They might think that, Bush said, "but it is certainly not true." Exasperated by Shamir's obstinacy, Jim Baker jumped in, waving his figurative dead cat. "We've been faithful to Israel's needs. We have bent over backwards," he grumbled. "We have made it clear . . . that we do not support an independent Palestinian state. What more can we do?" Was Shamir "worried about outside pressure?" Bush wondered. "He is worried about you and me being honest," Baker shot back. "I will be honest," Shamir replied as the Oval Office meeting drew to a close. "We worry about the media and the Arabs who will come to talk to you and not to us."[95]

Israeli-American relations grew even frostier during Shamir's final seven months as prime minister. On 4 December, the Labor Party leader Yitzhak Rabin, the man Bush's national security team hoped would defeat Shamir in the Israeli elections scheduled for the following November, paid a visit to the White House, where he chatted with Brent Scowcroft. Noting that America's firm stand against Iraq had reshaped the geopolitical landscape of the Middle East and, perhaps, paved the way for peace, Rabin confessed that "for several years it has been clear to me that the Palestinians want to deal with Israel." Scowcroft nodded, adding that "we hope direct contact will transform the dialogue" and increase the "self-confidence and courage" of Palestinian moderates. American officials realized that "there is no magic answer," yet greater flexibility on Israel's part would prove enormously helpful. Rabin agreed but urged the United States to "let the parties confront each other and do not interfere" or play favorites. "We will try very hard, very hard," Scowcroft replied, but so must Israel, especially on matters like the West Bank settlements. "As for the loan guarantees, we postponed the problem until January," he warned Rabin. "We will not postpone it again." Then Scowcroft posed a question that was on both men's minds: "Will Shamir call new elections?" Rabin doubted it, because "Shamir is not a risk taker." Instead, he would likely bide his time, and so must the Bush administration.[96]

There was another election scheduled for November 1992, of course, and many of Israel's American friends were determined to prevent George H. W. Bush from winning a second term. Ten months before election day, a group of Jewish leaders contacted Dennis Ross, whom Jim Baker had asked to oversee the peace process, to complain that the Bush administration was anti-Israel. Ross insisted that this was not the case. "We're entering a different world," he told his visitors, in which "there isn't a Cold War anymore." They must realize that the special relationship "was not just a function of our commitment to Israel" but rather a reflection of "a certain kind of strategic reality." With the decline of Russian influence in the Middle East, Ross explained, "we have to rethink that part of the world including the former Soviet states in Central Asia."[97] When a Jewish Republican fund-raiser from New York wrote President Bush directly in mid-March to express his unhappiness about withholding American loan guarantees until Israel halted its expansion into the Occupied Territories, the man in the Oval Office did not mince his words: "We say that settlements are an obstacle to peace, and they are. I do not exaggerate when I tell you that more than anything else Israel is saying or doing, settlements are undermining those forces in the Arab world that at long last are ready to reach out and live in peace with Israel." Resolving the standoff between Tel Aviv and Washington would "quite frankly . . . depend upon the priorities of those in Israel's government," Bush concluded. "I have come to believe that the measure of a good relationship is not the ability to agree, but rather the ability to disagree on specifics without placing fundamentals at risk. We do this all the time with Britain; we should manage to do it with Israel."[98]

Convinced that both specifics and fundamentals were at risk, AIPAC's executive director Thomas Dine told his organization's national conference a month later that resolving the Israeli-American impasse depended on the priorities of the Bush administration. "September 12, 1991, will be a day that lives in infamy for the American pro-Israel community," Dine vowed. "Like the Indian elephant, we shall not forget."[99] Samuel Lewis, who had recently stepped down after serving more than a decade as U.S. ambassador in Tel Aviv, told an interviewer that same April that Bush's policies might signal the demise of "the icing on the cake—what the Reagan administration [had] called 'the strategic relationship'" between Israel and America. "Now that the Cold War has been swept away, the icing doesn't look so colorful and impressive anymore," Lewis observed. "You take it away, and you see the cake is a bit moldy. It needs renewing."[100] Hoping to bake a better cake, in mid-May Yitzhak Shamir surprised everyone in Israel by scheduling early elections. In the end, however, the other Yitzhak had a better recipe, and Israeli voters repudiated Shamir and his Likud coalition by a wide margin on 24 June 1992. One of Rabin's first decisions as prime minister was to halt construction of Israeli settlements on the West Bank, and the White House responded by releasing the first tranche from the frozen $10 billion loan guarantee package.

If Bush expected these actions to restore even a modicum of support among Jewish Americans, he was mistaken. "Any Jew voting for Bush must be doing it for the sake of his pocket book," Morris Amitay, one of Thomas Dine's AIPAC colleagues, remarked acidly on the eve of the U.S. presidential balloting. ""It certainly isn't for Israel's sake." Indeed, just 10 percent of American Jews voted for Bush on 3 November, a sharp drop from the 27 percent he had received four years earlier.[101] Did Bush's confrontation with Shamir cost him the election? The postmortems on the 1992 campaign revealed that U.S. voters were far more concerned with domestic matters than with foreign policy, suggesting that the president's plummeting popularity among Jewish Americans played only a marginal role in the outcome. After all, the favorite rallying cry for the challenger, Bill Clinton, had been: "It's the economy, stupid." Yet looking back on the battle with Israel, George H. W. Bush was not so sure. "Look at the loan guarantees," he recalled many years later. "I didn't ride in here on a watermelon truck." Bush had realized that "the politics would be tough," and he knew "that when the head of AIPAC came down that we were in for a fight." Yet he expressed no regrets. "Some people have said that this cost you the Jewish vote," Bush remarked wistfully. "I don't know if that's true or not, but I can't whine about that."[102] Two things were indisputably true, however. America's long-standing special relationship with Israel looked very different after 1989. And so did U.S. relations with Russia's former Arab clients like Saddam Hussein. While the Bush national security team was busy developing a new approach to the Arabs and the Israelis in the aftermath of the Cold War, Islamic radicals were quietly making their own plans for Central Asia and the Middle East.

Islam, the End of History, and the Rise of the Green Threat

Not long after George H. W. Bush took the oath of office, Francis Fukuyama, a RAND corporation analyst who would soon join the State Department's policy planning staff, delivered the John Olin Lecture at the University of Chicago. Back in Washington, the new administration was cautiously developing its blueprint for moving beyond containment. Eight hundred miles to the west, on the shores of Lake Michigan, Fukuyama was proclaiming "the end of history." With the Soviet Union clearly in decline and the Kremlin's empire in Eastern Europe on the verge of collapse, he told a packed house on 8 February 1989, it seemed obvious that capitalism had triumphed over communism. Moreover, even bigger changes might be afoot. "What we may be witnessing is not just the end of the Cold War, or the passing of a particular period of post-war history, but the end of history as such," Fukuyama explained in the published version of his lecture in the summer 1989 issue of the *National Interest*. The world had quite likely reached "the end point of mankind's ideological evolution and the universalization of Western liberal democracy as the final form of human government." Fukuyama detected just one potential threat to this emerging New World Order—religious fundamentalism, particularly in Muslim societies. "In the contemporary world only Islam has offered a theocratic state as a political alternative to both liberalism and communism," he pointed out. "But the doctrine has little appeal for non-Muslims, and it is hard to believe that the movement will take on any universal significance."[103]

Despite this rose-colored forecast, however, radical Islam would have far greater appeal inside the Muslim world and far greater significance outside than Fukuyama imagined. A week after he gave the Olin Lecture, the Red Army withdrew from Afghanistan, but fighting dragged on between the Soviet-backed regime of Mohammed Najibullah and mujahedin guerrillas supported by the United States. Islamic radicalism, Kremlin officials warned their American counterparts repeatedly throughout 1989, posed a grave threat to political stability, not merely in Central Asia but also in the Middle East. Worried that radical Islam might spread to the Arabian Peninsula, the Yemeni president Ali Abdullah Saleh warned George H. W. Bush on 24 January 1990 that Najibullah's departure was no more welcome in Sana'a than in Moscow. "The Soviets," Bush conceded, "say we should stop cooperating with the Mujahedin, but as long as they are supplying Najib, then the freedom fighters should not be let down and deserted." Of course, Bush was quick to add, "if he leaves, there would be an instant solution."[104]

After reviewing the future of Afghanistan and other post–Cold War problems with the Soviet foreign minister Eduard Shevardnadze two months later, however, Secretary of State Jim Baker seemed more ambivalent. "If Najibullah were to go, we could immediately accept the principle of negative symmetry, a ceasefire, and national elections," he asserted. Maybe so, Shevardnadze retorted, but "no one could force Najibullah out." Therefore the next-best solution was nationwide balloting in which everyone, including the Kremlin's man in Kabul, could participate. "The mujihaddin would never accept it if Najib could run in the elections," Baker replied. Yet privately he was having second thoughts about America's clients in Afghanistan. "Frankly, I have got to say, there is something paradoxical and indefensible about us opposing elections that are free and fair," Baker cabled Bush on 20 March 1990. "If the mujihaddin won't participate in such elections, how can we justify continued support for them?"[105]

The threat posed by Muslim radicals was also becoming quite obvious two thousand miles to the west-southwest in the Holy Land, where American officials watched as Hamas, a homegrown Palestinian Islamist organization, adopted increasingly violent tactics against the Israeli occupation. Hamas had been founded in Gaza during the first months of the Palestinian intifada, and according to Philip Wilcox, the U.S. consul general in Jerusalem, it enjoyed broad support among the poorest refugees, was highly critical of the corruption and secularism of Fatah, Yasser Arafat's branch of the PLO, and appeared "genuinely committed to the goal of creating an Islamic state in all of Palestine." Relying on the same "enemy of my enemy is my friend" logic that led the United States to support the anti-Soviet mujahedin in Afghanistan, Israel briefly "turn[ed] a blind eye to Hamas activities" and treated Palestinian Islamists as convenient foils to Fatah.[106] Then suddenly in September 1989, Yitzhak Shamir banned Hamas and jailed its leaders. "Some Israeli occupation officials indicated that Hamas served as a useful counter to the secular organizations loyal to the PLO," Ambassador William Brown explained from his post in Tel Aviv, but "outlawing the organization indicates that [Israel] no longer sees—if it ever did—utility in allowing Hamas to operate." A year later, Fatah and Hamas buried the hatchet and formed a united front against Israel. Their reconciliation, Consul General Wilcox reported from Jerusalem on 25 September 1990, "is widely viewed here as reflecting gains made by Islamic fundamentalists in the occupied territories following the breakdown of the peace process and the eruption of the Gulf crisis."[107]

Earlier that month, a high-profile article written by Bernard Lewis, one of America's leading experts on the Middle East, had appeared in the *Atlantic* with a disturbing title—"The Roots of Muslim Rage"—and with an even more disturbing explanation for the recent rise of Islamic fundamentalism. Lewis did not draw the illustration that graced the magazine's cover, which depicted a turbaned, bearded, and hawk-nosed Muslim scowling back at readers while the stars and stripes shimmered in his eyes. Nor did he draft the blurb in the magazine's table of contents, which described the "intense—and violent—resentment of the West" then sweeping the Middle East as merely the latest in "a long series of attacks and counterattacks, jihads and crusades, conquests and reconquests." The British-born and Princeton-based public intellectual did insist, however, that the wave of anger surging through the region resulted less from Muslim bitterness about European imperialism or Israeli expansionism than from "the revival of ancient prejudices" about the Judeo-Christian heritage manipulated by theocratic Arab and Iranian zealots, for whom "America has become the archenemy, the incarnation of evil." The Koran, Lewis claimed, was based on an us-versus-them view of the world, in which the "House of Islam" must be perpetually at war with "the House of Unbelief." The article ended with a bleak prognosis that confirmed Fukuyama's worst nightmare. "We are facing a mood and a movement far transcending the level of issues and policies and the governments that pursue them," Lewis warned Americans. "This is no less than a clash of civilizations."[108]

Although Lewis did not mention Saddam Hussein, and although the roots of the Iraqi dictator's rage were rather different from the grievances of the angry Muslim on the cover of the *Atlantic*, during its final two years in office, the Bush administration became increasingly concerned about the specter of radical Islam. One reason that the White House vetoed General Schwartzkopf's proposal to occupy Baghdad and depose Saddam in March 1991, for example, was the danger that any successor regime would be dominated by Iraqi Shias, who might have aligned themselves with their Iranian coreligionists across the Shatt al-Arab. "Iraq," Jim Baker explained in his memoirs, "might fragment in unpredictable ways that would play into the hands of the mullahs in Iran, who could export their brand of Islamic fundamentalism with the help of Iraq's Shiites and quickly transform themselves into the dominant regional power."[109] After the Soviet Union collapsed later that year and was replaced by a new Commonwealth of Independent States (CIS), U.S. policy makers feared that this sprawling, decentralized entity would be overwhelmed by ethnic feuds and religious rivalries fueled by Muslim extremists. When Baker met with the new leaders of Ukraine and Belarus on 18 December, he stressed that "the danger of radical Islamic fundamentalism sweeping into what had been Soviet Central Asia" made it more important than ever to secure the Kremlin's atomic weapons and prevent loose nukes from making their way into the wrong hands.[110]

The fate of the CIS was just one of many woes that complicated Washington's policies in the Muslim world in 1992. In Gaza, Hamas looked relatively tame when compared to a new extremist organization, Islamic Jihad, which was calling for a holy war to destroy Israel and replace it with a theocratic Palestinian state. In the Balkans, Yugoslavia's rickety multiethnic regime was slowly unraveling into a grisly civil war, with Serbian militias striving to cleanse Bosnia of its Muslim population and with Islamic volunteers from Iran to Libya vowing to fight and die in Sarajevo to halt the slaughter. Meanwhile in Africa, the end of the Cold War produced a sharp decline in Soviet and American economic and military assistance, triggering the collapse of civil order and igniting brutal outbursts of violence from Somalia to the Congo. "The resulting turmoil provides opportunities to terrorists and their state sponsors," an NSC staff study pointed out at the end of the year, and "there are indications that Iran is seeking recruits within Islamic communities in Africa." Noting that "Libyan subversion has long been a problem throughout the continent," the NSC's Africa watchers also suspected that the anti-Western regime in Sudan intended to export its brand of radical Islam to its neighbors.[111] Judging from recent statements by Sudanese leaders, such suspicions were not unfounded. In a blistering anti-American speech in Khartoum on 14 September 1992, Hassan al-Turabi, the founder of Sudan's ruling National Islamic Front, urged Muslims "to use their religion as a shield against the power of the West" and "to apply Islam as a system to protect themselves against the New World Order." Six days later, the Sudanese president Omar al-Bashir denounced "the West's indifference to the suffering of Muslims in Bosnia and Hercegovina, Iraq, Libya and Somalia" and alleged that "the New World Order" was mounting "intrigues against Islam."[112]

The most troubling Muslim challenge to the New World Order, however, would come in Algeria, where by early 1992 the radical Islamic Salvation Front, known throughout North Africa by its French acronym FIS, seemed poised to win the country's first elections in three decades. The FIS had been founded during the late 1980s by Islamists eager to end the corrupt and autocratic reign of the National Liberation Front, or FLN, which had held power continuously since Algeria's war of independence against France. Underestimating the appeal of the FIS, the Algerian president Chadli Benjedid had scheduled parliamentary elections for late 1991. Islamist candidates won nearly half the votes in the first round of balloting and were expected to sweep to victory in the finale on 12 January 1992. Although Benjedid was willing to permit the Islamists to form a government, Mohammed Boudiaf, the FLN army chief of staff, thought otherwise. Just twenty-four hours before the final round was scheduled to begin, Boudiaf staged a military coup d'état, arrested Benjedid, and cancelled the elections. The Bush administration shed few tears for the FIS, whose promise to establish an Islamic state and whose support for Saddam Hussein it found deeply troubling. Whether or not rumors that Boudiaf had alerted the American embassy in Algiers before deposing Benjedid were true, the United States did extend recognition to the new regime and refused to condemn it for halting the balloting.

Five months later, Edward Djerejian, the assistant secretary of state for Near Eastern affairs, summarized the Bush administration's approach to the Middle East at the dawn of the post–Cold War era in a speech at Meridian House International, just a mile north of the White House. Aggressors like Saddam Hussein would not be tolerated. The Israeli-Palestinian peace process would go forward. And oil would continue to flow from the Persian Gulf to consumers in Western Europe and the United States. Djerejian's comments about Islam and democracy, on the other hand, were far less categorical. "The US Government does not view Islam as the next 'ism' confronting the West or threatening world peace," he declared on 2 June 1992. "That is an overly simplistic response to a complex reality." To be sure, from North Africa to the Persian Gulf, there were "movements seeking to reform their societies in keeping with Islamic ideals," but "we detect no monolithic or coordinated international effort" among them. Then, without mentioning Algeria by name, Djerejian explained why the United States had not condemned the FLN for thwarting the political aspirations of the FIS. "Those who seek to broaden political participation in the Middle East will," he insisted, "find us supportive, as we have been elsewhere in the world," but America would not support "those who would use the democratic process to come to power, only to destroy that very process in order to retain power and political dominance." In short, Djerejian concluded, "while we believe in the principle of 'one person, one vote,' we do not support 'one person, one vote, one time.'"[113] Twenty-seven days after the Meridian House speech, Boudiaf was assassinated by one of his own bodyguards, an Islamist with loose ties to the FIS, and Algeria was plunged into a bloody civil war.

While Algeria was imploding, Francis Fukuyama's *The End of History and the Last Man,* a revised and expanded version of his earlier essay, rose toward the top of the *New York Times* best-seller list. Fukuyama, who had resigned his State Department post shortly after the fall of the Berlin Wall, spent the early 1990s pondering the place of radical Islam in the emerging New World Order. He recognized that Muslim regimes seemed relatively immune from the "crisis of authoritarianism" spawned by the "worldwide liberal revolution" that rocked the Soviet Bloc and much of East Asia and Latin America during the late 1980s. "There have been pressures for greater democracy in various Middle Eastern countries like Egypt and Jordan, following the Eastern European revolutions of 1989," Fukuyama conceded. "But in this part of the world, Islam has stood as a major barrier to democratization." Although it did not contain color-coded language, *The End of History* offered a cautionary tale with a rather straightforward moral: the demise of the Red Threat, international communism, would come as cold comfort if it were replaced by an even more dangerous Green Threat—radical Islam. "As demonstrated by the Algerian municipal elections of 1990, or by Iran a decade earlier," Fukuyama pointed out, "greater democracy may not lead to greater liberalization because it brings to power Islamic fundamentalists hoping to establish some form of popular theocracy." Then, like the White House national security team, he alluded to a lesson from the 1930s. "The current revival of Islamic fundamentalism," Fukuyama asserted, "can be seen as a response to the failure of Muslim societies generally to maintain their dignity vis-à-vis the non-Muslim West" during the twentieth century. "In this respect," he concluded ominously, "Islamic fundamentalism bears a more than superficial resemblance to European fascism."[114]

Fukuyama's former colleagues at Foggy Bottom had mixed feelings as the Bush administration drew to a close. Jim Baker, Larry Eagleburger, Dennis Ross, and Edward Djerejian had, like Dean Acheson and George Kennan four decades earlier, been "present at the creation" of a new world order. Moving beyond containment, they had orchestrated some remarkably nonviolent transitions from the Brezhnev to the Sinatra Doctrine in Moscow and the capitals of Eastern Europe at the end of the Cold War. They had pressed President Bush to stand firm and face down Hitler on the Euphrates during Operation Desert Storm. And they had jumpstarted the stalled Arab-Israeli peace process while making enemies out of AIPAC and many American Jews. Yet they bequeathed to their successors a world every bit as unstable and unpredictable as the one they had inherited in 1989. The Middle East, where Islamic radicals sought to launch an anti-American jihad, constituted a primary case in point. During the autumn of 1992, another of Fukuyama's former colleagues, the assistant secretary of state for politico-military affairs, Richard Clarke, had begun keeping close tabs on a little-known Muslim extremist who had fought alongside the Afghan mujahedin during their anti-Soviet jihad before returning home to Saudi Arabia in 1989. While the Bush administration was busy expelling Saddam Hussein from Iraq, Osama Bin Laden kept busy organizing Arab veterans of the Afghan war to fight non-Muslims in Bosnia, Chechnya, Egypt, Algeria, and the Philippines. Bin Laden's ultimate goal, however, was to use his own secret terrorist organization—al-Qaeda—to drive the United States out of the Middle East. On the eve of the new millennium, al-Qaeda would replace the Kremlin as the quintessential them that threatened and terrified us.[115]

CHAPTER THREE

Bill Clinton and the Middle East
From "Enlargement" to "Dual Containment"

Inauguration Day 1993 dawned crisp and clear. There was a festive mood among the crowd of 800,000 who milled around the National Mall under blue skies, their gaze riveted on the west terrace of the U.S. Capitol, where President Bill Clinton celebrated "the mystery of American renewal" and, with a nod to the past, praised George H. W. Bush for having fought and won the good fight against both fascism and communism. Then, pivoting toward the future, Clinton signaled that he and his fellow baby boomers born after the Second World War were ready to lead. "Today, a generation raised in the shadows of the cold war assumes new responsibilities in a world warmed by the sunshine of freedom but threatened still by ancient hatreds and new plagues," he intoned, but beyond some boilerplate about the United States not shirking its responsibilities as the greatest power in the world, Clinton's inaugural address offered few clues about the incoming administration's approach to foreign policy. Having come of age during the 1960s, however, Clinton was skeptical of the us-versus-them paradigm that had led Cold Warriors to waste so much blood and treasure in the rice paddies and rain forests of Vietnam, and he hoped that the demise of the Red Threat abroad would bring a peace dividend, freeing up the resources necessary for Americans to fix what was broken at home.

Once his move to 1600 Pennsylvania Avenue was complete, Clinton emerged as a pragmatist who had little time for ideologies of the right or the left and who envisioned instead a post–Cold War world in which free markets and free elections would trump militarism and autocracy. Achieving this new world order, Clinton-style, meant not only investing in the technological and commercial infrastructure necessary to retain America's competitive edge in an age of economic globalization but also demonstrating the political determination and the military prowess necessary to contain "backlash states," to combat international outlaws, and to control ethnic violence. Early in his first term, Clinton was preoccupied with domestic affairs and other matters close to home—pushing health-care reform, ramping up spending on basic scientific research, and expanding markets for U.S. exports in North America—which overshadowed foreign policy. When the new president did turn his attention overseas, he usually focused on European problems—German reunification, instability in Russia, and the bloody war in Bosnia—where the stakes seemed higher and where the rewards seemed greater than in Africa, Asia, or the Middle East. By October 1993, the infamous Black Hawk Down (Battle of Mogadishu) episode in Somalia would confirm the Clinton administration's worst fears about just how dangerous the Third World had become since the end of the Cold War.

Yet when Clinton learned a month earlier that Israeli and Palestinian negotiators had secretly reached tentative agreement on a framework for peace, he saw an opportunity to reassert America's role as an honest broker in the Middle East and, perhaps, to reorient America's relationship with the Muslim world. During the following seven years, the Clinton administration nudged Israel and the PLO toward a peace-for-land deal that had eluded U.S. policy makers for half a century. To this end, Clinton reversed his predecessor's confrontational approach toward Tel Aviv, assuaging Israeli anxieties and winning kudos from AIPAC, all the while offering Palestinian leaders financial incentives to make peace. The Clinton national security team linked these efforts to a broader initiative in the region that included a policy of "dual containment" designed to isolate both Iraq and Iran, two rogue regimes that simultaneously threatened Israel's security and America's access to Persian Gulf oil. Containing a secular tyrant like Saddam Hussein and religious extremists like the Iranian mullahs, however, proved more complicated than the Clinton administration had imagined, especially after Israeli and Palestinian fundamentalists used guns and bombs to disrupt the peace process. In an eleventh-hour bid to secure a comprehensive settlement between Israel and the PLO that might also serve as his administration's most significant diplomatic legacy, Bill Clinton brought the two sides together one last time at Camp David in July 2000, but after ten days of intense negotiations, he came away empty-handed.

Although the high-profile deadlock at Camp David revealed that the Arab-Israeli conflict remained as intractable as ever, the failed summit also concealed some more disturbing trends in the Muslim World that had ominous implications for the United States. From South Asia to North Africa, Islamic radicals appalled by westernization, angered by American support for Israel, or outraged by the growing U.S. military presence in the Persian Gulf had taken up arms during the 1990s. Sometimes, as in Algeria and Afghanistan, Muslim extremists sought to depose secular regimes and impose sharia law. At other times, militant Islamists embraced narrower objectives, as with Hamas and Hezbollah, both of which sought the destruction of Israel. One group—Osama Bin Laden's al-Qaeda—explicitly took aim at the United

States. During Clinton's second term, al-Qaeda unleashed an escalating campaign of violence against U.S. targets from the Arabian Peninsula to the Horn of Africa and made plans to strike at the American homeland. As the decade drew to a close, some observers prophesied that radical Islam was destined to become during the twenty-first century what bolshevism had been a hundred years earlier—an existential threat to be destroyed if it could not be contained. The Harvard political scientist Samuel P. Huntington, for example, forecast an apocalyptic "clash of civilizations," while neo-conservative critics of Clinton's Middle East policies established the Project for a New American Century. Despite all the brave talk about a new world order, by the time Clinton left office, "us versus them" had returned with a vengeance.

Elvis Goes to Washington

"I loved Elvis," Bill Clinton confessed in his memoirs. That someone born in Hope, Arkansas, in August 1946 should make such a confession about the self-styled King of Rock and Roll, who hailed from Tupelo, Mississippi, is hardly surprising. Indeed, for members of the postwar baby boom generation, Elvis Presley—his music, his swagger, his sensuality—became the symbol of an age that began in peace, prosperity, and optimism but ended in war, recession, and debauchery. That someone like Clinton, whose widowed mother struggled to reach the middle class and whose alcoholic stepfather had a taste for fast women and faster cars, should eventually become America's forty-second president, however, appears somewhat surprising. Smart, ambitious, and manipulative, sixteen-year-old Bill won a coveted spot as Arkansas's representative to Boy's Nation and traveled to Washington, D.C., where he managed to shake hands with John F. Kennedy during a White House reception in July 1963. A year later, Clinton returned to the nation's capital to attend Georgetown University, intending to pursue a career in the U.S. foreign service.

Clinton began rethinking these plans during his sophomore year, when the number of American troops in Vietnam reached two hundred thousand. By the autumn of 1966, he had secured a part-time position on the staff of the Senate Committee on Foreign Relations, whose chairman, the Arkansas Democrat J. William Fulbright, was a leading critic of U.S. intervention in Southeast Asia and elsewhere in the Third World. With Fulbright's help, Clinton spent the two years after graduation from Georgetown in England on a Rhodes Scholarship at Oxford University, where in his spare time, like so many young men of his generation, he concocted a successful scheme to avoid the draft. He returned home to Arkansas in the summer of 1970, then headed back east later that autumn to attend law school at Yale University and dabble in antiwar politics.

Two years later, Clinton took a break from his legal studies and moved to Austin, Texas, where he served as statewide coordinator for George McGovern's quixotic campaign to unseat Richard Nixon. Clinton admired the South Dakota Democrat for challenging the Cold War us-versus-them thinking that had put the United States on the path to disaster in Vietnam, but the results on election day 1972 showed that most Americans did not. Following McGovern's landslide defeat, Clinton returned to New Haven to complete his law degree, wooing his classmate Hillary Rodham and building a political network along the way. Already displaying early symptoms of Potomac fever, the freshly minted Ivy League lawyer plunged into politics in his native Arkansas, relying on his good-old-boy habits and his southern drawl to reassure voters that he had not joined the East Coast elite. They responded in November 1978 by making Clinton America's youngest governor at the age of thirty-two. Because Arkansas, like most other states, did not have a foreign policy, Governor Clinton spent the following decade dealing with what mattered most to his constituents—building schools and roads, balancing economic growth and environmental protection, and budgeting wisely. He made no secret of his national ambitions, however, aligning himself with the centrist Democratic Leadership Council in 1985 and briefly toying with a run for the White House in 1988. Basking in glory after expelling Saddam Hussein from Kuwait, George H. W. Bush looked unbeatable three years later, but Bill Clinton—now nicknamed "Elvis" by his staff—believed that the incumbent was quite vulnerable on the home front despite his many accomplishments overseas.

"Elvis" launched his presidential campaign in late 1991 as the country was sliding into recession, and his laserlike focus on Main Street's economic woes was obvious from the very start. Yet candidate Clinton was convinced that "good jobs at good wages" at home would also require good policies abroad that took advantage of America's competitive edge in an age of globalization. "We need a New Covenant for American Security after the Cold War," Clinton told a cheering crowd at Georgetown University on 12 December, and "a new economic policy to serve ordinary Americans by launching a new era of global growth." He saw a post–Cold War world bright with promise. "If individual liberty, political pluralism and free enterprise take root in Latin America, Eastern and Central Europe, Africa, Asia, and the former

Soviet Union," Clinton explained, "we can look forward to a grand new era of reduced conflict, mutual understanding, and economic growth." One area likely to require special attention was the Middle East, where Operation Desert Storm could easily become a Pyrrhic victory unless the United States embraced a policy that "promotes democracy and human rights, and preserves our strategic relationship with the one democracy in the region: Israel." Clinton ended on a note of caution: "The collapse of communism does not mean the end of danger," he warned those gathered at his alma mater. "A new set of threats in an even less stable world will force us, even as we restructure our defenses, to keep our guard up."[1]

That new set of threats played almost no role during the 1992 election campaign, however. To secure the Democratic nomination, Clinton had to persuade voters in the spring primaries that he was not a skirt-chasing, dope-smoking, draft-dodging opportunist, something he managed to accomplish by keeping his inner Elvis in check. Winning the general election the following autumn, by contrast, proved far easier than the Arkansas Democrat had expected, thanks in large measure to a third-party challenge mounted by H. Ross Perot, a gnomelike Texas billionaire who attacked Bush from the right for a host of economic sins, most notably a broken pledge made four years earlier not to raise taxes. Foreign policy rarely came up, and when it did, as during a presidential debate on 11 October, Clinton offered up bromides suitable for a bumper sticker. Asked to describe the most important issues confronting the United States abroad, he summed up the "three fundamental challenges" this way: "national security, economic strength, democracy."[2] To be sure, Clinton would skewer Bush during the final weeks for doing too much for China, where trade had trumped human rights, and for doing too little for Bosnia, where Serbian militias had reduced Sarajevo to a charnel house, but as the Democratic campaign guru James Carville had predicted, the outcome hinged on one issue: "It's the economy, stupid."[3] Although Clinton won just 43 percent of the vote, nearly one-fifth of the electorate opted for Perot, making Bush the odd man out and putting Elvis in the White House.

The new national security team would be composed mostly of Democratic insiders and retreads from the Carter administration. Warren Christopher, the number two man at Foggy Bottom during the late 1970s, became Clinton's secretary of state. A taciturn corporate lawyer born in North Dakota and raised in southern California, Christopher was a skilled but colorless technocrat whose friends described him as "Dean Rusk without the charisma," a cruel reference to the laconic and inscrutable mandarin who had run Lyndon Johnson's State Department.[4] To head the Pentagon, Clinton turned to Les Aspin, a Yale-educated Rhodes Scholar and twelve-term congressman from suburban Milwaukee with a well-deserved reputation as a relentless foe of the military-industrial complex. To counterbalance his dovish secretary of defense, Clinton relied on his more hawkish vice president Albert Gore Jr., a Tennessee Democrat, Vietnam veteran, and one of the most outspoken supporters of Operation Desert Storm in the U.S. Senate. And to lead the American delegation at the United Nations in New York City, Clinton tapped Gore's friend and fellow hawk Madeleine Albright, an elegant Czech-born political scientist who would become secretary of state after Warren Christopher stepped down in early 1997.

The most influential political scientist in the Clinton administration, however, was National Security Adviser Anthony Lake, who held a B.A. from Harvard and a Ph.D. from Princeton. After joining the U.S. foreign service for an extended stint in Vietnam during the 1960s, Lake served briefly on Henry Kissinger's NSC staff before resigning in protest over the American invasion of Cambodia in May 1970. He returned to Washington during the Carter years as the State Department's director of policy planning and worked closely with Warren Christopher. Following the Reagan landslide, Lake joined the faculty of Mount Holyoke College in western Massachusetts, where he taught international relations and authored several books critical of America's Cold War policies in the Third World. Lake was recruited to advise Clinton on foreign affairs in 1992 by Samuel R. "Sandy" Berger, a well-connected attorney, international trade consultant, and long-time "Friend of Bill" who had first met the future president during the McGovern campaign in Texas twenty years earlier. Once Lake secured the White House national security portfolio in January 1993, he chose Berger as his deputy, and together they began to map out a new American approach to the post–Cold War world.

Throughout that first winter, Lake and Berger focused their attention on Bosnia, where a UN arms embargo sponsored by the Bush administration had backfired, leaving thousands of Muslims defenseless against heavily armed Serbian forces bent on "ethnic cleansing," a euphemism for genocide. A week before Inauguration Day, Lake received a long memo from Richard Holbrooke, an old friend and foreign service comrade just back from a whirlwind visit to the Balkans, who urged the Clinton administration to adopt a policy of "lift and strike" in Bosnia. By lifting the embargo and striking the Serbs, Holbrooke explained, Washington would save lives, demonstrate a commitment to human rights that extended to Muslims as well as

Christians, and ensure that *"Bosnia's outside support no longer comes solely from the Islamic nations."*[5] Lake and Berger liked the lift-and-strike option, as did Secretary of Defense Les Aspin. So did Clinton, at least until he read Robert Kaplan's best-selling *Balkan Ghosts* later that spring. Attributing the gruesome strife in Bosnia to ancient ethnic hatreds, not to garden-variety political rivalries of more recent vintage, Kaplan quoted a line from Shakespeare's *Life and Death of King John*—"so foul a sky clears not without a storm"—and implied that the United States should steer clear of the Balkans until the storm had passed. Clinton evidently took the point and directed the Pentagon and the NSC staff to explore other options. "Holy shit," Aspin warned Lake in late May. "He's going south on 'lift and strike.'"[6]

Disappointed by Clinton's U-turn on Bosnia, Lake was elated later that summer when his boss signed off on a broad new framework to guide U.S. foreign policy after the Cold War. "The successor to a doctrine of containment must be a strategy of enlargement—enlargement of the world's free community of market democracies," Lake declared at Johns Hopkins University on 21 September 1993. The world remained a dangerous place, and a military coup in Haiti or saber rattling in North Korea were still worth worrying about, but "absent a reversal in Russia, there is now no near-term threat to America's existence." The specter of terrorism and ethnic conflict might loom large, but Lake insisted that "none of these threats holds the same immediate dangers for us as did Nazi conquest or Soviet expansionism." The Clinton administration's grand vision was breathtaking. "During the Cold War, even children understood America's security mission; as they looked at those maps on their schoolroom walls, they knew we were trying to contain the creeping expansion of that big, red blob," Lake explained. "Today, at great risk of oversimplification, we might visualize our security mission as promoting the enlargement of the 'blue areas' of market democracies." The only real opponents of "Mission: Enlargement," he predicted confidently, would be atavistic "backlash states" from the Balkans to the Persian Gulf, where "every dictator, theocrat, kleptocrat or central planner in an unelected regime has reason to fear their subjects will suddenly demand the freedom to make their own decisions."[7]

Events in the Horn of Africa, however, soon demonstrated that so-called failed states could pose an even greater challenge to enlargement than backlash states. In late January 1991, while Americans watched with grim fascination in real time as Operation Desert Storm exploded in the skies over Baghdad, Siad Barre, the U.S.-backed dictator and kleptocrat who had ruled Somalia for more than a decade, fled Mogadishu one step ahead of Mohamed

Farah Aideed and a well-armed band of insurgents from his Habr Gidr clan. During the following year and a half, one of America's most visible Cold War client states in the Third World imploded as vicious clan warfare spawned an epic famine that claimed eight hundred thousand lives. "Since Siad's overthrow," CIA analysts reported in September 1992, "Somalia—the only ethnically and linguistically unitary country in Africa—has disintegrated into a patchwork of feuding clans" and might eventually become a playground for "Islamic fundamentalists" backed by Iran, Libya, or Sudan.[8] Three months later, the lame duck Bush administration sent twenty-eight thousand GIs to Mogadishu in Operation Restore Hope, part of a broader humanitarian effort to prevent mass starvation known as UNOSOM (United Nations Operation in Somalia). The morning after the American troops waded ashore near the Somali capital, Sudan's Islamist president Omar al-Bashir denounced the humanitarian intervention as "imperialism," pure and simple, "an international conspiracy aiming for a military presence in the Horn of Africa region, which overlooks the most important waterway in the world."[9]

Clinton and his national security team felt uneasy about Operation Restore Hope. To be sure, the new president had singled out Somalia in his inaugural address as one of those places where the United States "will not shrink from the challenges or fail to seize the opportunities" of the post–Cold War world, but he was also determined to avoid being drawn into a Somali civil war. The presence of ten thousand UN peacekeepers, mainly from Pakistan and Malaysia, made matters even more complicated, because Secretary General Boutros Boutros-Ghali, a former Egyptian diplomat who knew the players in Somalia well, considered Mohamed Farah Aideed a thug and ordered the blue helmets to track him down. In March 1993, Clinton sent Robert Oakley, one of America's few "Somali hands," to Mogadishu to size up the situation. Oakley came back convinced that the UN vendetta against Aideed would backfire. "Treat a warlord like a statesman and he will behave like a statesman," he warned Clinton. "Treat a warlord like a warlord and he will behave like a warlord."[10] The president responded by reducing the U.S. presence in Somalia to just forty-five hundred troops in April, but six weeks later gunmen loyal to Aideed brazenly ambushed a Pakistani convoy on the outskirts of Mogadishu, killing and mutilating twenty-four peacekeepers. Jonathan Howe, a retired U.S. admiral and former NSC staffer whom Boutros-Ghali had recently named to oversee UN operations in Somalia, vowed to put Aideed out of business, either dead or alive, and began to badger the Pentagon to provide Army Rangers and Delta Force snipers necessary to do the job.

At the White House, where Admiral Howe was fast becoming known as "Jonathan Ahab," Tony Lake counseled caution. "We should try to avoid turning this into an us-versus-Aideed struggle," he told a reporter, adding that State and Defense Department officials agreed that "we shouldn't hype it" and preferred to work through the UN Security Council.[11] The CIA's Somalia watchers, however, warned in mid-July that "if the threat from Aideed is not dealt with quickly—either by arresting him or chasing him from the capital—UNOSOM's credibility as a peacemaking force could be fatally undermined."[12] Against his better judgment, Clinton agreed to send an elite team of commandos to help apprehend Aideed a month later. "We've just made a fateful decision," Secretary of Defense Aspin told Richard Holbrooke in late August. "We're sending the Rangers to Somalia." Aspin was not happy. "We're not going to be able to control them, you know," he noted ruefully. "They're like overtrained pit bulls." Holbrooke, who was about to embark on a White House fact-finding trip to Europe, shook his head sadly, and recalling his own bitter experience in Southeast Asia a quarter of a century earlier, began referring to the Horn of Africa as "Vietmalia."[13]

In broad daylight on Sunday afternoon, 3 October 1993, a dozen U.S. Black Hawk helicopters carrying more than one hundred Army Rangers swooped down on the Bakara Market in the heart of Mogadishu, where Aideed was rumored to be meeting his top lieutenants. The snatch-and-grab mission did not go as planned. Somali guerrillas trained by Arab veterans of the recent jihad against the Red Army in Afghanistan managed to shoot down two Black Hawks with rocket-propelled grenades, and in the ensuing melee eighteen GIs and several hundred Somalis died. Clinton was shocked and appalled. "How could this happen?" he thundered. "It strikes me as dumb at a minimum to put U.S. troops in helicopters in urban areas where they were subject to ground fire."[14] Yet Clinton was not inclined to cut bait. "We are not running away with our tails between our legs," he told Richard Clarke, the NSC's counterterrorism expert, after the fog of war lifted. "We are also not gonna flatten Mogadishu to prove we are the big bad-ass superpower." Instead, the Pentagon would send in more tanks, aircraft, and whatever other military hardware U.S. troops needed. "We are going to show force. And we are going to keep delivering food," Clinton vowed. "If anybody fucks with us, we will respond massively."[15]

The GIs would return home in March 1994 without further incident, and UN forces followed suit a year later without having captured the elusive Aideed. Mass starvation may have been averted, but Somalia was still wracked by vicious clan warfare, and Islamic radicals had free rein throughout the Horn of Africa. "In ten years' time, you'll be able to buy fucking *plutonium* in Bakara market," one reporter muttered as he watched the last blue helmets depart from Mogadishu.[16] Madeleine Albright urged her boss not to be discouraged. "We had to turn the lesson of Somalia into a positive one," she recalled in her memoirs. "Our defeat there didn't mean we should never get involved; it meant we needed to be better prepared."[17] Clinton agreed and reaffirmed his commitment to what he called "Engagement and Enlargement" in a July 1994 statement on national security strategy. "The end of the Cold War fundamentally changed America's security imperatives," he pointed out. "The dangers we face today are more diverse. Ethnic conflict is spreading and rogue states pose a serious danger to regional stability in many corners of the globe." Notwithstanding these dangers, however, his administration stood ready to employ armed force whenever necessary "credibly [to] sustain our security."[18] Who knows? Perhaps Clinton recalled a line from "I'm All Shook Up," one of Elvis Presley's earliest chart-busters: "Please don't ask me what's on my mind; I'm a little mixed up, but I'm feelin' fine." In any case, eighteen months into his first term, the man whose aides called him "Elvis" was a bit shaken but largely unfazed. "The challenge of dealing with complicated problems like Somalia, Haiti, and Bosnia inspired one of Tony Lake's best lines," Clinton remarked long afterward: "Sometimes I really miss the Cold War."[19]

Yitzhak, Yasser, and Bibi: The Rise and Fall of the Oslo Peace Process

Although the Clinton administration worried that the end of the Cold War was making Somalia and other parts of the Third World safe for religious feuds and ethnic violence, many in Washington detected signs favorable to peace between Palestinians and Israelis. Candidate Clinton had been openly critical of the Bush administration's "public pressure tactics against Israel," which had "raised Arab expectations" and "fed Israeli fears" about "an American-imposed solution." Israel's friends inside the Beltway liked what they heard about the Arkansas Democrat. "I've known Bill [Clinton] for seven, eight years," AIPAC's president David Steiner told a friend in October 1992. "We have a dozen people in that campaign, in the headquarters," he added, "and they're all going to get big jobs" after the election. "I talked with Bill Clinton," Steiner explained, and whether the issue was more economic assistance for Israel or less pressure to withdraw from the Occupied Territories, "he's going to be with us."[20]

Among the people inside the Clinton campaign whom Steiner mentioned by name was Martin Indyk, an Australian political scientist who had served as AIPAC's chief of research before becoming executive director of the Washington Institute for Near East Policy (WINEP). Originally recruited by Tony Lake and Sandy Berger during the summer of 1992 because of his expertise on the Arab-Israeli conflict, Indyk and a WINEP associate, Robert Satloff, joined the Clinton transition team after the election and drafted an issues paper on the Middle East. Indyk's and Satloff's recommendations reflected their AIPAC and WINEP lineage. The new administration must stop badgering Israel about West Bank settlements and must start acting more like an "Honest Broker" willing to let the two sides resolve their disputes themselves. This would make Clinton the region's "new viceroy," a catalyst for "a moderate, stable, prosperous and democratic Middle East." It would not be easy, however. "The Arabs view Bill Clinton as pro-Israel," and even worse, "Islamic fundamentalists in southern Lebanon, the West Bank and Gaza have embarked on a bloody campaign of violence." In short, there were "two competing futures" on the horizon, "one in which peace prevails," and the other in which "Islamic extremists dictate events." For Indyk and Satloff, the choice was a no-brainer: "Working with regional allies—Israel, Egypt, Saudi Arabia and Turkey—the Clinton administration has the ability to tip the balance decisively in favor of a more peaceful Middle East."[21]

Determined that peace must prevail, Clinton assembled a national security team well suited to getting the negotiations back on track. Indyk, whom Clinton once playfully described as "AIPAC's candidate," became the point person for Arab-Israeli affairs on the NSC staff.[22] Dennis Ross, a holdover from the Bush administration, accepted a newly created position as special Middle East coordinator. And Aaron Miller, another State Department veteran well acquainted with the region, signed on as Ross's chief deputy. Publicly the trio embraced an evenhanded approach favoring neither Arab nor Jew, but privately they tilted toward Tel Aviv. "Whatever else we disagreed on," Miller confessed long afterward, "Dennis, Martin, and I brought a clear pro-Israel orientation to our peace-process planning."[23] This did not bother the man in the Oval Office, whose own sympathies for Israel were well known. During an NSC meeting on 3 March 1993, Indyk laid out a "Syria first" initiative designed to tame Hafez al-Assad, "the Lion of Damascus," and bring Israel's most dangerous Arab neighbor to the bargaining table, leaving the Palestinians with no choice but to sue for peace on Tel Aviv's terms. "You cannot make war in the Middle East without Egypt," Indyk explained, "and you cannot make peace without Syria." Clinton liked the idea a lot. "We shouldn't minimize the advantage of concentrating on Syria first," he remarked as the meeting broke up. "If we have a chance to do that we ought to take it while pushing the other tracks too."[24]

Israel's prime minister Yitzhak Rabin and PLO chairman Yasser Arafat, however, believed that the surest and swiftest track ran through Oslo, not Damascus. Meeting secretly in the Norwegian capital throughout the summer, Israeli and Palestinian negotiators drafted a "Declaration of Principles" outlining parameters for a peace-for-land settlement that came to be known as "Oslo I," which they shared with the Clinton administration in early September. The PLO renounced terrorism and recognized the Jewish state, while Israel promised to withdraw from Gaza and portions of the West Bank and, without saying so explicitly, agreed to accept a Palestinian state. Clinton invited both sides to the White House, where on 13 September 1993 he emceed a stilted diplomatic dance that culminated in the Rose Garden with Rabin stiffly shaking Arafat's hand. During a brief chat after the ceremony, the PLO leader told Clinton that the Palestinians were stuck somewhere between "Soweto and Singapore," but that with America's help, their new homeland would eventually resemble a Southeast Asian city-state, not a South African ghetto.[25] Clinton had a more extensive conversation with Rabin over lunch, during which the Israeli prime minister revealed that his rationale for peace was not much different from Arafat's. "If Israel were to hold on to the West Bank permanently, it would have to decide whether to let the Arabs there vote in Israeli elections," Rabin sighed. "If the Palestinians got the right to vote, given their higher birthrate, within a few decades Israel would no longer be a Jewish state." The alternative was equally unpleasant. "If they were denied the right to vote," Rabin confessed, "Israel would no longer be a democracy but an apartheid state."[26]

Nevertheless, not everyone was as enamored of the Oslo peace process as Clinton, Rabin, and Arafat. From the Galilee to the Negev, Israeli religious extremists denounced as treason plans to abandon the settlements and hand over most of the West Bank to the Arabs. Clinton and his advisers were horrified on 25 February 1994 when Baruch Goldstein, an American-born settler who lived in Kiryat Arba not far from Hebron, strode into a mosque adjacent to the Tomb of the Patriarchs armed with an assault rifle and opened fire on several hundred Palestinian worshippers, killing twenty-nine. This was "an act of murder designed also to kill the Oslo process," Dennis Ross recalled a decade later. "Instead of peace, we would hear calls for holy war, and Arafat would be under pressure not to negotiate with those whose purpose was to attack Islam."[27] Retribution came quickly courtesy of Hamas, the Islamic fundamentalist group and blood enemy of the PLO, which ordered a pair of suicide bombings inside Israel that killed fifteen and maimed more than seventy. Yet despite the escalating violence, Rabin remained more determined than ever to bury the hatchet with Israel's Arab neighbors, and so he did, signing a peace treaty with Jordan's King Hussein in October 1994 and hammering out a second, broader "Oslo II" agreement with Arafat a year later. Clinton admired the Israeli leader for his wisdom, his courage, and his stubbornness. "Rabin and I had developed an unusually close relationship, marked by candor, trust, and extraordinary understanding," he recalled in his memoirs. "I had come to love him as I had rarely loved another man." [28] Clinton liked to say that Rabin was blessed with "an incredible set of brass *baytzim* [balls]," which according to Aaron Miller made him something of a "Jewish lobby of one" at the White House.[29]

On 4 November 1995, that Jewish lobby of one was shot dead by Yigal Amir, an Israeli extremist with ties to West Bank settlers, following a rally for peace in downtown Tel Aviv. Rabin had been a marked man ever since he had signed "Oslo I" two years earlier, not merely because he was willing to trade land for peace but also because he possessed the clout with the Israeli armed forces and the credibility with the Israeli public necessary to make a two-state solution happen. Stunned and saddened by Rabin's death, Clinton assured his successor, Shimon Peres, that the United States remained committed to the Oslo process. No one doubted that Peres would continue talking with Yasser Arafat, but few believed he could ever match Rabin's heroic tenacity, and fewer still believed he could overcome his reputation as a shifty maker of backroom deals. Clinton and his national security team were quite fond of Peres and shared his vision of "a new Middle East," where Israelis and Arabs lived together peaceably, side by side. "Peres saw the global community becoming increasingly interconnected, with fewer barriers to information, investment, and economic growth," White House Middle East troubleshooter Dennis Ross observed many years later. "He believed globalization could be a powerful force for peace" and a catalyst for prosperity in the region, particularly for the Palestinians.[30]

Israeli elections were scheduled for May 1996, however, and Peres would have to resort to more than buzzwords like "globalization" if he wished to keep his job as prime minister. Hamas unleashed a fresh round of grisly suicide attacks that spring, targeting schools, shopping malls, and bus stops in Tel Aviv, while Hezbollah guerrillas battered Israeli farmers and soldiers along the border with Lebanon with mortar shells and roadside bombs. Peres responded with lethal force, authorizing the Mossad to assassinate

Hamas operatives like Yahya Ayyash, a bomb maker known as "The Engineer," and approving Operation Grapes of Wrath, an extended aerial foray into southern Lebanon that was supposed to punish Hezbollah but that ended in tragedy on 18 April after an Israeli F-15 mistakenly bombed a UN refugee center at Qana, killing more than one hundred women and children. When the ballots were counted six weeks later, Peres came up short, losing to Likud Party leader Benjamin Netanyahu by less than 1 percent of the vote. "On May 29, I stayed up until well after midnight watching the election returns in Israel. It was a real cliffhanger," Clinton recalled in his memoirs. Netanyahu had eked out his narrow victory "by promising to be tougher on terrorism and slower with the peace process," which led Clinton to wonder "whether and how he and I could work together."[31]

The president would get some answers when Netanyahu paid a visit to the White House on 9 July. Known as "Bibi" by friend and foe alike, Israel's new prime minister was the son of Benzion Netanyahu, a founding father of "Revisionist Zionism" who claimed that God had granted all of Palestine, including the West Bank and Gaza, to the Jews in biblical times. Bibi's older brother Yonathan had led the legendary raid on Entebbe in July 1976 and was killed in action rescuing a planeload of Israelis held hostage by Palestinian terrorists in Uganda. Bibi himself was born in Tel Aviv but attended high school just outside Philadelphia, where his father taught Judaic studies at a local college. After serving in the Israeli special forces, Netanyahu returned to the United States in 1972 to attend MIT, where he completed an undergraduate degree in architecture and an MBA. Following a brief stint with the Boston Consulting Group, he handled public relations for the Israeli embassy in Washington during the 1980s and established himself as an expert on international terrorism. A vitriolic critic of the Oslo peace process, Netanyahu ridiculed Rabin and Peres as hopelessly naive for having permitted the PLO to return to the Occupied Territories. "Gaza under Arafat" was little more than "a clearinghouse and stepping-stone" for radical Muslim groups like Hamas and Hezbollah, Bibi declared in a 1995 screed titled *Fighting Terrorism*, while the West Bank was fast becoming "a much enlarged base for militant Islam in the heart of the Arab world."[32]

Clinton did not need to read *Fighting Terrorism* to know that Netanyahu viewed Israel's relations with its Arab neighbors through the lens of us versus them. Bibi might speak English with an accent acquired in the City of Brotherly Love, but the message he delivered during his first visit to the Oval Office was as blunt as anything in the Old Testament. In matters of war and peace with the Arabs, Israel would make its own decisions based on what was best for the Jewish state, not what was best for the United States. Referring to America as Israel's "strategic asset," Netanyahu noted that many on Capitol Hill felt uneasy about White House support for the Oslo Accords, which seemed to be bringing more terrorism than peace.[33] Much later, when asked how his initial meeting with Clinton had gone, Bibi first recalled the moment four decades earlier when Dwight Eisenhower had forced David Ben Gurion to withdraw from the Sinai following the Suez Crisis and then snapped at the interviewer: "That was the first and last time an Israeli Prime Minister succumbed to an American diktat."[34] For his part, Clinton made nice during a joint press conference with Netanyahu immediately afterward, telling reporters that "our commitment to Israel's security remains rock solid" and that he personally remained confident that the Oslo process would "bring security, dignity, and a better life for Arabs and Israelis alike." Privately, however, the president was furious about Bibi's arrogance and impulsiveness. "Who the fuck does he think he is?" Clinton growled. "Who's the fucking superpower here?"[35]

Netanyahu answered those questions with provocative actions that threatened to derail the peace process. In September 1996, Bibi sparked violent Palestinian protests by reopening the long abandoned Hasmonean Tunnel to provide Jews with access to ancient archaeological sites beneath Jerusalem's al-Aqsa mosque. Six months later, Netanyahu approved plans for a massive new housing complex at Har Homa designed to separate Arab East Jerusalem from the rest of the West Bank. While Yasser Arafat and the PLO cried foul, their rivals in Hamas sent suicide bombers into Jewish West Jerusalem and other Israeli population centers, prompting Bibi to authorize another round of targeted killings against leading Islamic extremists. "The Palestinians believed in the peace process, but they did not believe in Bibi," Ami Ayalon, who headed Shin Bet, Israel's internal security agency, told a journalist many years later. "They knew that Bibi was cheating them, but they believed in the American president."[36] Madeleine Albright, whom Clinton had just appointed secretary of state, urged Netanyahu to reverse course at Har Homa, but to no avail. "Pugnacious, partisan, and very smooth, he reminded me of Newt Gingrich," Albright remarked in her memoirs, referring to the Georgia Republican who had become Speaker of the House after the 1994 off-year elections. "We would think we had reached an understanding and were moving toward an agreement [with Bibi], only to find that that wasn't his intention at all."[37]

Determined to reach an agreement that both Israelis and Palestinians could believe in, Albright's boss summoned Netanyahu and Arafat to a mini summit at Wye Plantation on Maryland's eastern shore in October 1998. Things got off to a bad start when Ariel Sharon, Bibi's foreign minister, refused to shake Arafat's hand and called the PLO "a gang of thugs." Albright agreed that the Palestinian leadership was far from perfect, but she warned Sharon that "if you think of them as a gang, there's no hope: they will act like a gang." With an assist from Jordan's ailing King Hussein, who happened to be in Washington for chemotherapy, Clinton managed to persuade the two sides tentatively to agree on the next steps in the Oslo process. The Palestinians would get more land and more U.S. economic assistance, while the Israelis would get unprecedented cooperation in halting terrorism and explicit repudiation of anti-Israel language in the PLO Covenant. The deal nearly fell apart at the last minute, however, when Netanyahu refused to release five hundred PLO prisoners unless Arafat liquidated a "particularly prominent" Palestinian firebrand. "Just execute him?" the PLO chairman asked. "I won't ask, you won't tell," Bibi replied. Clinton exploded. "This is just chicken shit," he told Netanyahu. "I am not going to put up with this kind of bullshit." Flushed from the barnyard, Netanyahu relented and initialed the Wye Agreement on 23 October.[38]

Seven weeks later, Clinton flew to the Middle East and reaffirmed America's commitment to the Oslo process. His first stop was Jerusalem, where he confirmed that despite recent progress, the path to peace would be long and hard. "We knew in the Wye agreement it would be difficult for both sides to comply," he told Israeli reporters on 13 December. "But the fact that this has been hard to implement doesn't mean it was a mistake. It means it was real."[39] Clinton delivered a similar message the next day in Gaza City, where he told a cheering crowd that he was "profoundly honored to be the first American President to address the Palestinian people in a city governed by Palestinians." Much still remained to be done to achieve lasting peace, and it would require "good faith, mutual respect, and compromise to forge a final agreement." Clinton, however, remained optimistic. "I think there will be more breakdowns," he confessed, "but I think there will be more breakthroughs, as well."[40] Privately, the president was much less upbeat, largely because he questioned whether Netanyahu could deliver. After returning to Washington, Clinton telephoned King Hussein to report that "the political situation in Israel is quite unstable." Members of Bibi's own cabinet were demanding that he halt further Israeli withdrawals from the West Bank, which "may well delay the Wye implementation process." Insisting that the peace process remained "on track," Clinton nevertheless admitted that "we'll need to keep pushing the Israelis to implement." Yet the United States might not have to push quite so hard, he told the Jordanian monarch, if ongoing American air strikes against Israel's blood enemy, Saddam Hussein, had the desired effect.[41]

Containing the Backlash States: Clinton, Iraq, and Iran

It was no coincidence that Clinton linked Operation Desert Fox, as the latest U.S. campaign against Iraq was known, to the Palestinian-Israeli peace process. For more than five years, the Clinton administration had pursued a policy of dual containment in the Persian Gulf, where anti-American regimes in Baghdad and Tehran fulminated against "the Zionist entity in Palestine" as Washington's stalking horse and the world's leading oppressor of Muslims. The chief architect of dual containment was Martin Indyk, the NSC's resident Middle East expert who became U.S. ambassador to Israel in 1995. He had first spelled out the logic of this approach during a skull session on Iraq and Iran with candidate Clinton in July 1992. "I had argued that both nations were hostile to our interests," Indyk recalled, and "we should therefore work to contain them while we pressed ahead with Arab-Israeli peacemaking."[42]

The NSC adviser Tony Lake and his staff fleshed out dual containment during the first half of 1993 as the perfect antidote to America's security dilemmas in the Middle East. The most pressing issue was how to handle Saddam Hussein, whose ham-handed attempt to have former President Bush assassinated during a visit to Kuwait prompted the Clinton administration to demolish Iraqi intelligence headquarters in Baghdad with Tomahawk cruise missiles in late June. Indyk's prescription for Iraq was "aggressive containment"—broader UN sanctions, an expanded no-fly zone over Kurdistan, and a fresh round of covert action designed to spark regime change—not unlike America's "get tough" approach toward the Kremlin during the early years of the Cold War. "The policy of containment of the Soviet Union, first articulated by George Kennan, was based on the idea that the Soviet system was rotten to the core and would collapse of its own weight if the United States could only keep the pressure on it," Indyk explained. "Containment of Iraq was based on a similar calculation." The way the CIA's Iraq watchers and the NSC staff saw it, "if we pressed Saddam's regime hard enough, it would eventually collapse," provided the United States was willing to "contain him through sanctions and the occasional resort to force."[43]

The theocratic regime in Iran, which bankrolled Hamas and Hezbollah and threatened the pro-American Arab petro-kingdoms along the Persian

Gulf, required a slightly different approach, which Indyk dubbed "active containment." Inside Clinton's national security team, "a consensus quickly emerged that Iran was the archetype of a hostile, rogue regime" whose leaders would resort to subversion, subterfuge, and assassination to damage U.S. interests in the Middle East. Because Iran's supreme leader Ayatollah Ali Khamenei shied away from overt Saddam-style armed confrontation, however, active containment relied more on diplomatic isolation and unilateral U.S. economic sanctions than covert operations or military threats.[44] According to Indyk, Washington's goal in Tehran was behavior change, not regime change. "We have no problem with the Iranian government per se," he told an interviewer in March 1994, but the United States did take issue with the Khamenei regime's desire for nuclear weapons, its opposition to the Oslo peace process, and its subversive policies "designed to threaten and undermine Western interests."[45]

In a cover article published in *Foreign Affairs* that same month, Indyk's boss, Tony Lake, revealed that "dual containment" was a key component of the Clinton administration's broader strategy of enlargement. Iran and Iraq were charter members of "a defiant bunch" of "backlash states" that also included Libya and North Korea. As the world's sole remaining superpower, America had a responsibility to "contain" them. "Dual containment does not mean duplicate containment," however, because the threats emanating from Baghdad and Tehran were somewhat different. "In Saddam Hussein's regime, Washington faces an aggressive, modernist, secular avarice," Lake explained, while "in Iran, it is challenged by a theocratic regime with a sense of cultural and political destiny and an abiding antagonism toward the United States." The White House was customizing its policies toward Iraq and Iran to reflect these differences, but in each case the ultimate goal was the same. "Slowly but surely they are coming to understand that there is a price to pay for their recalcitrant commitment to remain on the wrong side of history," Lake concluded. "This is not a crusade, but a genuine and responsible effort, over time, to protect American strategic interests, stabilize the international system and enlarge the community of nations committed to democracy, free markets and peace." In short, America's role in the New World Order would not differ much from its role during the Cold War. "Forty-seven years ago, George Kennan, writing under a pseudonym, made the case for containment of an outlaw empire" in these very pages, Lake reminded the readers of *Foreign Affairs*. "Containing the band of outlaws we refer to as 'the backlash states'" might present "a less formidable challenge" than the one Kennan described, but the Clinton administration was convinced that "it is still very much within our power to prevail."[46]

The first real test of dual containment came that autumn, when Saddam Hussein beefed up Iraq's military presence along the Kuwaiti border with two battalions of his crack Republican Guard, which had spearheaded the invasion four years earlier. The White House responded with Operation Vigilant Warrior, a joint Saudi-American maneuver that saw U.S. forces move north from their encampment at Dhahran toward the border with Iraq. It is unclear whether or not Saddam was actually planning another round of smash and grab in Kuwait, but he beat a hasty retreat once the American cavalry arrived. Indyk later claimed that Clinton and his national security team briefly toyed with the idea of supplementing the existing no-fly zone with a no-drive zone in southern Iraq, where the anti-Saddam Shia resistance was spoiling for a fight, but "none of them was prepared to open this Pandora's box," which would have been likely to enhance Iranian influence. Nevertheless, "the outcome of the October 1994 Iraq crisis represented a victory for Clinton's policy of 'dual containment,'" Indyk noted in his memoirs, because America "had demonstrated, through its ability to move large forces rapidly to Iraq's borders, that it could effectively deter Saddam from threatening or attacking his neighbors."[47]

The challenge posed by the other backlash state in the Persian Gulf, by contrast, proved more subtle and, in some ways, more dangerous. According to Indyk, the White House "viewed the containment of Iran as [just as] important as containing Iraq," not least because the mullahs in Tehran were trying to derail the Oslo peace process by arming anti-Israeli extremists in Lebanon and Gaza.[48] The Iranians had embraced the Palestinian cause "as a critical means both of promoting their interests in the Arab and Muslim worlds, and conversely, of preventing a hostile power from asserting dominance there," Indyk explained. For his part, "Clinton had identified the Iranian regime's motives as hostile and had therefore determined to contain its influence in the Persian Gulf." It seemed to be a classic case of us versus them, with the Ayatollah Khamenei and his Shia followers harboring "hegemonic ambitions" that rivaled those of Cyrus the Great or Xerxes. Yet from the Iranian point of view, Indyk remembers thinking, "the greatest obstacle to the achievement of their aspirations is the alliance between the United States and Israel—what they call 'the Great Satan' and 'the little Satan.'" Simply put, for the mullahs in Tehran "a Pax Americana in the Middle East based on a resolution of the Arab-Israeli conflict represents a strategic threat to their interests."[49]

For their part, Indyk and many other Americans worried that a new Pax Iranica could easily emerge as the greatest obstacle to the achievement of U.S. aspirations in the Middle East since the height of the Cold War. The neoconservative pundit Charles Krauthammer sounded the first alarm at the dawn of the Clinton administration when he declared on New Year's Day 1993 that "Iran is the center of the world's new Comintern." Pointing to Tehran's links to Hezbollah and Hamas and its support for the Islamist regime in Khartoum, Krauthammer warned that "the new threat is as evil as the old Evil Empire."[50] A year later, Richard Nixon branded the Iranians the new "them" most likely to challenge "us" in his final book, *Beyond Peace.* "Iran's tactics are ominously similar to those of the Soviet Union's infamous Comintern before World War II," the old Cold Warrior intoned. "Rather than going over a border, Iran in effect goes under a border and enlists citizens of the target nation who share its extreme religious faith to carry out its designs for conquest."[51]

Iran's purchase of a reactor capable of producing weapons-grade uranium from Russia in late 1994, ostensibly for the purpose of generating nuclear energy, merely reinforced the analogy between the Red and Green Threats and created high anxiety from Washington to Riyadh. "Iran was doing a number of things it should not be doing," Assistant Secretary of State for Near Eastern Affairs Robert Pelletreau told Prince Saud al-Faisal, the Saudi foreign minister, in February 1995. Not only was the Khamenei regime "trying to acquire weapons of mass destruction," it was also "carrying out wider subversive activities, such as conducting actions against Egypt and supporting Hizbullah." Suggestions from America's European allies that a "critical dialogue" with Tehran might encourage moderation among the mullahs were just wishful thinking, Pelletreau assured Prince Saud, because "there do not appear to be any moderates when it comes to Iran's external policy."[52]

This was not quite true. While the Ayatollah Khamenei was busy lambasting the United States as the Great Satan, the Iranian president, Hashemi Rafsanjani, announced deals with two American oil companies in March 1995 and asked European intermediaries to let it be known that Tehran was interested in restoring diplomatic relations with Washington. Rafsanjani's gestures, however, did not impress Martin Indyk, who detected Iran's "fingerprints" on everything from "the arming of Islamic insurgents in Algeria" to "Shiite dissent in Bahrain." As a result, the Clinton administration concluded that the best way "to curb Iran's appetite for regional troublemaking" was to ban U.S. firms from investing in Iranian petroleum.[53]

Ironically, by snubbing Rafsanjani and the moderates, the White House may have inadvertently strengthened the hand of Iranian extremists, who helped Shia radicals in Saudi Arabia build the truck bomb that destroyed the Khobar Towers housing complex outside Dhahran in June 1996, killing nineteen Americans and injuring nearly two hundred others. Washington was convinced that Iran used terrorism as "a tool of statecraft" to "spread its version of Islamic 'revolution'" throughout the region, but confirming Tehran's role in the Khobar bombing took time.[54] Clinton's first instinct was "to whack the shit out of Iran," Deputy National Security Adviser Sandy Berger told a reporter several years later, but in the absence of hard evidence, the White House had to sit tight.[55] With no diplomatic representation in Tehran, by early 1997 some of the best American intelligence about Iran was coming from the listening post at the U.S. consulate in Dubai on the Arabian side of the Strait of Hormuz. Later that spring, Consul General David Pearce fired off a cable titled "The Lion and the Cage," which urged the Clinton administration to rethink its approach toward Iran. "In effect, the U.S. has attempted to design a cage of sanctions and pressure to contain Iran," he began, "but there is little point in keeping the Persian lion in a cage and just prodding him, getting him madder and madder." While Pearce had no aversion to prodding, he did believe that "at some point, the door to the cage must be opened so that the lion knows which way to go."[56]

The Persian lion invited American policy makers to reexamine its cage on 23 May 1997 when Mohammed Khatami, an English-speaking Islamic moderate with strong support among women and young people fed up with the Ayatollah Khamenei's repressive ways, won 70 percent of the votes in Iran's presidential election. Noting that "we are sorry that America's policies have always been hostile to us," Khatami told reporters that he would try to change that by endorsing the Oslo peace process and resuming scholarly and cultural exchanges with the United States. For their part, Secretary of State Madeleine Albright and Bill Clinton "were intrigued by the possibility of better relations with Iran" and hoped that "the time was ripe to move beyond dual containment."[57] After all, Khatami's Iran and Clinton's America had much in common—desire for a more inclusive political system at home, faith in market-oriented trade expansion abroad, and mistrust of the Taliban, the Sunni extremists in Kabul who brutalized Afghanistan's Shia minority after seizing power in late 1996. One big obstacle to normalization was Iran's access to Russia's nuclear secrets. "We'd call the Russians' attention to a company or an institute that was trafficking in dangerous technology, and they'd do something about it for a while," Strobe Talbott, ambassador-at-large and a longtime Clinton associate, recalled. "Sandy Berger likened our efforts to the children's game of Whac-A-Mole, and we felt we were losing."[58] An even bigger obstacle was Iran's schizophrenic foreign policy, with President Khatami's conciliatory words at odds with the Ayatollah Khamenei's "Death to America" rhetoric. Once the FBI confirmed that the Saudi Hezbollah had received Iranian help in planning the attack on the Khobar Towers, all bets were off. "We could have achieved a breakthrough only by abandoning our principles and interests on nonproliferation, terrorism, and the Middle East," Albright remarked wistfully, "far too high a price."[59]

Albright and Clinton never even considered reversing their policy of dual containment on the other side of the Shatt al-Arab, where Saddam Hussein threatened the same set of U.S. principles and interests but showed no trace of Khatami's moderation. Indeed, by the autumn of 1998, Iraq had become the quintessential backlash state, terrorizing its own people, bullying its Arab neighbors, and seeking unconventional weapons for its arsenal. The Clinton administration could take comfort, however, that UN economic sanctions deprived Saddam of the resources he needed to rebuild his war machine and that UN inspectors prevented him from acquiring poison gas or atomic bombs. The U.S. Congress complicated matters in early October by passing the Iraq Liberation Act, which endorsed regime change in Baghdad but appropriated a paltry $97 million to accomplish the task. Saddam Hussein responded on cue, expelling the United Nations Special Commission (UNSCOM) on 3 November 1998 and hinting that Iraq would resume its quest for weapons of mass destruction. An angry Bill Clinton asked the Pentagon to develop a military option, and a week later he approved Operation Desert Viper, which called for American B-52s to bombard Baghdad.

Clinton was forced to postpone the attack at the eleventh hour when Saddam wrote UN Secretary General Kofi Annan to say that UNSCOM would be permitted to return. "The letter is bullshit," Clinton told his national security team on 14 November. "I think we should bomb tomorrow." Yet with UN inspectors headed back to Iraq, "Kofi Annan will disagree with us." Vice President Al Gore believed it was time for Annan to stop his pussyfooting. "He stabbed you in the back by announcing that the Iraqi letter was acceptable," Gore growled. "You should call him and tell him, 'Listen you little [prick], you're screwing around with the national interests of the United States and we won't put up with it.'" In the end, Clinton called off Desert Viper but vowed that the next time Saddam Hussein acted up, the United States would hit him hard.[60] With this in mind, Clinton's top advisers met again on 20 November 1998 to consider covert ways of "engaging and strengthening the Iraqi opposition" to the anti-American regime in

Baghdad. The minutes of the meeting hint at even more extreme measures: "We will not rule out the option of training and arming the opposition."[61]

When Clinton learned in mid-December that the Iraqis were once again interfering with UN inspections and firing missiles at U.S. aircraft patrolling the no-fly zones, he approved Operation Desert Fox, the heaviest American attack since the end of the First Gulf War in 1991. The president spelled out his thinking in a series of telephone calls to Jordan's King Hussein, Britain's Tony Blair, and other world leaders. Clinton put it this way when he thanked Egyptian president Hosni Mubarak on 17 December for permitting U.S. warplanes to fly across the Sinai on their way to Baghdad: "The strike will be significant and will continue for some time, but I think it is important to degrade [Saddam's] capacity to develop weapons of mass destruction and his ability to threaten his neighbors as much as possible."[62]

As Operation Desert Fox wound down, Clinton pondered the final two years of his presidency with mixed feelings about recent U.S. confrontations in the Middle East. The good news was that Iraq remained too weak to attack its neighbors and Iran seemed quite willing to talk peace. The bad news was that both Saddam Hussein and the Iranian mullahs had proved far more resilient and far more ruthless than most Americans had anticipated. The two halves of U.S. policy—dual containment and the Oslo peace process—were supposed to complement each other. By isolating and containing Iraq and Iran, the White House had hoped to buy time for the Arab-Israeli negotiations to bear fruit. Clinton and his advisers did not have to wait long to learn whether or not their quest to convert lemons into lemonade in Palestine had succeeded.

Who Killed the Peace Process at Camp David?

Despite endless delays and frequent Israeli and Palestinian backsliding, the White House troika of peace processors—Dennis Ross, Aaron Miller, and Martin Indyk—remained confident that they could broker a deal between the two sides before the end of Clinton's second term. Continuing to keep Iran and Iraq off balance was one component of the equation. "The more we succeeded in making peace, the more isolated [Iran and the rogue states] would become," Indyk told an interviewer five years later, and "the more we succeeded in containing [Iran], the more possible it would be to make peace."[63] Of far greater importance, however, was persuading Benjamin Netanyahu to fulfill Israel's obligations under the Wye Agreement, which by early 1999 had begun to unravel thanks to the steady expansion of Jewish settlements on the West Bank. In mid-January, the Israeli Knesset delivered a vote of no confidence and forced Netanyahu to call new elections. "Across the political spectrum, everybody agreed that Bibi had driven the United States and the Palestinians together," Ross recalled, and "advanced the cause of Palestinian statehood with an American emblem of support for the first time." Netanyahu expected a serious challenge from Labor Party leader Ehud Barak, a war hero and former army chief of staff who embraced the Oslo process, and he got it. Much to the delight of the Clinton administration, Barak won a landslide victory on 17 May, with 56 percent of the popular vote. The Palestinians were even more optimistic than the Americans. "We can now make peace," Mahmoud Abbas, Arafat's chief lieutenant who was widely known as Abu Mazen, told U.S. officials as they watched Bibi concede defeat. "These are our natural partners."[64]

Nevertheless, within fifteen months the partnership between Barak and Arafat would seem quite unnatural. Part of the problem was Arafat's inability to rein in Hamas, whose armed wing continued to stage hit-and-run attacks against Israeli targets. A much larger concern, however, was Barak's refusal to freeze construction of new settlements on the West Bank, which led the PLO to question his commitment to a two-state solution. In the six years since Rabin and Arafat had shaken hands in the Rose Garden, the number of Jewish settlers had nearly doubled, and with more than two hundred thousand Israelis living in an area designated for Palestinian control under the Oslo Accords, the settlements were becoming ever bigger obstacles to peace. Barak tried to circumvent the stalemated Oslo process by pursuing a "Syria First" strategy designed to secure a peace agreement with Hafez al-Assad and to isolate Yasser Arafat and the PLO. Assad "was everything Arafat wasn't," Barak told Ross. "He commanded a real state with a real army." To be sure, "he was a tough enemy," but Israelis saw Assad as someone "who kept his word and was respected and feared by other leaders in the region." Barak realized that peace with Assad would come at a high price—Israel's withdrawal from Syria's Golan Heights—yet he claimed he could muster the necessary support for such a deal in the Knesset.[65]

Ross and his fellow peace processors were not so sure, but Barak, whose ego and ambition were legendary, badgered the White House on a daily basis until Clinton agreed to broker negotiations between Tel Aviv and Damascus in early 2000. After grueling talks with Israeli and Syrian officials in Shepherdstown, West Virginia, and a whirlwind trip to Geneva, Switzerland, to meet Assad, however, Clinton had little to show for his efforts. "I went to Shepherdstown and was told nothing by you for four days," he growled at

Barak shortly afterward. "I went to Geneva and felt like a wooden Indian doing your bidding."[66] Despite all the Israeli promises, pursuing "Syria First" had proved to be a wild goose chase.

Even worse, the dead end in Damascus delayed the resumption of negotiations between Israel and the PLO for nine months and dealt the entire Oslo peace process a major blow that Clinton's national security team feared might be fatal. Yasser Arafat was outraged by what he regarded as Israel's bait-and-switch tactics. "Barak shouldn't take me for granted," he warned Aaron Miller in early 2000.[67] Yet that was exactly what the Israeli leader did after talks with Assad fell apart. Rather than approaching Arafat to resume negotiations, Barak turned instead to Beirut. On 24 May, he announced that Israel would withdraw its troops from southern Lebanon, where they had stood guard since 1982, with the Lebanese government assuming responsibility for policing the no-man's-land south of the Litani River that Hezbollah called home. Arafat regarded Barak's unilateral decision to pull out of Lebanon as a tactical maneuver calculated not only to reduce international pressure to end the Israeli occupation of the West Bank, which was about to begin its thirty-fourth year, but also to embarrass the PLO. "Barak is screwing me," Arafat complained to U.S. officials, by making jaw-dropping concessions to the Lebanese while simultaneously maneuvering to hang onto important pieces of Palestinian real estate.[68]

By the summer of 2000, time was running out for Bill Clinton, who hoped to restore a reputation sullied by fallout from a sordid sex scandal by securing a more positive historical legacy for himself in the Middle East. The time seemed ripe, and Ehud Barak seemed ready. The Israeli public was unhappy about the deadlock in Damascus, uneasy about the situation in Beirut, and increasingly unimpressed with the prime minister responsible for both. On 1 June, Barak "intercepted" Clinton in Lisbon, Portugal, the first stop on a ten-day presidential trip to Europe, to "plead" that the United States summon Israel and the PLO to Camp David to hammer out an agreement. Eager to "leap over the backward drift of his negotiations with the Palestinians," Barak hinted that Israel was ready to make unprecedented concessions to achieve a lasting peace. Seeing an opportunity to salvage the Oslo Accords at the eleventh hour, Clinton liked the idea of holding a summit at Camp David, but the PLO did not. "Arafat fumed that Barak had parked him behind Assad, for nothing, and withdrawn Israeli troops from Lebanon, for free, which rendered Arafat a laughingstock among Arabs," Clinton confided to Taylor Branch, an old friend who was serving as the administration's unofficial historian-in-residence.[69]

On 26 June, Dennis Ross arrived in Jerusalem to discuss the ground rules for a possible summit with Ahmed Qurei, the PLO's chief negotiator whose nom de guerre was Abu Ala. Ross revealed that the Israelis were willing to withdraw from most of the West Bank, provided the PLO approved territorial swaps that would incorporate several heavily populated settlement blocs into the Jewish state. In return, the Palestinians would receive a small amount of land previously belonging to Israel. The PLO was not interested in such an exchange. "In principle, we refuse it," Abu Ala told Ross. "Israelis can stay and apply for Palestinian citizenship, but they must live under Palestinian law."[70] Unwilling to take no for an answer, Ross's boss invited Arafat to the White House at the end of the month. According to Abu Ala, "Arafat told Clinton he needed more time." The two sides were still too far apart on too many matters, not just the territorial swaps but also the Palestinian right of return to Israel and the status of Muslim holy sites in Jerusalem. "Clinton said, 'Chairman Arafat, come try your best. If it fails, I will not blame you,'" Abu Ala recalled ruefully. "But that is exactly what he did."[71]

Had Yasser Arafat been privy to Ehud Barak's state of mind on the eve of the summit, he would not even have bothered to show up at Camp David. "If you just look at the Israeli-Palestinian situation, it appears that the Palestinians are the victims and Israel has all the cards," Barak told Martin Indyk, who was serving a second stint at the U.S. embassy in Tel Aviv, on 10 July. "But in the bigger picture, we are a very small country in a much larger Arab world." The president needed to "widen his lens" and consider matters from the Israeli point of view. "Our borders with the Arab world will be determined at Camp David," Barak continued. "Israel will at most become a city-state with a large park in the south." Above all, he added, "I don't want [Bill Clinton] to allow Arafat to pocket our concessions." The PLO chairman "uses his unhappiness as a tactic," Barak quipped. "He should get an Oscar for his performances."[72]

The next day, Barak and Arafat arrived at Camp David, where Clinton vowed to broker a landmark peace agreement. Yet when the three men departed two weeks later, nobody had won an Academy Award. As the days passed, U.S. negotiators grew increasingly impatient with both sides. For his part, Barak impressed the Americans as brilliant and brave but also as manipulative and obstinate. "He was willing to go a long way on Jerusalem and on territory," Clinton recalled in his memoirs. "But he had a hard time listening to people who didn't see things the way he did," which left the Palestinians bitter and mistrustful. "Barak wanted others to wait until he decided the time was right," Clinton observed, "then, when he made his best offer, he expected it to be accepted as self-evidently a good deal."[73] After the Israeli prime minister reneged on a promise to turn three West Bank villages over to the PLO and asked the United States to break the bad news to the Palestinians, Clinton was not amused. "I can't go to see Arafat with a retrenchment. Maybe you can sell it to him; there's no way that I can," he exploded at Barak. "This is not real. This is not serious."[74]

The man in the Oval Office was even unhappier with Yasser Arafat. Shortly after his blowup with Barak, Clinton handed the Palestinians an Israeli offer that he felt they could not refuse. Israel would relinquish 91 percent of the West Bank, it would swap 1 percent of its own territory to create a narrow land bridge connecting the West Bank with Gaza, it would grant Palestinian autonomy in East Jerusalem, and it would recognize PLO custodianship over the al-Aqsa mosque and other Muslim holy sites in the Old City. Although the president managed to convince himself that at long last the two sides had finally gotten to "yes," Arafat said "no," insisting that the territorial swap was unbalanced, that the PLO could accept nothing less than complete control of East Jerusalem, and that the Israelis must recognize the Palestinian right of return. According to the NSC adviser Sandy Berger, the six-foot-two Clinton proceeded to subject the diminutive PLO chairman to "the full Lyndon Johnson treatment," towering over him while shouting: "This is the best deal you're gonna get. For God's sake, don't turn it down."[75] But despite Clinton's bullying, Arafat stood his ground. A year later, he explained his thinking to a reporter this way: At Camp David, Clinton and Barak had offered the PLO "less than a Bantustan," a non-viable state whose borders, airspace, and aquifers would remain firmly under Israeli control. "They have to divide the West Bank in three cantons. They keep 10 percent of it for settlements and roads and their forces," Arafat complained. "And refugees, we didn't have a serious discussion about."[76] The way Arafat saw it, this had clearly been an offer that the Palestinians could refuse, and that is precisely what they had done.

Desperate to salvage the summit, Clinton made one last attempt to win Palestinian approval during a marathon session on July 18. Arafat and Abu Ala, however, continued to insist that Israel must relinquish the entire West Bank, including East Jerusalem, as specified by several UN Security Council resolutions. At this point, "Clinton became boiling mad and started shouting terribly," the Israeli foreign minister Shlomo Ben Ami recalled. "He told Abu Ala that this wasn't a speech at the United Nations, and that the Palestinians had to come up with positive proposals of their own." After reminding the PLO negotiators that "no one would be able to get everything he wanted," the president "turned completely red and finally got up and stalked out." According to Ben Ami, "Abu Ala was deeply offended," and "from that moment, almost the only thing he did at Camp David was drive around the lawns in a golf cart."[77]

The next day Clinton flew to Okinawa for the annual G-8 summit, and when he returned a week later, he blamed the Palestinians for the stalemate at Camp David. "I don't like to fail," he confessed to Madeleine Albright.[78] "Arafat wanted 100 percent of Jerusalem and gave Barak nothing," Clinton told his national security team. "Barak on the other hand was courageous and creative. He was willing to take less than one hundred percent and Arafat wasn't."[79] In an interview conducted long afterward, Sandy Berger confirmed that Clinton found the PLO leader exasperating: "There was frustration always with Arafat because he was a master of victimhood, at grievance, and you'd listen to him for hours at a time talking about how poorly the Palestinians had been treated." Was it fair to say that the White House had double-crossed Arafat at Camp David? "I think it was Clinton's intent going in that we would not blame Arafat if it failed," Berger replied, but "it ultimately was not the way things played out." So, had Clinton broken his promise? "I don't think that he was disingenuous with Arafat at the time," Berger explained, but "I think as things unfolded he went in a different direction on that."[80]

The Palestinians, on the other hand, insisted that the Americans were at fault because they had abandoned the principle of peace for land by acquiescing to Israel's territorial requirements. "Clinton was angry at me and told me I was personally responsible for the failure of the summit," Abu Ala remembered. "I told him even if occupation continues for 500 years, we will not change."[81] Aaron Miller, who served alongside Dennis Ross and Martin Indyk on the U.S. negotiating team, confessed that the three of them frequently served as "Israel's lawyers" during the late 1990s and helped put a black hat on the PLO after the debacle at Camp David. "Barak's and Clinton's anger [was] understandable, and the politician in Clinton was eager to do something for the bold and beleaguered prime minister," Miller noted. "But I can't help thinking our behavior in blaming the Palestinians and facilitating Barak's campaign to delegitimize Arafat as a partner was immature and counterproductive."[82] Some high-ranking Israelis agreed. "Ten years later, there are still people who say, 'We gave them everything at Camp David and got nothing,'" Tal Zilberstein, one of Barak's closest political advisers, told a reporter. "That is a flagrant lie." Barak's foreign minister, Shlomo Ben Ami, offered this blunt postmortem on the peace that never was: "If I were a Palestinian, I would have rejected Camp David as well."[83]

Although there was much dispute about what caused the summit to crash and burn, there was widespread agreement about the consequences. With election day just three months away, some Democrats worried that fallout from the Camp David fiasco might undermine Vice President Al Gore's bid for the White House. "I want the shit dry by September," Clinton told his advisers.[84] Events in the Holy Land soon made that impossible. Convinced that Arafat was no longer interested in peace, Barak did nothing to discourage the Likud Party's new leader, Ariel Sharon, from making a provocative visit to Jerusalem's al-Aqsa mosque on 28 September accompanied by eight hundred police officers. After young Palestinians pelted the Israeli entourage with stones and bottles, Sharon's security detail fired live ammunition into the crowd, killing thirteen protestors and touching off what came to be known as the "al-Aqsa Intifada." Convinced that Barak was no longer interested in peace, Arafat did nothing to halt the spiral of violence, permitting armed militias loyal to the PLO to attack Israeli police and soldiers and refusing to condemn Hamas for sending suicide bombers into Israeli cities. By the end of the year, nearly three hundred Palestinians and forty-one Israelis had died.

Two days before Christmas, Clinton invited representatives of the two sides to the White House, where he handed them a set of parameters outlining a last-minute peace deal. The terms were much more favorable to the PLO than what had been on offer at Camp David—Israel would relinquish 95 percent of the West Bank, it would share control of Jerusalem, and it would permit a few Palestinian refugees to reunite with their families inside the Jewish state. With less than a month left in his second term, Clinton said he was still willing to mediate one final round of peace talks. "These are my ideas," he told his visitors. "If they are not accepted, they are not just off the table, they also go with me when I leave office."[85] Ehud Barak reluctantly endorsed the parameters on 27 December, but when Yasser Arafat paid a call at the White House on 2 January 2001, he haggled over the details. Pressed to follow Barak's lead, the PLO chairman responded instead with "the Arafat answer" that Dennis Ross and other Americans had heard so often: *La-Na'am* (no and yes in Arabic).[86] Clinton was furious. Two weeks later, he sat down with Colin Powell, secretary of state–designate in the incoming administration, for a presidential gripe session about the Palestinians, whom he held responsible for the deadlocked peace process. "Don't let Arafat sucker punch you like he did me," Clinton snarled. "Don't you ever trust that son of a bitch. He lied to me and he'll lie to you."[87] As the Arkansas Democrat prepared to pass the torch to George W. Bush, he clearly regarded the "missing peace" between the Israelis and the Palestinians as his biggest disappointment in the Middle East. Before long, however, Arafat would have a serious rival as "public enemy number one."

Radical Islam, Osama Bin Laden, and the Clash of Civilizations

The Israeli-Palestinian deadlock was just one of many irritants that bedeviled American relations with the Muslim world during the Clinton era. From the moment he settled into his office in the West Wing, Tony Lake had smelled trouble from the Eastern Mediterranean to the Red Sea and from the Persian Gulf to the Hindu Kush. His biggest worry was the deepening crisis in Bosnia, where the Serbs were perpetrating genocide in everything but name while the Iranians were providing arms and advisers to the embattled Muslims. "What could be more classic than concerns about a new Balkan war with spillover that could draw in the Greeks and the Turks?" Lake asked a reporter in the spring of 1993. "And with all this you have tensions between the Islamic world and the Christian world that are filled with ancient dangers." By taking a hard line with the Serbs, of course, the Clinton administration might merely be playing into the hands of the Iranians. "Containment of Iran requires our working to contain Muslim extremism, and we have to find a way of being firm in our opposition to Muslim extremism while making it clear we're not opposed to Islam." There were no easy answers. "If we are seen as anti-Muslim, it's harder for us to contain Muslim extremism," Lake sighed. "If we stand by while Muslims are killed and raped in Bosnia, it makes it harder to continue our policy of dual containment."[88]

Manifestations of mounting Islamic radicalism seemed to be everywhere during 1993. In late February, Muslim extremists exploded a truck bomb in the parking garage beneath the World Trade Center in New York City, killing six and injuring hundreds. In March, Algerian Islamists staged brutal attacks on both soldiers and civilians, slitting throats and gouging eyes, and the military government in Algiers responded with a dirty war of its own, complete with torture and mass executions. By early summer, Hamas and Hezbollah had ratcheted up their anti-Israeli rhetoric while Islamic radicals like Gulbuddin Hekmatyar edged closer to power in Afghanistan. Meanwhile, the Egyptian Islamic Jihad launched a terrorist campaign directed at foreigners, slicing Egypt's tourism revenues by 50 percent, and Abu Sayyaf, a militant Filipino Muslim group, stepped up its guerrilla war against the pro-American regime in Manila.[89]

Just as this wave of Islamic radicalism was reaching a crescendo, Samuel P. Huntington framed it in a post–Cold War context in "The Coming Clash of Civilizations," the cover article in the summer 1993 issue of *Foreign Affairs*. An academic expert on national security and a self-styled big thinker who had served on Jimmy Carter's NSC staff, Huntington argued that the end of the Cold War had brought both good news and bad news. On the bright side, the disintegration of the Soviet Union confirmed the wisdom of containment and signaled the demise of ideology as the most explosive source of conflict in the international system. Nevertheless, Huntington foresaw serious trouble ahead, largely because the ideological antagonism between communism and capitalism was being rapidly replaced by something far more dangerous. The "'us' versus 'them' relation" at the center of the Soviet-American rivalry had not disappeared but had rather been reformatted to reflect the two most powerful engines of change during the 1990s, religion and culture. According to Huntington's multipolar model, seven civilizations—Western, Slavic-Orthodox, Confucian, Japanese, Hindu, Latin American, and Islamic—would interact with increasing intensity in the new millennium. "Faith and family, blood and belief, are what people identify with and what they will fight and die for," he wrote. "And that is why the clash of civilizations is replacing the Cold War as the central phenomenon of global politics."[90]

Huntington claimed that the most problematic fault line was the one separating the West from the Muslim world, a geopolitical subduction zone where secularism and modernization collided with theocracy and tradition. Taking his cue from Bernard Lewis, the Princeton Orientalist who had first attributed the "the roots of Muslim rage" to "a clash of civilizations" three years earlier, the Harvard don made a case for irrepressible conflict. Huntington explained the clash this way in a subsequent book-length version of his article: "Wherever one looks, along the perimeter of Islam, Muslims have problems living peaceably with their neighbors." Simply put, "Islam's borders are bloody, and so are its innards."[91] Critics, however, dismissed Huntington's Islamophobia as unfounded. Kishore Mahbubani, Singapore's deputy foreign minister, probably spoke for many when he noted that "in all conflicts between Muslims and pro-Western forces" from Bosnia to Iraq, "Muslims are losing, and losing badly."[92]

Huntington's prophecy created quite a stir, not only in the Muslim world but also inside the Clinton administration. In early August, Indonesia played host to representatives from two dozen nations, who gathered in Jakarta for a forum titled "Asia Pacific and the New World Order." The gathering was supposed to showcase the benefits of economic globalization, but it was clear to the U.S. ambassador Robert Barry that most of the delegates had read the latest issue of *Foreign Affairs*. "Sam Huntington's thesis about the 'coming clash of civilizations' has caught on in Asia like wildfire," Barry cabled Washington on 16 August, with troubling implications for the United States. "The danger is that the prophecy will become self-fulfilling as more people believe it and act on it," he warned. "This is particularly true in the Islamic world, where anti-Western paranoia is already at a high pitch." The best antidote to "Huntingtonism," the ambassador insisted, was not more military muscle but rather better public diplomacy focusing on "what we are rather than what we are against." Although the problem was most acute in the Middle East, it reverberated throughout Asia and Africa. "To counter the 'we versus they' mentality," Barry concluded, Washington must do more to highlight "our cooperative programs with Muslim states and the way in which Muslims are integrated into American society."[93]

When Tony Lake unveiled the Clinton administration's strategy of engagement and enlargement at Johns Hopkins University a month later, he tried to put some distance between Huntington and the White House. "We have arrived at neither the end of history nor a clash of civilizations, but a moment of immense democratic and entrepreneurial opportunity," he declared on 21 September 1993. America was certainly not looking to pick a fight with the Muslim world. "Let me emphasize this point: our nation respects the many contributions Islam has made to the world over the past 1300 years, and we appreciate the close bonds of values and history between Islam and the Judeo-Christian beliefs of most Americans." The United States was, however, looking to distinguish between good Muslims and bad Muslims. "We will extend every expression or friendship to those of the Islamic faith who abide in peace and tolerance," Lake promised. "But we will provide every resistance to militants who distort Islamic doctrines and seek to expand their influence by force."[94]

Clinton and his top advisers reiterated this distinction at every opportunity. During an Arab-Israeli economic summit in Casablanca, for example, then Secretary of State Warren Christopher argued that "the roots of extremism and terror" were to be found in "economic stagnation and poverty," not religion. "The United States has a friendly relationship with Islam and not an adversarial one," he told a group of Americans doing business in Morocco. "If I can borrow a line from Humphrey Bogart's famous comment, I think we may be beginning a beautiful friendship."[95] From her perch at the United Nations, Madeleine Albright downplayed the danger that "one person, one vote, one time" might thwart democracy in the Arab world, emphasizing that "there are many voices of Islam" and appealing for a "true dialogue of civilizations" between Muslims and Americans.[96] The president himself dismissed "those who insist that between America and the Middle East there are impassable religious and other obstacles" as completely wrongheaded. "America refuses to accept that our civilizations must collide," Clinton remarked during a visit to Amman, Jordan. "We respect Islam."[97]

One of the most sophisticated advocates for separating good and bad Muslims during the Clinton era was the State Department's Robert H. Pelletreau, who had previously held ambassadorial appointments in Bahrain, Tunisia, and Egypt. "We, as a government, have no quarrel with Islam," he told a gathering of academic experts in May 1994, and "the United States does not view Islam as the next 'ism' confronting the West or threatening world peace." To be sure, "we're concerned about third countries' exploitation of Islamic extremist groups throughout the region, and over Sudan's role, for example, in supporting such groups in North Africa, either in its own right or as a cat's-paw for Iran," but Pelletreau was very clear that "we see no monolithic international control being exercised over the various Islamic movements active in the region."[98] He was even clearer a year later during an interview with Daniel Pipes, the neoconservative editor of the *Middle East Quarterly*. "The phenomenon of Islamic fundamentalism," Pelletreau told Pipes in June 1995, "is not monolithic." U.S. officials were deeply troubled but hardly surprised by violent outbursts that threatened America's partners in the region from Egypt to the Palestinian territories. "In an era when the 'isms' of communism and socialism, even of Arab nationalism, have lost their luster, it is quite understandable that many people return to their religious roots for meaning and for values," Pelletreau confessed. Nevertheless, "we don't believe that everybody who says he's an Islamist falls necessarily in the terrorist category."[99]

One Islamist who clearly did fall in that category by 1995 was Osama Bin Laden, a wealthy Saudi renegade whose radical brand of Islam had initially caught the attention of U.S. policy makers when he helped found al-Qaeda, a global jihadist group, in Afghanistan. "We had been following bin Laden for years," Bill Clinton recalled in his memoirs. At first, the al-Qaeda leader seemed to be merely "a financier of terrorist operations," but over time the White House learned that Bin Laden actually headed a "highly sophisticated" organization with ties to Islamic extremists from Bosnia to the Philippines and that his "transnational network continued to grow."[100] Bin Laden had floated onto the NSC counterterrorism team's radar screen as early as 1993, when rumors surfaced in the aftermath of the Black Hawk Down fiasco in Somalia that "al Qaeda had been sending advisors to Aideed and had helped engineer the shoot-down of the U.S. helicopters."[101] Three years later, after U.S. intelligence confirmed that Bin Laden was orchestrating plots to blow up American airliners over the Pacific and attack GIs stationed in Saudi Arabia from his new headquarters in Khartoum, the Clinton administration pressured the Sudanese government to expel him. White House al-Qaeda watchers Daniel Benjamin and Steven Simon later remembered that "separating bin Laden from his archipelago of training camps, his import-export companies, his construction firm, and his other cash cows, as well putting distance between him and Sudan's passport printing office, was extremely attractive." On 18 May 1996, Bin Laden packed his bags and "returned to the site of his earlier glory, Afghanistan."[102]

Despite Bin Laden's abrupt departure from Sudan, U.S. policy makers worried that he would simply wage the same old jihad from a new base in Kabul. "His prolonged stay in Afghanistan—where hundreds of Arab mujahedeen receive terrorist training and key extremist leaders often congregate," State Department experts warned on 18 July, "could prove more dangerous to U.S. interests in the long run than his three-year liaison with Khartoum." Even worse, Bin Laden's ties to "radical Islamists extend[ed] well beyond the Middle East." French officials, for example, suspected that he had helped Algeria's Armed Islamic Group plan a recent series of bombings in Paris and Lyon, while British intelligence had detected signs that there might be an al-Qaeda cell operating in London.[103] Bin Laden's prospects brightened once the Taliban, a group of anti-Western extremists led by the one-eyed Mullah Omar, triumphed in the Afghan civil war and established an Islamist regime based on sharia law later that summer. Because Washington refused to recognize the new regime in Kabul, all face-to-face American diplomatic contact with the Taliban occurred next door in Pakistan, where the CIA worked closely with the Interservice Intelligence Agency (ISI), Islamabad's chief spy agency. On 18 September 1996, U.S. officials met with Mullah Abdul Jalil, the Taliban's deputy foreign minister, in the Pakistani capital to express concern about al-Qaeda's presence in Afghanistan and to ascertain the whereabouts of Osama Bin Laden. Although Jalil claimed to have no information about al-Qaeda or its leader, "he made all the right sounds about terrorism," insisting that "the Taliban did not support terrorism in any form and would not provide refuge to Osama bin Laden."[104]

During the following eighteen months, however, evidence mounted that Bin Laden was organizing an anti-American jihad stretching from North

Africa to the Persian Gulf. Judging from several heavily redacted intelligence reports prepared during 1997, the CIA seems not only to have realized that al-Qaeda was behind a series of recent terrorist attacks against U.S. targets in Egypt and Yemen but also to have suspected that al-Qaeda might have had a hand in the deadly Khobar Towers bombing in Saudi Arabia the previous June.[105] Any remaining doubts about Bin Laden's malevolent intentions disappeared on 23 February 1998, when he promulgated a fatwa against "the Jews and Crusaders," calling for the destruction of Israel, condemning the presence of U.S. troops in Saudi Arabia as a mortal threat to the Islamic holy places in Mecca and Medina, and insisting that "to kill the Americans and their allies—civilians and military—is an individual obligation incumbent upon every Muslim who can do it and in any country."[106] Three days later, U.S. diplomats in Pakistan informed Taliban officials that "Usama bin Laden's inflammatory remarks and anti-American rhetoric" were "unacceptable and will not be tolerated" and warned that the Clinton administration would hold Mullah Omar and his regime in Kabul responsible should the al-Qaeda leader carry out his violent threats.[107]

On 7 August 1998, two truck bombs exploded in quick succession outside the U.S. embassies in Kenya and Tanzania, killing more than two hundred people, including eight Americans, and injuring thousands. After U.S. intelligence confirmed that Bin Laden's fingerprints were all over the bombings in East Africa, the Clinton administration launched Tomahawk cruise missiles against his headquarters outside Kabul and against a factory near Khartoum, where al-Qaeda was rumored to be developing chemical weapons. These retaliatory attacks, the State Department explained on 20 August, were intended to destroy the terrorist infrastructure and to kill Bin Laden, who "directs a network that organizes, funds, and inspires a wide range of Islamic extremist groups" and who was waging an anti-American jihad from Afghanistan to Yemen and from Algeria to the Philippines. Tipped off by radical Islamists inside the Pakistani ISI, however, Bin Laden escaped unharmed, prompting President Clinton to seek a more effective way to fight terrorism. "What I think would scare the shit out of these al Qaeda guys more than any cruise missile," he told General Hugh Shelton, who chaired the Joint Chiefs of Staff, in late August, "would be the sight of U.S. commandos, Ninja guys in black suits, jumping out of helicopters into their camps, spraying machine guns." Clinton realized that this would be quite risky, but he was convinced that "even if we don't get the big guys, it will have a good effect."[108]

Although cruise missiles and commandos might be attractive tools for combatting terrorism in theory, U.S. policy makers worried that in practice such tactics would merely fan the flames of anti-Americanism throughout the region. When American diplomats ventured outside Islamabad later that fall to take the pulse of rural Pakistanis, they discovered a surprising amount of support for al-Qaeda. "Bin Laden and the Taliban appeared to ordinary folk as Islamic heroes who had not only stood up to the anti-Islamic West but were successful in so doing," the deputy chief of mission John Schmidt reported on 27 October. That these Sunni extremists should become "cultural icons" throughout much of Pakistan reflected "the cumulative impact of years of what has been perceived here as anti-Islamic behavior by the United States."[109] As the CIA learned more about Bin Laden's whereabouts early in 1999, some in Washington pushed for preemptive action before he could strike again. With U.S. Air Force jets already leading NATO's aerial campaign to repel Serbian aggression in Kosovo, however, Clinton's national security team worried that new attacks on al-Qaeda or its Taliban hosts would merely guarantee that "the United States was increasingly seen as the world's mad bomber." Unable to build a compelling case for a fresh round of retaliatory strikes against Kabul, American officials resorted to black humor. "The frequent morbid refrain in these discussions, inverting General Curtis LeMay's famous remark," two NSC counterterrorism experts recalled afterward, "was that an attack would bomb Afghanistan *up* to the Stone Age."[110]

As the year drew to a close, disturbing evidence of an al-Qaeda plot to strike multiple targets in the Middle East and the United States surfaced. On 4 December, the CIA learned that Jordanian intelligence had captured sixteen Islamic extremists who were planning an attack against the American community in Amman and whose motto was: "The season is coming, and bodies will pile up in stacks." Ten days later, immigration officers arrested an Algerian national trying to smuggle explosives into Washington State from Canada for an attack on Los Angeles International Airport on New Year's Eve.[111] As the "millennium crisis" unfolded, alarm bells sounded in Washington, D.C., and the Clinton administration zeroed in on Osama Bin Laden. "I spoke with the President and he wants you all to know," NSC adviser Sandy Berger told CIA director George Tenet, Attorney General Janet Reno, and the FBI's Louis Freeh shortly before Christmas, "this is it, nothing more important, all assets. We stop this fucker."[112] A threat that Bill Clinton had dismissed as ridiculous and far-fetched when he entered the White House now seemed all too real at the start of his final year in office. "*Foreign sleeper cells are present in the US,*" Berger's staff warned on 3 January 2000, "*and attacks in the US are likely.*"[113]

At the dawn of the new millennium, most U.S. policy makers regarded Islamic extremism as the gravest threat facing the world's sole remaining superpower. In *Six Nightmares*, a book that was part memoir and part crystal ball, Tony Lake, Clinton's former NSC adviser, urged any doubters among his old colleagues to direct their attention to the Hindu Kush. "Religious zealots based in Afghanistan have started to spread throughout Central Asia and the Caucasus, hoping that economic hardship will make radical appeals more popular," the father of enlargement wrote. "Such radical Islamic activism is setting off alarm bells in Moscow and Beijing, who fear its spillover into their territories. And it should be setting off louder bells than it has in Washington and throughout Europe."[114] As the presidential campaign heated up later that fall, Ben Bonk, a CIA counterterrorism specialist, flew to Crawford, Texas, to brief the Republican candidate about the dangers posed by al-Qaeda and other Muslim extremists. "I can say one thing for sure without any qualification," Bonk warned George W. Bush on 2 September 2000: "Sometime in the next four years, Americans will die as a result of a terrorist incident."[115] Three weeks before election day, suicide bombers loyal to Osama Bin Laden rammed a small boat loaded with half a ton of C-4, a deadly plastic explosive, into the USS *Cole* while the guided-missile frigate was refueling at Aden harbor in Yemen en route to the Persian Gulf. The explosion killed seventeen sailors, wounded thirty-nine others, and nearly sent the warship to the bottom.

Immediate suspicion fell on Bin Laden, and by late November the CIA was almost certain that he was indeed the evil mastermind behind the attack. With less than two months left in his second term, however, Bill Clinton was reluctant to embroil the United States in an undeclared war against al-Qaeda and their Taliban hosts without ironclad proof. Nothing about the *Cole* episode sat well with officials like Mike Sheehan, a retired colonel who had earlier spent time with the U.S. special forces in Somalia and who now served as Clinton's ambassador-at-large for counterterrorism. "Yemen is a viper's nest of terrorists," Sheehan thundered. "What the fuck was the *Cole* doing there in the first place?" Moreover, it was a huge mistake not to hit al-Qaeda's base camps in Afghanistan hard. "Who the shit do they think attacked the *Cole*, fuckin' Martians?" Sheehan asked his fellow Bin Laden watcher Richard Clarke. "Does al Qaeda have to attack the Pentagon to get their attention?"[116] Clinton and Berger would brief their successors on the al-Qaeda threat early in the New Year, but it would be up to the incoming Bush administration to answer Sheehan's questions.[117]

Bill Clinton had entered office eight years earlier bursting with post–Cold War euphoria and largely unconcerned about events in the Muslim world. The president nicknamed Elvis, along with Tony Lake and the rest of his national security team, embraced the doctrine of enlargement. Following the abrupt demise of the Soviet Union, the hoary Red Threat had suddenly disappeared, and in its wake the Clinton administration proposed a new paradigm based not on the Cold War logic of us versus them but rather on multilateral democratization, economic globalization, and a computer-driven "revolution in information." Well aware of the perils of military intervention in the Third World, Clinton intended to rely on soft power to promote peace and prosperity, and he was determined that foreign policy not distract him from pressing economic matters closer to home.

Things started well enough for Clinton in the Middle East. During his first term, the Israelis and Palestinians seemed on track to conclude a just and lasting peace while backlash states like Saddam Hussein's Iraq and the Islamic Republic of Iran were held in check by a policy of dual containment. The Oslo peace process suffered a fatal blow, however, when Yitzhak Rabin was assassinated by a Jewish extremist in November 1995, unleashing a bloody spiral of reciprocal violence that played into the hands of Hamas, who used Islam as a weapon against secular Palestinian rivals while sending suicide bombers into Israeli cities to maim and kill tourists and schoolchildren. By late 1996, the Israeli prime minister Benjamin Netanyahu seemed to have abandoned the peace process, while Saddam Hussein seemed to have sped up his quest for nuclear weapons.

Throughout Clinton's second term, the foreign policy conversation inside the Beltway revolved increasingly around the Green Threat posed by radical Islam and the growing likelihood of a supposed clash of civilizations between America and the Muslim world. To be sure, had Elvis managed to broker a peace agreement between Ehud Barak and Yasser Arafat at Camp David in the summer of 2000, he could have erased a major grievance among the many Muslims who held the United States responsible for the plight of the Palestinians. During his final three years in the Oval Office, however, Clinton faced an ever escalating confrontation with Islamic extremism in general and with al-Qaeda in particular. Osama Bin Laden may not have been a household name on 20 January 2001, but the bombings of two U.S. embassies in East Africa in August 1998, the millennium crisis in late 1999, and the attack on the USS *Cole* in October 2000 had certainly made him a White House name. The key question for the new president seemed obvious. Would George W. Bush seek to reinvigorate Clinton's post–Cold War paradigm, or would he revert to us-versus-them verities of the world before 1989?

CHAPTER FOUR

Containment on Steroids?

George W. Bush and Rogue State Rollback

George W. Bush was sworn in as America's forty-third president on 20 January 2001 under gray skies in a cold rain, the first chief executive to receive fewer popular votes than his opponent in more than a hundred years and the first to follow his father into the White House since John Quincy Adams in 1825. Having eked out a victory in the Electoral College thanks to Florida, which he carried by just 537 votes, President Bush could claim no clear mandate either at home or abroad. Even though the United States was prosperous and at peace, the Texas Republican regarded his predecessor as a callow usurper who had defamed the House of Bush in 1992 and plunged the country into diplomatic disaster and moral depravity. Dismissing Bill Clinton's formula of economic globalization, multilateralism, and soft power as a recipe for weakness and decline, George W. Bush insisted that post–Cold War America must remain what it had been throughout its long confrontation with the Kremlin—the most dominant force in world affairs and the only nation capable of protecting us from them. "The stakes for America are never small," Bush declared in his inaugural address. "If our country does not lead the cause of freedom, it will not be led." Whatever "new horrors" the new millennium might hold, "the enemies of liberty and our country" should remember that "America remains engaged in the world, by history and by choice, shaping a balance of power that favors freedom."[1]

The way the new president saw it, "rogue states" posed the biggest threat to the cause of freedom. Some of these "enemies of liberty" were great powers in their own right like Russia and China, which combined impressive military arsenals with oppressive political systems, while others were regional troublemakers like Iraq or North Korea, whose brutal and volatile leaders reveled in anti-American bluster and bragged about weapons of mass destruction (WMD). Although Bush recognized that containment was the only realistic option for preserving the balance of power with Moscow or Beijing, he stocked his national security team with hard-line Cold Warriors whose strategy for handling smaller rogue regimes like the ones in Baghdad and Pyongyang came straight out of Eisenhower's America—rollback. Rolling back rogue states would mean ramping up U.S. defense spending and reaffirming Washington's willingness to act unilaterally whenever and wherever it wished. From his first days in office, President Bush promoted a high-tech missile shield to protect America from a nuclear-armed North Korea while embracing Israel as a de facto sheriff to help corral outlaw regimes like the one in Iraq.

Yet none of this mattered when Arab terrorists literally flew in under the radar to attack the U.S. homeland on 11 September 2001. For many months, CIA counterterrorism experts had been warning that stateless groups like al-Qaeda could be far more dangerous than rogue states such as Iraq, but until the day the Twin Towers fell, the White House was fixated on a rogue's gallery filled with old-fashioned autocrats like Saddam Hussein, not new-age thugs like Osama Bin Laden. Reeling from an unprecedented assault on the American homeland that claimed 2,977 lives, the Bush administration moved swiftly to meet the new threat, unleashing a "global war on terror" against violent Islamic extremists and their supporters, expanding the Cold War national security state to grant the White House sweeping new powers, and embracing the doctrine of preventive war as the surest guarantee that they would never get the chance to inflict a second 9/11 on us. In the process, the new Green Threat of radical Islam would replace the old Red Threat of international communism.

The implications for American relations with the Muslim world were far-reaching. Before the year ended, the CIA and the Pentagon had joined forces to topple the Taliban regime in Kabul, depriving al-Qaeda of its safe haven in the Hindu Kush. Bush and his senior advisers made it clear that the swift victory in Afghanistan constituted merely a prelude to a much broader crusade against Islamic terrorists from North Africa to Southeast Asia. Then in early 2002, the president branded Iraq as a charter member of what he called the Axis of Evil, lumping Saddam Hussein, a secular radical, together with religious terrorists like Osama Bin Laden, and began calling for regime change in Baghdad. Meanwhile, the Israelis managed to persuade the Bush administration that the Palestinians presented the same kind of existential threat to the Holy Land that al-Qaeda posed to America, enabling Prime Minister Ariel Sharon to send troops and tanks back onto the West Bank, where they laid siege to PLO headquarters in Ramallah.

One year after the 9/11 attacks, George W. Bush unveiled an ambitious new national security strategy modeled on Harry Truman's Cold War call to arms in NSC-68. The world's sole remaining superpower would combat terrorism and achieve rogue state rollback by waging preventive war and exporting democracy. The initial testing ground for the Bush Doctrine was Iraq, where an American blitzkrieg overwhelmed Saddam Hussein's forces in the spring of 2003, paving the way for what was supposed to be a quick-and-dirty round of nation-building on the Euphrates. Before long, however, U.S. troops became bogged down in a brutal low-intensity war against Iraqi insurgents, some of whom pledged fealty to Osama Bin Laden and formed al-Qaeda in Iraq (AQI). The first two years of Bush's second term proved a nightmare. Grisly sectarian violence enveloped Iraq, radical jihadis threatened pro-American regimes in Pakistan and Afghanistan, and anti-American forces like Hamas and Hezbollah kept Israel, Washington's chief partner in the region, off balance. A surge of fresh U.S. troops into Iraq would quell some of the violence after 2007, but many Americans worried that Bush's global war on terror had morphed into Mission Impossible. In this latest round of us versus them in the Muslim world, they seemed to be winning.

Dubya and His Team of Vulcans

When George W. Bush entered the GOP primaries in early 2000, he seemed like a long shot to follow his namesake to the Oval Office. Born in New Haven, Connecticut, in July 1946, "Little George" had grown up idolizing his future-president father, retracing "Big George's" career path, first to Phillips Andover, then to Yale University, and finally to the oil fields of West Texas. Known affectionately as "Dubya" by his pals in the Lone Star State, Bush probably regarded Jack Daniel as his best friend until he managed to quit drinking cold turkey in 1986. Although Dubya held no official post during the first Bush administration, he served as his father's de facto political enforcer, plotting new tactics and settling old scores. Stunned by Bill Clinton's triumph in November 1992, Dubya headed home to Texas and redeemed the family name with an impressive victory in the gubernatorial election two years later. Governor Bush despised President Clinton, not only because the Arkansas Democrat could not keep his fly zipped but also because he spoke softly and carried a small stick. Shortly after winning a second term at the State House in November 1998, Dubya set his sights on the White House, where he hoped to emulate his personal hero, Theodore Roosevelt, by wielding a big stick.

Having come of age at the height of the Cold War, George W. Bush viewed the world through the lens of us versus them. "My passion was history," Dubya observed in his memoirs, and as a result, he took courses at Yale on the American Revolution, the British Empire, and Nazi Germany. His favorite teacher, however, was an East German exile who taught the history of Soviet Russia. "The class was an introduction to the struggle between tyranny and freedom," Dubya recalled, "a battle that has held my attention for the rest of my life."[2] Two years at the Harvard Business School, "the West Point of capitalism," left him with an abiding faith in free enterprise, a deep disgust for government meddling in the economy, and an avid interest in the "Reagan Revolution" of the 1980s.[3] Although Dubya would wince when the first Bush administration unveiled its "status quo plus" approach toward the Kremlin in early 1989, he was proud of his father's deft handling of the collapse of the Soviet Union in December 1991.

Governors of Texas seldom say much about foreign policy, but once George W. Bush became a presidential contender, his rhetoric often evoked the binary logic of the Cold War. During an Iowa campaign stop in January 2000, for example, candidate Bush confessed that the challenges facing America in the new millennium would be daunting. "When I was coming up, it was a dangerous world, and you knew exactly what they were. It was us versus them, and it was clear who them was." Then came the punch line in syntax so convoluted that some wags would later claim that English was Dubya's second language: "Today, we are not so sure who the they are, but we know they're there."[4] Senator John McCain, Bush's chief rival for the Republican nomination, displayed a better grasp of who they were and where to find them on 16 February during a debate on the eve of the South Carolina primary. Blasting Bill Clinton for not being tough enough with outlaw regimes in Iraq, Libya, and North Korea, McCain called for a policy of "rogue state rollback" to arm and train pro-American forces to overthrow thugs like Saddam Hussein and replace them with "free and democratically elected governments." Dubya, who truly could not have said it better himself, nodded in agreement.[5]

Bush's come-from-behind victory over McCain in the Palmetto State cleared the way for a showdown with Al Gore on 7 November 2000. Foreign policy did not figure prominently during the campaign, which became a referendum on Clinton's peccadilloes, Gore's prissiness, and Bush's mojo. During one of the presidential debates, however, Dubya did chide the Clinton administration for its prolonged military involvement in the Balkans, where U.S. soldiers and warplanes had prevented Serbia from completing the ethnic cleansing of Bosnia and Kosovo. "The vice president and I have a disagreement about the use of troops. He believes in nation building," Bush remarked on 3 October. "I believe the role of the military is to fight and win war and therefore prevent war from happening in the first place." Before putting Americans in harm's way, he added, a president must determine "whether or not . . . our defense alliances are threatened, whether or not our friends in the Middle East are threatened," and "whether or not there was an exit strategy."[6] Helping Bush make such determinations was Condoleezza Rice, a Stanford Russian specialist who had served on his father's NSC staff. The only child of middle-class African American parents from Birmingham, Alabama, "Condi" was an unabashed realist who saw international affairs as a struggle between us and them and believed that the best defense was a good offense.[7] She revealed her prescription for what ailed U.S. foreign policy in the first issue of *Foreign Affairs* in the new millennium. Americans must stop trying to save the world and start promoting the national interest, Rice informed her readers in January 2000, not merely by supporting free elections and free markets overseas but also by stepping up funding for the Pentagon and the CIA. Pooh-poohing the Clinton administration's preference for soft power and public diplomacy, she insisted that the next president must "deal decisively with the threat of rogue regimes and hostile powers, which is increasingly taking the forms of the potential for terrorism and development of weapons of mass destruction."[8]

With a bow to the Roman god of fire, whose statue towered above her hometown, Condi Rice staffed the Bush campaign with a band of self-styled "Vulcans," hardheaded national security analysts who shared her belief that when dealing with rogues and outlaws, it was often necessary to shoot first and ask questions later. Chief among the Vulcans was Paul Wolfowitz, a hawkish veteran of the first Bush administration who had helped found the Project for a New American Century, a noisy coterie of neoconservatives who intended to replace what they regarded as Bill Clinton's feckless diplomacy with "a Reaganite policy of military strength and moral clarity" necessary "to shape circumstances before crises emerge, and to meet threats before they become dire."[9] The project's chairman, William Kristol, was a second-generation neocon whose father, Irving, had famously defined a neoconservative as "a liberal who has been mugged by reality."[10] Having helped establish a network of foreign policy hawks, Kristol the Younger opened up his Rolodex for the Bush team. From Palo Alto to Kennebunkport, Rice and Wolfowitz brainstormed with Richard Perle, the Pentagon's legendary "Prince of Darkness" who had helped engineer a massive increase in U.S. military spending during the final decade of the Cold War, Robert Zoellick, the mastermind behind Washington's dollar diplomacy in the early 1990s, and Richard Armitage, a sailor-statesman who had served both Ronald Reagan and George H. W. Bush as a diplomatic troubleshooter in Asia and the Middle East.

The most influential Vulcans, however, were Dick Cheney and Donald Rumsfeld, two Cold Warriors who had become fast friends during the mid-1970s when they ran the White House staff and the Pentagon for Gerald Ford. Robert Hartmann, who worked closely with both men during the Ford administration, found that Rumsfeld held less extreme views than his pal from Wyoming. "Whenever [Cheney's] private ideology was exposed," Hartmann recalled, "he appeared somewhat to the right of Ford, Rumsfeld, or, for that matter, Genghis Khan."[11] Not surprisingly, Rumsfeld and Cheney both became charter members of the Project for the New American Century and outspoken advocates of big-stick diplomacy. Although the two friends did their share of Clinton-bashing in early 2000, unlike the other Vulcans, they seemed destined for cabinet-level positions in the next Republican administration. Intrigued by Cheney's mastery of inter-service rivalries at the Pentagon, George W. Bush was even more impressed by the no-nonsense managerial style that his father's secretary of defense displayed after becoming the CEO of Halliburton, the Houston-based oil services giant, in 1995. Once Dubya nailed down the GOP nomination in June 2000, he asked Cheney to screen potential vice presidential candidates, and in a bizarre twist that would have made Machiavelli proud, the screener maneuvered himself into the number two slot on the Republican ticket. Gruff, laconic, and battle-tested, Cheney lent gravitas to a campaign whose headliner was occasionally tongue-tied and always vulnerable to questions about his inexperience.

Although the Sunshine State's electoral votes would not wind up in the Republican column until 12 December, shortly before Thanksgiving Dubya tapped Cheney to lead a shadow transition team to fill the top jobs in a potential Bush administration. Just after Christmas, the newly crowned vice president–elect convinced Bush to make Donald Rumsfeld the Grover Cleveland of the Pentagon. Much had changed since Rumsfeld's first stint as secretary of defense a quarter of a century earlier, but Rumsfeld remained what he had been ever since he accepted his first government post in Richard Nixon's Washington—an arrogant and impatient bureaucratic infighter whose views on foreign policy ran more toward rollback than containment. "He's a ruthless little bastard," Nixon himself remarked in 1971 after meeting with "Rummy," high praise from someone whose own name would soon be synonymous with Watergate in the American political lexicon.[12] When Gerald Ford named him secretary of defense four years later, Rumsfeld employed alarmist anti-Soviet rhetoric to build a case for a massive increase in U.S. military spending. Following Ford's defeat in the 1976 election, Rummy left Washington to become a corporate CEO in Chicago, where he acquired a small fortune and a bad case of Potomac fever during the 1980s. Throughout his exile from government, however, Rumsfeld stayed in touch with neoconservative action intellectuals like Wolfowitz and Andrew Marshall, the longtime director of the Pentagon's Office of Net Assessment, who was heralding a "revolution in military affairs" based on speed, stealth, and surprise. By the time Cheney got Bush to make him an offer he couldn't refuse in late 2000, Donald Rumsfeld was determined to implement Marshall's bold ideas and revolutionize the way America fought its wars.

Based on the composition of the rest of Bush's foreign policy team, Rumsfeld had every reason to believe that, with Cheney's help, he would be successful. Bush made Condi Rice his national security adviser, and the "founding Vulcan" gave every indication that she shared Rummy's ambitious agenda, even though she resented his sharp elbows and his short fuse. Dubya's secretary of state, Colin Powell, was a more complex figure—a Vietnam veteran and a longtime critic of the Pentagon "Whiz Kids" who were seldom around when the body bags came home, but also a loyal team player and the architect of Operation Desert Storm from his perch as chairman of the Joint Chiefs of Staff during the first Bush administration. The CIA director George Tenet, a holdover from the Clinton years, was a savvy political operator who played well with others and who was eager to upgrade his agency's intelligence-gathering infrastructure and its covert action capability. One level down from the cabinet, the Bush administration was loaded with even more Vulcans. Richard Armitage became Powell's confidant and corner man at Foggy Bottom, Wolfowitz served as Rumsfeld's chief deputy at the Pentagon, and Richard Perle headed the President's Foreign Intelligence Advisory Board. Because Cheney demanded a greater role in making foreign policy than his predecessors, his national security team was nearly as large as the president's. Before long, rumors flew that the vice president's two neoconservative acolytes—David Addington and I. Lewis "Scooter" Libby—wielded more influence on White House decision making than Condi Rice and her NSC staff.

Rice, Cheney, and the other Vulcans confirmed George W. Bush's own belief, fueled by his muscular born-again Christianity, that foreign policy must be understood as a battle between good and evil. This became obvious during Bush's marathon run for the White House, when he repeatedly charged that the Clinton administration's handling of resurgent rivals like Russia and China and rogue states like Iraq and North Korea was naive, misguided, and a serious threat to U.S. national security. Dubya had set the tone in September 1999 during a well-publicized speech at the Citadel, South Carolina's vaunted military academy, where he accused President Clinton of assuming that just because the Cold War was over, the world would automatically become a safer place. Squeezing defense spending to create a peace dividend was a bad idea, candidate Bush told his listeners, not just because there were regimes in Baghdad and Pyongyang "that hate our values and resent our success," but also because there were autocratic rulers in Moscow and Beijing who encouraged the anti-American antics of Saddam Hussein and Kim Jong-il. With the world about to enter "an era of car bombers and plutonium merchants and cyber terrorists and drug cartels and unbalanced dictators—all the unconventional and invisible threats of new technologies and old hatreds," Dubya vowed that if he were elected, his administration would "build America's defenses on the troubled frontiers of technology and terror" and create an "agile, lethal, [and] readily deployable" arsenal worthy of the new millennium.[13] Sixteen months later, Bush and his Vulcan advisers would get their chance.

Under the Radar: The Road to 9/11

Despite having lost the popular vote, George W. Bush believed that the electorate had delivered a real mandate for change, and he spent his first nine months in the Oval Office seeking to reverse Clinton's policies and restore America's credibility in the global arena. One area of particular concern was the Pentagon's aging arsenal, which according to Secretary of Defense Rumsfeld and other foreign policy hawks, was too small and too conventional to meet emerging challenges. In particular, Pentagon planners felt hamstrung by the restrictive language of the 1972 Soviet-American Anti-Ballistic Missile (ABM) Treaty and hemmed in by the tight budgets of the 1990s, which denied them the technology and the resources necessary to intimidate rogue states like North Korea or to outmaneuver competitors like Russia. Dubya heralded a new approach during his first White House press conference. "There are new threats in the post-cold-war era, threats that require theater-based antiballistic missile systems," he told reporters on 22 February 2001, "threats from an accidental launch or threats as a result of a leader in what they call a rogue nation."[14] Four months later during a summit meeting with Russian president Vladimir Putin in Slovenia, Bush proposed abandoning the ABM Treaty as an outmoded relic from the Cold War. Putin disagreed, insisting that the treaty remained "the cornerstone of the modern architecture of international security," but he did not rule out a major renovation. Afterward, Bush told reporters that he detected a hint of common ground. "Our nations are confronted with new threats in the 21st century," he explained on 16 June. "Terror in the hands of what we call rogue nations is a threat."[15]

Despite his nostalgia for Cold War diplomatic architecture, Putin soon proved amenable to scrapping the ABM Treaty, evidence that he too was haunted by the specter of a rogue's gallery early in the new millennium. Sergei Ivanov, Putin's minister of defense, told Rumsfeld in mid-June that Russia was eager to shed its reputation as an international pariah and become "a significant global economic power and a partner with the West."[16] For that to happen, came the reply, Moscow must distance itself from radical regimes in places like Havana and Pyongyang and move closer to Washington on nuclear nonproliferation. "Russia can consort with Cuba, North Korea, Iran, Iraq—the world's walking wounded—to show that they have a new bloc and try to put pressure on the former Soviet republics to knuckle under," Rumsfeld remarked on 12 July. "Or Russia can turn to the West, learn from Germany, Japan and Italy after World War II, create an environment that is hospitable to enterprise, demonstrate respect for contracts, the free press, free political and economic systems."[17] Although Putin termed Bush's decision to pull out of the ABM Treaty in December 2001 a "mistake," his relatively mild reaction signaled that, at least on this issue, Russia preferred to cast its lot with the West.

Even with Russia's help, the Bush administration realized that riding herd on the world's walking wounded would not be a cakewalk. In April 2001, Rumsfeld asked Andrew Marshall, the Pentagon's resident defense intellectual, to brief the White House national security team on "what the future might hold." Although the details of Marshall's briefing remain classified, he evidently argued that meeting the challenges posed by rogue states in the twenty-first century would require a more nimble fighting force with a lighter footprint on the battlefield. Because anticipating new threats was likely to become much more difficult, Marshall also called for a less rigid decision-making process with fewer bureaucratic barriers between the four branches of the military.[18] Bush's secretary of defense agreed. "It is a difficult world, it is a dangerous, world, it is an untidy world," Rumsfeld reckoned on 31 May in one of the haiku-like "snowflake" memos he frequently wrote to himself or his subordinates. "It is a world where more and more nations and non-state entities are going to have weapons of mass destruction and the ability to deliver them at great distances." Rumsfeld saw just one way forward: "We can only live in this world if we resolve to invest what is necessary to assure that we can deter and dissuade and, if necessary, defend and prevail."[19]

One region where the Bush administration was determined to defend and prevail was the Middle East, whose ratio of rogue states per capita was higher than anywhere else in the world. When Bush convened his National Security Council for the first time on 30 January 2001, the main item for discussion was "Mideast Policy." His chief foreign policy adviser framed matters in stark terms. "I thought that in light of the breakdown of Camp David and the launching of the second Intifada," Condi Rice remembered long afterward, "there was absolutely no prospect of a Middle East peace process that was going to lead to anything."[20] Dubya agreed. "Clinton overreached, and it all fell apart," he told his NSC team. "We're going to correct the imbalances of the previous administration" and "tilt it back toward Israel." Noting that he had flown over the Palestinian refugee camps during a prepresidential visit to Israel in late 1998, Bush recalled that it "looked real bad down there." The best option at present was to cut bait. "I think it's time to pull out of that situation," Bush said grimly. Colin Powell worried that the Israelis would interpret American disengagement as a green light to crack down on the Palestinians, with dire consequences for the peace process. The president responded with a shrug, observing that "sometimes a show of strength by one side can really clarify things."

The next item requiring clarification startled Powell and several others sitting around the table. "What's on the agenda?" Dubya asked Rice. "How Iraq is destabilizing the region, Mr. President," came the reply. For nearly an hour, Bush grilled his advisers about Saddam Hussein's recent behavior. The Iraqi dictator was skimming funds from the UN oil-for-food program to purchase black-market weapons; he was harassing U.S. aircraft in the no-fly zones over Kurdistan and Basra; and, according to the CIA, he was secretly developing chemical and biological weapons. Moreover, there were unconfirmed reports that Saddam was paying bounties to the families of Palestinian suicide bombers who killed Israelis in the Occupied Territories. "We need to know more about this," Bush replied, "and also his destructive weapons." As the meeting broke up, Dubya ordered the CIA's director, George Tenet, to monitor Saddam's activities much more closely and instructed Rumsfeld and Hugh Shelton, the chairman of the Joint Chiefs of Staff, to "examine our military options" in the Persian Gulf.[21]

Back at the Pentagon, Undersecretary of Defense Paul Wolfowitz was already hard at work. One of the most vocal neoconservative critics of Bill

Clinton's handling of Saddam Hussein, as early as November 1997 Wolfowitz had written a blistering op-ed in the *Wall Street Journal* accusing the White House of coddling "a maniacal and vengeful tyrant, who has already slaughtered tens of thousands of his own people using chemical weapons."[22] A year later, he told a congressional committee that the Baathist strongman "inflicts horrendous suffering on the Iraqi people" and recommended that the United States create "a safe area to which Iraqi army units could rally in opposition to Saddam, leading to the liberation of more and more of the country."[23] Kenneth Pollack, who oversaw Persian Gulf affairs during the final two years of the Clinton administration and briefed the incoming Bush team, confirmed that Wolfowitz and the Vulcans had Iraq in the crosshairs from day one. "This band had an almost obsessive fixation on getting rid of Saddam's regime," Pollack recalled. "Their dogma was that the Iraqi regime was the root cause of nearly every evil to befall the United States (from the Arab-Israeli violence to international terrorism), while the Iraqi people were waiting to rise up against Saddam and would do so if the United States demonstrated that it was serious about overthrowing him."[24]

One of Wolfowitz's most important bureaucratic allies was the undersecretary of defense for policy, Douglas Feith, a fellow founder of the Project for the New American Century, who also dismissed Clinton's efforts to contain Iraq as weak and misguided. "By the time the Bush administration was preparing to take office," Feith wrote in his memoirs, "incoming officials knew they would soon have to shore up the Clinton administration's policy of containment, or replace it."[25] During inter-agency meetings and Pentagon skull sessions, Wolfowitz and Feith employed us-versus-them rhetoric to brand Saddam Hussein as the most serious threat to U.S. interests in the Middle East. White House counterterrorism chief Richard Clarke, a holdover from the Clinton years, begged to differ and insisted that Osama Bin Laden and al-Qaeda were far more dangerous, but his warnings were drowned out by loose talk about regime change in Iraq, the outdated ABM Treaty, and other "vestigial Cold War concerns."[26]

Vice president Dick Cheney, Wolfowitz's longtime friend and mentor, agreed that potential Iraqi aggression must rank high on the list of dangers that America faced in the new millennium. With the Cold War over and the Soviet menace gone, Cheney recognized that "the threat's much different today." The United States was increasingly vulnerable to "terrorist attacks" at home, he told an interviewer in early May, "with weapons of mass destruction—bugs or gas, biological or chemical agents, potentially even, someday, nuclear weapons." Bigger dangers lurked abroad. "There are still regions of the world that are strategically vital to the U.S., where we care very much about whether or not they're dominated by a power hostile to our interests," Cheney explained. One such region was the Middle East, where "you've got to worry about the Iraqis." Despite UN inspections, Saddam Hussein was still seeking WMDs and the ballistic missiles necessary to deliver them. The Bush administration stood ready "to defend the United States against a missile launch from a rogue state" and also to repel any "threat that would be directed at our allies," the vice president declared. "Just ask yourself how successful we would have been in 1990 and '91, putting together a coalition of thirty nations to roll back Iraqi aggression in the Gulf, if Iraq had been in possession of a handful of ballistic missiles with nuclear weapons on board." For Cheney, the answer to that question from the past was self-evident. "You're going to have to deal with that kind of threat in the future."[27]

In late June, Cheney and other senior policy makers got a thinly fictionalized look at how Saddam might make that threat materialize during Operation Dark Winter, a creepy simulation hosted by Johns Hopkins University, where Wolfowitz had been the dean of the School for Advanced International Studies before joining the Bush administration. The script for Dark Winter read like the screenplay for a B movie. Out of the blue, twenty Americans come down with smallpox in Oklahoma City, where the Alfred P. Murrah federal building had been bombed six years earlier. Newsreel footage reveals the horrifying effects of the virus in graphic detail. Within two weeks, smallpox has spread to twenty-five states, hundreds are dead because there is not enough vaccine, and "profound economic losses are crippling the nation." Meanwhile, "Iraq is deploying forces on [the] border with Kuwait." The U.S. government must curb the epidemic and determine whether the outbreak is an act of God or a case of bioterrorism. The cast included the former U.S. senator Sam Nunn as president, the former CIA chief James Woolsey as his own fictional successor, and the *New York Times* reporter Judith Miller as herself in the ensuing faux media frenzy ignited by the "NCN" cable network. The voice-overs could have been written by Wolfowitz or Cheney. Although the United States recently lifted sanctions and ceased enforcing the no-fly zones, "most Americans agree that Saddam's Iraq regime represents a real threat to stability in the region and to American interests." President Nunn quickly learns that a "prominent Iraqi defector is claiming that Iraq arranged the bioweapons attacks on the US through intermediaries," and before long NCN is reporting that "Iraq may have provided the technology behind the attack to terrorist groups based in Afghanistan."[28]

Although the simulators at Johns Hopkins intended merely to gin up support on Capitol Hill for biosecurity research, Dark Winter did not go unnoticed inside the Bush administration, where Saddam Hussein was fast emerging as the foremost public enemy. "Even before 9/11, Scooter Libby talked often about 'Dark Winter,' noting that Vice President Cheney considered it a particularly significant study," Feith recalled in his memoirs. "What would President Bush tell the American people if a 'Dark Winter'– type attack occurred, and the biological weapons agent were traced to Iraq?"[29] The Dark Winter scenario also reinforced claims made by Laurie Mylroie, a neoconservative conspiracy theorist, whose tendentious book, *A Study of Revenge*, asserted that Saddam Hussein had ordered the bombing of the World Trade Center in February 1993 as payback for Operation Desert Storm. One of Mylroie's good friends was Paul Wolfowitz, who not only read the first draft of *A Study of Revenge* but later blurbed the book and praised its author for "proving" that Ramzi Yousef, the mastermind behind the truck bomb that rocked lower Manhattan on Bill Clinton's watch, "was in fact an agent of Iraqi intelligence."[30]

Throughout the summer of 2001, the key players on Bush's national security team worked overtime to build a compelling case for regime change in Baghdad. On 13 July, Wolfowitz proposed establishing a "Free Iraq" in oil-rich Kurdistan, which would make Saddam Hussein "vulnerable to overthrow by increasingly strong domestic forces."[31] A week later, State Department officials recommended that President Bush "discuss regime change policy" during his upcoming meeting with British prime minister Tony Blair. At the end of the month, Rumsfeld told Rice that it was time to "stop the pretense of having a policy that is keeping Saddam 'in the box,'" when we know he has crawled a good distance out of the box." The Persian Gulf was a dangerous neighborhood, and U.S. passivity would only make it more likely that "somebody, whether Iran, Iraq, or Usama Bin Laden, could take out the royal family in one or more of the Gulf states" and trigger a military free-for-all.[32] Looking back on the final weeks before Bin Laden took out two skyscrapers overlooking New York harbor, Rice later regretted devoting so much attention to Saddam Hussein. "We spent an inordinate amount of time—and this I really want to be understood—from the time we came in until after 9/11 trying to figure out something else on Iraq," she told a reporter long afterward. "I went to more meetings about strengthening sanctions than I did on anything else."[33]

Had Rice and Rumsfeld attended fewer meetings on Iraq and had they paid greater attention to Osama Bin Laden, his terrorist acolytes might not have flown in under the radar on 11 September 2001. Al-Qaeda first showed up on George W. Bush's radar screen shortly after he became president-elect, when he sat down with Bill Clinton to review the most important dangers America faced abroad. Based on "credible threat reporting" that "new attacks" might well be in the offing, CIA director Tenet had placed al-Qaeda at the top of the list just before Christmas. The most likely targets were "US facilities in the Middle East especially the Arabian peninsula, in Turkey and Western Europe," but Tenet reminded Clinton that "Bin Ladin's network is global" and that al-Qaeda was "capable of attacks in other regions, including the United States."[34] Clinton relayed this grim news to Dubya during a two-hour meeting in the Oval Office. "I think you will find that by far your biggest threat is Bin Ladin and the al-Qaeda," he told his successor. "One of the great regrets of my presidency is that I didn't get him for you, because I tried to."[35] Sandy Berger, Clinton's national security adviser, delivered the same message to Condi Rice. "I want to underscore how important this issue is," Berger told his successor in early January 2001. "You're going to spend more time during your four years on terrorism generally and al-Qaeda specifically than any other issue."[36] Brian Sheridan, who oversaw special operations at Clinton's Pentagon, was even blunter, telling Rice to keep close tabs on Bin Laden and company, because "these guys are not going to go away."[37]

Five days after she settled into her new office in the West Wing of the White House, Rice received a melodramatic report from Richard Clarke, whom Dubya had retained as head of the Counterterrorism Security Group (CSG) at Clinton's suggestion, reiterating what Berger and Sheridan had said about Bin Laden. "Al Qida [*sic*] is not some narrow, little terrorist issue that needs to be included in broader regional policy," Clarke explained on 25 January, but rather a "transnational challenge" to American interests in the Middle East and beyond. Osama Bin Laden intended "to drive the US out of the Muslim world," he explained, and "to replace moderate, modern Western regimes in Muslim countries with theocrats modeled along the lines of the Taliban." Reminding Rice just who had been responsible for the bombing of two U.S. embassies in East Africa in August 1998 and the attack on the USS *Cole* in October 2000, Clarke urged the Bush administration to consider more aggressive options to combat al-Qaeda, including Predator drone strikes on Bin Laden's hideouts and expanded military assistance to the CIA-backed Northern Alliance in Afghanistan and the pro-American regime in Uzbekistan. Rice did alert the president, but she suspected that Clarke was exaggerating the al-Qaeda threat to gain leverage over the new administration's national security agenda.[38]

So did Paul Wolfowitz, who exploded in early April when Clarke continued to insist that Osama Bin Laden posed a far greater threat than Saddam
Hussein. "I just don't understand why we are talking about this one man bin
Laden," Wolfowitz snapped, when there were much bigger problems, such
as "Iraqi terrorism for example." Insisting that Saddam had not been responsible for a single anti-American terrorist attack for at least eight years, Clarke
proceeded to recite a long list of Bin Laden's bloody misdeeds. "We are
talking about a network of terrorist organizations called al Qaeda," Clarke
concluded, "because it alone poses an immediate and serious threat to the
United States." Wolfowitz remained unpersuaded. "You give bin Laden
too much credit," he grumbled. "He could not do all these things like the
1993 attack on New York, not without a state sponsor," say, someone like
Saddam Hussein. Clarke was livid. "I could hardly believe it but Wolfowitz
was actually spouting the totally discredited Laurie Mylroie theory that Iraq
was behind the 1993 truck bomb at the World Trade Center," he recalled in
his memoirs, "a theory that had been investigated for years and found to be
totally untrue."[39]

Clarke was not the only holdover from the Clinton administration
who tried to sound the alarm about al-Qaeda. General Don Kerrick, who
remained on the NSC staff until mid-April to wrap up the investigation of
the attack on the USS *Cole*, remembers warning Stephen Hadley, Rice's chief
deputy, that "we are going to be struck again," but to no avail. "I don't think
it was above the waterline," Kerrick recalled later. "They were gambling that
nothing would happen."[40] Later that spring, Tenet called on Rice to reiterate
the grim prophecy he had given Bill Clinton five months earlier and to tell
her that on a scale of one to ten, the likelihood of another al-Qaeda attack in
the near future now stood at "about seven."[41] Meanwhile, Richard Clarke had
become so frustrated by the apparent lack of interest in Bin Laden inside the
Bush White House that he asked to be transferred to a newly created post
as head of cybersecurity. "Perhaps," he told Rice and Hadley in May, "I have
become too close to the terrorism issue." Having spent nearly a decade mon-
itoring al-Qaeda, "to me it seems like a very important issue, but maybe I'm
becoming like Captain Ahab with bin Laden as the White Whale." Clarke's
reassignment was approved, effective 1 October 2001.[42]

For his part, the man in the Oval Office appeared concerned but not
alarmed. As scouting reports about al-Qaeda's game plan piled up on his
desk that spring, Bush told both Rice and Clarke that he was "tired of swat-
ting at flies" and that he wanted to play offense, not defense, against Team
Bin Laden.[43] Yet throughout the summer of 2001, Dubya seemed much

more interested in ballistic missile defense and stem cell research than in international terrorism. George Tenet remembers making several visits to the White House in June and July to warn that "the system was blinking red."[44] After an especially vivid PowerPoint slide show during which "Rich B," one of the CIA's top al-Qaeda watchers, predicted that "Usama Bin Ladin [UBL] will launch a significant terrorist attack against the U.S. and/or Israeli interests in the coming weeks," Tenet asked Rice to schedule an emergency NSC meeting. On 10 July, Rich B repeated his prediction and declared that it was high time to "take the battle to UBL in Afghanistan" before it was too late, but according to Tenet, White House officials rejected CIA counterterrorism chief Cofer Black's recommendation that "this country needs to go on a war footing *now*."[45] During another fruitless meeting about al-Qaeda with Rice and the NSC staff at the end of the month, an exasperated Rich B shouted: "They're coming here!"[46]

Not long afterward, George W. Bush headed to his ranch in Crawford, Texas, where he soaked up some sun and put the finishing touches on a speech about stem cells. On 6 August, Dubya's daily CIA briefing included an eye-catching subject line: "Bin Ladin Determined to Strike in US." After recapping al-Qaeda's terrorist attacks and recalling Bin Laden's vow to "bring the fighting to America," the briefing memo concluded on an ominous note. During the summer, the FBI had detected "patterns of suspicious activity in this country consistent with preparations for hijackings or other types of attacks, including recent surveillance of federal buildings in New York."[47] The White House would subsequently downplay the significance of this warning, with Bush pointing out that it contained nothing specific about suicide attacks on the World Trade Center and Rice dismissing it as merely "a historical memo."[48] Al-Qaeda would nevertheless be on the agenda when Rice convened the Principals Committee, a standing NSC group composed of all the top policy makers except the president, in early September.

But time was running out. Preoccupied with his impending transfer to his new job in cybersecurity, Richard Clarke fired off one last jeremiad about al-Qaeda. "Decision makers should imagine themselves on a future day when the CSG has not succeeded in stopping al Qida [*sic*] attacks and hundreds of Americans lay dead in several countries, including the US," he warned Rice just before the Principals Committee met on 4 September. Unless the Bush national security team moved fast, "you are left waiting for the big attack, with lots of casualties, after which some major US retaliation will be in order." In a classic case of too, little too late, the Principals Committee approved a draft presidential directive instructing the CIA and the Pentagon to develop plans for more aggressive action against al-Qaeda. That directive was still sitting on the president's desk awaiting his signature when an American Airlines Boeing 767 passenger jet plowed into the World Trade Center's north tower at 8:46 A.M. on Tuesday, 11 September.[49] Although crackpot theories soon surfaced on the Internet claiming that the 9/11 attacks were an inside job orchestrated by malevolent U.S. officials seeking a pretext for war in Afghanistan and Iraq, the truth was devastatingly simple. Bush and his Vulcan advisers had entered office locked into an us-versus-them view of the world view in which "they" were no longer Soviet-backed subversives but rather rogue states like North Korea and Iraq, which "we" must prevent from acquiring WMDs and ballistic missiles at all cost. In a colossal failure of imagination, the White House had let Saddam Hussein become its White Whale, distracting policy makers from a far graver danger lurking high in the mountains of Southwest Asia.

Combatting the Green Threat: Bush's Global War on Terror

President Bush was at a grade school in Sarasota, Florida, promoting his No Child Left Behind initiative when he learned of the aerial assault on the World Trade Center. "My blood was boiling," he recalled long afterward. "We were going to find out who did this, and kick their ass." While Dubya prepared to return to the nation's capital, his advisers confirmed that al-Qaeda was responsible. "We are at war against terror," Bush declared at the end of a secure NSC video conference a few hours after the 9/11 attacks. "From this day forward, this is the new priority of our administration." The president decided to frame the crisis as a case of us versus them on steroids. "We had to force nations to choose whether they would fight the terrorists or share their fate," Bush wrote in his memoirs, "and we had to wage this war on the offense, by attacking the terrorists overseas before they could attack us again at home." After Air Force One touched down at Andrews air force base, Bush turned to White House chief of staff Andrew Card and said: "You're looking at the first war of the twenty-first century."[50]

Without mentioning al-Qaeda by name, the president assured the American public later that evening in a nationally televised address that he would find those responsible for the 9/11 attacks and bring them to justice. "We will make no distinction between the terrorists who committed these acts," Bush vowed, "and those who harbor them."[51] A few minutes later, he convened an emergency NSC meeting to consider the broader implications of the day's events. It went without saying that the United States intended to strike al-Qaeda's base camps in Afghanistan and pressure Pakistan to cut its ties with Bin Laden's Taliban hosts. Bush, however, outlined a far more ambitious scheme. "This is an opportunity beyond Afghanistan," he told his advisers. "We have to shake terror loose in places like Syria, and Iran, and Iraq."[52] The way Bush saw it, 11 September 2001 was a day of infamy unparalleled since 7 December 1941. "The Pearl Harbor of the 21st century," Bush confided in his diary, "took place today."[53]

In the days that followed, the president approached the global war on terror with remarkable singleness of purpose. On 12 September, Senate majority leader Thomas Daschle cautioned Bush against framing the 9/11 attacks as "an act of war." Dubya bristled. Then what was it, he asked the South Dakota Democrat, "a breach of protocol?"[54] Two days later, he visited Ground Zero in lower Manhattan. After a New York City firefighter looked him in the eye and said, "George, find the bastards who did this and kill them," Bush grabbed a bullhorn. "I can hear you," he shouted to the rescue workers digging through the smoldering ruin of the World Trade Center, "and the people who knocked these buildings down will hear all of us soon."[55] During a phone conversation with the British prime minister Tony Blair that same afternoon, Bush let it be known that the war on terror would quite likely target people well beyond al-Qaeda and the Taliban. "It'll be like circles coming from pebbles dropped in the water," he told Blair. "The next step is to look at other countries, including Iraq."[56]

Bush spent the weekend at Camp David, where he and his national security team decided to defer any discussion of Iraq and concentrate instead on Afghanistan. The outline of what would become Operation Enduring Freedom quickly came into focus. The White House would issue an ultimatum demanding that the Taliban turn over Osama Bin Laden, the CIA would expand covert support for the pro-American Northern Alliance, and the Pentagon would prepare a massive bombing campaign, paving the way for regime change in Kabul. "Our enemy is a radical network of terrorists and every government that supports them," President Bush told a joint session of Congress on 20 September. Groups like al-Qaeda, the Egyptian Islamic Jihad, and the Islamic Movement of Uzbekistan were "traitors to their own faith, trying, in effect, to hijack Islam itself." Yet Bin Laden and company were doomed, because "they follow in the path of fascism and Nazism and totalitarianism" that ends in "history's unmarked grave of discarded lies." For those Americans wondering "why do they hate us," Dubya had a simple answer. "They hate our freedom—our freedom of religion, our freedom of speech, [and] our freedom to vote." Although "our war on terror begins with

Al Qaida," Bush explained that "it will not end until every terrorist group of global reach has been found, stopped, and defeated." His message could not have been clearer. "Every nation in every region now has a decision to make," he warned. "Either you are with us, or you are with the terrorists."[57]

Among those applauding most loudly inside the U.S. Capitol that night were Secretary of Defense Donald Rumsfeld and Vice President Dick Cheney, whose subordinates had begun mapping out the global war on terror not long after the Twin Towers imploded. On 11 September, Douglas Feith and two other top Pentagon officials, Peter Rodman and William Luti, were in Moscow discussing the ABM Treaty with the Russians. The next day, during the long flight home via Frankfurt, Germany, the trio conducted an impromptu seminar on international terrorism in the cargo hold of a U.S. Air Force KC-135 transport. One of the key items on their informal syllabus was Claire Sterling's controversial classic from the Reagan era, *The Terror Network*. Feith argued that Sterling's approach was as valid in the wake of 9/11 as it had been two decades earlier. "Many international terrorist groups of the time were operating not as a unified, corporate-style hierarchy but as a network," he remembered telling Rodman and Luti, and "their network served the interests of the Soviet Union, which provided them with funds, training, explosives, and other support." Once the Cold War ended, Feith observed, the Kremlin had relinquished its role as the impresario of global terrorism, only to be succeeded by a more decentralized network of Muslim extremists with regional hubs from North Africa to Southwest Asia. The color of the threat might have changed during the past ten years from communist red to Islamic green, but the specter of international terrorism loomed larger than ever.[58]

Back in Washington, Feith would find some very sympathetic ears. Indeed, just five hours after American Airlines Flight 77 had plowed into the Pentagon, Rumsfeld declared that Osama Bin Laden posed a global threat that required a global response. "Go massive—sweep it all up," Rumsfeld told his top aides while smoke billowed outside his window, and get the "best info fast" to determine whether to "hit S.H. [Saddam Hussein] @ same time—not only UBL."[59] When Feith checked in with his boss on 14 September, Rumsfeld said "don't over-elevate the importance of al Qaida" and urged him to think big. "As we saw it, 9/11 did not mean simply that the United States had an al Qaida problem. We had a terrorism problem," Feith recalled in his memoirs. "A strategic response to 9/11 would have to take account of the threat from other terrorist groups—Jemaah Islamiya in Southeast Asia, Lebanese Hezbollah, various Africa-based groups—and state sponsors beyond Afghanistan, especially those that pursued weapons of mass destruction," such as Iraq. Before the day was out, he handed Rumsfeld a game plan for a global war against "the entire network of states, non-state entities, and organizations that engage in or support terrorism against the United States." Noting that "the objective is not punishment but prevention and self-defense," Feith emphasized that the Bush administration must "force the terrorists to play defense" and make them "run [and] hide," so that they could never employ "political blackmail against America and our interests."[60]

Rumsfeld liked what he read and incorporated some of Feith's ideas into a long memo for President Bush dated 19 September. Although America was responding to a "systematic, uncivilized assault on a free way of life" launched by Muslim extremists, he reminded Dubya that "this is not a war against Islam or any other religion." U.S. forces were certain to prevail in Afghanistan, but the American public must recognize that regime change in Kabul would be only round one in a broader war on terror. "This campaign is a marathon, not a sprint," Rumsfeld concluded. "No terrorist or terrorist network, such as the Al-Qaida network, is going to be conclusively dealt with by cruise missiles or bombers."[61] Just how long that marathon might last was obvious in another memo that Rumsfeld sent to the chairman of the Joint Chiefs of Staff, Hugh Shelton, later that same day. Because "our field of action is much wider than Afghanistan," the Pentagon must be ready to strike "targets worldwide, such as UBL Al Qaida cells in regions outside Afghanistan and even outside the Middle East."[62] Reverting to "CEO speak," Rumsfeld summed up the implications four days later in a snowflake memo to himself. "We should not talk about attacks, but effects," he wrote. "We [should] look interested not in inputs but outcomes." Most important, the Bush administration must shy away from phrases like "occupying territory" and remember that America would soon be waging a different kind of war, one with "no beachheads; no physical battlefields; no D-Days; no long marches and no Wellington at Waterloo."[63]

By late September, the key elements for the global war on terror were in place. President Bush had issued an ultimatum to Afghanistan and authorized a sophisticated plan combining covert action with surgical air strikes if, as expected, the Taliban refused to expel al-Qaeda. Having decided "to use our air power in a way that could be truly effective instead of merely pounding sand," the Pentagon's Paul Wolfowitz believed that the Bush administration must demonstrate "we know how to fight smart."[64] Feith crowed that "we" were about to win a huge victory against "them" in the opening round of a long war. "As I saw it," he remembered many years later, "the President decided that, in dealing with the terrorists, he had the choice of changing the way *we* live or changing the way *they* live."[65] Rumsfeld, however, probably put it best in some "Strategic Thoughts" that he passed along to Dubya on 30 September. Settling scores with the Taliban was all well and good. America, however, must also make sure to "capitalize on our strong suit, which is not finding a few hundred terrorists in the caves of Afghanistan, but is the vastness of our military and humanitarian resources, which can strengthen enormously the opposition forces in terrorist-supporting States." The stakes were incredibly high. "If the war does not significantly change the world's political map, the U.S. will not achieve its aim." Among the cartographic revisions that Rumsfeld anticipated were "new regimes in Afghanistan and another key State (or two) that supports terrorism" and the "dismantlement of WMD capabilities."[66]

On Sunday, 7 October, while the secretary of defense was unleashing Operation Enduring Freedom against the Taliban in Afghanistan, his alter ego, Vice President Dick Cheney, relayed some chilling news to the White House. The Centers for Disease Control (CDC) in Atlanta had just confirmed that a mysterious ailment responsible for sickening people in three states and killing a newspaper reporter in Boca Raton, Florida, was in fact anthrax, a lethal toxin and favorite ingredient for biological weapon-makers. Having endured an awful autumn, the vice president wondered, was America about to undergo a Dark Winter? A few days after the 9/11 attacks, Scooter Libby, Cheney's chief of staff, had screened the Dark Winter bioterrorism video for his boss, prompting the vice president to arrange a "gruesome briefing" for Bush and the entire NSC team on 20 September.[67] Well aware of "the horrifying consequences of a bioweapons attack" involving smallpox, Dubya reacted to the news about anthrax by asking himself: "Was this the second wave, a biological attack?"[68] Condi Rice answered with a resounding "yes" and remembers learning at the height of the anthrax scare "of another plotline suggesting that the United States was facing the threat of a smallpox attack."[69]

A bacterium like anthrax in the hands of terrorists would be bad enough, but a virus like smallpox would be far worse, because it was transmitted by human contact, not by aerosol spores. In mid-October, Bush and Cheney ordered the CDC to launch a crash program to rebuild its depleted supply of smallpox vaccine in case mass immunization became necessary. Although no smallpox epidemic ever materialized and although the FBI eventually attributed the anthrax attacks to a disgruntled American scientist, not to al-Qaeda, the specter of a real-life Dark Winter rattled Washington and helped rev up the global war on terror. "It's hard to remember what it was like in the aftermath of 9/11," Eric Edelman, Cheney's deputy national security adviser, recalled years later. "Anthrax. Smallpox. Loose nukes. Al-Qaeda. Pakistan. Iraq."[70]

Indeed, for both Edelman's boss and the man in the Oval Office, the only scenario more frightening than al-Qaeda launching germ warfare was Osama Bin Laden getting his hands on an atomic bomb. Rumors flew throughout the autumn of 2001 that the mastermind of the 9/11 attacks was close to obtaining a small nuclear device from North Korea or Pakistan. Then in late November, the CIA's George Tenet informed the NSC principals that an al-Qaeda operative captured in Afghanistan had recently revealed that Ummah Tameer-e-Nau (UTN), a Pakistani extremist group whose members included several prominent nuclear physicists, was willing to provide Bin Laden with what he needed to construct a radiological weapon. "This is the thing we all feared the most," Tenet groaned. "This changes everything." Cheney, who chaired the meeting, spelled out the implications. "If there's a one percent chance that Pakistani scientists are helping al Qaeda build or develop a nuclear weapon, we have to treat it as a certainty in terms of our response," the vice president growled. "It's not about our analysis, or finding a preponderance of evidence." Bush agreed and sent Tenet to Pakistan for a come-to-Jesus talk with President Pervez Musharraf. "Al Qaeda has said for years that they want a nuclear device," the CIA director told Musharraf on 1 December. "Now it is within reach," thanks to the UTN. "The President needs to be assured you will not let your country's scientists act on behalf of Bin Laden." Musharraf clasped Tenet's hand and said: "You have my assurance."[71]

For Cheney and his staff, the "1 percent doctrine" soon became the central feature of a bold new operational code for national security decision making in the post-9/11 world that challenged long-standing constitutional restraints on presidential power. Just hours after al-Qaeda had attacked New York and Washington, David Addington, the vice president's chief counsel, began insisting that America needed a "unitary executive" empowered to do whatever was necessary, both abroad and at home, to make us safe from them. A neoconservative lawyer with the reputation of a ferocious bureaucratic infighter, Addington argued that the threat posed by radical Islam required a new paradigm granting the president unprecedented authority to hold suspected terrorists indefinitely without trial, order warrantless electronic surveillance, and expand covert operations inside and outside the United States. Nicknamed "Cheney's Cheney" by friend and foe alike, Addington was a leading proponent of the USA Patriot Act, under which Congress incorporated much of the new paradigm in October 2001. "A lot of the things around Watergate and Vietnam both, in the seventies, served to erode the authority I think the President needs," Cheney himself told reporters several years after the 9/11 attacks. "I believe in a strong, robust executive authority, and I think the world we live in demands it."[72]

Meanwhile, David Wurmser, another neoconservative who would soon become Cheney's chief Middle East adviser, was arguing that in a world in which al-Qaeda had become a household name, the United States must develop closer relations with Israel, whose battle with Palestinian extremists was a microcosm of America's global war on terror. Wurmser had first come to Cheney's attention during the late 1990s when he helped Richard Perle and Douglas Feith draft "A Clean Break," a shrill white paper charging that the American-backed Oslo peace process jeopardized Israel's security.[73] After Feith invited him to join the Pentagon's new Policy Counter Terrorism Evaluation Group in late 2001, Wurmser helped write a tendentious report linking both Osama Bin Laden and Saddam Hussein to an alphabet soup of radical groups in Gaza and the West Bank who were determined to destroy Israel and establish an independent Palestine. "Iraq trains Palestinian terrorists associated with PFLP, PIJ, Hamas, ANO, PLF," Wurmser claimed in an account that circulated widely inside the Bush administration, and also "Ansar al-Islam *which has direct ties to Al Qaeda*."[74]

During the first months of 2002, Hamas, the largest of these Palestinian extremist groups, launched a new wave of deadly suicide attacks inside the Jewish state, killing dozens of civilians. Prime Minister Sharon responded by launching Operation Defensive Shield and sent Israeli troops into Jenin, Ramallah, and other West Bank cities, igniting bloody street fighting that left hundreds dead and prompting calls from Western Europe and the Arab world for the United States to broker a cease-fire. President Bush, who blamed the Palestinian president Yasser Arafat for the carnage and regarded Sharon as "a leader who understood what it meant to fight terror," sent Dick Cheney on a fact-finding mission to Israel and the Occupied Territories in early March.[75] On his way to the Holy Land, the vice president stopped in London to confer with Tony Blair. When the British prime minister warned that Operation Defensive Shield might fuel anti-Western extremism throughout the Middle East, Cheney refused to be distracted by what he regarded as a red herring. "The United States would certainly remain engaged in attempting to find a solution to the Israeli-Palestinian crisis, but we would not do so at the expense of the War on Terror," Cheney grumbled, because even if Arabs and Jews buried the hatchet tomorrow, "the terrorists would simply find another rationale for continuing jihad."[76]

Six months after the 9/11 attacks, the White House was molding elements of Cheney's "1 percent doctrine," Rumsfeld's blitzkrieg tactics in Afghanistan, and Sharon's "best defense is a good offense" model for combatting Islamic terrorism into a comprehensive new national security strategy that in tone, scope, and cost resembled NSC-68, Harry Truman's legendary game plan for winning the Cold War. President Bush revealed an ambitious agenda during his State of the Union address on 29 January 2002. He began by pointing out that Operation Enduring Freedom had delivered on two fronts—toppling the Taliban and forcing al-Qaeda to run and hide—and he praised Hamid Karzai, America's favorite Afghan, whose new regime in Kabul was building a democracy. More must be done, however, to eradicate the Green Threat. "What we have found in Afghanistan confirms that, far from ending there, our war against terror is only beginning," Bush explained. "Thousands of dangerous killers, schooled in the methods of murder, often supported by outlaw regimes, are now spread throughout the world like ticking time bombs, set to go off without warning."

Friendly regimes in Pakistan and the Philippines were helping "eliminate the terrorist parasites who threaten their countries and our own," but elsewhere in the Muslim world, the situation was much bleaker. "A terrorist underworld, including groups like Hamas, Hizballah, [and] Islamic Jihad," Bush observed, "operates in remote jungles and deserts and hides in the centers of large cities," wreaking havoc with help from rogue regimes in North Korea, Iran, and Iraq. "States like these and their terrorist allies constitute an axis of evil," Dubya declared. "By seeking weapons of mass destruction," this axis would eventually "provide these arms to terrorists." The stakes were simply too high to adopt a wait-and-see approach. "I will not stand by as peril draws closer and closer," Bush told the nation, and he would "not permit the world's most dangerous regimes to threaten us with the world's most destructive weapons." This new Axis of Evil must be defeated and dismantled, because "if we stop now, leaving terror camps intact and terrorist states unchecked, our sense of security would be false and temporary."[77]

Although no proof existed that Iraq or Iran possessed WMDs or that they intended to give such weapons to al-Qaeda, the Bush administration insisted otherwise and launched a broad antiterrorist campaign. By early 2002, the White House had approved two controversial initiatives—"extraordinary rendition," which permitted the CIA to hand suspected terrorists over to foreign intelligence services for torture, and "enhanced interrogation," which authorized the CIA's own counterterrorism unit to employ water-boarding and other brutal techniques banned by the Geneva Convention. "What are we now, the Huns?" Dan Coleman, a veteran FBI interrogator, wondered after learning about the CIA programs. "If you don't talk to us, we'll kill you?"[78] Not to be outdone, the National Security Agency (NSA), the CIA's fraternal twin, secretly obtained White House approval to intercept the phone calls and e-mails of U.S. citizens, a clear violation of the Foreign Intelligence Surveillance Act (FISA) that Congress had passed following the Watergate scandal. When critics complained that the Bush team was waging a neoconservative crusade that ran contrary to basic American values, the Pentagon's Douglas Feith sneered that defeating the Axis of Evil was not for the faint of heart. "Some argued against viewing the war on terrorism as ideological," he observed in his memoirs. "But the last two hundred years have seen a number of successful international ideological campaigns," culminating in "confrontations with fascism and communism in the 20th century."[79]

Like Feith, the old history major in the White House believed that in the post-9/11 world, the ends justified the means. On 1 June, Dubya traveled to West Point, where he informed the class of 2002 that the old rules no longer applied. "For much of the last century, America's defense relied on the cold war doctrines of deterrence and containment," but today new thinking was in order. "Deterrence—the promise of massive retaliation against nations—means nothing against shadowy terrorist networks with no nation or citizens to defend," Bush told the cadets. "Containment is not possible when unbalanced dictators with weapons of mass destruction can deliver those weapons on missiles or secretly provide them to terrorist allies." Americans had learned a painful lesson nine months earlier. "We are in a conflict between good and evil," and the best antidote was rogue state rollback. "The war on terror will not be won on the defensive," Bush concluded. "We must take the battle to the enemy, disrupt his plans, and confront the worst threats before they emerge." America must be ready to play offense. "In the world we have entered, the only path to safety is the path of action, and this Nation will act."[80]

Inside the Pentagon, Bush's Vulcan advisers were mapping out a path of action unprecedented in American history—preventive war. "Al-Qaeda is not a snake that can be killed by lopping off its head," Wolfowitz told the Senate Foreign Relations Committee in late June. "It is more analogous to a disease that has infected many parts of a healthy body." His prescription was predictable: more aggressive military action. "There is no one, single solution," Wolfowitz confessed. "You cannot simply cut out one infected area and declare victory, but success in one area can lead to success in others, and our success in Afghanistan has contributed to the larger campaign."[81] Two months later, a blunt rationale for such a campaign landed on Rumsfeld's desk. Reiterating Bush's claims that rogue states and WMDs had made Cold War concepts like containment and deterrence irrelevant, Pentagon planners warned that "a hostile power may be able to use terrorist groups to deliver weapons in an unattributable, and hence undeterrable, manner." These realities led "inevitably to a doctrine of anticipatory self-defense," where in certain situations, America must strike first. Defense Department officials recognized that "this doctrine is unsettling to many people" because "it appears to authorize the unchecked use of military power against any country that the U.S. President dislikes or suspects." In a world where al-Qaeda was rumored to be shopping for smallpox or tactical nukes, however, an ounce of prevention was worth a pound of cure.[82]

By the autumn of 2002, anticipatory self-defense had strong support, not only at the Pentagon but also at the White House, where Vice President Cheney urged the president to embrace the concept publicly and acknowledge that rollback had replaced containment in the national security catechism. "After the attack on the homeland that had killed three thousand people, the world had changed," Cheney remembers thinking. "We were at war against terrorist enemies who could not be negotiated with, deterred, or contained, and who would never surrender."[83] In early September, Condi Rice provided Dubya with a bold national security doctrine that reflected these new realities. "We took as the model the historic NSC-68," she wrote in her memoirs, the "seminal statement of U.S. objectives and strategy at the outset of the Cold War." Brimming with "brilliant but baroque" language courtesy of Philip Zelikow, one of Rice's closest confidants, "NSC-2002" argued that America could win the war on terror by promoting democracy around the world, beefing up homeland security, and pursuing proactive nonproliferation to prevent rogue states or terrorist groups from acquiring WMDs. George W. Bush liked the proposal but not the prose. "I thought this document was supposed to be *my* strategy," he told Rice. "The boys in Midland will never believe it. It doesn't sound like me."[84]

The White House released NSC-2002 on 20 September, with a preface written by the president himself in the vernacular of West Texas. Warning that "the gravest danger our Nation faces lies at the crossroads of radicalism and technology," Bush vowed that "as a matter of common sense and self-defense, America will act against such emerging threats before they are fully formed." The section titled "Prevent Our Enemies from Threatening Us, Our Allies, and Our Friends with Weapons of Mass Destruction" contended that what would soon be known as "the Bush Doctrine" merely updated America's traditional policy of preemption to address the grave threat posed by "rogue states and their terrorist clients" in the post-9/11 world.[85] Condi Rice later insisted that "the only novel aspect of our articulation of the preemption strategy was the way in which we had to adapt the concept of 'imminent threat' to contemporary realities."[86]

Yet that was precisely the point. Prior to 2001, "imminent" had typically evoked images of an army poised to invade or nuclear missiles ready to launch, but now the word conjured up a nightmare world of us versus them, where terrorists might inflict harm next week or next month or next year. Chastened by the 9/11 attacks, Rice and the drafters of NSC-2002 conflated preemption with prevention when they proclaimed that "to forestall or prevent such hostile acts by our adversaries, the United States will, if necessary, act preemptively."[87] Seven decades earlier, Japan had bombed Pearl Harbor to *prevent* America from thwarting its imperial ambitions in Asia, and Franklin D. Roosevelt might have *preempted* that attack had he received more timely intelligence. In the early stages of the war on terror, however, the Bush White House focused on Roosevelt's successor. To no one's great surprise, Rice beamed when John Lewis Gaddis, one of the country's leading Cold War historians, called NSC-2002 "the most important foreign policy document since NSC-68 of Harry Truman's administration."[88]

The Baghdad Express: The Bush Doctrine and Preventive War in Iraq

For Bush and Rice, Iraq would become the testing ground for their new and improved version of NSC-68. Saddam Hussein proved to be the perfect villain for U.S. national security managers early in the new millennium. Having emerged at the height of the Cold War as a high-profile Soviet client who would later shock the world by using poison gas against Iraqi Kurds and by invading Kuwait, Saddam seemed like just the sort of ruthless thug who might one day turn WMDs over to al-Qaeda. Nicknamed "the Butcher of Baghdad" by Donald Rumsfeld, the Iraqi dictator was the subject of nasty bureaucratic infighting between Pentagon advocates of rollback and State Department proponents of containment prior to the 9/11 attacks.[89] "For my first eight months in office, my [Iraq] policy focused on tightening the sanctions—or, as Colin Powell put it, keeping Saddam in his box," Bush recalled later. "Then 9/11 hit, and we had to take a fresh look at every threat in the world," from rogue states who sponsored terrorism and regional bullies who threatened their neighbors to psychopaths who brutalized their own people and reckless autocrats who pursued unconventional weapons. "Iraq combined all those threats."[90]

The Vulcans at the Pentagon and elsewhere inside the Bush administration were eager to connect Saddam Hussein with al-Qaeda. During an NSC meeting on 12 September, Rumsfeld blamed Saddam for the events of the previous day and stressed the importance of "getting Iraq." Irritated but hardly surprised, Powell managed to steer the conversation back to Osama Bin Laden. Richard Clarke, who would complete his stint as White House counterterrorism chief at the end of the month, just shook his head. "Having been attacked by al-Qaeda," he said, "for us now to go bombing Iraq in response would be like our invading Mexico after the Japanese attacked us at Pearl Harbor."[91] According to Clarke's heir apparent, Lisa Gordon-Hagerty, however, as the skull session drew to a close, President Bush indicated that he took rumors of Saddam Hussein's involvement in the 9/11 attacks very seriously. "He was very adamant," she would subsequently tell an MSNBC interviewer, about "seeing whether or not Iraq could conduct such an operation against the United States." Puzzled by the president's sense of urgency, Gordon-Hagerty could only conclude that "Secretary Wolfowitz got to him."[92]

Wolfowitz and his neoconservative sidekick, Douglas Feith, were indeed lobbying very hard for American retaliation against Iraq. According to Feith, during yet another NSC meeting on 13 September, President Bush "wanted to know whether Saddam was implicated in the 9/11 attack or otherwise connected to al Qaida" and was intrigued by the idea of bombing Iraq, whose massive military infrastructure offered a richer array of targets than Afghanistan, where the Taliban waged war with rocket-propelled grenades launched from a fleet of Toyota pickup trucks. "There might be a connection between Saddam Hussein and Osama bin Laden," Dubya told Britain's Tony Blair the next day.[93] During the NSC retreat at Camp David the weekend immediately after 9/11, Bush recalled in his memoirs, "Paul Wolfowitz suggested that we consider confronting Iraq as well as the Taliban."[94] Condi Rice listened with interest. "His argument was not without merit, focusing on the relative strategic importance of Iraq over Afghanistan," she remembers thinking. "The war in Afghanistan would be so much more complicated than a 'straightforward' engagement against a real army such as Saddam's," and the Iraqi strongman "was clearly an enemy of the United States and had supported terrorism."[95] Colin Powell, on the other hand, regarded Wolfowitz's suggestion as premature and foolhardy. "Going after Iraq now would be viewed as a bait and switch," he warned Bush on 15 September. "We would lose the UN, the Islamic countries, and NATO." Like Powell, the CIA's George Tenet thought "it would be a mistake" to hit Saddam. Finally, the vice president weighed in, reminding everyone that Iraq remained a clear and present danger and that "we had to address it" sooner or later. "But now is not a good time to do it," Cheney concluded. "We would lose our momentum." Bush agreed and settled matters, at least for the time being, by ordering his advisers to concentrate on the impending campaign against the Taliban.[96]

Nevertheless, throughout the autumn of 2001 and into the New Year, regime change in Baghdad would repeatedly find its way onto the agenda for Bush's national security team. Critics later speculated that this fixation on Iraq boiled down to one three-letter word—oil. Because both Dubya and his vice president had close ties to the Texas oil business, the rumor mill revved up when the White House refused to reveal whether or not the National Energy Policy Development Group (NEPDG) that Dick Cheney convened in the spring of 2001 had met with petroleum industry executives. The eighty-page report that the NEPDG released on 1 May made no specific mention of Iraq, but it highlighted the importance of the Persian Gulf, which was projected to supply two-thirds of the world's oil by 2020. Noting that the quota system adopted by Arab members of the OPEC cartel was constraining oil output in the face of rising demand and pushing prices higher, the NEPDG recommended pressuring Algeria, Saudi Arabia, and the Persian Gulf sheikhdoms "to open up areas of their energy sectors to foreign investment."[97] Noticeably absent from the list was Iraq, whose 112 billion barrels of proven reserves ranked second in the world behind Saudi Arabia's. Thanks to American-backed UN sanctions, however, Iraqi oil output had fallen dramatically during the 1990s, leaving Baghdad without the funds necessary to exploit its existing reserves or to tap offshore sources of the black gold that some U.S. experts believed lay undiscovered beneath the Shatt al-Arab.

Just one week after the 9/11 attacks, Ahmad Chalabi, a leading Iraqi exile well known to Richard Perle and other neoconservatives inside the Bush administration, sat down with the President's Foreign Intelligence Advisory Board and made a passionate case for regime change. After cataloguing the sins of Saddam Hussein in great detail, Chalabi argued that the costs of toppling the Baathist tyrant would be easily covered by privatizing Iraq's state-owned oil industry and channeling some of the revenue to a new pro-American provisional government. As the White House completed round one of the war on terror in Afghanistan, Secretary of Defense Rumsfeld arrived at the headquarters of the U.S. Central Command (CENTCOM) in Tampa, Florida, on 27 November 2001 to congratulate General Tommy Franks on toppling the Taliban and to propose an encore performance directed against Saddam Hussein. Among the key objectives inside Iraq would be "oil fields in the north" and "oil fields in the south," whose output would finance a successor regime in Baghdad. "Unlike in Afghanistan," Rumsfeld explained, it was "important to have ideas in advance about who would rule afterwards." While his talking points did not mention Chalabi, they did suggest that the United States should "give control over oil sale proceeds from liberated fields" to a "Provisional Government" that would prosecute Saddam for war crimes and hand over Iraq's alleged stockpile of WMDs.[98]

Ahmed Chalabi made his case directly to Rumsfeld's old friend Cheney at a private gathering in Aspen, Colorado, during the summer of 2002. "He and Cheney spent long hours together," White House speech writer David Frum recalled long afterward, "contemplating the possibilities of a Western-oriented Iraq: an additional source of oil, an alternative to U.S. dependency on an unstable-looking Saudi Arabia."[99] Six months later during an interview for *60 Minutes*, Rumsfeld dismissed rumors that petro-politics was behind Bush's confrontation with Saddam Hussein as "nonsense" and insisted that the looming war with Iraq had "literally nothing to do with oil." Yet in that same broadcast, Chalabi himself painted a different picture of what might lie ahead. "American companies did well by abstaining from dealing with the illegal regime of Saddam," he told a CBS reporter, "and American companies, we expect, will play an important role and leading role in the future oil situation in Iraq."[100]

Once the shooting started on 18 March 2003, U.S. officials cringed at any mention of oil. After Press Secretary Ari Fleischer referred in passing to Operation Iraqi Liberation and produced an embarrassing acronym, for example, White House public relations experts quickly substituted the word "freedom" to yield a more benign OIF.[101] Yet when looters descended on Baghdad in late April, smashing storefronts and stealing archeological treasures, Fleischer and company could not deny that the only Iraqi government agency to receive U.S. protection was the Ministry of Oil. By mid-July, Chalabi's friend and lobbyist, Francis Brooke, saw no reason to downplay the importance of oil. "We have a new ally in the Middle East—one that is secular, modern, and pro free market," he grinned. "It's time to replace the Saudis with the Iraqis."[102]

By early 2003, however, the Vulcans on Bush's NSC team clearly regarded the prospect of free elections for Iraqis as a more compelling reason for fomenting regime change in Baghdad than the possibility of a free market for oil. Three of them—Cheney, Rice, and Wolfowitz—had held important posts during the first Bush administration, when Dubya's father had decided not to order U.S. troops to march on the Iraqi capital and depose Saddam Hussein, and they felt a bit guilty for having failed to prevent the bloody reign of Baathist terror that enveloped the Shias in the marshlands of southern Iraq. Cheney in particular was delighted to have a chance to settle old scores. "When we looked around the world in those first months after 9/11, there was no place more likely to be a nexus between terrorism and WMD capability than Saddam Hussein's Iraq," he wrote in his memoirs. "We could not ignore the threat or wish it away, hoping naïvely that the crumbling sanctions regime would contain Saddam" and end his brutal treatment of the Iraqi people. "The security of our nation and of our friends and allies required that we act. And so we did."[103] Rice, who usually bristled when Cheney meddled in NSC affairs, agreed that toppling Saddam would not only help make the world safe from terrorism but also help make the Middle East safe for democracy. Wolfowitz was even more outspoken about the "freedom agenda" than Rice. "If some kind of constitutional government gets established in Iraq," he would later remark, "then I think it's a huge gain for us in the Arab world and in the overall war on terrorism." To be sure, America was taking a big gamble, but if post-Saddam Iraq came to resemble "the new democracies in Eastern Europe," then "it's a much better world for us." In short, according to Wolfowitz, "after 9/11 the importance of beginning to push that kind of change in the Muslim world is huge."[104]

George W. Bush's views on Iraq were less abstract but more heartfelt. "Before 9/11, Saddam was a problem America might have been able to manage," he recalled many years later, but afterward, everything was different. "I had just witnessed the damage inflicted by nineteen fanatics armed with box cutters," Bush explained. "I could only imagine the destruction possible if an enemy dictator passed his WMD to terrorists."[105] The simplest and least costly way to prevent Iraq's dictator from ever making such a nuclear baton pass was to engineer a coup d'état in Baghdad. With Dubya's blessing, in early 2002 the CIA launched Operation DB/Anabasis, a $400 million scheme that called for Kurdish separatists and dissident Iraqi army officers to join forces and bump Saddam off. "We wanted that fucker dead," John

Maguire, a covert operator who had been the CIA's man in Kurdistan for many years, told reporters. "We were willing to do anything to get Saddam." The CIA's friends, however, were no match for Saddam's secret police, and DB/Anabasis fizzled.[106] The prospect of military intervention soon prompted sharp questions about the Bush administration's ultimate intentions in Iraq. On 1 May, Helen Thomas, the dean of the White House press corps, tangled with Ari Fleischer, who tried to brush off her questions about Saddam Hussein with lighthearted banter. Fleischer's boss, by contrast, was in no mood for levity and said so privately in language that would have made Maguire proud. "Did you tell her I don't like assholes who lie to the world?" Bush snarled. "Did you tell her I'm going to kick his sorry motherfucking ass all over the Mideast?"[107]

Before 2002 was out, the president would tell the world in language much less salty that Saddam Hussein did indeed have a huge bull's eye on his hind end and that the new Bush Doctrine was designed to deliver the mother of all swift kicks. The decision for war seems to have come as a snap judgment, with little fanfare and even less forethought. Richard Haass, the State Department's policy planning chief, remembers sharing his concerns about the drift toward war with Condi Rice, an old friend from the first Bush administration, in early July. "Are you really sure you want to make Iraq the centerpiece of the administration's foreign policy?" Haass asked. "You can save your breath, Richard," she replied. "The president has already made up his mind on Iraq."[108] Later that month, Richard Dearlove, the head of Britain's MI6 whose nom de guerre was "C," arrived in Washington to compare notes with the CIA director Tenet about Iraqi WMDs. Because British intelligence officers were much less certain than their American counterparts that Saddam possessed chemical and biological weapons or that he was close to acquiring a nuclear arsenal, "C" felt troubled by the gung ho attitude at the White House. "Military action was now seen as inevitable. Bush wanted to remove Saddam, through military action, justified by the conjunction of terrorism and WMD," Dearlove warned Prime Minister Tony Blair and the British cabinet on 23 July. "The intelligence and facts were being fixed around the policy," and even worse, "there was little discussion in Washington of the aftermath of military action." Foreign Secretary Jack Straw echoed Dearlove's concerns. "It seemed clear that Bush had made up his mind to take military action, even if the timing was not yet decided," Straw told his colleagues. "But the case was thin. Saddam was not threatening his neighbours, and his WMD capability was less than that of Libya, North Korea or Iran."[109]

Back across the pond, the momentum for war had become overwhelming. Not long after "C" returned to London, Haass concluded that the die had been cast. "Although the formal decision to go to war would not be made for six more months," he wrote in his memoirs, "by mid-2002 the president and his inner circle had crossed the political and psychological Rubicon."[110] Haass's boss had one last chance to throttle down the Baghdad Express during a private dinner with Bush and Rice on 5 August 2002. The "Pottery Barn rule" applied to Iraq, Colin Powell reminded the president: "You break it, you own it." Noting that war in the Persian Gulf was "not going to be a walk in the woods," Bush's secretary of state pointed out that "you are going to be the proud owner of 25 million people." Dubya was unfazed. "My reaction to that, is that my job is to secure America," Bush told a reporter who later asked about Powell's words of warning. "I also believe that freedom is something people long for," he continued. "And that if given a chance, the Iraqis over time would seize the moment."[111]

Bush would express similar views to a much wider audience on 12 September during an address to UN General Assembly. He started by insisting that Iraq already possessed WMDs and might give them to terrorist groups. "If we fail to act in the face of danger, the people of Iraq will continue to live in brutal submission," Bush warned. "The regime will have new power to bully and dominate and conquer its neighbors, condemning the Middle East to more years of bloodshed and fear."[112] Dubya reiterated all this more colorfully eight days later during a private White House dinner for GOP governors. Sounding like a Texas sheriff, Bush told his fellow Republicans that "Saddam is a guy who is liable to have his head show up on a platter." He was "a brutal, ugly, repugnant man who needs to go." Yet the governors could rest assured that regime change in Baghdad would not create a political vacuum, nor would it disrupt the flow of Persian Gulf oil. Rather, it would pay huge dividends. "I'm gonna make a prediction," Bush said with a smile, "write this down." With America's help, "Afghanistan and Iraq will lead that part of the world to democracy," he vowed. "They are going to be the catalyst to change the Middle East and the world."[113]

Thirteen months after the 9/11 attacks, George W. Bush himself was emerging as the world's most potent catalyst for change. Following intense White House lobbying on Capitol Hill focusing on Saddam's brutality and duplicity, Dubya secured congressional approval for a joint resolution on 16 October authorizing the use of armed force as "necessary and appropriate in order to defend the national security of the United States against the continuing threat posed by Iraq." Three weeks later, the UN Security Council passed Resolution 1441, which found Iraq in "material breach" of its disarmament obligations and demanded that Saddam permit the International Atomic Energy Agency (IAEA) to resume its inspections of his country's nuclear facilities. Saddam reluctantly agreed to cooperate with the IAEA in mid-December, but early in the new year, Bush made it clear that this was too little, too late. Regime change in Baghdad was the only acceptable solution. "What reaction do you expect from the Iraqis to the entry of U.S. forces in their cities?" he asked Kanan Makiya, one of Ahmed Chalabi's close allies, during a meeting with a group of exiles at the White House on 10 January 2003. "The Iraqis will welcome U.S. forces with flowers and sweets when they come in," Makiya replied.[114]

The case for rogue state rollback as the preferred option rested on three controversial claims. First, high-ranking U.S. officials, including the president himself, repeatedly asserted that the Butcher of Baghdad had a close working relationship with al-Qaeda despite the absence of any corroborating evidence. As a result, on the eve of Operation Iraqi Freedom, opinion polls showed that 45 percent of Americans believed that Saddam Hussein had been "personally involved" in the 9/11 attacks.[115] Second, Bush and the Vulcans relied on tainted intelligence, including wild stories from a CIA source ironically code-named "Curveball" and forged documents suggesting that Iraq had purchased yellow-cake uranium in West Africa, to prove that Baghdad had already acquired the key ingredient for an atomic bomb. After the CIA director George Tenet termed the evidence that Saddam had WMDs "a slam dunk," the White House sent Colin Powell to New York City, where he tried but failed to secure UN Security Council authorization to invade Iraq. And third, the Bush administration insisted that demolishing the Baathist dictatorship in Baghdad would trigger a political chain reaction, toppling other radical anti-American regimes in the region like a row of dominoes. "Iraq is a sophisticated society," Dubya told a group of conservative supporters on 28 January 2003, "that can emerge and show the Muslim world that it's possible to have peace on its borders without rallying the extremists." Other good things would follow on Saddam's demise. "There will be less exportation of terror out of Iraq—which will provide more comfort and stability for a country like Israel," Bush added, which would make it "easier for us to achieve a peace in the Palestinian-Israel issue."[116]

As the countdown proceeded inexorably toward war during the winter of 2003, State Department officials dismissed the al-Qaeda connection as specious and doubted that invading Iraq would spark democratic change elsewhere in the Arab world. In late February, Wayne White, the deputy director of the Bureau of Intelligence and Research at Foggy Bottom, pre-pared a secret report entitled "Iraq, the Middle East, and Change: No Dominoes" warning that "liberal democracy would be difficult to achieve" in Iraq and "could well be subject to exploitation by anti-American ele-ments." The risks were quite clear, White would later recall. "The region's populations were (and are) predominantly more anti-American, anti-Israeli, and militantly Islamic than their existing governments." As a result, "EVEN A SUCCESSFUL EFFORT IN IRAQ, both militarily and politically, would not only fail to trigger a tsunami of democracy in the region, but potentially could endanger longstanding U.S. allies in the Middle East, like Jordan, not the region's anti-U.S. autocrats."[117] When Thomas Warrick, who coordi-nated the State Department's "Future of Iraq Project," incorporated these concerns into a 250-page report detailing the challenges that America would face once the shooting stopped, Secretary of Defense Rumsfeld banned him from serving in the Office of Reconstruction and Humanitarian Assistance (ORHA), the new agency responsible for handling the aftermath of the Pentagon's looming campaign of "shock and awe." Jay Garner, the retired general who oversaw ORHA, was troubled by the Defense Department's lack of postwar planning and its aggressive timetable for withdrawing U.S. forces. "It sounded like they were going to package up five pounds of shit in a nice foil wrapper and hand it off and say, 'Good luck,'" Paul Hughes, Garner's planning chief, later told a reporter. "It might look nice, but it would still be a package of shit."[118]

Despite growing uneasiness at ORHA and Foggy Bottom, Operation Iraqi Freedom began on 18 March 2003 with air strikes against targets throughout Saddam's realm and ended three weeks later when American tanks rolled into Baghdad and toppled a forty-foot statue of the Baathist dictator. The Bush administration declared victory on 14 April, and on May Day, Dubya himself announced the end of hostilities just off the coast of Southern California beneath a huge "Mission Accomplished" banner on the flight deck the USS *Abraham Lincoln*, an aircraft carrier that had recently returned from the Persian Gulf. Although the president recycled the spe-cious allegation that Saddam was tied to the 9/11 attacks and reasserted the dubious claim that Iraq possessed a dangerous arsenal of WMDs, what stood out most during his remarks was his unwavering faith in freedom at the core of the new Bush Doctrine. From the Truman era through the age of Reagan, America had waged and won a Cold War against "an evil empire," and Bush vowed that the good guys would prevail once again in the global battle against terrorism. "Everywhere that freedom arrives, humanity

rejoices," he declared, "and everywhere that freedom stirs, let tyrants fear."
This truth was now self-evident in Kabul and Baghdad, and soon it would
resonate throughout the entire Middle East. "We are committed to freedom in Afghanistan, in Iraq, and in a peaceful Palestine," Bush explained,
because "the advance of freedom is the surest strategy to undermine the
appeal of terror in the world."[119] In this latest conflict between us and them,
he implied, preventive war against Iraq was merely the most compelling way
we could demonstrate that they would pay a huge price for threatening the
United States. The Bush administration was about to discover, however,
that exporting democracy at gunpoint to the Muslim world could prove
quite costly to America as well.

Democracy at Gunpoint; or, The Arabian Nights of Thomas Jefferson

Twelve days after Bush's "Mission Accomplished" moment aboard the
Abraham Lincoln, L. Paul "Jerry" Bremer, a veteran national security man-
ager and longtime friend of Paul Wolfowitz and other neoconservatives,
arrived in Baghdad to take charge of the Coalition Provisional Authority
(CPA), yet another new agency that replaced Garner's short-lived ORHA.
Arrogant and sanctimonious, Bremer assumed that transplanting democracy to Iraq would be a simple matter of creating free markets and holding
free elections. During his first ten days on the job, Bush's proconsul made
two major mistakes that virtually guaranteed that his year in Iraq would
become Mission Impossible. First, Bremer launched a de-Baathification
campaign banning all members of the Baath party from employment in the
CPA-backed interim government in Baghdad. Because party membership had
been a job requirement for tens of thousands of school teachers, municipal
employees, and other government workers prior to 2003, the CPA's ruling
hurt far more people than Saddam and his Baathist inner circle. Second,
Bremer disbanded the Iraqi army and with the stroke of a pen put 250,000
heavily armed men out of work. Because the officer corps was composed
almost entirely of Sunni Muslims, the CPA's action created an opportunity
for Iraq's Shia majority to settle old scores with its ethnic rivals and paved
the way for civil war. Both decisions had strong support at the Pentagon,
however, where Bremer's neoconservative friends had a bold game plan.
"We've got to show all the Iraqis that we're serious about building a new
Iraq," Douglas Feith explained. "And that means that Saddam's instruments
of repression have no role in that new nation."[120]

Things looked very different on the ground in Baghdad, where U.S. officers commanding an undermanned occupation force had been counting on Iraqi troops to keep order. Paul Hughes, who had made the transition from Garner's ORHA to Bremer's CPA, was stunned. "I turned on the morning news and there's NBC announcing that Bremer had abolished the Army and I thought, 'Holy shit! How can he have done that?'" Hughes recalled. "The Joint Chiefs of Staff didn't find out until after Feith sent them a hand-written note."[121] Anthony Zinni, Tommy Franks's predecessor as head of CENTCOM, was appalled. "The neocons didn't really give a shit what happened in Iraq and the aftermath," Zinni told a reporter. "There's some bloodshed, and it's messy. Who cares? I mean, we've taken out Saddam." For true believers like Feith and Wolfowitz, the costs in Baghdad were far outweighed by the benefits elsewhere. "We've asserted our strength in the Middle East. We're changing the dynamic," Zinni continued. "We're now off the peace process as the centerpiece and we're not putting any pressure on Israel."[122] Franks agreed, calling Feith "the fucking stupidest guy on the face of the earth."[123] Colonel Paul Arcangeli, who spent much of 2003 at the Pentagon, pointed the finger at Wolfowitz. "I blame him for all this shit in Iraq. Even more than Rumsfeld, I blame him," Arcangeli growled. "Dangerously idealistic. And crack-smoking stupid."[124]

Yet however misguided their decisions, Wolfowitz, Feith, and Bremer actually did care deeply about what happened in Baghdad, because they wanted to transform post-Saddam Iraq into a beacon of capitalism and democracy in the Arab world. Bremer, for example, insisted that the best cure for "Saddam's economic mismanagement, lack of investment, and cockeyed socialist economic theory" was a healthy dose of private enterprise. "It's a full-scale economic overhaul," he told a reporter in the summer of 2003. "We're going to create the first real free market economy in the Arab world." One early manifestation of this economic sorcery was a series of ten-figure, no-bid contracts for U.S. firms like Halliburton, which moved in to resurrect the Iraqi oil industry, and Bechtel, which focused on rebuilding the country's power grid and transportation network that had been pulverized by American bombs. When Iraqi officials claimed that it was illegal for an occupying power to sell government assets to private firms, Thomas Foley, the chief sorcerer's apprentice at the CPA, retorted that "I don't give a shit about international law," because "I made a commitment to the president that I'd privatize Iraq's businesses." Meanwhile, hundreds of twenty- and thirty-something Bush administration loyalists flooded into Baghdad's Green Zone, where they imposed American-style antismoking regulations, privatized the pharmaceutical industry, and enacted a carbon copy of Maryland's traffic code to cope with the sudden arrival of 950,000 imported automobiles. "This doesn't feel like Iraq," Mahmud Ahmed, a translator for the CPA, snapped. "It feels like America."[125]

Many other Iraqis felt the same way, especially after the Americans turned their attention to political reform. When Bremer convened a "governing council" to oversee Iraq's transition to democracy, he assigned the majority of the seats to Shia politicians, in part because this apportionment reflected the country's demographic reality, but also because his de-Baathification program excluded many influential Sunni leaders, most of whom had ties to Saddam's regime. By mid-summer, several thousand Sunni insurgents led by Baathist officers forced into retirement by the CPA were waging a low-intensity war against the American occupation. Back in Washington, Bush's national security team found it hard to square the enthusiastic crowds who had welcomed GIs in April with the shadowy guerrillas who killed and maimed those same troops two months later. Rumsfeld blamed a small group of Baathist "dead-enders" and Islamic fanatics, as did the cowboy in the White House. "There are some who feel like the conditions are such that they can attack us there," Dubya snapped on 2 July. "My answer is, bring 'em on."[126] Yet Tim Carney, the CPA's official historian, provided a better explanation for what seemed to be Mesopotamian mass political schizophrenia by quoting al-Mutanabi, Iraq's most famous poet: "When a lion shows his teeth, do not assume he's smiling at you."[127]

During the following eighteen months, a pride of angry Iraqi lions accepted Bush's invitation and "brought it" to the U.S. occupiers. The best organized and most dangerous were the Baathist-led militias that controlled Fallujah, Samara, and other cities in the Sunni Triangle. After Sunni guerrillas repelled an American assault on Fallujah in March 2004, hundreds of foreign jihadis flocked into the city, prompting U.S. marine commander John Toolan to remark that "it was like the bar in *Star Wars*."[128] The largest of the insurgent groups was the Jaish al Mahdi, an Islamic army founded in Baghdad's Shia slums by Muktada al-Sadr, a black-turbaned cleric with close ties to Iran, who was determined to impose theocratic rule. His ferocious anti-Americanism and his urgent desire to export Iranian-style revolutionary Shiism throughout the Persian Gulf prompted Mike Gfoeller, the CPA's Arabic- and Russian-speaking regional coordinator for southern Iraq, to brand al-Sadr "a Bolshevik Islamist."[129] Easily the most brutal of the bunch, however, was al-Qaeda in Iraq (AQI), a ruthless band of Sunni thugs led by Abu Musab al-Zarqawi, a one-legged Jordanian trained by the Afghan mujahedin and loyal to Osama Bin Laden. Although Zarqawi did not even arrive in Iraq until after the fall of Saddam Hussein, he and the AQI quickly became infamous for bombing Shia mosques and for kidnapping Americans and then beheading them while video cameras whirred.

The quagmire on the Euphrates did not derail Bush's bid for a second term, but his ill-advised attempt to impose democracy in Baghdad did set in motion a self-fulfilling prophecy whose irony was inescapable. In theory, rogue state rollback was supposed to prevent dictators like Saddam Hussein from supporting jihadis like Osama Bin Laden, yet in practice, the Bush Doctrine had transformed Iraq into a breeding ground for Islamic radicals like Muktada al-Sadr and terrorist groups like AQI . The naïveté of top U.S. officials like John Bolton, the neoconservative lawyer who served as Bush's ambassador to the United Nations, would have been laughable had the results not been so tragic. "My thought was," Bolton admitted during an interview about the future of Iraq, "we hand 'em a copy of the Federalist Papers, say good luck, and then we're out of there."[130] John Agresto, an old friend of Cheney's who served as a CPA educational consultant, shared Bolton's faith in American exceptionalism, but threw up his hands when Iraqi universities refused to adopt a classic liberal arts curriculum. "I'm a neoconservative who's been mugged by reality," Agresto confessed, with a nod to Irving Kristol, after a year in Baghdad. "We think democracy is easy—get rid of the bad guys, call for elections, encourage 'power-sharing,' and see to it somebody writes a bill of rights," but few tasks were as complicated as building a good government. "Until this country [Iraq] can find a Madison," Agresto growled, "it would be far better off with just a good ruler."[131] It was an anonymous CPA official, however, who offered the most honest postmortem as the occupation drew to a close in May 2004. "We were so busy trying to build a Jeffersonian democracy and a capitalist economy that we neglected the big picture," he sighed. "We squandered an enormous opportunity and we didn't realize it until everything blew up in our faces."[132]

Undaunted by all this, Dubya was convinced that historians would eventually regard the Bush Doctrine as his most important legacy. To this end, he made "promoting democracy" the centerpiece of his second inaugural address in January 2005. "It is the policy of the United States to seek and support the growth of democratic movements and institutions in every nation and culture," Bush declared, "with the ultimate goal of ending tyranny in our world."[133] While he did not mention Iraq or terrorism even once, Bush did use the word "freedom" twenty-seven times. Dubya would, however, make the connection to Iraq explicit in his memoirs. Insisting that the United

States had "an obligation to help the Iraqi people replace Saddam's tyranny with a democracy," he continued to predict that regime change "would have an impact beyond Iraq's borders," because "once liberty took root in one society, it could spread to others."[134] Condi Rice, Bush's new secretary of state, upped the ante four months later during a high-profile speech at the American University in Cairo outlining a bold agenda for the Muslim world. "For 60 years, my country, the United States, pursued stability at the expense of democracy in this region here in the Middle East—and we achieved neither," she confessed on 6 May 2005. "Now, we are taking a different course. We are supporting the democratic aspirations of all people." Thanks to regime change in Iraq, a revolution of rising expectations was spreading throughout the region, forcing Syria to end its thirty-year occupation of Lebanon, making the mullahs in Tehran think twice about exporting radical Islam, and encouraging conservative regimes in Egypt and Saudi Arabia to implement modest reforms.[135]

Rice's words no doubt made her host Hosni Mubarak and other pro-American autocrats nervous, yet with no end in sight to the costly war in Iraq and no sign of any WMDs, political reform in the Arab world could provide the Bush administration with a much more achievable benchmark for success. State Department counselor Philip Zelikow, the chief author of NSC-2002 and the godfather of the Bush Doctrine, connected these dots in a "long memo" dated 26 September 2005. He began by pointing out that "Iraqis had exaggerated hopes about what we would do in their country" and that Bush's failure to deliver had produced "profound disillusionment about America." Only by breaking the back of the insurgency and rebuilding the country's infrastructure could the White House reverse this trend, but Zelikow believed that if Washington doubled down in Baghdad, a 70 percent chance of success existed. The payoff would be huge. Success would mean "an independent Iraqi government, able to maintain enough public order so that Iraq is not a significant base for Islamist terrorism against the United States, and is not an open field for violent subversion and interference with world oil supplies." Equally important, it would also mean "an Iraqi government that demonstrates some positive potential for democratic processes in the Arab and Muslim world."[136]

The logic of Zelikow's approach seemed compelling in the abstract, but when Arabs actually put those democratic processes into action, the Bush administration received some rude surprises. Developments in the Palestinian territories proved an early case in point. U.S. officials pressed Mahmud Abbas, who had become Palestinian president after Yasser Arafat's death in November 2004, to schedule parliamentary elections for early 2006, fully anticipating that his party, Fatah, would defeat Hamas, thwart the radical Islamists, and jump-start the peace process. Nevertheless, thanks to widespread unhappiness with Fatah's corruption on the West Bank and broad popular support for Hamas's delivery of badly needed social services in Gaza, Palestinian voters awarded the Islamists seventy-four legislative seats, while Abbas and company received only forty-five. Condi Rice saw the results on a CNN news flash during her morning aerobic workout and nearly fell off her treadmill. "I've asked why nobody saw it coming," she told a reporter. "I don't know anyone who wasn't caught off guard by Hamas's strong showing." Across the Potomac at the Defense Department, Rumsfeld's aides were stunned. "We sat there in the Pentagon," one of them recalled a year later, "and said, 'Who the fuck recommended this?'"[137]

Disappointed by Palestinian democracy in action, Washington refused to treat Hamas as a legitimate government, citing its violent opposition to Israel and its close ties with Iran. Instead, the Bush administration pressed Fatah to isolate the Islamists in their Gaza stronghold. "The United States is like the prince in search of Cinderella," Osama Hamdan, an aide to Hamas leader Khaled Meshaal, observed ruefully. "The Americans have the shoe, and they want to find the kind of people who fit the shoe," he explained. "If the people who are elected don't fit the American shoe, then the Americans will reject them for democracy."[138] Hoping to reverse the outcome at the ballot box, CIA officials secretly channeled arms and dollars to Muhammad Dahlen, Fatah's man in Gaza, to oust the Hamas regime. Meshaal's men struck first, however, and crushed the American-backed Fatah security forces in a bloody shootout in June 2007.

Bush's plan to foster democracy, American-style, fared little better elsewhere in the Muslim world. When Iraqis went to the polls shortly after Dubya's second inaugural and gave Shias a parliamentary majority that paved the way for Nuri al-Maliki to become prime minister, U.S. officials were ecstatic. Yet Maliki soon proved to be a feckless autocrat prone to crony capitalism and religious favoritism. Iraqi Sunnis responded by blowing up the Golden Mosque at Samarra, one of the country's most sacred Shia shrines, in February 2006, touching off a grisly civil war. "Where's George Washington? Where's Thomas Jefferson?" the historian in the White House snapped a month later. "Where's John Adams, for crying out loud? He didn't even have much of a personality."[139] With ethnic violence and American casualties escalating rapidly, Stephen Hadley, who had replaced Rice as NSC adviser, visited Baghdad in late October and returned with a blistering evaluation of the Shia prime minister that must have left Bush with no doubt as to which U.S. president Maliki most closely resembled: James Buchanan. Because Maliki had "limited ability to command Iraqi forces against terrorists and insurgents," Iraq, like America 150 years earlier, faced an impending crisis. "The reality on the streets of Baghdad," Hadley reported on 8 November, "suggests Maliki is either ignorant of what is going on, misrepresenting his intentions, or that his capabilities are not yet sufficient to turn his good intentions into action."[140]

Another crisis loomed 1,500 miles to the east in Pakistan, where America's partner, Pervez Musharraf, stood accused of bad intentions by secular reformers demanding free elections and religious extremists endorsing an Islamic republic. Anti-Americanism ran deep in the Land of the Pure, where Pakistanis complained bitterly that their country's contributions to the war on terror next door in Afghanistan had gone largely unrecognized in Washington. Islamic militants like Liaqat Baloch insisted that Musharraf's pro-American policies made him unfit to lead Pakistan. "The rulers should read the writing on the wall!" Baloch thundered. "The friend of Bush is our enemy!"[141] By late 2007, the rising tide of political instability inside the only Muslim nation to possess an atomic bomb was leading top American officials to think twice about exporting democracy to South Asia. "While Pervez Musharraf might not be a Jeffersonian Democrat," Bolton, Dubya's recently retired ambassador to the United Nations, told the *New York Times* in November "he is the best bet to secure the nuclear arsenal."[142]

Indeed, everywhere Bush's national security team turned, they detected signs that democracy was playing into the hands of Islamic radicals. After Israel invaded Lebanon in July 2006 to root out extremists responsible for a recent wave of kidnappings, Hezbollah fought back and soon emerged as a symbol of self-determination throughout the Arab world. A month later, Islam Karimov, who had ruled Uzbekistan with an iron fist for more than a decade, warned American diplomats visiting Tashkent that "by promoting democracy in the region, the U.S. helped create the conditions for Hamas and Hezbollah to succeed," with dire implications for Central Asia. "The day will come when Uzbekistan is ready for democracy and human rights," Karimov said, "but it would be a mistake to 'impose' them prematurely."[143] When Gurbanguly Berdymukhammedov, a Turkmen thug with a long name and a short fuse, seized power one thousand miles to the west in Ashgabat in June 2007, State Department spokesman Evan A. Feigenbaum merely shrugged and said: "Rome wasn't built in a day and we don't expect that Turkmenistan is going to turn into a Jeffersonian democracy by next

Thursday."[144] Of potentially greater significance that summer was the bleak situation in Hosni Mubarak's Egypt, where a nasty crackdown on Islamic activists was making the Bush administration's claim that "Egyptian democracy and human rights issues are enduring, core American interests" ring increasingly hollow.[145]

With political turmoil brewing from Cairo to Tashkent, with Osama Bin Laden still on the loose, and with a "surge" of 30,000 additional troops bringing the total number of GIs in harm's way in Iraq to more than 160,000, by early 2008 neither Bush's freedom agenda nor his war on terror had worked out quite the way he had imagined seven years earlier. Rogue state rollback, as enshrined in NSC-2002, promised that exporting democracy through preventive war would make America and the world safe from terrorism. Profane, judgmental, and intolerant of ambiguity, the Texan in the White House surrounded himself with an arrogant band of neoconservative intellectuals who exaggerated the danger of germ warfare, ginned up mythical Islamic sleeper cells lurking in the heartland, and fabricated links between Saddam Hussein and Osama Bin Laden to bring popular anxiety to a fever pitch following the 9/11 attacks. Yet like the old us-versus-them paradigm that had fueled the Red Scare at the height of the Cold War, Dubya's mantra—"either you are with us or you are with the terrorists"—would set in motion a self-fulfilling prophecy that guaranteed only greater insecurity and perpetual war.

Two old soldiers, both of whom had worked for Bush, summed up the consequences very well in late 2006, the grimmest moment since the fall of the Twin Towers. "Look, 9/11 was a huge traumatic shock to us," Colin Powell told a reporter, "but the Cold War is gone." Noting that "all the theologies and ideologies that were going to supplant ours are gone," Bush's first secretary of state insisted that "we can't let terrorism suddenly become the substitute for Red China and the Soviet Union as our all-encompassing enemy, this great Muslim-extremist, monolithic thing from somewhere in Mauritania all the way through Muslim India."[146] Anthony Zinni, like Powell a combat veteran of America's fool's errand in Southeast Asia, saw ominous parallels between the Cold War and the war on terror. "When it came to engage in conflicts like Iraq and Vietnam," Zinni explained in a personal account of his own failed peace mission to the post-9/11 Middle East, "we must have bad guys we can demonize." In both eras, U.S. policy makers had no trouble identifying those demons— Asian communists during the 1960s and Islamic extremists early in the new millennium. "Our leaders cooked up the Gulf of Tonkin incident to justify our war in Vietnam," Zinni concluded, and "our leaders cooked up Saddam Hussein's secret weapons of mass destruction and collaboration schemes with Al Qaeda to justify our war in Iraq." To a great degree, the Red Threat outlined in the Truman Doctrine begat the Green Threat at the core of the Bush Doctrine half a century later. "We had to cook up the rationale," Zinni concluded. "We had to follow the model."[147]

The rationale that America's forty-third president concocted after 9/11 was a strange brew that combined idealistic commitments to free markets and free elections with a muscular sense of self-righteousness and a willingness to shoot first and ask questions later. By defining his approach to the Muslim world as a global battle against terror, George W. Bush subordinated democratic principles and traditional concepts of international law to a troubling set of new tactics such as enhanced interrogation, cybersurveillance, and preventive war. Moreover, his obsession with rogue state rollback in Iraq meant that his policies elsewhere in the region suffered from diplomatic attention deficit disorder. Operation Enduring Freedom toppled the Taliban but did not provide Afghanistan with good government. The Palestinian-Israeli peace talks that Bush convened in Annapolis, Maryland, late in his second term were stillborn in part because he subliminally equated the PLO with al-Qaeda. Despite talking the talk of democracy in the Middle East, the Bush administration proved reluctant to walk the walk when Islamic radicals used the ballot box to challenge America's friends in Tel Aviv or in Arab capitals. Thanks to Dubya, the old red-colored paradigm of us versus them was now tinted green.

CHAPTER FIVE

The Obama Doctrine
"Contagement" and Counterterrorism in the Muslim World

The raw north wind that whipped across the Potomac on 20 January 2009 could not chill the enthusiasm of the 2 million Americans gathered in the shadow of the Washington Monument to watch Barack Obama take the oath of office. The nation's first African American president was inheriting the worst economic crisis since the Great Depression and the most divisive war since Vietnam. Eight years of rolling back regulations on Wall Street and rolling up terrorists in the Middle East had left George W. Bush's administration dead in the water. With a quick glance to his left, where the man who made these messes was seated, President Obama dismissed Republican rhetoric as stale, cynical, and inadequate in the midst of a great recession. "The question we ask today," the Illinois Democrat declared, "is not whether our Government is too big or too small but whether it works." Turning to foreign policy, Obama "reject[ed] as false the choice between our safety and our ideals" and vowed instead to usher in "a new era of peace" in which America's unmatched military power would be tempered by "humility and restraint." He promised to withdraw U.S. troops from Iraq, stabilize the situation in Afghanistan, and chart a new course toward the Muslim world "based on mutual interest and mutual respect." Those who resorted to terror should realize that "we will defeat you," but those who resented the United States should also know that "we will extend a hand if you are willing to unclench your fist."[1]

When dealing with the wider world, Obama's watchword was "engagement," a concept designed to reposition U.S. foreign policy midway between interventionism and isolationism. Well versed in the lessons of Vietnam and Iraq, his new national security team was convinced that George W. Bush's reliance on tough talk, torture, and preventive war had squandered an opportunity to exert America's moral leadership after the 9/11 attacks. Yet Obama also recognized that in an age of globalization, where ocean barriers offered little protection from terrorist violence, remaining underinvolved was almost as risky as becoming overcommitted. Rather than rolling back rogue states or ignoring rival powers, Obama and his advisers preferred what might be called "contagement," a complex mixture of containment and engagement that they pursued cautiously, first with China and later with Iran and the Arabs.

The recipe for contagement in the Middle East seemed quite simple—the United States must embrace the moderates and isolate the extremists. Ramping down the wars in Iraq and Afghanistan while ramping up the Israeli-Palestinian peace process would reverse the tide of anti-Americanism sweeping the Muslim world. Refocusing Bush's global war on terror solely on al-Qaeda and rethinking his rigid approach to nuclear proliferation would permit greater flexibility in handling the Green Threat. Implementing contagement, however, proved a nightmare, largely because engagement and containment frequently worked at cross-purposes. Iraq's prime minister Nuri al-Maliki and Afghanistan's president Hamid Karzai, neither of whom could have survived without U.S. help, vacillated wildly between moderation and extremism. Getting Israel and the PLO back to the bargaining table proved impossible after both sides laid out non-negotiable preconditions. And the Iranian mullahs kept their fists tightly clenched.

Pursuing contagement grew far more complicated after a wave of political upheavals swept through the region in early 2011, first in Tehran, then in Tunis, and eventually in five other Arab capitals. Having declared in his inaugural address that Middle Eastern tyrants and theocrats were "on the wrong side of history," Barack Obama proved reluctant to pick winners and losers from North Africa to the Persian Gulf, not because he preferred dictatorship over democracy, but because he worried that the demise of strongmen like Egypt's president Hosni Mubarak would open the door to Muslim extremists or Islamic radicals linked to al-Qaeda. Yet Obama was not reluctant to play God when dealing with Osama Bin Laden and others intent on doing great harm to America. Although he outlawed torture and promised to close the notorious prison camp at Guantánamo Bay, Obama also authorized almost eight hundred drone strikes from Central Asia to southwest Arabia during his first three years in office, killing more than two thousand militants, including several U.S. citizens, and causing the death of nearly one thousand innocent civilians. His most spectacular feat of counterterrorism came in May 2011, when he sent Navy SEALs deep inside Pakistan to kill Bin Laden and decapitate al-Qaeda. "SEALs and Drones" proved quite popular on Main Street and helped insulate Obama from charges that his foreign policy was incoherent during his successful bid for reelection in November 2012.

Yet even as he savored his victory and prepared for a second term, America's forty-fourth president faced growing criticism from both sides of the aisle. Outraged by mob violence in Benghazi, Libya, that had killed four

Americans, including the U.S. ambassador, just two months before election day, Republican lawmakers howled that Obama was soft on terrorism. For their part, many Democrats chided him for authorizing electronic surveillance at home and drone warfare abroad. The rise of radical jihadist movements from Mali, a huge North African state bordering Algeria, to Yemen, which shared a border with Saudi Arabia, revealed that al-Qaeda was alive and well, while a gruesome attack on the Boston Marathon made rumors about Islamic sleeper cells in America seem less far-fetched. Meanwhile, Israeli leaders and their supporters on Capitol Hill accused the Obama administration of appeasing the Islamist regime in Iran and abetting its quest for nuclear weapons. In short, despite President Obama's good-faith attempt to reshape the U.S. relationship with the Muslim world via contagement, and despite his stealth efforts to promote U.S. security via more aggressive counterterrorism, by early 2013 he would find himself back in the familiar world of us versus them.

A Black Man Playing on the White Man's Court

When Barack Obama came into the world in August 1961, the odds that he would ever call 1600 Pennsylvania Avenue home were about as long as they could be. The son of a black exchange student from Kenya and a white woman from Kansas who had met at the University of Hawaii, young Barack would spend most of his childhood and adolescence sorting out his racial identity. Obama's parents separated soon after his birth. His mother filed for divorce in 1964, married an Indonesian cartographer eighteen months later, and headed for Jakarta in early 1967 with her five-year-old son in tow. Obama remembers being struck by the "otherness" of Indonesia—the unbridgeable gap between the haves and the have-nots, the enchanting sound of the Muslim call to prayer, and the menacing atmosphere of military repression in a land where the army had recently butchered half a million communists. By day, his mother taught English to Indonesian businessmen, but by night she rubbed elbows with U.S. diplomats and oil company executives, who exerted considerable influence over the country's dictator, General Suharto. "*Power*: The word fixed in my mother's mind like a curse," Obama recalled long afterward in his memoir *Dreams from My Father*. "In America, it had generally remained hidden from view until you dug beneath the surface of things; until you visited an Indian reservation or spoke to a black person whose trust you had earned." In Indonesia, however, "power was undisguised, indiscriminate, naked, always fresh in the memory."[2]

In July 1971, Obama's mother sent him to live with her parents in Honolulu, where he would attend an exclusive prep school. An indifferent student, the skinny kid nicknamed "Barry" spent most of his free time shooting hoops with older classmates like "Ray" and coming to terms with being black in Cold War America. "We were always playing on the white man's court," Ray explained one day, which meant accepting "the white man's rules." The school principal or the basketball coach would insist on making all the decisions "because of that fundamental power he held over you," and should you push back or "lash out," he would be quick to place a label on you: "Paranoid. Militant. Violent. Nigger."[3] For the most part, Obama played by the rules, winning a scholarship to Occidental College in Los Angeles, where he organized protests against South African apartheid before transferring to Columbia University in 1981 to major in international relations. After graduation, Obama moved to Chicago, where he worked to empower the local African American community and came to appreciate the appeal of black nationalism as preached by the Nation of Islam. He headed back east in 1988 to enroll at Harvard Law School and returned to the Windy City three years later to direct Illinois Project Vote, teach part-time at the University of Chicago, and court and marry Michelle Robinson.

Barack Obama was elected to the state senate in 1996, and before long he was playing very well on the white man's political court in Springfield, where his exotic background and his silver tongue made him hard to miss. Sometime early in the new millennium, he developed a serious case of Potomac fever. After securing the nomination for a vacant U.S. Senate seat in March 2004, Obama startled the Democratic National Convention in Boston with an electrifying keynote address in July, won 70 percent of the vote in the election the following November, and joined the upper house in January 2005. Few Democrats expected Obama to remain in the Senate very long, and once his second book, *The Audacity of Hope*, soared to the top of the best-seller list in 2006, most insiders expected him to make a run at the White House. As his subtitle—"Thoughts on Reclaiming the American Dream"—suggested, the Illinois Democrat blamed George W. Bush for slow growth and stagnant incomes at home, a message that resonated with middle-class voters when financial panic on Wall Street created economic chaos on Main Street three months before election day.

In a chapter titled "The World beyond Our Borders," however, Obama also took aim at the Bush administration's foreign policies. He began with a short course in diplomatic history, starting with George Washington, who urged Americans to avoid risky foreign entanglements, then applauding

Woodrow Wilson, who claimed that "spiritual power" was more potent than military force, and finally praising the Cold War generation, who "married Wilson's idealism to hardheaded realism, an acceptance of America's power with a humility regarding America's ability to control events around the world." Based on these criteria, Professor Obama awarded George W. Bush a grade of "F," not because he had let the nation's guard down on 11 September 2001, but because he had ginned up an ill-conceived preventive war against Iraq in the aftermath of 9/11 and branded his critics "soft on terrorism" in rhetoric echoing the Cold War Red Scare.[4] "I don't oppose all wars," Obama had declared in Chicago's Federal Plaza on 2 October 2002. "What I am opposed to is a rash war." Emphasizing his own support for Bush's earlier decision to go after al-Qaeda and the Taliban, Obama called war with Iraq a "cynical attempt" orchestrated by "armchair, weekend warriors in this administration to shove their own ideological agendas down our throats" and warned that the impending invasion was likely to "encourage the worst, rather than the best, impulses in the Arab world."[5] Four years later in *The Audacity of Hope*, candidate Obama told his readers, in not so many words, "I told you so." The debacle in Iraq reflected not only "bad execution" in Baghdad but also "a failure of conception" inside the Bush White House, which "still lacks a coherent national security policy" and which was pursuing "a series of ad hoc decisions, with dubious results" that had fueled the fires of radical Islam. "Why invade Iraq," Obama wondered, "but not North Korea or Burma?"[6]

There were no easy answers, of course. "I don't presume to have this grand strategy in my hip pocket," Obama admitted, but his prescription for a better foreign policy began with a simple truth. The United States stood to gain more by "engaging" both friend and foe alike than by rejecting them or, even worse, by insisting that they take all their cues from us. America must withdraw from Iraq, reframe the global war on terror as a much narrower battle against al-Qaeda, and reject Bush-style unilateralism if it ever hoped to regain credibility with its NATO partners or improve its reputation among the peoples of Asia, Africa, and the Middle East. Yet Obama cautioned his liberal supporters not to be too quick to draw parallels between Southeast Asia during the 1960s and the Muslim world today. "It's useful to remind ourselves," he pointed out, "that Osama bin Laden is not Ho Chi Minh, and that the threats facing the United States today are real, multiple, and potentially devastating." In short, although Obama remained convinced that Iraq was the wrong war in the wrong place at the wrong time, he also recognized that "there will be times when we must again play the role of the world's reluctant sheriff."[7]

Exit polls in November 2008 showed that the role that most voters wanted Barack Obama to play was America's enthusiastic economic wizard, but the president-elect devoted much time during the transition to assembling a national security team committed to engaging the world. He persuaded his onetime political rival Hillary Clinton to become secretary of state, hoping that the celebrity status she had acquired as first lady during the 1990s and the hard work she had done in the U.S. Senate since 2001 would pay big dividends in world capitals and on Capitol Hill. To placate conservatives inside and outside the Republican Party and to preserve recent military gains in Iraq, Obama asked Robert Gates, whom Bush had appointed secretary of defense in 2006, to stay on at the Pentagon. James Jones, a retired four-star general who had commanded NATO troops in Europe, seemed at first blush an odd choice for NSC adviser, but the new president lacked military experience and hoped that placing an ex-Leatherneck in charge of the West Wing would reassure the armed forces. Three veterans from Bill Clinton's administration signed up with Team Obama—Leon Panetta as the director of central intelligence, Susan Rice as U.S. ambassador to the United Nations, and Thomas Donilon as Jones's chief deputy at the National Security Council.

The most intriguing component of the new president's foreign policy apparatus, however, was a self-styled group of youthful, brainy, and often brash "Obamians" who were eager to employ social media like Facebook and Twitter to further a new agenda that included climate change, financial transparency, and human rights. Benjamin Rhodes, a thirty-something NYU alum who had caught Obama's eye as an eloquent critic of the war in Iraq, wrote speeches on global matters and encouraged his boss to view the world from the bottom up, not from the top down. The Stanford University political scientist Michael McFaul, a specialist on Russia under Boris Yeltsin and Vladimir Putin, provided insight on the perils of regime change in authoritarian societies. Samantha Power, a sharp-tongued Irish-born Pulitzer Prize–winning journalist, served as Obama's resident expert (and de facto conscience) on matters related to human rights. The most influential of the Obamians was probably Denis McDonough, a tough-talking and hard-hitting former college football star from Minnesota who headed the NSC's Office of Strategic Communication before becoming White House chief of staff in January 2013.

Contagement in Asia and the Middle East: The Obama Doctrine

With such a diverse array of players on the new national security team and with so many urgent domestic matters demanding instant attention, the contours of Obama's foreign policy emerged slowly. The president-elect had made clear during the transition that whether the issue was educational reform or nuclear nonproliferation, his motto was: "Let's engage, not attack."[8] Sorting through the tangled web of international problems that they had inherited from the Bush administration, however, Obama and his advisers soon recognized that they must temper their instinct to engage the world with a willingness to contain foreign threats posed by rival powers, rogue states, or radical groups. Although no one inside the White House ever employed the term "contagement," their approach combined elements of engagement and containment.

This first became apparent not in the Middle East but in East Asia, where the Obama administration quickly found itself at odds with China, whose economic and military power challenged America's supremacy in the Pacific. Earlier in the new millennium, Liu Jianfei, the director of the Central Party School in Beijing, had asserted that the United States was pursuing a counterrevolutionary agenda designed to contain China. "The U.S. has always opposed communist 'red revolutions' and hates the 'green revolutions' in Iran and other Islamic states," Liu told two visiting American academics in 2005, but "it supported the 'rose,' 'orange,' and 'tulip' revolutions" as part of a long-standing strategy "to spread democracy further and turn the whole globe 'blue.'"[9] After several rounds of head-butting with Washington over everything from digital piracy to the fate of the Spratly Islands in the South China Sea, Beijing was ready to give America's policy a new name— "contagement." The Taiwan-based *China Times*, for example, reported that the Chinese vice president Xi Jinping, President Hu Jintao's heir apparent, had tried to smooth ruffled feathers during a White House visit in February 2012. "Many Chinese strategists are of the view that Washington will go out of its way to undermine China's rise to the world stage," the Taiwanese newspaper explained. "They have termed the US strategy as 'contagement'—a combination of 'containment' and 'engagement.'"[10] An Huihou, who headed the government-funded China Foundation for International Studies, was far blunter a few months later. "The United States has followed a 'contagement' policy vis-à-vis China and [has] created trouble for us on multiple fronts," he grumbled. "Therefore China should stick to the non-interference principle and oppose the West's 'interventionism'" in Asia.[11]

Meanwhile, a slightly different version of contagement was starting to shape American policies toward the Muslim world, where Obama's verb of choice still appeared to be "engage" rather than "contain." The new president had raised a few eyebrows by granting his first Oval Office interview to a Muslim reporter, Hishem Melhem, the Washington bureau chief for

Al Arabiya, on 26 January 2009. Thanks to the U.S. invasion of Iraq, Melhem reminded Obama, "there is a demonization of America," not only among Islamic radicals but also among Arab moderates. Was there a way to reverse that? The short answer was "yes," Obama said, but it would take time. Winding down the war in Iraq and stabilizing Afghanistan would be two big steps in the right direction, and restarting the stalled Israeli-Palestinian peace process would be a third. He went on to reiterate what he had said six days earlier in his inaugural address: "If countries like Iran are willing to unclench their fist, they will find an extended hand from us." The United States was after something even larger, however. "My job to [*sic*] the Muslim world is to communicate that the Americans are not your enemy," he told Melhem. "If you look at the track record," Obama explained, it was clear that "America was not born as a colonial power," which meant that "the same respect and partnership that America had with the Muslim world as recently as 20 or 30 years ago, there's no reason why we can't restore that." There was a rumor, Melhem remarked as the interview wound down, that the president would soon say these things in a Muslim capital. This was true, Obama replied, but he would not say where.[12]

"Where" would actually come in two places, Ankara and Cairo. In early April, Obama arrived in the Turkish capital, where he praised Prime Minister Recep Tayyip Erdoğan, a moderate Islamist, for making Turkey "a critical strategic partner with the United States, not just in combatting terrorism" but also in developing the economic, political, and cultural links "that will allow both countries to prosper."[13] He went even further during an address to the Turkish parliament. "The United States is not, and will never be, at war with Islam," Obama declared. "America's relationship with the Muslim community, the Muslim world, cannot, and will not, just be based upon opposition to terrorism." Rather, America sought "broader engagement based on mutual interest and mutual respect."[14]

Obama reiterated these themes two months later in a speech at Cairo University that was broadcast live throughout Egypt and much of the Arab world. "I've come here," he told the cheering crowd on 4 June 2009, "to seek a new beginning between the United States and Muslims around the world . . . based upon the truth that America and Islam are not exclusive and need not be in competition." Indeed, they shared a set of "common principles," including "justice and progress" and "tolerance and the dignity of all human beings." Without using the word "contagement," Obama outlined a new American approach to the region that would simultaneously contain Islamic radicals and engage Islamic moderates. His administration remained committed to fighting "violent extremism in all its forms" and to "preventing a nuclear arms race in the Middle East," but it was also reversing three of George W. Bush's most controversial policies in Baghdad, Kabul, and Jerusalem. It was time "to leave Iraq to the Iraqis," it was time for a little less killing and a lot more nation-building in Afghanistan, and it was time for peace in the Holy Land based on security for the Israelis and justice for the Palestinians. "We should choose the right path," Obama concluded, "not just the easy path."[15]

Obama's desire to choose the right path made him somewhat more popular among the world's Muslims than his predecessor. The Pew Research Global Attitudes Project, for example, reported a modest "Cairo Effect," especially among Palestinians, whose favorability index for America's first black president had risen from 27 to 39 percent by late July.[16] The man in the Oval Office had chosen the harder path with his eyes wide open and was well aware that Muslims would judge him by what he did, not by what he said in Ankara or Cairo. "Our objective was not to get some signed agreement from the Muslim world that they were all going to align with us against terrorism," Obama told a reporter a few months later. "The question was, are you starting to affect the Arab street in a way that creates a different environment?"[17]

Creating that different environment started in Iraq, where the Obama administration handed responsibility for security in Baghdad back to Prime Minister Nuri al-Maliki on 30 June 2009 and confirmed that all U.S. troops would return home within two years. "We now have an Iraqi government that has gained its balance and thinks it knows how to ride the bike in the race," Colonel Timothy R. Reese, the Pentagon's chief military liaison with Maliki, explained in an edgy e-mail that he fired off in early July, but "our hand on the back of the seat is holding them back and causing resentment." As far as Reese was concerned, there was only one good option: "We need to let go before we both tumble to the ground." Otherwise, the Iraqis "will continue to squeeze the US for all the 'goodies' that we can provide" and "suckle at Uncle Sam's bounteous mammary glands."[18] Obama's national security team may have cringed at Reese's mixed metaphor, but they would terminate America's military presence in Iraq on schedule.

Extricating the United States from the mess that Bush had left behind in Afghanistan would prove much more complicated. Throughout the 2008 election campaign, candidate Obama had distinguished between the "war of choice" against Saddam Hussein and the "war of necessity" against the Taliban, who sought to topple Afghan president Hamid Karzai with help from radical Islamists backed by Pakistani intelligence. In late November, the president-elect spelled out for Admiral Mike Mullen, the chairman of the Joint Chiefs of Staff, what he thought was necessary in Kabul. "I want to get Afghanistan and Pakistan right," Obama said, "but I don't want to build a Jeffersonian democracy."[19] By the time he took the oath of office, he realized that getting it right would almost certainly mean doubling or perhaps even tripling the number of U.S. troops, which stood at 30,000 in January 2009. Obama reluctantly agreed to send an additional 17,000 GIs to Afghanistan on 13 February and spent the rest of the year debating the merits of two strategies going forward—"counterterrorism lite," favored by Vice President Joe Biden, which would require only a modest increase in troop levels, and "counterinsurgency plus," favored by Generals David Petraeus and Stanley McChrystal, who wanted at least 100,000 American boots on the ground. Everyone knew what was at stake. "If you don't succeed in Afghanistan," NSC adviser James Jones told a reporter in June 2009, "you will be fighting in more places" like "Africa, South America, you name it." Even worse, a Taliban victory would mean that "organizations like NATO, by association the European Union, and the United Nations might be relegated to the dustbin of history." Yet Jones was quick to admit that the most important lesson to be learned from Bush's recent folly in Iraq was, "Be careful you don't over-Americanize the war."[20]

On 13 September 2009, President Obama convened the first in a series of ten special NSC meetings to determine how to avoid repeating his predecessor's mistakes. Vice President Biden urged his boss to worry less about Hamid Karzai in Kabul and more about the volatile political situation next door in Islamabad. "If you don't get Pakistan right, you can't win," Biden warned. "You own this war" just as soon as more GIs arrive in Afghanistan. "I already own it," Obama replied.[21] When the NSC met again, however, the president sided with Biden and decided to "start where our interests take us, which is really Pakistan, not Afghanistan." This might require less war fighting and more nation-building. "We need to drain the swamp and reduce the appeal of violent extremism to young Muslims," Obama told his national security team. "We need to elevate our public affairs and our civilian affairs."[22] At the next NSC session on 9 October 2009, Richard Holbrooke, Obama's special envoy for Afghanistan and Pakistan, held center stage. Having watched Ngo Dinh Diem fiddle while Saigon burned in 1963, Holbrooke was well aware of how perilous it could be rely on feckless and corrupt clients like Hamid Karzai, yet he cautioned against leaving Kabul too soon. "I'm concerned about setting timelines," he told Obama. "This is a long war. It will be longer than Vietnam."[23]

That scenario, of course, was precisely what worried the White House. An unreliable regime wholly dependent on U.S. support, some highly motivated guerrillas operating out of base camps next door, and a malevolent neighbor fishing in troubled waters—the key ingredients from Lyndon Johnson's recipe for catastrophe in Indochina—now confronted Barack Obama in Central Asia. Deputy NSC adviser Thomas Donilon, who had experienced the disabling pathology of "the Vietnam Syndrome" firsthand as a young intern during the Carter years, came up with some required reading for Team Obama in the autumn of 2009—Gordon Goldstein's *Lessons in Disaster*, an inside account of how the Johnson administration crashed and burned in Southeast Asia. During the mid-1990s, Goldstein had collaborated with McGeorge Bundy, LBJ's NSC adviser, on what was supposed to have been a memoir and primer about the limits of American power. After Bundy died, however, Goldstein reworked the material into a cautionary tale whose principal lesson was that "intervention is a presidential choice, not an inevitability."[24]

Identifying the right choice meant being realistic about what was possible in Kabul. The stakes remained incredibly high. "Taliban success in taking and holding parts of Afghanistan against the combined forces of multiple modern Western armies (above all, the United States) ... would dramatically strengthen the extremist Muslim psychology and popular perceptions of who is winning and who is losing," Secretary of Defense Gates explained on 13 October 2009.[25] "No government in Central Asia is a democracy and delivers services well. We can't aim too high," he added the next day. "The key is to blend with local Afghan culture and not to impose Western democracy."[26] America's credibility as a great power was in jeopardy in Kabul, just as it had been in Saigon forty years earlier. "For Islamic extremists to defeat a second superpower in Afghanistan would have devastating and long-lasting consequences," Gates recalled in his memoirs, with "grave implications for our standing in the world."[27] Obama reluctantly agreed and approved a quick spike in troop levels modeled on Bush's "surge" in Iraq to stabilize the situation just long enough to permit a graceful American exit. "We're not making Afghanistan a long-term protectorate," he told his national security team on 29 November.[28] Obama unveiled the "Afghan surge" two days later at West Point—another 50,000 GIs would be deployed to keep the Taliban in check for the next two years, after which the Pentagon would begin winding down its operations, with the U.S. combat mission scheduled to terminate no later than 2014.

With more troops on the way and with a deadline for withdrawal now in place, General McChrystal secured Obama's approval in February 2010 for an all-out assault on Marja, a guerrilla stronghold in Helmand Province 150 miles west of Kandahar, the Taliban's informal capital. Three months later, with American forces mired down in Marja, McChrystal was urging the White House to authorize a much broader offensive against Kandahar. "This reminds me of Chicago politics," Obama informed the general on 6 May, where one had "to understand the interrelationships and interconnections between ward bosses and district chiefs and tribes" in order to accomplish anything. "I've got to tell you, I've lived in Chicago for a long time, and I don't understand that." Unfazed by Obama's words of caution, McChrystal pushed back hard. "If we're going to do Chicago, we're going to need a lot more troops," he said, and even then, "we're not going to make Kandahar a shining city on the hill."[29]

Shining city-building had never been part of the plan, of course, nor was having an arrogant field commander call the shots. Not long after the seminar on Chicago politics, another acolyte of McChrystal's brand of counterinsurgency told the *New York Times* that Americans should "compare the Afghan people to sheep," who "fall over and have a heart attack" when startled. "When they're scared, they'll just huddle with the shepherd," Lieutenant Colonel Guy Jones remarked. "As soon as they hear the sound of his voice, they'll calm down."[30] Then in June a reporter for *Rolling Stone* magazine revealed that McChrystal and his top aides had taken to calling Vice President Biden "Joe Bite Me," that they ridiculed White House troubleshooter Richard Holbrooke as a pompous know-it-all, and that they clearly believed that the occupant of the Oval Office himself was in over his head.[31] Before the month was out, the president forced McChrystal to resign and asked General David Petraeus, the hero of the surge in Iraq, to replace him. Obama was making it very clear that his administration had no interest in becoming a good shepherd. Eighteen months into his first term, the black man in the White House had barely managed to keep his policy of contagement with the Muslim world on track in Iraq and Afghanistan. The challenges he faced in the Holy Land would prove even more daunting.

Eating Pizza in the Holy Land: Obama, Israel, and Palestine

Two days after Christmas, President-elect Obama learned that Israel had launched Operation Cast Lead against Hamas, the Islamist group based in Gaza. With national elections scheduled for February 2009, Israel's lame-duck Prime Minister Ehud Olmert was retaliating for sporadic Palestinian rocket attacks on Sderot and other cities in the Negev Desert. For more than three weeks, Israeli jets and helicopters pounded Gaza with bombs and rockets, Israeli tanks sealed the border with Egypt, and Israeli commandos tracked down Hamas leaders, house to house. When the shooting stopped forty-eight hours before Obama took the oath of office, thirteen Israelis and more than twelve hundred Palestinians (many of them women and children) had died, much of Gaza had been reduced to rubble, and the Middle East peace process remained where it had been throughout most of the previous eight years—hopelessly deadlocked. Rumors flew that Olmert had decided to attack Gaza during the waning days of George W. Bush's administration because the incoming American president was anti-Israel.

The Arab-Israeli conflict had become an issue a year earlier during primary season, when some American Jews in key states like California whispered that the Illinois Democrat was "unreliable" on Israel. Thanks to help from such high-profile friends of Israel as his fellow Chicagoan Rahm Emanuel, however, Barack Obama captured three-quarters of the Jewish vote in November 2008.[32] Speculation that the new president might prove to be tougher on Israel than his predecessor was not entirely unfounded. As a community organizer and state legislator in the Windy City, Obama had been influenced by liberal Zionists like Rabbi Arnold Wolf and Judge Abner Mikva, who were quite critical of Israel's expansion into the Occupied Territories. According to Ali Hasan Abunimah, an Arab American activist and onetime "Friend of Barack" who later founded the Web site *Electronic Intifada*, Obama called for "an even-handed approach to the Palestinian-Israeli conflict" during an unsuccessful bid for a congressional seat in 2000 and vowed to "be more upfront" on Palestine after winning election to the U.S. Senate four years later.[33] Abunimah himself had gained a bit of national attention during a debate with a supporter of Israel in August 2001 by resorting to a colorful analogy to explain how Jewish settlements on the West Bank undermined the peace process. Reminding listeners of Radio Pacifica that Israel was continuing to confiscate Palestinian land and demolish Palestinian houses, Abunimah pointed out that "if you and I are going to decide how to slice a pizza, and I start gobbling the pizza up as fast as I can there's no way we can negotiate in that situation."[34]

Shortly after moving into the Oval Office, Obama tried to establish better ground rules for eating pizza in the Holy Land. In mid-February he urged Mahmoud Abbas, the president of the Palestinian Authority (PA), to do more to control Hamas and other Islamic militants in Gaza and pressed Israel to stop building new settlements on the West Bank. One month later, Israeli voters made Obama's task much more difficult when they brought

Benjamin "Bibi" Netanyahu back for a second term as prime minister. On the eve of his first visit to Obama's Washington in May 2009, Bibi publicly rejected a settlement freeze and hinted privately that a "two-state solution" based on the principle of "peace for land" might no longer be feasible. Obama and Netanyahu spent their time together reviewing Israel's worries about Iran's quest for nuclear weapons and discussing the fate on the West Bank. Reporters attending the press briefing immediately afterward could see that the two men had agreed to disagree on both issues. To no one's great surprise, Bibi bristled when Obama reaffirmed America's willingness to "reach out to Iran" via "direct talks" on nuclear nonproliferation and when he reiterated the long-standing U.S. position that "settlements have to be stopped in order for us to move forward" toward peace.[35]

Abbas got his turn to review the peace process with Obama on 28 May 2009. The PLO leader had just two questions. First, "are you serious about the two-state solution?" If Obama was, Abbas could "not comprehend that you would allow a single settlement housing unit to be built in the West Bank." Further Israeli expansion into the Occupied Territories would only mean more "chaos, extremism, [and] violence," and Hamas "would shoot me and other moderates in the head and make this Bin Laden's region." The second question was even more pointed than the first. "If you cannot make Israel stop settlements," Abbas wondered, "who can?" A little taken aback, Obama insisted that "the establishment of a Palestinian state is a must for me personally" and suggested that the first step might be a "partial freeze" on Israeli expansion into the West Bank.[36] The best deal that Obama could get, however, was Israel's pledge not to confiscate any additional Palestinian land and to confine all new construction to existing settlement blocs. When Washington broke the news later that summer, the Palestinians were furious. "I know you did your best, and it's not the outcome you wanted," Saab Erekat, the PLO's chief negotiator, told U.S. officials on 17 September, but "with this deal Bibi will say settlements will continue, and they *will* continue." After one of the Americans insisted that "no new confiscation" was a big step in the right direction, the Palestinian diplomat lost his temper. "I'm not coming from Mars! 40% of the West Bank is already confiscated. They can keep building for years," Erekat roared. "What I don't want is the US to acquiesce to settlements and take me on a ride."[37]

A month later Erekat paid a call at Foggy Bottom, where he met with George Mitchell, a former U.S. Senate majority leader and an informal Middle East envoy who was helping Secretary of State Hillary Clinton revive the peace process. Arguing that the Israelis were not bargaining in good faith, Erekat complained that nearly two decades after the first peace talks in Madrid in October 1991, "there is no light at the end of the tunnel." President Abbas felt the same way and would resign rather than accept a partial freeze. "Without him," Erekat told Mitchell, "only Hamas remains." With that, Mitchell called upstairs to Clinton, who rushed down from the seventh floor. Eager to prevent Abbas from resigning, she was also irritated by his inflexibility. Why, Clinton wondered, are the Palestinians "always in a chapter of a Greek tragedy?" Was it really the case that "if no settlement freeze, no negotiations?" Erekat did not mince words: "Yes. Cut the story short. It is a non-starter." A few minutes later, Clinton relayed the news to her boss in the Oval Office, who managed to persuade Abbas not to step down by reaffirming America's commitment to a two-state solution based on UN Security Council Resolution 242.[38]

Obama's gesture may have reassured Abbas, but it did not sit well with Netanyahu, who had no interest in making Resolution 242 the starting point for peace talks. Whatever residual good feelings the partial freeze on settlements may have inspired in Washington were dissipated in March 2010 when the Israelis broke ground on sixteen hundred new housing units in East Jerusalem at the very moment that Vice President Joe Biden was in Israel for talks with Netanyahu. Holding his legendary Irish temper in check, Biden would only say that this was "precisely the kind of step that undermines the trust we need right now."[39] Other members of Team Obama were far less restrained. Secretary of State Clinton called the new settlements "an insult to the US" that had sent a "deeply negative signal" to the Muslim world, while David Axelrod, one of the president's most trusted advisers, told *Meet the Press* on 15 March that the Israeli announcement was a "very destructive" move that "undermined this very fragile effort to bring peace to that region."[40]

Obama and Netanyahu hoped to stay above the fray, but Israel's supporters took aim at what they regarded as the pro-Palestinian tilt of U.S. policy. The Obama administration "may want to consider the fact that their relationship with their Israeli wife is more valuable than their newfound relationship with their Arab mistresses," Haim Saban, a Hollywood media mogul with close ties to AIPAC, warned Vice President Biden at a gathering of American Jewish leaders.[41] Meanwhile, Bibi's brother-in-law, Hagai Ben-Artzi, was telling Israel's *Army Radio* that "there is an anti-Semitic president in the United States."[42] Tempers flared when Netanyahu arrived at the White House on 23 March. Skipping the small talk, Obama insisted that Israel rescind its plans for new settlements, and when Bibi balked, the president cut the meeting short and headed to the family quarters for lunch with Michelle and his daughters. Netanyahu departed later that afternoon without the usual joint statement, press briefing, or photographic fanfare.

Palestinian officials were heartened by this Israeli-American contretemps, but they refused to resume peace negotiations without categorical guarantees that all construction of new settlements on the West Bank, including East Jerusalem, would halt. A briefing paper prepared by the PLO's Negotiations Services Unit (NSU) summed up the pluses and minuses succinctly. "President Obama has framed Palestinian-Israeli peace both as a US national strategic interest and central to achieving regional peace and stability," but he was learning that "translating optimism and opportunity into concrete progress on the ground is not easy." Sixteen hundred new units of housing in East Jerusalem showed that the Israelis were still more interested in eating pizza than in dividing it fairly. "Without an immediate and comprehensive settlement freeze and the eventual dismantlement of settlements, there will be no Palestinian state left to negotiate and no two-state solution to speak of," the NSU concluded. "Time is running out for the two-state solution. Palestinians cannot keep waiting for Israel to catch up."[43]

Time also seemed to be running out for Barack Obama. In early July, he sat for a television interview with Yonit Lavi of Israel's *Channel 2*, who observed that many of her viewers "feel like you don't have a special connection to Israel." Insisting that top advisers like Rahm Emanuel and David Axelrod could vouch for his "closeness to the Jewish American community," the president confessed that he and Bibi did not see eye to eye on settlements. Yet there was also a larger problem related to his efforts to improve ties with the Palestinians and the Iranians. "I think that sometimes, particularly in the Middle East, there's the feeling of the friend of my enemy must be my enemy," Obama explained. "The truth of the matter is that my outreach to the Muslim community is designed precisely to reduce the antagonism and the dangers posed by a hostile Muslim world to Israel and to the West."[44] He made many of the same points to a worldwide audience two months later during his address to the UN General Assembly in New York City, where he reaffirmed the importance of a two-state solution in the Holy Land. "Those of us who are friends of Israel must understand that true security for the Jewish state requires an independent Palestine—one that allows the Palestinian people to live with dignity and opportunity," Obama declared. "And those of us who are friends of the Palestinians must understand that the rights of the Palestinian people will be won only through peaceful means—including genuine reconciliation with a secure Israel."[45]

After Republicans regained control of the U.S. House of Representatives in the 2010 off-year elections, however, Obama grew more pessimistic about his ability to broker peace in the Middle East. The new House majority leader would be Eric Cantor, an ultraconservative from Richmond, Virginia, with close ties to AIPAC and Netanyahu. "The new Republican majority understands the special relationship between Israel and the United States," Cantor assured Bibi just days after the ballots were counted, and "will serve as a check on the [Obama] Administration."[46] Emboldened by the GOP's gains on Capitol Hill, Israeli officials began eating what remained of the Palestinian pizza. Avigdor Lieberman, Netanyahu's 's Islamophobic foreign minister, made it clear that restoring the Green Line, the 1967 border separating Israel from the West Bank, was no longer an option. "The right approach is not peace for territory," he told *Newsweek* in late 2010, "but exchanging territory and populations."[47] When critics branded Lieberman's proposal "ethnic cleansing," Bibi toned down the rhetoric early in the new year while pushing ahead with plans to build still more housing in East Jerusalem. In February, the Obama administration stepped in to veto a UN Security Council resolution that would have declared Netanyahu's actions illegal, but Ambassador Susan Rice also condemned "the folly and illegitimacy of continued Israeli settlement activity."[48]

President Obama followed up later that spring by reiterating America's support for a two-state solution based on the Green Line. "We believe the borders of Israel and Palestine should be based on the 1967 lines with mutually agreed swaps," he told a packed house at the State Department on 19 May 2011, "so that secure and recognized borders are established for both states." Whether Israeli leaders like Avigdor Lieberman wanted to admit it, Obama insisted that "the Palestinian people must have the right to govern themselves, and reach their full potential, in a sovereign and contiguous state."[49] Halfway around the world, Netanyahu was about to board an El Al jetliner for a flight to Washington, where he was scheduled to visit the White House the following day. Insisting that Obama's comments ran counter to previous assurances from the Bush administration, Bibi told his aides to post an icy response on Twitter. "Prime Minister Netanyahu expects to hear a reaffirmation from President Obama of U.S. commitments made to Israel in 2004, which were overwhelmingly supported by both Houses of Congress," they tweeted, commitments that specified "Israel not having to withdraw to the 1967 lines."[50]

By all accounts, the meeting in the Oval Office on 20 May was frosty. A White House insider reported that Obama regarded Bibi's use of the verb "expects" as "insulting." Nor was he pleased by the history lesson that Netanyahu insisted on delivering. "Before 1967, Israel was all of nine miles wide," Bibi lectured. "These were not the boundaries of peace; they were the boundaries of repeated wars."[51] The president kept his cool and clarified his own position when he spoke to AIPAC's annual policy conference two days later. Because his earlier comments about "the 1967 lines—with mutually agreed swaps" had received so much attention, Obama parsed his language carefully. "It means that the parties themselves—Israelis and Palestinians— will negotiate a border that is different than the one that existed on June 4, 1967," one that reflects "the new demographic realities on the ground," but it also it meant that a two-state solution must be achieved via mutual agreement, not via unilateral action by Israel.[52]

Not to be outdone, Netanyahu delivered a rejoinder before a joint session of Congress on 24 May 2011. His message was unequivocal. "I will accept a Palestinian state," Bibi declared, but "Jerusalem must never again be divided" and Israel "will not return to the indefensible boundaries of 1967." Because most of the 650,000 settlers now living beyond the Green Line "reside in neighborhoods and suburbs of Jerusalem and Greater Tel Aviv," that territory must become part of Israel. Finally, Netanyahu reserved the right to strike rogue nations like Iran or terrorist groups like Hezbollah and Hamas should they threaten Israel's security. Thanks to AIPAC's connections on Capitol Hill, the audience in the House gallery was overwhelmingly pro-Israel and greeted Bibi's remarks with thunderous applause. Down on the floor, senators and congressman from both sides of the aisle gave Bibi multiple standing ovations. "We're not talking about a peace process anymore," Robert Malley, Bill Clinton's principal liaison with the PLO, told a reporter after the cheering stopped, "we're talking about a P.R. process."[53]

Further evidence that AIPAC and public relations trumped the PLO and foreign relations surfaced later that summer. Locked in a ferocious battle with majority leader Eric Cantor and House Republicans, who opposed raising the U.S. government's debt ceiling, the Obama administration thwarted a French-sponsored plan to grant the Palestinians "observer status" in the UN General Assembly as the first step toward statehood. Although there was no explicit quid pro quo linking the GOP's eleventh-hour budget compromise and American maneuvering at the United Nations, Cantor was quite satisfied with the outcome on both fronts. "What you have on the Hill is a bipartisan demonstration for the U.S./Israeli relationship," he told reporters, "and frankly I think it's in contrast to the signals being sent from the White House."[54] Frustrated to have come away empty-handed at the United Nations, the French president Nicholas Sarkozy blamed Israel. "I cannot bear Netanyahu, he's a liar," Sarkozy whispered inadvertently into an open microphone during the G-20 Summit at Cannes on 8 November 2011. "You're fed up with him," Obama replied, "but I have to deal with him even more often than you."[55]

By early 2012, the issue on which Obama was dealing with Netanyahu most often was not peace with the Palestinians but rather the specter of nuclear proliferation in Iran. Twice during the previous three decades, the Israeli air force had destroyed atomic reactors in the Muslim world—first in Iraq in 1981 and then in Syria in 2007. When Tehran stepped up its efforts in 2009 to acquire enough enriched uranium to build a bomb, Bibi let the White House know that he was quite willing to make the third time a charm. After all, the Iranian president Mahmoud Ahmadinejad was a Holocaust denier who regarded Israel as a blood enemy. For his part, Obama worried that an Israeli preventive strike against Iran would unleash a fresh wave of anti-American-ism throughout the Middle East, where everyone knew that Tel Aviv had already developed nuclear weapons of its own while Washington looked the other way. Throughout 2009 and into 2010, Team Obama orchestrated ever tighter economic sanctions against Tehran while American and Israeli intel-ligence teamed up for Operation Olympic Games, a joint venture to disrupt the Iranian nuclear project via Stuxnet, a computer virus that disabled the centrifuges that produced enriched uranium. When asked to identify the most important diplomatic problems President Obama confronted as the country headed into the 2010 off-year elections, Deputy Secretary of State James Steinberg had replied: "Iran, Iran, Iran and Iran."[56]

Once the 2012 presidential election campaign moved into full swing, Obama's GOP rivals took turns bashing him for not being tough enough with Tehran. "If we reelect Barack Obama, Iran will have a nuclear weapon," Republican front-runner Mitt Romney declared on the eve of the New Hampshire primary, but "if you elect me as the next president, they will not have a nuclear weapon."[57] After he sewed up the GOP nomination, Romney delivered another blistering critique at a private fund-raising dinner on 17 May. Thanks to the neophyte in the Oval Office, candidate Romney told Republican high rollers in Boca Raton, Florida, "America could be held up and blackmailed by Iran, by the mullahs, by crazy people."[58] Meanwhile, Prime Minister Netanyahu rattled Israel's sabers ever more loudly at Iran and encouraged Eric Cantor and other friends on Capitol Hill to keep the pressure on the White House. Bibi made no secret that if he could cast a ballot on election day, it would be for Romney, an old colleague with whom he had worked at the Boston Consulting Group almost forty years earlier. Clearly, there was no love lost between the Israeli prime minister and the American president. The *Haaretz* editor Aluf Benn probably put it best in September 2012 when he said that "Bibi looks at Obama and sees his ideological opposite," while "Obama looks at Bibi and sees Eric Cantor."[59]

Iranian Summer, Arab Spring: Finding the Right Side of History

Unlike Netanyahu and Cantor, whose motto for dealing with Islamic radicals in Tehran and elsewhere seemed to be "the best defense is a good offense," Obama remained convinced that the most effective prescription for peace and stability in the Middle East was to engage Muslim moderates while containing Muslim extremists. The first experiment with contagement had come in Iran during the spring of 2009. Eager to open a diplomatic dialogue and end three decades of estrangement, President Obama sent greetings via YouTube to the Iranian people and their government on Nowruz, the Persian New Year. America wanted "constructive ties" and "engagement that is honest and grounded in mutual respect," he declared on 19 March, but for its part, Iran must recognize that the "ability to build and create" was more powerful than "a capacity to destroy."[60]

Dismissing Obama's message as a clever diplomatic ploy, Ayatollah Ali Khamenei, the Islamic Republic's supreme leader, asked whether the United States stood ready to lift its "cruel sanctions" and cease its "negative propaganda" against Iran. "Change has to be real," Khamenei snapped. "You change, and we will change as well."[61] Others in Iran, however, seemed more willing to take Obama at his word, especially after he acknowledged the "tumultuous history" between Washington and Tehran during his address at Cairo University on 4 June 2009 and admitted that "the United States [had] played a role in the overthrow of a democratically elected Iranian government." Things had changed since the CIA toppled Mohammed Mossadegh half a century earlier. "America respects the right of all peaceful and law-abiding voices to be heard around the world," Obama told Muslims everywhere, "even if we disagree with them."[62]

Just eight days later, Iranians would let their voices be heard during their country's fourth presidential election in twelve years. From their listening post in Dubai on the Arab side of the Strait of Hormuz, the State Department's Iran watchers had detected signs of serious political discontent in Tehran, where Mir Hossein Mousavi, a moderate Islamist, and his Green

Path movement seemed poised to deny President Ahmadinejad a second term. Mousavi and his followers hoped to curb the power of the mullahs and erase Iran's reputation as a rogue state by transforming the Islamic Republic into a responsible regional power. Early returns showed the Green Path with a big lead, but shortly after the polls closed on 12 June, Ayatollah Khamenei stopped counting the ballots and declared Ahmadinejad the winner. The Iran Regional Presence Office in Dubai reported widespread popular resentment and warned Washington that "many opposition supporters will likely look to the US—particularly after the Cairo speech—for inspiration."[63] In the days that followed, pro-Mousavi demonstrators surged into the streets of Tehran, where they were beaten by Iranian Revolutionary Guards or shot and killed by the Basij, a shadowy band of motor cycle–riding thugs loyal to the regime. By the time the protests subsided, Khamenei had ordered the arrest of several hundred Green Path leaders and the Basij had killed at least fifty demonstrators, including twenty-six-year-old Neda Agha-Soltan, who bled to death while the world watched on a cell phone video that went viral on YouTube.

Less than three weeks after his Cairo speech heralding democracy in the Muslim world, Barack Obama confronted an embarrassing dilemma in Iran. Americans were "appalled and outraged by the threats, the beatings, and imprisonments of the last few days," he told reporters on 23 June. Adding insult to injury, the Iranian government was "accusing the United States and others in the West of instigating protests over the election" in a crass effort "to distract people from what is truly taking place within Iran's borders." The United States had paid a high price for meddling in Iranian politics during the Cold War, however, and the White House was not about to make that mistake again. Rather, Americans could only "bear witness to the courage and the dignity of the Iranian people," reminding themselves that "those who stand up for justice are always on the right side of history."[64] Privately, Team Obama seems to have hoped that the electoral fiasco and its brutal aftermath would discredit the Ahmadinejad regime and force it to accept international oversight of Iran's nuclear program. Yet any such American negotiations with Iran could easily result in a "lose-lose scenario" elsewhere in the Middle East, where "Arab moderates may argue that the U.S., for the sake of its own national interests, has cut a deal at the expense of pro-democracy advocates."[65] There were hints during the autumn of 2009 that Tehran might indeed allow the International Atomic Energy Agency to monitor its uranium enrichment operations, but in the end the Iranians preferred to work through Turkish or Brazilian intermediaries. With no acceptable deal in sight, Washington persuaded the UN Security Council to impose stiffer economic sanctions on 9 June 2010.

Embarrassed by the lose-lose scenario that he had just witnessed in Iran, Obama was determined to be on the right side of history the next time violent unrest rocked the Muslim world. In early August, he personally drafted a memo entitled "Political Reform in the Middle East and North Africa," complaining that progress toward democracy had stalled and expressing concern over "growing citizen discontent with the region's regimes," many of which were supported by the United States. In what became known as Presidential Study Directive 11 (PSD-11), Obama asked his national security team for specific recommendations, "tailored . . . country-by-country," to encourage Arab autocrats to prepare for peaceful change. "Increased repression could threaten the political and economic stability of some of our allies, [and] leave us with fewer capable, credible partners who can support our regional priorities," the president pointed out. "Our regional and international credibility will be undermined if we are seen or perceived to be backing repressive regimes and ignoring the rights and aspirations of citizens."[66]

During the next four months, a self-styled "Nerd Directorate" that included human rights advocate Samantha Power, the Middle East troubleshooter Dennis Ross, and the Russia expert Michael McFaul wrestled with the dilemmas spelled out in PSD-11. President Obama's concern that the Arab world was ripe for revolution did not seem unfounded. Democracy was still an alien concept absent from the vocabulary of the oil-rich Sunni elites who ruled Saudi Arabia and Bahrain, where any political discontent was attributed to Shia subversives backed by Iran. When human rights protests erupted in Manama in February 2009, Bahrain's King Hamad blamed Tehran.[67] Likewise, when John Brennan, Obama's counterterrorism chief, arrived in Riyadh in mid-March, he was reminded that "the Saudis are surrounded by Iranian intrigues."[68] Six months later Brennan visited Yemen, a key ally in the war on terror whose president, Ali Abdullah Saleh, had ruled with an iron fist for more than thirty years. Dismissing half a million dollars in U.S. military assistance as "insufficient" to root out current al-Qaeda operations in Yemen, Saleh claimed he faced an even bigger threat from rivals in the Houthi tribe, who had recently launched an insurrection along the northern border with Saudi Arabia. "If you don't help," he warned Brennan, "this country will become worse than Somalia."[69]

Even in Jordan, easily the most moderate of the Arab states, unrest was spreading among the kingdom's Palestinian majority, who were angry about Israel's continuing expansion on the West Bank, and among Jordanian

Islamists, who were appalled by Washington's botched attempt at regime change next door in Baghdad. In November 2009, King Abdullah II, Jordan's American-educated monarch, had dissolved parliament, and three months later he ordered the arrest of five hundred Islamic militants.[70] "We moderates have very little voice to be heard," he told Jon Stewart during an interview on *The Daily Show* on 23 September 2010. "We describe ourselves as being between Iraq and a hard place." With U.S. boots already on the ground in Afghanistan and Iraq, and with U.S. drones already prowling the skies from Pakistan to Yemen, Abdullah worried that "potential crisis number five, six, or seven" was just around the corner.[71]

Obama's Nerd Directorate was beginning to suspect that the most likely location for crises five, six, and seven was North Africa. In Morocco, for example, high unemployment and widespread bureaucratic corruption were producing explosive conditions. King Mohammed VI was trying to placate his critics with cosmetic top-down reforms, but U.S. diplomats reported that "the political system is sick."[72] Farther down the Mediterranean coast, Muammar Qaddafi, who had long ruled Libya through a brutal and bizarre cult of personality, was squandering immense oil wealth and converting his country into "a kleptocracy in which the regime has a direct stake in anything worth buying, selling, or owning."[73] Of far greater concern in Washington was Egypt, the most populous Arab state and the first to have signed a peace treaty with Israel. Hosni Mubarak, the eighty-two year-old air force general who had held power in Cairo for nearly three decades, scoffed at the idea of democracy and relied on crony capitalism, a ruthless intelligence apparatus, and $2 billion per year in U.S. military assistance to keep his critics in check. U.S. Ambassador Margaret Scobey described Mubarak in May 2009 as "a classic Egyptian secularist who hates religious extremism and interference in politics" and who knew how to "keep the domestic beasts at bay." The cocksure Egyptian strongman's favorite adage seemed to be: "It is far better to let a few individuals suffer than risk chaos for society as a whole."[74] Yet by February 2010, there were signs of serious trouble. With Mubarak relying more and more on "arrests, harassment and intimidation" to silence his opponents while ignoring calls for political reform, Scobey suspected that Egypt's aging president was more interested in grooming his son Gamal to succeed him than in addressing his country's economic woes. Some Egypt watchers in Washington began to worry that Hosni Mubarak might not last the year.[75]

The first tremor of the political earthquake that would eventually turn the Arab world upside down, however, did not strike Cairo but Tunis. For nearly a quarter of a century, Tunisia had been ruled by Zine el Abidine Ben Ali, a seventy-five-year-old self-styled populist who enriched himself and his family while creating a one-party state complete with rigged elections, secret police, and a corrupt bureaucracy. Seven months before Obama took the oath of office, Ambassador Robert Godec remarked that the Tunisian government's informal motto seemed to be "What's Yours Is Mine." Greed had become the coin of the realm. "Whether it's cash, services, land, prop- erty, or yes, even your yacht," Godec reported, "President Ben Ali's family is rumored to covet it and reportedly gets what it wants." Ordinary Tunisians were hit with petty fees and arbitrary taxes while foreign investors routinely paid big bribes and bigger kickbacks. In short, "corruption is the elephant in the room; it is the problem everyone knows about, but no one can publicly acknowledge."[76] After Ben Ali won an unprecedented sixth term with more than 90 percent of the vote on 25 October 2009, Gordon Gray, Godec's suc- cessor at the U.S. embassy in Tunis, warned Team Obama that "the elephant is getting bigger and the room smaller." Although the Ben Ali clan pretended that the outcome was "an incremental step toward democracy," Ambassador Gray believed that "the opposite is closer to the truth."[77] In February 2010, Ben Ali's opponents took to the streets of the capital to demand democratic reforms and privately pressed U.S. diplomats for help "in keeping pressure on the [government of Tunisia] to improve its human rights record and its tolerance for dissent."[78]

Ten months later in Sidi Bouzid, a market town two hundred miles south of Tunis, Mohammed Bouazizi, a street-smart fruit vendor and chief bread- winner for his family of seven, tangled with a petty official, who confiscated the young man's pears, bananas, and produce scale because he could not afford the necessary municipal permit. Shortly afterward, Bouazizi doused himself with paint thinner and set himself on fire outside city hall while his friends watched in horror.[79] By the time he died on 4 January 2011, chaos reigned throughout Tunisia, with tens of thousands of protestors demand- ing regime change from the bottom up. President Ben Ali fought back, branding his foes as Islamic radicals and ordering his riot police to snuff out "the Jasmine Revolution," but tear gas, clubs, and rubber bullets were no match for the antigovernment crowds, who smelled victory. Having lost the support of the Tunisian army, which refused to fire on the protestors, Ben Ali abruptly stepped down on 14 January and fled into exile in Saudi Arabia. Startled by this dramatic turn of events, NSC adviser Thomas Donilon told the White House press corps that "each nation gives life to the principle of democracy in its own way" and that the Obama administration expected

Ben Ali's successors to show "respect for basic human rights in a process of much needed political reform."[80]

At almost the same moment that Mohamed Bouazizi was having his rendezvous with martyrdom in Tunisia, the NSC's Nerd Directorate was completing its assessment of political instability in the Muslim world that President Obama had requested in PSD-11. Samantha Powers, chief among the NSC's first responders, recalled that "the premise of the directive was that there were profound costs to allowing the status quo," that "the social drivers of discontent were becoming uncontainable," and that "it was just getting harder and harder to keep a lid on things." Ben Ali's fate proved a cautionary tale. "We were more and more implicated by our friendships with authoritarian regimes that were using ever more brutal tactics to repress their people," Powers sighed.[81] She and her fellow nerds were even more concerned about the volatile situation in Egypt, where Hosni Mubarak had stuffed the ballot boxes to stack parliament with pro-regime figures in November 2010. Appalled by runaway corruption and frightened by resurgent repression, tech-savvy reformers like Wael Ghonim, an Egyptian computer whiz who managed Google's marketing operations in the Middle East, began using Facebook and other social media to call for regime change in Cairo. "It was clear from the time of the parliamentary elections that something was going to happen there," Deputy Secretary of State James Steinberg told a reporter several months later. "Everyone recognized that Egypt was going to be a crisis sometime in the next couple of years," but no one knew exactly when things would "come to a head."[82] Steinberg's boss, who had flown to Doha, Qatar, early in the new year to attend the seventh annual Forum on the Future, provided a bleak forecast for Mubarak and other Arab autocrats. "We have to come up with a way to wake these people up," Secretary of State Clinton remarked privately. "They are sitting on a time bomb."[83]

The Egyptian time bomb exploded a few days after Clinton returned home from Doha. On 25 January 2011, the fifty-ninth anniversary of Black Friday, when a bloody clash between British troops and local police had sounded the death knell for Egypt's King Farouk, fifty thousand protestors jammed Tahrir Square in downtown Cairo to demand change. Many wanted an end to crony capitalism, most wanted free elections, and a few wanted sharia law, but everyone wanted Mubarak gone. For several years, Egyptians had been captivated by Alaa al-Aswany's *The Yacoubian Building*, a best-selling fictionalized account of Mubarak's regime whose leader, the unnamed "Big Man," resembled a modern-day Pharaoh. "Our Lord created the Egyptians to accept government authority," the Big Man's chief enforcer informed a hapless political dissident. "It says so in the history books." The Big Man's regime was just as cynical as Mubarak's. "Egyptians are the easiest people in the world to rule," his enforcer sneered. "The moment you take power, they submit to you and grovel to you and you can do what you want with them."[84] The history books, however, were about to change. When Mubarak ordered the protestors to disperse in late January, they refused to grovel. Instead, Tahrir Square, whose name means "liberation" in Arabic, became a sprawling tent city as the crowd swelled to more than one hundred thousand. Google's Wael Ghonim and dozens of other anti-Mubarak activists tweeted, blogged, and posted real-time videos on the Internet while the outlawed Muslim Brotherhood helped student radicals build barricades. Hoping to buy some time, Mubarak agreed that he would not be a candidate for reelection but insisted on remaining in power until voters chose his successor in September. Convinced that Hosni Mubarak's most likely successor would be his son Gamal, the protestors demanded that he step down immediately.

Disappointed by Mubarak's long goodbye, Team Obama decided that Egypt's Big Man had to go. As the crisis deepened in late January, an NSC staffer asked the president what he thought would happen next. "What do I want to happen, or what do I think?" came the reply. "What I want is for the kids in the square to win and that Google guy to be president," Obama quipped. "What I think is we're going to be in for a long, protracted transition."[85] After watching Mubarak unveil his scheme during a televised speech on 1 February, however, he telephoned the Egyptian leader and advised him to keep the transition very short. According to one White House aide, Mubarak urged Obama to remain patient and outwait the demonstrators in Tahrir Square, who would eventually go home. Instant regime change, Mubarak explained, merely guaranteed that the big winner would be "Muslim Brotherhood, Muslim Brotherhood, Muslim Brotherhood."[86] Unfazed by this apocalyptic mantra, Obama retorted that "we don't believe the protests are going to die down," and then politely delivered some bad news. "I always respect my elders," he told Mubarak. "You've been in politics for a very long time." Nevertheless, "there are moments in history that, just because things have been the same way in the past, doesn't mean they will be the same way in the future."[87] This was one of those moments. After making it clear that Mubarak must resign sooner rather than later, Obama hung up and went on U.S. television to declare that change in Cairo "must begin now."[88]

The end came soon enough. The Big Man hoped to persuade high-ranking military officers to launch a crackdown, but as in Tunisia, the army showed remarkable restraint, and some Egyptian soldiers actually began to fraternize with the demonstrators. Then, in an ill-advised act of desperation, during the wee hours of 2 February, Mubarak's secret police sent thugs on camels into Tahrir Square, where they killed thirteen and injured more than a hundred. As far as the White House was concerned, the "Battle of the Camels" was the straw that broke Hosni's back. "History was moving here," Obama told Donilon, "and we needed to be on the right side."[89] Nine days later, after much back-channel maneuvering, Vice President Omar Suleiman announced that Mubarak was turning power over to the Supreme Council of the Armed Forces (SCAF), which would maintain order and oversee national elections. Steven Cook, an American Egypt watcher who witnessed the slow-motion revolution from a hotel not far from Tahrir Square, remarked afterward that many of the demonstrators worried that the United States would find a way to prevent regime change because, after all, "Mubarak was Washington's man in Cairo."[90] Obama, however, was convinced that American thinking about the region was "out of date" and urged his national security team to prepare for more change in the Middle East, not less. Secretary of State Clinton, who had earlier tried to defuse the time bomb without forcing Mubarak out, now sought "a soft landing rather than a hard thud" after his departure. "It may all work out in twenty-five years," she told the president, "but I think the period between now and then will be quite rocky for the Egyptian people, for the region, and for us."[91]

The Obama administration's handling of the crisis in Egypt led some observers to speculate that the era during which America supported friendly tyrants through thick and thin was over, but events elsewhere in the Middle East suggested that it would not be easy to stay on the right side of history. Just a few hours after Mubarak's resignation on 11 February, Sheikh Issa Qassim, Bahrain's leading Shia cleric, declared during Friday prayers that "the winds of change in the Arab world were unstoppable" and demanded that his country's Sunni minority, including King Hamad and the royal family, relinquish some of their power.[92] Word of Qassim's sermon spread quickly via Facebook, and on 14 February, several thousand Shia activists poured into Pearl Square in downtown Manama, where they were roughed up by Bahraini security forces. By the end of the month, the crowd had swelled to more than one hundred thousand, one-fifth of the tiny island nation's entire population. A short distance to the west on the Saudi Arabian mainland, a very nervous King Abdullah worried that the "Pearl Revolution" was about to send King Hamad packing. Claiming that Bahrain was the target of Iranian subversion, Hamad appealed to Abdullah for help, and on 14

March a thousand Saudi troops boarded armored personnel carriers for the twenty-mile ride across the causeway to Manama. Two days later, Bahraini and Saudi forces stormed Pearl Square, killing eight protestors and injuring several hundred others. Shocked by the bloodshed, President Obama called both Hamad and Abdullah to express "deep concern over the violence in Bahrain" and to urge "maximum restraint."[93] Privately, Team Obama dismissed the notion that Iran was behind the trouble. "If you see every Shiite as an Iranian agent," one unidentified White House aide said later, "it can become a self-fulfilling prophecy." Yet once King Abdullah made it clear that Saudi Arabia regarded Bahrain as "the reddest of red lines," U.S. officials dialed back their criticism.[94]

While the Obama administration waited for things to sort themselves out in the Persian Gulf, a far more explosive situation was developing on the shores of the Gulf of Sidra, where angry Libyans hoped to make Muammar Qaddafi the Arab world's next Hosni Mubarak. On 15 February 2011, just one day after Shia protestors occupied Pearl Square in Manama, rioting erupted in Benghazi, Libya's second-largest city, after Qaddafi's secret police broke up a human rights demonstration. Within days, anti-Qaddafi protests had spread throughout eastern Libya, and soon the entire country was engulfed in a full-scale civil war. Unlike Ben Ali in Tunisia or Mubarak in Egypt, Libya's self-styled "Brother Leader" had no qualms about employing massive doses of lethal force to put down the disturbances. In mid-March, Qaddafi ordered his air force to bomb and strafe Benghazi, making it clear that he intended to fulfill an earlier vow to hunt down his opponents "like rats and cockroaches."

When Team Obama could come up with nothing stronger by way of response than a no-fly zone, the president lost his temper. "Is a no-fly zone going to stop anything we just heard about from happening?" Obama bellowed. "If you're telling me that this guy is tearing through his country, about to overrun this city of seven hundred thousand people, and potentially kill thousands of people—why is the option I'm looking at one that will do nothing to stop that scenario?" After more brainstorming, he got the option he wanted—Western air strikes to prevent Qaddafi's troops from overrunning Benghazi—and quickly secured the necessary support from the UN Security Council and America's NATO allies. "If we don't act," Obama explained on 15 March, "it will have consequences for US credibility and leadership, consequences for the Arab Spring, and consequences for the international community." The United States simply could not stand by and watch Qaddafi slaughter his own people. "That's just not who we are."[95]

With the blessing of the United Nations, Operation Odyssey Dawn began a few days later. American pilots flew most of the early sorties, but soon British, French, and Italian warplanes moved into action, with the United States "leading from behind."[96] By mid-summer, the NATO air war had tilted the balance against Qaddafi, who was forced to abandon Tripoli, the Libyan capital, in August. Two months later, insurgents captured Brother Leader in a drainage ditch, shot him dead, and then posted their handiwork on the Internet.

At the same moment that U.S. policy makers were helping engineer regime change from the bottom up in Libya during a high tide for the Arab Spring, however, they could also see the low watermark emerging 1,500 miles to the east in Syria. On 15 March 2011, while the Obama administration was putting the finishing touches on plans for Operation Odyssey Dawn, a "Day of Rage" exploded in Damascus and other Syrian cities, where protestors demanded that President Bashar al-Assad begin the transition from dictatorship to democracy. A British-educated ophthalmologist who had presented himself as a reformer when he succeeded his father Hafez eleven years earlier, Bashar now revealed that he was every bit as ruthless as the Assad clan's patriarch. He let the secret police torture and maim children who spray-painted anti-regime graffiti, he sent the Syrian army into action with orders to shoot to kill unarmed demonstrators, and he warned his fellow Alawites that the opponents of the Assad regime were not aspiring democrats but rather brutal religious extremists manipulating the country's Sunni majority. By the summer of 2011, Bashar had set in motion a self-fulfilling prophecy, plunging Syria into a nasty civil war that looked more and more like the grisly sectarian bloodbath that had enveloped Iraq during the American occupation. Wendell Steavenson, an American journalist who arrived in Damascus in late July, likened the conflict to mob warfare, with the Assad family determined to fight to the death. "I asked three Western diplomats, separately, whether the best analogy might be the Sopranos sitting around their dining room table," she reported as the bodies began to pile up. "Each of them replied, 'Exactly!'"[97]

While Bashar al-Assad channeled his inner Tony Soprano, Team Obama struggled to square two contradictory aspects of its approach to the Arab world—encouragement for democracy and containment of radical Islam. Although Bashar exaggerated the threat posed by Sunni extremists, there were al-Qaeda members among his opponents, and as recently as February 2010 his regime had stood shoulder to shoulder with Washington in the war on terror, proposing a "blueprint" for "security and intelligence cooperation between Syria and the U.S."[98] When a reporter asked Secretary of State Clinton fifteen months later whether she would welcome the fall of the House of Assad, her reply revealed considerable ambivalence: "Depends on what replaces it."[99] The Obama administration's cautious handling of the crisis in Damascus was understandable, not just because Islamic extremists stood ready to pounce on any misstep but also because Bashar al-Assad had friends in Moscow, where Russia's once and future president Vladimir Putin was not about to allow an American-backed coalition to make the Kremlin's sole remaining client in the Arab world the next Muammar Qaddafi.

Yet Obama's indecisiveness made America's friends elsewhere in the Middle East very nervous. When Kim Ghattas, the BBC's Beirut-born State Department correspondent who had shadowed Clinton on her trips around the world, returned home to Lebanon during the summer of 2011, everyone wanted to know what Washington planned to do next door in Syria. The answer seemed to be "not much," Ghattas replied. "What do you mean there is no plan?" one of her friends retorted. "If the Americans don't have a plan, then who the hell is in charge of everything?"[100] Based on their reading of recent events in Arab capitals, top U.S. officials thought that restless and bitter Muslim millennials were most likely to be in charge. "Increasing numbers of young people unable to find work; rising income disparities; deepening anger at corruption; [and] alienation from ossified regimes," the CIA director Leon Panetta sighed, "were the underpinnings of the Arab Spring" that had ignited revolutions of rising expectations throughout the region.[101] For too long and "in too many countries, power has been concentrated in the hands of a few," Barack Obama declared on 19 May 2011, but now "the people of the Middle East and North Africa had taken their future into their own hands."[102] Echoing her boss, Hillary Clinton told a reporter that Arab autocrats were "trying to stop history, which is a fool's errand." Rather than "walk away from Saudi Arabia" or other friendly regimes, however, "we encourage consistently, both publicly and privately, reform and the protection of human rights."[103]

SEALs and Drones: Obama and the War on Terror

Just after midnight local time on 2 May 2011, two U.S. Blackhawk helicopters made history by swooping into a darkened compound in Abbottabad, Pakistan, where for several years Osama Bin Laden had been hiding in plain sight right under the noses of Washington's friends in Islamabad. In less than an hour, seventy Navy commandos from SEAL Team Six stormed the fortified villa, killed the al-Qaeda leader, and seized a treasure trove of data on laptop computers, thumb drives, and DVDs before hightailing it back to their home base in Afghanistan, one step ahead of Pakistani security forces. Operation Neptune Spear should have come as no surprise to anyone in either the Land of the Free or the Land of the Pure, for Barack Obama had long made it very clear that he would decapitate al-Qaeda if he ever got the chance. "If we have Osama bin Laden in our sights and the Pakistani government is unable or unwilling to take them out, then I think that we have to act," candidate Obama had declared during a town-hall presidential debate in Nashville in October 2008. "We will kill bin Laden; we will crush Al Qaeda."[104] After settling in at 1600 Pennsylvania Avenue three months later, President Obama made no secret that defeating al-Qaeda would require the Pakistanis to do a much more effective job policing the Pashtun no-man's-land along their border with Afghanistan. Pakistan's president Asif Ali Zardari bitterly resented allegations that his country was coddling terrorists, as did the army chief of staff Ashfaq Pervez Kayani, who warned the new administration that "if you keep suspecting and insinuating against us publicly, we will find it difficult to motivate our rank and file."[105] Denial, however, was not one of Obama's favorite words. "We need to make clear to people that the cancer is in Pakistan," he told his national security team on 25 November 2009. America must first "excise the cancer," Obama the oncologist added, and then "connect this to our counterterrorism efforts in the homeland."[106]

At the same time that the White House was stepping up pressure on Pakistan, it was toning down the us-versus-them rhetoric so central to the battle against Islamic extremism since 9/11. John Brennan, Obama's counterterrorism chief, laid out the new rationale in late 2009. "There was a tendency on the part of some to view the world through that prism—you know, are you with us or against us, black and white, this global war on terror." Yet while acknowledging "that there's still a very serious threat . . . from organizations like Al Qaeda," Brennan insisted that "what we have to do is make sure that we're not pouring fuel on the flames by the things we do."[107] In practice, this meant fewer Code Red alerts at home and more vigorous surveillance of Islamic extremists abroad. "What you've seen is a metastasizing of al Qaeda, where a range of loosely affiliated groups now have the capacity and ambition to recruit and train for attacks that may not be on the scale of 9/11, but obviously can still be extraordinary," President Obama told a reporter in July 2010. "One man, one bomb," he pointed out, "could still have, obviously, an extraordinary traumatizing effect on the homeland."[108]

For his part, Osama Bin Laden taunted Obama and vowed to wage jihad for thirty years if necessary. "How will you win a war whose cost is like a hurricane blowing violently at your economy," he sneered in an open letter to the American people in early 2010, "and which has no connection to your security?"[109] Later that year, the CIA's Counterterrorism Center (CTC) began tracking an al-Qaeda courier in Pakistan who would eventually lead them to Bin Laden. By early 2011, unarmed CIA surveillance drones had gathered enough electronic data to suggest there was a good chance that the man behind the 9/11 attacks was holed up in Abbottabad, less than a mile from the Pakistani national military academy. "This was not," CTC chief Michael Leiter told Team Obama on 28 April, "a slam dunk," and he estimated the likelihood that the CIA had finally found Bin Laden at somewhere between 40 and 70 percent. The president liked those odds. "At the end of day," he told his top advisers, "it's fifty-fifty," but this was "the best evidence we've had since Tora Bora" ten years earlier.[110] After sleeping on it, Obama decided to send SEAL Team Six into action. "I had fifty-fifty confidence that Bin Laden was there," he told the U.S. commandos afterward, "but I had one-hundred-per-cent confidence in you guys."[111] Operation Neptune Spear not only killed the al-Qaeda leader; it also revealed much about the inner workings of the world's most dangerous terrorist organization. "Bin Laden really wasn't the CEO of a multinational corporation," the CTC's Michael Leiter concluded. "He was a slightly out-of-touch coordinator of a broad, dysfunctional family, who were frankly operating more on their own agendas than his agenda."[112] It was still good to have him dead.

Although the Navy SEALs captured most of the headlines, the CIA's Predator drones proved an equally important tool for disabling Bin Laden's dysfunctional family and curtailing the al-Qaeda threat. Armed with small but lethal Hellfire missiles and flown by "pilots" at video consoles half a world away in the Nevada desert, Predators had become the Obama administration's weapon of choice in Afghanistan and Pakistan by May 2011. During his first twenty-eight months in office, Obama authorized two hundred drone strikes, five times as many as his predecessor had approved in eight years. Targets included terrorist training camps, high-profile figures in the Afghan and Pakistani Taliban, and al-Qaeda militants. In Pakistan alone, the death toll stood at 2,200, including at least 400 civilians with no connection to Islamic extremism. Despite such collateral damage, however, the Obama White House found remote-control drone warfare very attractive, not only because it minimized American casualties but also because it maximized the element of surprise. For their part, the people of Afghanistan and Pakistan bitterly resented the Predators, which rained sudden death indiscriminately from the sky, violated national sovereignty, and humiliated Presidents Hamid Karzai and Asif Ali Zardari, both of whom threatened to sever relations with the United States over the drone attacks.

The Obama administration responded by throttling back drone warfare in Central Asia—there were just forty-eight Predator strikes in Pakistan during 2012—while expanding remote-control attacks in Yemen, which soared from eighteen in 2011 to eighty-three the following year. The shift from Pakistan to Yemen reflected growing White House concern about al-Qaeda in the Arabian Peninsula (AQAP), a franchise operation determined to destabilize the monarchy next door in Saudi Arabia. Its leader was Anwar al-Awlaki, an American-born cleric whose fiery calls to strike targets inside the United States had inspired Nidal Malik Hasan, an army psychiatrist who killed thirteen GIs at Fort Hood, Texas, in November 2009, and Umar Farouk Abdulmutallab, the Nigerian "Underwear Bomber" who tried to blow up an American jetliner over Detroit six weeks later on Christmas Day. "Jihad," Awlaki declared from his hideout near the Yemeni border with Saudi Arabia in March 2010, "is becoming as American as apple pie and as British as afternoon tea."[113] Eighteen months later, Awlaki and three other AQAP members died when a Reaper drone, the Predator's larger and more powerful cousin, hit their SUV with Hellfire missiles in northern Yemen. Determined to refute President Ali Abdullah Saleh's grim prophecy that his country was about to become the next Somalia, Washington escalated its drone war in Yemen during the autumn of 2011, killing dozens of AQAP fighters and several civilians, including Anwar al-Awlaki's sixteen-year-old son, Abdurahman, a U.S. citizen born in Denver, Colorado, who according to the *New York Times* "had no connection to terrorism."[114]

When Saleh was forced to step down in February 2012 after sustaining severe injuries in a terrorist attack, his successor, Abd Rabbuh Mansur al-Hadi, agreed to expand the drone war. The body count soared during the next six months, with CIA Predators and Reapers pounding suspected terrorist bases in so-called signature strikes that left more than six hundred dead. U.S. officials tried hard to limit collateral damage and claimed that 85 percent of those killed in the drone strikes were militants, but critics suspected that the body counters had in effect resurrected and revised a gruesome rule of thumb from the Vietnam War: "If it's dead and it's Muslim, it's AQAP." In May 2012, the *New York Times* revealed that the White House maintained a top-secret "kill list" of high-value al-Qaeda targets, that President Obama himself reviewed and approved every drone attack in Yemen, and that he personally authorized approximately one-third of the Predator and Reaper strikes in Pakistan. Relying on classic "just war theory," Obama and his counterterrorism chief John Brennan simply went down a list that some-times included a few American citizens and decided who should live and who should die. Most decisions were difficult, but some were not. "This is an easy one," the president allegedly remarked moments before a CIA drone killed Anwar al-Awlaki on 30 September 2011.[115]

Some on Capitol Hill wondered, however, whether these targeted kill-ings violated the ban on assassinations that Congress had imposed three decades earlier. The State Department's legal adviser Harold Koh, a consti-tutional scholar who had previously served as dean of the Yale Law School, insisted that the Obama White House had put appropriate safeguards in place. "If John Brennan is the last guy in the room with the president, I'm comfortable, because Brennan is a person of genuine moral rectitude," Koh assured reporters. "It's as though you had a priest with extremely strong moral values who was suddenly charged with leading a war."[116] Skeptics nevertheless questioned the morality of targeted killings when America was not actually at war and worried that officials responsible for promoting homeland security might be tempted to authorize drone strikes inside the United States.[117]

Although the White House downplayed the potential threat to civil liberties at home as far-fetched and highlighted the grim effectiveness of the Reapers abroad, remote-control warfare sparked a backlash among those on the receiving end of the drone strikes and undermined Obama's efforts to improve relations with the Muslim world. Pakistani women in hijabs picketed the U.S. embassy in Islamabad clad in T-shirts showing a Predator emblazoned with the "universal symbol for no"—a red circle with a backslash. Anti-American protests erupted in Yemen, where clerics claimed that the United States was not battling terrorism but rather waging war on Islam. In Afghanistan, suicide attacks on American military instal-lations frequently followed drone strikes against Taliban guerillas. When Israel used a homegrown version of the Predator to assassinate high-ranking members of Hamas in Gaza, Palestinians connected the dots and blamed the United States. Some American Muslims evidently embraced the ancient motto "don't get mad, get even." Faisal Shahzad, a South Asian immigrant who tried but failed to blow up Times Square in May 2010, justified his deci-sion to target ordinary New Yorkers by pointing to the hundreds of civilian casualties in his native Pakistan. "When the drones hit," he told a packed courtroom in Manhattan, "they don't see children."[118]

Despite the anti-American backlash among the peoples of the Middle East, Obama regarded his "Drones and SEALs" approach to combatting terrorism as an important asset in his bid for a second term. In keeping with his nickname, "No Drama Obama" had no qualms about employing deadly force against terrorists like Bin Laden or Awlaki, but he avoided alarmist rhetoric and took quiet pride in having kept America safe. "One of the things for which I am proudest of this administration is that we haven't demagogued these issues," he told his top aides at the height of the controversy over the kill lists in the summer of 2012. "We haven't been playing to people's fears and we haven't been playing politics with terrorism."[119]

Obama's Republican critics, on the other hand, had made much of his lack of foreign policy experience during the 2008 campaign and claimed that as president, he seemed to believe that diplomacy was synonymous with apology, especially when it came to the Muslim world. Mitt Romney, the rich and smug management consultant who hoped to unseat Obama in November 2012, had conjured up the bogeyman of radical Islam again and again during his marathon quest to secure the GOP nomination. "It's this century's nightmare. Jihadism—violent, radical Islamic fundamentalism," Romney intoned during a television ad as early as April 2010. "Their goal is to unite the world under a single jihadist caliphate. To do that, they must collapse freedom-loving nations like us."[120] He repeatedly accused Obama of conducting an "apology tour" across the Middle East that left America vulnerable to Islamic terrorism and of blaming Israel instead of the Palestinians for the stalemated peace process in the Holy Land.

When Islamic extremists sacked and burned the U.S. consulate in Benghazi, Libya, on 11 September 2012, killing Ambassador Christopher Stevens and three other Americans, Romney was sorely tempted to say, "I rest my case." Eager to prevent the tragedy from becoming an issue in the final weeks of the presidential election campaign, the White House claimed that most of the Libyan attackers had been inspired by an American-made Islamophobic video that had gone viral, which was true, and that none of the Libyan attackers was connected to al-Qaeda, which was not. In July 2012, anti-Islam activists in California had posted a fourteen-minute clip on YouTube, purportedly from a full-length video titled *The Innocence of Muslims*, which depicted the Prophet Mohammed as a bisexual imposter who surrounded himself with thugs and whores. The video itself was so poorly made that almost no one noticed it until Morris Sadek, an Egyptian American Coptic Christian and vocal critic of the Muslim Brotherhood living in northern Virginia, e-mailed a link to friends in Cairo, who forwarded it to other Arab capitals. By early September, angry mobs gathered outside U.S. diplomatic facilities throughout the region, lighting the fuse for the explosion in Benghazi.[121] When reporters caught up with Steven Klein, a self-styled "radical Muslim hunter" who had helped promote the video, at his home southeast of Los Angeles, he claimed to have visited "every Mosque in California" and to have encountered "500 to 750 of these people who are future suicide bombers and murderers." Sipping a Coors Light, Klein asked: "What do I get out of this? I get to die one of these days hoping my granddaughters and my grandsons will be safe from these monsters."[122]

Even without the incendiary actions of Sadek and Klein, however, Islamic extremism was surging through North Africa, where Libyan jihadis who had recently fought alongside anti-American insurgents in Iraq were returning home to challenge their secular rivals. In the immediate aftermath of the deaths of the four Americans in Benghazi, White House officials publicly emphasized the spontaneity of the assault, which they linked to the inflammatory video. Privately, however, U.S. policy makers were well aware that "Islamic extremists with ties to al-Qaeda participated in the attack," something that the talking points prepared by the State Department failed to acknowledge.[123] Twenty-four hours after the carnage, the president himself mourned those who died in Benghazi without mentioning either al-Qaeda or the Islamophobic video. "Yesterday was already a painful day for our nation as we marked the solemn memory of the 9/11 attacks," Obama told a gaggle of reporters gathered in the Rose Garden on 12 September 2012, but "no acts of terror will ever shake the resolve of this great nation." Vowing that America would never cut and run, Obama instructed the CIA to deploy Predator drones in the skies over eastern Libya.

Underwhelmed by all this, Mitt Romney chided the Obama administration, not only for failing to take adequate precautions prior to the attack in Benghazi but also for implying afterward that anti-Muslim activists in America had provoked the jihadists. Out on the stump, the GOP nominee accused President Obama of covering up a series of State Department miscues in Libya to conceal a larger truth—that the policy of contagement toward the Muslim world was misguided and dangerous. During a nationally televised debate on 17 October, however, Romney went too far, insisting that his opponent had refused to call the assault on Benghazi what it was—an act of terror—only to appear foolish when the moderator quoted from the transcript of the president's news conference in the Rose Garden a month earlier. By splitting hairs about the meaning of the word "terror," Romney not only failed to brand Obama as weak or dishonest, he also made himself seem petty and insensitive. When polls showed that undecided voters were paying almost no attention to the events in Benghazi, Romney's advisers ratcheted back their attack ads. In the end, terrorism proved only a minor issue on 6 November, when the president won a second term by a comfortable margin.

Nevertheless, there was growing uneasiness both on Main Street and on Capitol Hill, where many Americans wondered whether Obama's reliance on "SEALs and Drones," and his tilt toward the us-versus-them thinking that justified their use, were increasing rather than decreasing the threat posed by radical Islam. While U.S. casualties in Afghanistan fell from 418 in 2011 to 310 in 2012 as the Obama administration made good on its promise to end U.S. ground combat operations on schedule, CIA drone strikes nearly doubled during the same period from 294 to 506, prompting Taliban insurgents to respond with increasingly deadly suicide attacks directed at American targets.[124] The abrupt decline in drone warfare in the skies over Pakistan's Northwest Frontier Province during 2012 did little to reduce anti-Americanism on the streets of Karachi and Lahore, where angry protestors chanted the Urdu equivalent of "Yankee Go Home," or in the corridors of power in Islamabad, where President Zardari fumed.[125]

The new year would bring even more disturbing news. On 1 February 2013, the U.S. embassy in Ankara, Turkey, was demolished in a suicide attack that prompted much speculation as to whether the bomber was a Marxist or an Islamist.[126] Ten weeks later, two Chechen immigrants inspired by the Yemeni jihadist Anwar al-Awlaki used pressure cookers packed with black powder and roofing nails to wreak havoc during the Boston Marathon, killing three and injuring nearly two hundred. "The U.S. Government is killing our innocent civilians," nineteen-year-old Dzhokar Tsarnaev scrawled on the hull of the boat where he was hiding just before police captured him on 19 April; "I can't stand to see such evil go unpunished, we Muslims are one body, you hurt one you hurt us all."[127] Although the motives of the Brothers Tsarnaev remain murky, clearly the American homeland was not entirely safe from terrorism. Neither were Algeria or Mali, where al-Qaeda in the Islamic Maghreb staged hit-and-run attacks against secular governments supported by the United States during the first months of 2013.[128]

As he began his second term, Obama knew that his ambitious plan to improve relations with the Muslim world by reinventing U.S. foreign policy remained very much a work in progress. The first black man in the White House had promised that new faces and new ideas would produce a new beginning in the Middle East, and he worked hard to replace

George W. Bush's strategy of rogue state rollback with contagement—a more nuanced approach that combined elements of containment and engagement. By making dialogue rather than confrontation the centerpiece of his landmark speech at Cairo University, by keeping his promise to pull U.S. troops out of Iraq, and by gradually scaling back America's military footprint in Afghanistan, Obama signaled that Uncle Sam was less likely to shoot first and ask questions later. Team Obama also made a good-faith effort to restart the stalemated Palestinian-Israeli peace process and edged toward the right side of history when friendly tyrants came under fire in Tunisia, Egypt, and Yemen.

Nevertheless, abroad as well as at home, Barack Obama soon learned that promising people change that they could believe in was much easier than delivering it. By insisting that Prime Minister Benjamin Netanyahu freeze all settlement activity on the West Bank and then backing down under pressure from AIPAC, the president managed to aggravate both Israelis and Palestinians. By indulging in the rhetoric of reform from the bottom up, Obama helped unleash a revolution of rising expectations among Iranians and Arabs and left himself open to charges of hypocrisy when the cold calculus of realpolitik ruled out U.S. intervention in Tehran, Manama, and Damascus. Most troubling of all, by relying on SEALs and drones to do its dirty work, the Obama administration risked triggering a new wave of anti-Americanism throughout the Middle East that played into the hands of Islamophobic hate groups who claimed to have uncovered a vast Muslim conspiracy to destroy America.

CHAPTER SIX

Revelations

Islamophobia, the Green Threat, and a
New Cold War in the Middle East?

On a cloudy Tuesday afternoon in May 2015, Barack Obama sat down with Jeffrey Goldberg of the *Atlantic* to discuss the Middle East. The Islamic State in Iraq and Syria (ISIS), a ruthless band of Sunni thugs determined to establish a new caliphate, had just overrun Ramadi, sixty miles west of Baghdad. The deadline for U.S. negotiators to strike a deal with Iran to prevent the Islamic Republic from acquiring nuclear weapons was just six weeks away. And the Israeli prime minister Benjamin Netanyahu was still basking in the glow of his recent trip up Capitol Hill, where he had delivered a blistering attack on Obama for being soft on radical Islam. Despite all this, the president insisted that "I don't think we're losing." To be sure, "you have a Middle East that is turbulent and chaotic, and where extremists seem to be full of enthusiasm and momentum" from Syria to Yemen. Yet the president downplayed the fall of Ramadi and assured Goldberg that "ISIL has been significantly degraded."[1]

The prospect of more boots on the ground left Obama cold. For their part, Republicans claimed that he had "overlearned the mistake of Iraq" and that "just because the 2003 invasion did not go well doesn't argue that we shouldn't go back in." The president, however, remained convinced that it had been a huge error to think that "if we simply went in and deposed a dictator . . . and cleared out the bad guys, that somehow peace and prosperity would automatically emerge." Rather than sending in the Eighty-Second Airborne, America must "find effective partners" among Muslim moderates while working with Israel to confront the extremists. Viewing the world through the lens of us versus them only led to more military conflict and religious persecution. "When you are objectifying them and making them the Other," Obama explained, "you are destroying something in yourself, and the world goes into a tailspin."[2]

Nevertheless, as President Obama headed into the second half of his second term, many Americans worried that their country was heading into a diplomatic tailspin. A poll released by the Pew Research Center on 21 May 2015 showed that only 37 percent of the public approved of Obama's foreign policies.[3] Despite having vowed to put America "on the right side of history" during the Arab Spring, Obama had proven powerless to stop the wave of Islamic insurgencies sweeping much of the Arab world and chose to look the other way when the Egyptian army deposed a freely elected Islamist government in Cairo and Israel cracked down on Hamas in Gaza. More often than not, the president's personal efforts to engage Muslim moderates while relying on covert action and drone warfare to contain Muslim radicals merely confused both friend and foe, without winning much popular support on Main Street.

Even if conceptual shortcomings and poor execution had not hobbled Obama's ambitious initiatives in the Middle East, a complex new approach like "contagement" would have been no match for the surge of xenophobia coursing through U.S. popular culture. Resonating with the us-versus-them dialectic that had been a central feature of America's worldview for more than three centuries, radical Islam had come to embody the existential threat posed by a long line of bogeymen from Native Americans and African slaves to Nazis and Bolsheviks. Despite repeated assurances after 9/11 that Uncle Sam was not at war with Islam, American Muslims frequently found themselves treated like subversives. Before long, New York City police officers were staking out mosques and Islamic community centers in the Big Apple, while cyber-spooks at the National Security Agency monitored the e-mail and phone calls of Muslim activists categorized as "Mohammed Ragheads."[4] Hollywood attracted huge audiences by presenting fictionalized Islamic radicals, some homegrown and some from overseas, as relentless and implacable fiends determined to bring America to its knees via far-fetched plots involving sleeper cells and mind control. Meanwhile, right-wing bloggers and ultraconservative shock jocks spread bizarre conspiracy theories via the Internet and talk radio.

The fall of the Berlin Wall in November 1989 may have freed most Americans from four decades of Cold War high anxiety, but twenty-five years later many had fallen under the spell of a new ideology at least as potent as anticommunism—Islamophobia—a powerful cocktail of political, racial, and cultural assumptions that signaled a shift from Code Red to Code Green, the color of Islam. After 1945, the taint of Marxism-Leninism had encouraged the White House to designate popular governments in Latin America, Africa, and the Middle East as fair game for CIA covert action and had enabled the FBI to bully and smear left-wing radicals at home as fellow travelers or Soviet stooges. After 2001, the specter of radical Islam encouraged U.S. policy makers to regard movements for political change and social justice in the Muslim world with grave suspicion and enabled the Justice Department to treat critics of U.S. policies in Iraq or Afghanistan as potential terrorists under the auspices of the Patriot Act.

One of the most disturbing symptoms of the "green scare" was the growing number of Americans who insisted that their president was a Muslim—one of them, not one of us. After all, Obama did rhyme with Osama, and that unusual middle name—Hussein—did evoke memories of Saddam. Meanwhile, Tea Party zealots branded Obama as a "socialist" whose hatred of capitalism allegedly rivaled Lenin's. Once the jockeying for positon for the 2016 presidential election began in earnest, contenders from both sides of the aisle called for a post-Obama foreign policy that treated radical Islam the same way that Cold War leaders from Truman through Reagan had treated international communism. The merger of the Red and Green Threats recalled America's original encounter with an existential menace, when English settlers and Wampanoag warriors waged war without mercy in the wilderness of colonial Massachusetts.

Facing West: The Metaphysics of Indian-Hating and Other Racial Pathologies

Among the most controversial postmortems of the 9/11 attacks was Susan Faludi's *The Terror Dream*. Six years after the Twin Towers fell, Faludi compared contemporary Islamic extremists like Osama Bin Laden to Native American raiders from the past and likened George W. Bush to such "Cowboys of Yesterday" as John Wayne, who in John Ford's iconic Western, *The Searchers*, rescued us (and our women) from them. The "global war on terrorism" was merely the latest incarnation of four hundred years of combat with demonic others that began when the Puritans first encountered hostile Indian tribes in the forests of New England.[5] Long before 9/11, of course, historians like Richard Drinnon had detected a strong connection between what Herman Melville called "the metaphysics of Indian-hating" and more recent U.S. foreign policy, which combined frontier-style hypermasculinity with Anglo-Saxon racism to produce a lethal doctrine of counterinsurgency from colonial America to modern Southeast Asia.[6]

As early as 1630, John Winthrop claimed to have founded Massachusetts Bay colony not only to secure religious freedom for his Puritan followers but also to civilize the native inhabitants of North America. Four decades later, however, the Wampanoag chief Metacom, who called himself "King Philip," launched a bloody war against Winthrop's descendants, burning dozens of

New England towns to the ground and killing hundreds of English colonists.[7] The Puritan bard Philip Walker confirmed the terrifying legacy of King Phillip's War most succinctly in a poem he wrote shortly after the killing stopped in September 1676. "The murthres Rooges like wild Arabians thay," Walker observed long before Faludi connected the Algonquians with al-Qaeda, "lurke heare & there of every thing make prey."[8]

During the following two hundred years, American leaders worked relentlessly to drive "murderous rogues" like Metacom ever westward to secure an open frontier for white settlement. The most ruthless Indian fighter of all was General Andrew Jackson, whom the Creeks nicknamed "Sharp Knife" after militiamen under his command slaughtered nearly two thousand warriors and their families at Horseshoe Bend just north of Mobile, Alabama, in 1814. Sharp Knife saw Native Americans as "savages" and "barbarians" who must be relocated as soon as possible. "Our national security require it and *their* security require it," he explained on the eve of the Horseshoe Bend massacre.[9] Promoting national security would be the chief rationale not only for General Jackson's scorched-earth campaign against the Seminoles in Spanish Florida in 1818 but also for President Jackson's endorsement of the Indian Removal Act of 1830 and for former president Jackson's approval of the expulsion of the Cherokees from Georgia eight years later.

As the Cherokees trudged along their Trail of Tears, the locus of the Red Threat shifted to the arid borderlands between Texas and California, where Comanche and Kiowa warriors resisted white encroachment. The ensuing cycle of violence triggered the slaughter of thousands of Indians and Mexicans and culminated in America's invasion of Mexico in 1846. Few have captured the us-versus-them aspect of this episode better than novelist Cormac McCarthy, whose masterpiece *Blood Meridian* offers a chilling portrait of a renegade army captain who led a band of gringo marauders on a rampage through the no-man's-land of northern Mexico in the 1850s. "What we are dealing with," the captain said, "is a race of degenerates. A mongrel race, little better than niggers. And maybe no better." Promoting American security was futile in such an environment. "There is no government in Mexico," the captain concluded. "We are dealing with people manifestly incapable of governing themselves. And do you know what happens with people who cannot govern themselves? That's right. Others come in to govern for them."[10]

While Indian-hating and Mexican-bashing were central features of Uncle Sam's quest to build a continental empire and govern the ungovernable, nothing was more terrifying for white Americans, especially south of the Mason-Dixon Line, than the "black threat"—the possibility that "degenerate" African American slaves would rise up, slay their masters, and rape their masters' wives. The worst white fears, however, would materialize not in British North America but rather in the French colony of Saint-Domingue, as Haiti was then known, where a free black overseer named Toussaint Louverture launched an armed rebellion in 1791 and demanded "liberty, equality, and fraternity" for the island's four hundred thousand African slaves. After French troops captured Toussaint eleven years later, his chief lieutenant, Jean-Jacques Dessalines, unleashed a reign of terror that presented the island's white population with two options—exile or death. Thousands of French refugees fled to the United States, where their tales of African savagery horrified American slave owners and touched off a black scare throughout the South.

Determined to contain any Haitian contagion, most southern states banned the importation of slaves from Saint-Domingue during the early nineteenth century. Nevertheless, the legend of Toussaint Louverture inspired African Americans like Denmark Vesey, a free black carpenter born in the West Indies who was hanged in 1822 after local officials uncovered his plan to wipe out the master class in South Carolina, and Nat Turner, a self-taught slave minister who launched a rebellion in Southampton County, Virginia, that claimed sixty white lives in 1831. "The day is not far distant," the African American novelist William Wells Brown predicted in 1855, "when the revolution of St. Domingo will be reenacted in South Carolina and Louisiana."[11] Not long afterward, a very different Brown—the messianic white abolitionist John—would attempt to fulfill the novelist's prophecy by raiding the federal arsenal at Harpers Ferry, Virginia, to capture weapons necessary to launch a slave insurrection.

Alarmed by the specters of Haiti and Harpers Ferry, by early 1861 eleven slave states would secede from the Union, adding a south-versus-north dimension to the older us-versus-them paradigm. During the Civil War, more than 140,000 black men fled plantation life and joined the Union Army as it swept through the South, determined to achieve "self-emancipation" as in Saint-Domingue. "The name of Toussaint L'Ouverture has been passed from mouth to mouth until it has become a household word," one Union chaplain reported after encountering hundreds of fugitive slaves at Port Royal, South Carolina. "It has been felt that if it was right for the colored Haytiens to fight to be free, it is equally right for colored Americans."[12] Horrified by the prospect of living alongside freed blacks after Appomattox, white militants established the Knights of the Ku Klux Klan in 1866, terrorizing former slaves, thwarting halfhearted efforts by the White House to promote racial equality, and ushering in a century of Jim Crow. As he prepared to bring down the curtain on Reconstruction in early 1877, the newly elected president Rutherford B. Hayes evidently persuaded himself that the Klan's concerns about the black threat were not without foundation. "Conciliating Southern whites," Hayes concluded, was more important than stationing federal troops throughout the South to "protect the colored people."[13]

Uncertain whether blacks could be integrated into postwar America, President Hayes was also very skeptical about the three hundred thousand Chinese immigrants who had recently arrived on the West Coast to provide cheap labor to complete the transcontinental railroads. During the 1870s, white workers decried the "yellow peril" and demanded restrictions on further immigration. The man in the White House proved quite sympathetic. "The present Chinese labor invasion (it is not in any proper sense immigration—women and children do not come) is pernicious and should be discouraged," Hayes remarked in 1879. "Our experience in dealing with the weaker races—the Negroes and Indians, for example—is not encouraging."[14] Three years later, Congress obliged by passing the Chinese Exclusion Act, which banned all immigration from the Middle Kingdom and prevented Chinese already in the United States from obtaining American citizenship.

The second wave of immigrants who headed east across the Pacific from Japan would prove far more problematic. Unlike the Chinese, the Japanese usually came in family groups, they frequently possessed the financial resources necessary to compete with white Americans, and their homeland was rapidly emerging as Uncle Sam's chief rival in East Asia. By the early twentieth century, nearly fifty thousand Japanese immigrants had arrived, prompting fresh warnings about the yellow peril from Honolulu to San Francisco. Startled by the military prowess that the Japanese demonstrated by defeating Russia in 1904, President Theodore Roosevelt remarked privately that if "Japan seriously starts in to reorganize China and makes headway, there will result a real shifting of the center of equilibrium as far as the white races are concerned."[15] As Roosevelt feared, Japan wasted little time making serious headway at China's expense, seizing the Shantung peninsula in 1915, invading Manchuria in 1931, and soon thereafter threatening the colonial possessions of Britain, France, the Netherlands, and the United States. Then on 7 December 1941, Emperor Hirohito and General Hideki Tojo became the latest them in a long line of fiendish enemies, stretching from King Philip to Toussaint Louverture, who were bent on doing us serious harm. Japan's attack on Pearl Harbor would trigger a race war to end all race wars in the Western Pacific and pave the way for the internment of 125,000 Japanese Americans in detention camps that resembled slave quarters or Indian reservations.

Facing East: America Encounters the Islamic Other

On the eve of World War II, Americans were well acquainted with the red and the black threats as well as the yellow peril, but they paid little attention to the Muslim world. What the U.S. public knew about Islam was based largely on what they read about Aladdin, Sindbad, and Ali Baba in Scheherazade's *One Thousand and One Nights*, what they heard about the heroic Christian Crusaders who had once upon a time tried to liberate the Holy Land from the infidels, and what they recalled about the Barbary Wars, when Muslim pirates disrupted commerce in the Mediterranean and held several hundred American citizens hostage along the shores of Tripoli. The Founding Fathers regarded Islam as especially repellent because it allegedly stifled the imagination, stultified the intellect, and bred fatalism. Indeed, for statesmen from Thomas Jefferson to Theodore Roosevelt, the Muslim world constituted the very antithesis of John Winthrop's "city upon a hill," and the sins of Turkey's Ottoman Empire in particular—its reactionary royalism and its repression of Armenians and other religious minorities—confirmed that despotism and democracy were incompatible. "It is impossible to expect moral, intellectual and material well-being," Roosevelt remarked privately in 1907, "where Mohammedanism is supreme."[16]

The many ordinary Americans—a handful of explorers, hundreds of churchmen, and thousands of tourists—who actually traveled to the Middle East prior to World War I found little to contradict Roosevelt's harsh verdict. John Ledyard, a Connecticut Yankee who became the Indiana Jones of early America, marveled at Egypt's pyramids and great stone pharaohs but warned Thomas Jefferson that Muslims were "a superstitious, warlike set of vagabonds."[17] Inspired but frustrated by the challenge of spreading the gospel among Native Americans, missionaries like Eli Smith encountered even greater obstacles when they arrived in the Middle East, where the "arrogance and cruelty of Mohammedans" and the deceit and dishonesty of Ottoman officials made being rebuffed by Creeks or Cherokees seem tame by comparison.[18] Mark Twain, whose acerbic wit and acid tongue were legendary, accompanied a small band of self-styled American pilgrims to the Holy Land in 1867 and published a scathing account of the affair two years later that sold half a million copies. No fan of what would later be called "cultural imperialism," he lambasted his fellow travelers for throwing around their weight and their money. "He went through this peaceful land," Twain wrote of one well-armed sentimental pilgrim, "with one hand on his revolver, and the other on his pocket-handkerchief." Yet Twain also regarded the Muslims of Syria, Egypt, and Palestine as insolent and untrustworthy barbarians. "They reminded me much of Indians, did these people," he recalled later. "They sat in silence, and with tireless patience watched over every motion with that vile, uncomplaining impoliteness which is so truly Indian, and which makes a white man so nervous and uncomfortable and savage that he wants to exterminate the whole tribe."[19]

The collapse of the Ottoman Empire after World War I triggered rising expectations among Arabs and other non-Turkish Muslims, who were eager to win their independence and prove Twain and Roosevelt wrong. Among the first Americans to take notice was Lothrop Stoddard, a self-proclaimed expert on foreign affairs who applied Roosevelt's theory of Anglo-Saxon superiority to the Middle East in *The New World of Islam*, which became a must-read in 1921. Enthralled by European empire-building, Stoddard endorsed "the white man's burden" as a noble undertaking. "Given two worlds at such different levels as East and West at the beginning of the nineteenth century—the West overflowing with vitality and striding at the forefront of human progress, the East sunk in lethargy and decrepitude, it was a foregone conclusion that the former would encroach on the latter," he explained. For their part, Muslims responded by developing a "blind hatred of Western civilization," which played into the hands of militant "Pan Islamists," who were relying on "ultramodern concepts like feminism, socialism, [and] Bolshevism" to "stir up the fanatic passions of the ignorant masses." Russia's new Soviet leaders believed that "the golden opportunities vouchsafed them in the East" would pave the way for an unholy alliance between communism and Islamic radicalism. "Suffice it to remember here," Stoddard concluded, "that Bolshevik propaganda is an important element in the profound ferment which extends over the whole Near and Middle East."[20] Predictably, such an unapologetic brief for Anglo-Saxon domination drew considerable public attention. *The New World of Islam* won praise in the pages of the *American Historical Review* in January 1922, for example, as "remarkably illuminating and reliable," while nine months later President Warren G. Harding urged Americans to "take the time to read and ponder" one of Stoddard's earlier books, *The Rising Tide of Color*, which argued for racial separation at home and abroad.[21]

Stoddard's unified field theory highlighting the grave threat posed by Islamo-bolshevism would be called into question later in the decade by the more sympathetic and romantic portrait of the Muslim world that T. E. Lawrence offered in his best-selling *Seven Pillars of Wisdom*. A dashing British officer who had helped Sharif Hussein of Mecca launch an Arab revolt against the Turks during World War I, "Lawrence of Arabia" revealed Muslims to be a good deal more complex than Stoddard had allowed— puritanical but not xenophobic, bold but not fanatical, loyal but not entirely trustworthy. Yet surprisingly, few Americans had any direct contact with Islam prior to World War II. The Muslim immigrant population never exceeded two hundred thousand, and most of it clustered near much larger Arab American Christian communities in southeastern Michigan and north-western Ohio. As a result, the most visible Muslims in America belonged to the Nation of Islam, a black radical organization founded in 1930, which claimed a quarter of a million members by the end of the decade and whose leader, Elijah Muhammad, more closely resembled a stock character from one of Stoddard's screeds than a heroic freedom fighter from *Seven Pillars of Wisdom*. Indeed, an African American nationalist who embraced militant Islam was the ultimate nightmare for white America, as Muhammad discovered in 1942, when he was sentenced to four years in prison for sedition after urging his followers to resist the draft and to support Japan's war against U.S. imperialism.[22]

American officials would get their first sustained look at Arabs and Islam during World War II, and what they saw accorded more with Stoddard's version than with Lawrence's. Two weeks after Pearl Harbor, Franklin D. Roosevelt received a report titled "Axis Propaganda in the Moslem World," prepared by the newly established Office of Strategic Services (OSS), the predecessor to the CIA, warning him that German and Italian influence was growing in the Middle East. "The Arab," OSS Middle East watchers explained, "is a born dissenter and a lover of intrigue" who dreamed of living in an independent state free from British or French colonialism, "a miniature Reich with its Fuhrer or Duce" wielding "absolute power."[23] A year later on the eve of Operation Torch, the Anglo-American invasion of North Africa that counted heavily on tacit support from local Muslims to dislodge the Nazi occupation, General Dwight Eisenhower ordered U.S. aircraft to drop Arabic-language leaflets across Algeria exhorting the "sons of the Mughreb" to join "the great Jihad of freedom" alongside Uncle Sam's "Holy Warriors."[24] Privately, Eisenhower expressed considerable frustration. "Arabs are a very uncertain quantity, explosive and full of prejudices" he told his wife, Mamie, on 27 November 1942. "Many things done here that look queer are just to keep the Arabs from blazing up into revolt."[25]

Hollywood echoed Eisenhower's grim assessment of the Muslim world. *The Perils of Nyoka*, a Saturday afternoon serial that premiered in 1942, showed Arab warriors in Native American war paint waging jihad against "white infidels" from the United States. *The Desert Hawk*, another fifteen-episode cliffhanger from the summer of 1944, depicted Arabs as "treacherous dogs" who traded slaves, raped women, and tortured non-believers. Full-length B movies with bigger budgets and a broader audience focused on alleged ties between the Arabs and the Axis powers. *Adventure in Iraq*, a Warner Brothers potboiler released in 1943, saw an American pilot and his pretty English sidekick team up to outsmart a pro-German sheik and his "fanatical devil-worshipping" followers. A year later, RKO delivered *Action in Arabia*, a forgettable five-reeler originally titled *The Fanatic of the Fez*, which featured a journalist working undercover for U.S. intelligence in Damascus to prevent Syrian thugs from aligning themselves with "the new saviors of Islam—the Nazis."[26]

As the real-life fighting dragged on, the Roosevelt administration wondered whether Hollywood had captured an essential truth about the Muslim world. George Kennan, who had been appalled by Stalin's show trials and other evidence of "oriental despotism" in Moscow prior to the war, found more of the same during a brief stopover in Baghdad in late 1943. Despite Britain's efforts to keep its Iraqi protectorate Nazi-free, Kennan was struck by the "selfishness and stupidity" of the local Arabs, who seemed "inclined to all manner of religious bigotry and fanaticism."[27] An OSS report from May 1944 predicted that the Soviets would pose a bigger threat than the Nazis once the shooting stopped, because "the USSR is enjoying a rising curve of popularity throughout the entire Arab world" due to its support for "nationalist aspirations" from North Africa to the Persian Gulf.[28] The OSS experts did not mention Palestine, but one American diplomat who met with FDR's successor eighteen months later to discuss the Middle East did. All the Arabs, George Wadsworth, the U.S. ambassador to Saudi Arabia, warned Harry Truman in November 1945, were expecting America's help in ending colonial rule and resisting Zionism. "If the United States fails them," Wadsworth prophesied, "they will turn to Russia and will be lost to our civilization."[29] The February 1946 issue of *Intelligence Review*, the Pentagon's in-house journal of foreign affairs, included "Islam: A Threat to World Stability," which echoed Wadsworth's concerns. Claiming that Muslims had "an inferiority complex" that made them "restless" and "unpredictable," the article concluded that because of "the strategic position of the Moslem world," the entire region constituted "a potential threat to world peace."[30]

Once the Cold War began to heat up during the late 1940s, however, U.S. national security managers paid little attention to the potential Green Threat of Islam because they were preoccupied with the Red Threat of international communism. Harry Truman and his secretary of state, Dean Acheson, had read enough history to draw some parallels between Muslim expansion during the Middle Ages and the spread of bolshevism during their own time, but they were reluctant to launch a crusade against the Kremlin and opted instead for the containment of Soviet power as spelled out in NSC-68. Truman's successor briefly toyed with rolling back the Iron Curtain during the mid-1950s, but in the end Eisenhower shied away from the brinksmanship favored by his secretary of state, John Foster Dulles, and rededicated his administration to containing communism, which in the Middle East also meant containing radical Arab nationalism with help from Muslim conservatives in Riyadh and Tehran. Like their predecessors in the Oval Office, neither John F. Kennedy nor Lyndon B. Johnson spent much time worrying about Islam and concentrated on shoring up containment from Suez to the Strait of Hormuz with help from the Israelis and from "good Muslims" like the Shah of Iran. Through the mid-1970s, few American policy makers noticed the religious rumblings that were beginning to reverberate through the Muslim world, largely because Richard Nixon, Gerald Ford, and Henry Kissinger had convinced themselves that containing the Kremlin and combatting its secular Arab clients remained the only game in town.

The revolution that brought down the Shah of Iran in February 1979 and the Soviet invasion of Afghanistan ten months later would change all that, forcing the Carter and Reagan administrations to consider whether it was possible simultaneously to contain communism and radical Islam, and if it was not, which posed the greater danger to American national security. Assured by U.S. intelligence that dire predictions of a global jihad were "overdrawn" and that "various Islamic groups so far show no signs of developing a leadership or philosophy that crosses national boundaries," Jimmy Carter chose to rattle sabers at Moscow while running guns to Muslim guerrillas battling the Red Army in the Hindu Kush.[31] Yet after Iranian extremists seized fifty-two U.S. diplomats with the blessing of Ayatollah Khomeini and held them hostage throughout the 1980 election campaign, Muslim-bashing threatened to replace red-baiting as America's national pastime. Assisted by a coterie of devoted Cold Warriors who would later become prominent neoconservatives, Ronald Reagan hoped to square the circle by building a "strategic consensus" composed of Israel and pro-American

Arab regimes and designed to contain both Khomeini and the Kremlin. Publicly, Reagan adopted a muscular anti-Soviet approach from Central Asia to Central America during his first term, one that often looked more like rollback than containment, and he claimed vindication in his second term after Mikhail Gorbachev unveiled glasnost and perestroika. Privately, Reagan felt that hard-line policies had paid similar dividends in the Persian Gulf, where Iran "wanted to be a fundamentalist superpower" with influence extending from Morocco to Indonesia. "We stood up & contained Iran," he told George Shultz and Colin Powell in July 1988, as we "should have done w/Hitler."[32]

When the Berlin Wall came down sixteen months later, Reagan was safely retired and clearing brush at his ranch in southern California while the new occupant of the White House pronounced containment an incontrovertible success and pondered where to steer the American ship of state in the uncharted waters of a post–Cold War world. George H. W. Bush inched beyond containment, pursuing a "status quo plus" policy toward the Kremlin that ensured that half a century of Soviet-American rivalry would expire with a whimper rather than a bang. Yet despite much loose talk about "the end of history," America's forty-first president left office in January 1993 ill at ease, not just because a "Hitler on the Euphrates" threatened U.S. access to Persian Gulf oil but because from Algeria to Iran, Islamic radicals refused to accept Washington's proposed New World Order and embraced a much older way of organizing global society. According to Bill Clinton, the goal of U.S. diplomacy was no longer to contain communism but rather to enlarge the area of freedom by expanding trade, enhancing civil society, and accelerating technological change in every corner of the globe. When dealing with the Muslim world, however, the Arkansas Democrat proposed what amounted to old wine in new bottles and followed a policy of dual containment that may have kept Islamic militants in Tehran and secular radicals in Baghdad off balance but that did nothing to address the emerging threat posed by stateless Muslim extremists like Osama Bin Laden. After the 9/11 attacks convinced Clinton's successor that radical Islam could not be contained, George W. Bush would launch a global war on terror based on a strategy of rogue state rollback in Afghanistan and Iraq that many Muslims were quick to interpret as the second coming of the Crusades. Dubya's successor was left to pick up the pieces after the attempt to export democracy at gunpoint backfired, but Barack Obama's attempt to combine containment and engagement would find little favor in Middle America or the Middle East.

The Metaphysics of Muslim-Hating
in Contemporary America

On 10 March 2011, sixty years after Senator Joseph McCarthy, a Wisconsin demagogue who created his own "ism," claimed to have uncovered a communist "conspiracy so immense" as to jeopardize the very survival of the United States, Peter King, a Republican congressman from Long Island, convened the House Committee on Homeland Security to determine whether America faced a similar danger in the twenty-first century. Irked that his decision merely to schedule hearings had triggered "paroxysms of rage and hysteria" from critics who drew parallels with McCarthy's Cold War witch hunt for "un-American" subversives, King insisted that this time the threat of "homegrown radicalization" was real and pointed to recent plots to bomb Times Square and the New York City subway as proof that "Al Qaeda is actively targeting the American Muslim Community for recruitment."[33] Keith Ellison, an African American Democrat from Minneapolis and the first Muslim ever elected to Congress, begged to differ. Terming King's hearings "the very heart of scapegoating," he pointed out that since the 9/11 attacks, the global war on terror had gone hand in hand with the demonization of Islam, which not only served to legitimize harassment and discrimination against Black Muslims and Arab Americans but also to encourage young Somali immigrants from his own district in Minnesota to return home to Mogadishu to join extremist groups like Al Shabab. "We've seen the consequences of anti-Muslim hate," Ellison noted sadly. "The best defense against extreme ideologies is social inclusion and civic engagement."[34]

During the ten years preceding Ellison's exchange with King, the architects of Islamophobia had done a lot to make American Muslims feel excluded and disengaged. Steven Emerson was one of the first to turn Muslim-bashing into a cottage industry, publishing books like *American Jihad* in 2002 and *Jihad Incorporated* four years later before releasing *The Grand Deception*, a straight-to-video documentary describing alleged Muslim subversion in the United States, in late 2013. According to Emerson, the Muslim Student Association and the Council on American Islamic Relations (CAIR) were "legacy organizations" controlled by extremists groups like Egypt's Muslim Brotherhood.[35] David Horowitz, a recovering leftist from the 1960s who had led the right-wing charge against "political correctness" during the 1990s, claimed that "neo-communists" had formed an "unholy alliance" with al-Qaeda, Hamas, and other Islamic radicals to destroy the United States from within. "An underappreciated fact about the

War on Terror is that America itself is a primary base of Islamic terrorist operations," he warned in 2004, adding that those Americans who opposed the Bush administration's muscular policies in the Middle East were "reminiscent of Communist Party fronts of the Cold War era."[36]

Ann Coulter, the fire-eating femme fatale of the far right, sounded the alarm about Muslim subversion at home and Muslim extremism abroad in her syndicated columns, on her Web site, and in books with titles like *Treason* and *Godless*. The day after the 9/11 attacks she offered a simple solution for dealing with Muslims: "We should invade their countries, kill their leaders, and convert them to Christianity."[37] In response to widespread criticism of the Bush administration's reliance on waterboarding and other methods of enhanced interrogation during 2006, Coulter deemed such practices essential to defeat the "Arab savages" battling U.S. forces in Iraq.[38] Four years later during a talk at the University of Western Ontario, Coulter told Canadian students that if Muslims objected to racial profiling at American airports, they should find a "flying carpet," or better yet, "take a camel."[39]

Popular culture was saturated with Islamophobia. Political cartoons frequently employed caricatures of Osama Bin Laden in America to symbolize the Green Threat. Bumper stickers were available online with blunt messages like "I Learned All I Need to Know about Islam on 9/11" or calls to arms like "Time for Another Crusade" and "I ♥ Dead Terrorists!"[40] Right-wing talk radio fanned the flames with xenophobic fear-mongering not seen since the McCarthy era half a century earlier. When Faisal Shahzad, the Pakistani American who attempted unsuccessfully to bomb New York City's Times Square on 1 May 2010, nearly managed to escape aboard a plane bound for Dubai, Rush Limbaugh blasted the Obama administration for being soft on radical Islam. "Domestic terrorism, especially by *Muslim* terrorists," Limbaugh told his listeners, "is apparently an unwanted distraction to be swept under the rug, if possible."[41] Seven months later, Glenn Beck claimed that the "mainstream media" was refusing to acknowledge that 10 percent of American Muslims were terrorists "who want to violently overthrow the government" and impose sharia law. "We have revolutionaries here in America," he roared, "speaking—American citizens speaking—about an open violent revolution and no one will cover it!"[42]

Hollywood helped blur the lines between fact and fiction by bringing the Green Threat into America's living rooms. For several years following the 9/11 attacks, one of the most watched shows on network television was *24*, which featured Jack Bauer, a CIA counterterrorist superhero prepared to do whatever was necessary to thwart foreign terrorists and domestic evildoers, most of whom were Muslim. Joel Surnow, one of the creators of *24*, had no regrets about depicting American Muslims as potential subversives. "This is what we fear—Islamic terrorism," he told a *New York Times* reporter in January 2005. "This is what we are fighting."[43] Almost exactly a decade after the Twin Towers fell, *Homeland* premiered on Showtime, with Carrie Mathieson, a female Jack Bauer, battling super terrorist Abu Nazir week after week on cable television. "You can bomb us, starve us, occupy our holy places, but we will never lose our faith. We carry God in our hearts, our souls. To die is to join him," Nazir tells Mathieson in episode 10 of the 2012 season. "It may take a century, two centuries, three centuries, but we will exterminate you." In the finale two weeks later, Nazir's followers set off a car bomb at CIA headquarters, killing more than two hundred, including the vice president of the United States.[44]

Pulp fiction often imitated television. In late 2004, for example, Nelson DeMille's *Night Fall* soared to the top of the best-seller list with a fictionalized profile of the 9/11 terrorists, whose deadly plot was nearly foiled by the NYPD detective John Corey, who took a dim view of Islam. "What's the definition of a moderate Arab?" Corey asks his partner. "A guy who ran out of ammunition."[45] Five years later, Lee Child, the author of the best-selling Jack Reacher series of crime novels, published *Gone Tomorrow*, in which U.S. intelligence agents race against time to prevent an al-Qaeda sleeper cell from incinerating lower Manhattan with a suitcase-sized nuclear weapon. Then in 2011, Tom Clancy, whose Cold War potboilers had made him Ronald Reagan's favorite novelist, laid out the mother of all us-versus-them scenarios in *Against All Enemies*, in which Islamic extremists from the badlands of Baluchistan join forces with Mexican drug lords to bring terror back to American soil ten years after the 9/11 attacks. Not long afterward, in a bizarre case of life imitating pulp fiction, the FBI accused the Islamic Republic of Iran of attempting to hire Mexican hit men from the Los Zetas cartel as part of a Clancy-like scheme to blow up Saudi Arabia's ambassador to the United States while he dined at his favorite Georgetown eatery.[46]

The computer software industry outdid pulp fiction, bringing the Green Threat into the bedrooms of American teenage boys via virtual reality. During the decade after 9/11, best-selling first-person shooter video games like *Call of Duty: Modern Warfare*, *Muslim Massacre: The Game of Modern Religious Genocide*, and *Tom Clancy's Splinter Cell: Blacklist* pitted bloodthirsty Islamic radicals against Uncle Sam, with the winner determined by the highest body count. James Portnow, a celebrated video game designer whose credits include the hugely popular Facebook phenomenon *Farmville*, felt deeply disturbed by this trend. "Think of how many shooters today use Muslims as the default enemy. They've kinda become the American Indian of our generation," Portnow told viewers of his animated Internet documentary *Propaganda Games* in October 2011. "As much as we look back and cringe at the old Westerns that glorify the wholesale slaughter of Native Americans, someday I expect we'll probably look back with horror at this huge pile of shoddily made modern conflict games" filled with "racial slurs related to Muslims or Arabs" where "the main activity is shooting anybody with a turban on their head."[47] Two years later, researchers at Iowa State University studying the impact of violent video games confirmed that "the portrayal of Arabs as enemy/terrorist targets . . . caused an increase in implicit anti-Arab attitude." As a result, "for many within the United States, the word 'terrorism' has become coincident with Arabs, Muslims, and Islam."[48]

The Islamophobic hype over the air waves, on television, and in print left real-life American Muslims feeling marginalized and vulnerable. U.S. citizens with Arab surnames were subjected to racial profiling at airports and train stations, while those who frequented mosques or joined Islamic advocacy groups like CAIR became targets of secret government surveillance. Meanwhile, anti-Muslim hate crimes in the United States, which had averaged just 27 during the five years preceding 9/11, spiked to 481 in 2001, before sliding back to an average of 139 during the following decade, a fivefold increase from the late 1990s.[49] In one of the most notorious examples of Islamophobia running amok, in September 2005 Bush administration officials actually ordered the U.S. Army National Guard to round up several dozen Arab immigrants in the immediate aftermath of Hurricane Katrina and had them held incommunicado for two weeks just north of New Orleans at Camp Greyhound, which was modeled on Camp X-Ray, the U.S. detention center for suspected Islamic terrorists at Guantánamo Bay. Dave Eggers, whose account of one of the detainees, Abdulrahman Zeitoun, later won the 2009 American Book Award for non-fiction, discovered that as the Category 5 monster storm bore down on the Gulf Coast, law enforcement agencies throughout the region received an e-mail from the Department of Homeland Security (DHS) to beware of "possible terrorist exploitation" of the crisis. "Several types of exploitation or attacks may potentially be conducted throughout the hurricane cycle," DHS headquarters warned, including "hostage situations or attacks on shelters, cyber attacks, or impersonation of emergency response officials."[50]

Anti-Muslim anxieties proved especially potent in New York City, which many regarded as the once and future target of al-Qaeda terrorists.

When the American Society for Muslim Advancement (ASMA) acquired the old Burlington Coat Factory at 51 Park Place in Lower Manhattan, two blocks from Ground Zero, and announced plans in early 2010 to replace it with Cordoba House, a thirteen-story Islamic community center inspired by the Big Apple's famous Ninety-Second Street Y, Islamophobic groups cried foul. Claiming that ASMA was building "a Mosque at Ground Zero" that would be an affront to the families of the victims of the 9/11 attacks, two longtime right-wing bloggers, Pamela Geller and Robert Spencer, set up Stop Islamization of America (SIOA), with encouragement from like-minded anti-Muslim groups in Western Europe, to derail the project. Although Cordoba House was never intended as a mosque and would not have been built at Ground Zero, Geller and Spencer utilized talk radio, social media, and street protests to delay construction indefinitely. Among SIOA's strongest American supporters was another New Yorker, David Yerushalmi, who coordinated a national campaign against creeping Islam that managed to persuade legislators in North Carolina, South Dakota, and five other states to pass constitutional amendments banning sharia law, something that most neutral observers agreed was far down the list of serious threats to Middle America.[51] Appalled by the antics of Geller, Spencer, and Yerushalmi, the Anti-Defamation League, one of the nation's oldest human rights groups famous for battling anti-Semitism and other forms of bigotry, condemned SIOA for "promot[ing] a conspiratorial anti-Muslim agenda under the guise of fighting radical Islam" and for "consistently vilifying the Islamic faith and asserting the existence of an Islamic conspiracy to destroy 'American' values."[52]

After popular revolutions whose supporters included Islamic radicals brought down pro-American Arab autocrats in Tunisia and Egypt in early 2011, an Islamophobic chorus blamed the "crypto-Muslim" in the White House. Congressman Louie Gohmert, a Texas Republican backed by the Tea Party, ranked among the most outspoken. Recalling Barack Obama's claim to have visited fifty-seven states late in the 2008 election campaign, Gohmert insisted that this was not just a slip of the tongue by an exhausted candidate but rather a sign of something far more sinister. "I'm well aware that there are not 57 states in this country," he sneered in the House chamber on 16 June 2011, but "there are 57 members of OIC [Organization of Islamic Cooperation], the Islamic states in the world." Although candidate Obama might have confused the OIC with the USA, the Lone Star State's man in Washington did not. "We have an obligation to the 50 American states, not the 57 Muslim, Islamic states," he thundered, and certainly "not to the Muslim Brotherhood, who may very well take over Egypt and once they do, they are bent upon setting up a caliphate around the world, including the United States." Hyping the Green Threat to the max, Gohmert concluded that "this administration will [have] been complicit in helping people who want to destroy our country."⁵³

After Islamic extremists destroyed the U.S. consulate in Benghazi, Libya, in September 2012 and killed four Americans, right-wing talk radio joined Gohmert and ratcheted up its Obama-bashing. Rush Limbaugh took the lead. "We got democracy springing up, the Libyans love us, in Obama's world," Rush told his 20 million listeners in late October. "No, we don't. We've got the Muslim Brotherhood spreading Sharia and Islamic supremacy all over the Middle East."⁵⁴ Ten days after Obama was reelected, Rush not only howled that the White House had covered up al-Qaeda's role in the Benghazi attacks but also snarled that the president's "lack of a military response [was] emboldening terrorists" throughout the Muslim world.⁵⁵

Although Obama defeated Mitt Romney handily, there were signs that he was losing the battle against Islamophobia. Rumors that Obama was not a Christian had circulated inside the evangelical community for years. "Obama sounds too much like Osama," Kayla Nickel of Westlink, Kansas, told a reporter in October 2007. "When he says his name, I am like, 'I am not voting for a Muslim!'"⁵⁶ Five years later on the eve of the 2012 election, one-sixth of all registered voters and one-third of all Republicans remained convinced that the president was a Muslim.⁵⁷ Hank Williams Jr., a very popular and very opinionated country and western star, was among the loudest of the wild bunch who charged that the nation's first African American chief executive was an unpatriotic infidel. "We've got a Muslim president who hates farming, hates the military, hates the US," Williams roared after belting out his latest hit, "We Don't Apologize for America," at the Iowa state fair on 17 August 2012, "and we hate him!"⁵⁸ On occasion, Obama's own supporters lent credence to this urban legend, as when Madonna blurted out that "we have a black Muslim in the White House" during one of her raucous concerts six weeks before election day. "It means there is hope in this country," the aging diva exclaimed in a clip that was eventually downloaded from YouTube 2 million times. "Y'all better vote for fucking Obama, OK?"⁵⁹ Messages like Madonna's did not inspire much hope, however, among anti-Muslim activists such as the right-wing shock jock Michael Savage, who had been telling his 3 million radio listeners for years that Obama was a front man for the Islamization of America. "He's the first Muslim president," Savage bellowed on 2 August 2013 after ridiculing what he called a recent "Ramadan Party" at the White House, "everybody knows that."⁶⁰

ISIS, Partisan Politics, and the Irony of American History

Developing a coherent approach toward the Middle East or a compelling strategy for the wider world in such a bitterly partisan and ideologically charged atmosphere was not easy. Throughout Obama's first term, right-wing firebrands like Newt Gingrich, a former speaker of the House with a chronic case of Potomac fever, pandered to the most xenophobic elements in the GOP with Islamophobic us-versus-them rhetoric that recalled the worst kind of Cold War red-baiting. "The left's refusal to tell the truth about the Islamist threat is a natural parallel to the 70-year pattern of left-wing intellectuals refusing to tell the truth about communism," Gingrich screeched during a talk at the American Enterprise Institute in July 2010. Decrying a new age of "appeasement," he charged that Obama was soft on "stealth jihadis" who sought to destroy America from within. The United States now faced a crisis unsurpassed since the late 1940s, when Truman began "developing what became NSC-68," which Gingrich called "the most important single document in the Cold War." According to the Georgia Republican, Americans must be prepared for "a long struggle" with radical Islam that "may well last longer than the Cold War because it's a much more fundamental, I think much more difficult struggle requiring far more change." It was time for "us to say to the radical Islamists," he concluded, "as we said to Nazi Germany, as we said to the Soviet Union, freedom will prevail."[61]

Gingrich's reveille for a new NSC-68 updated for the war on terror won him few votes in the 2012 Republican primaries, but it was a shrill reminder for the man in the Oval Office that at the start of his second term, the Obama Doctrine in the Middle East—containment plus engagement—was increasingly unpopular, not only on the right but also on the left. In February, Limbaugh mocked the president for unleashing lethal drone strikes against renegade Americans like Anwar al-Awlaki without a court order and then blanching at the use of torture against bona fide al-Qaeda terrorists. "Barack Obama is demanding the right to kill American citizens without making his case to a judge, as long as he thinks the American in question is in an upper tier of operations of Al-Qaeda or a related group," Limbaugh roared. "You can kill him, but we can't waterboard him."[62] A month later, Tea Party extremists like Louie Gohmert joined forces with more moderate Republicans on Capitol Hill to demand hearings on the president's alleged mishandling of the Benghazi attacks. After the Chechen Tsarnaev brothers brought mayhem to the streets of Boston on 15 April 2013, right-wing pundits erupted again with charges that the White House was doing too little to protect America's borders. Was it really "a good idea to be letting in so many immigrants who then blow up the Boston Marathon," Ann Coulter wondered during a Fox News segment on how best to address the danger of Islamic extremism.[63] Meanwhile, U.S. drone strikes in Afghanistan, Pakistan, and Yemen were continuing to kill dozens of civilians, prompting left-wing activists and human rights groups to part company with a Democratic administration that they saw as increasingly ruthless and amoral. Later that spring, a hunger strike by more than one hundred Muslim detainees at Guantánamo Bay led some of Obama's own supporters to brand him as a hypocrite for failing to fulfill a campaign promise to shut down the notorious detention center that had become a black mark on America's reputation abroad.

Buffeted by criticism from both Republicans and Democrats, Barack Obama unveiled a diplomatic blueprint for his second term at the National Defense University at Fort McNair in Washington, D.C., on 23 May 2013. Despite his first term successes in the Muslim world—winding down the wars in Iraq and Afghanistan and decimating al-Qaeda—Obama acknowledged that "from Benghazi to Boston," Uncle Sam was "still threatened by terrorists." Americans, however, must "recognize that these threats don't arise in a vacuum" but rather from a conviction held by many Muslims "that Islam is in conflict with the United States and the West." The principal outcome of such us-versus-them thinking was reciprocal demonization that endangered everyone. Insisting that "the United States is not at war with Islam," the president proposed a two-pronged foreign policy predicated on destroying "specific networks of violent extremists" in the Muslim world while simultaneously "addressing the underlying grievances and conflicts that feed extremism—from North Africa to South Asia." In simple English, this would mean more drone attacks against al-Qaeda and its affiliates but also more "diplomatic engagement and assistance" for Muslim societies seeking to make the transition to democracy.

Things proved no less complex closer to home, where Obama confessed that balancing privacy and security would remain an ongoing challenge. Speaking just weeks after the Boston Marathon bombing and just days before Edward Snowden, a former CIA systems administrator, would leak thousands of documents revealing an elaborate program of domestic spying by the National Security Agency (NSA), the president pointed out that "thwarting homegrown [terrorist] plots presents particular challenges in part because of our proud commitment to civil liberties." He promised, however, "to keep working hard to strike the appropriate balance between our need for security and preserving those freedoms that make us who we are." Noting that, two centuries earlier, James Madison had warned the citizens of the modern world's first republic that "no nation could preserve its freedom in the midst of continual warfare," America's forty-fourth president vowed to heed the wisdom of its fourth.[64]

Even James Madison, however, would have been perplexed by the central dilemma that Barack Obama faced in the Middle East by the summer of 2013—how to square America's faith in democracy with its fear of Islamic extremism. Matters came to a head first in Cairo, where Mohammed Morsi, the only freely elected president in Egyptian history, unveiled a new constitution crafted largely by his comrades in the Muslim Brotherhood, who controlled parliament. Convinced that Egypt was on the verge of becoming an Islamic Republic, Morsi's secular critics launched a campaign called Tamarod, an Arabic word meaning "rebellion." Relying on the same Facebook strategy that had helped topple Hosni Mubarak two years earlier, Tamarod gathered 22 million signatures in June for a petition demanding that Morsi step down. To no one's great surprise, Abdel Fatah el-Sisi, the American-trained commander of the Egyptian army, seized power on 3 July and arrested Morsi on charges that he and the Muslim Brotherhood had intended to impose sharia law. Six weeks later, Sisi's troops gunned down eight hundred Islamist demonstrators in Cairo's Raba'a Square. Yet despite professions of "deep concern," the White House refused to suspend the $2 billion U.S. military aid package for Egypt. Instead, Obama chose to place much of the blame for the turmoil on Morsi himself, whose "government was not inclusive and did not respect the views of all Egyptians."[65]

Even more turmoil erupted elsewhere in the region. From Yemen came word in September that despite the Obama administration's aggressive campaign of drone warfare, al-Qaeda in the Arabian Peninsula (AQAP) was gaining the upper hand against President Abd Rabbuh Mansur al-Hadi and his pro-American government. A month later on the other side of the Red Sea, two Somali Americans loyal to the extremist group Al Shabab took part in a grisly attack on a shopping mall in Nairobi, Kenya, that left sixty-seven dead. Meanwhile, just two years after the fall of Muammar Qaddafi, Islamist radicals controlled the eastern half of Libya and embraced Muslim extremists like Mokhtar Belmokhtar, an Algerian veteran of the anti-Soviet jihad in Afghanistan who sought to destabilize American-backed regimes in Mali and Mauritania.

Not all the news from the Middle East during 2013 was bleak. In Jordan, for example, King Abdullah continued to work closely with the Obama administration to combat radical Islam and in July played host to the so-called "Special Forces Olympics" just outside Amman, where retired SEALs and CIA spooks compared notes with their counterparts from friendly Arab intelligence services.[66] Several months later Washington confirmed that the ruler of Qatar, the thumb-shaped, oil-rich emirate jutting into the Persian Gulf near Bahrain, had agreed to have the Pentagon establish a Combined Air and Space Operations Center in Doha to coordinate U.S. military communications throughout the region.[67] Even more encouraging were developments in Iran, where Hassan Rouhani, a moderate Islamist with a reputation as a reformer, was elected president in mid-June and named Javad Zarif, an affable American-educated political scientist, as his foreign minister, with responsibility for improving relations with the United States. Before the year was out, Zarif and John Kerry, who had recently succeeded Hillary Clinton as secretary of state, were discussing the possibility of lifting American economic sanctions on Iran. In return, the Iranians would abandon their program to produce enriched uranium, a crucial ingredient for nuclear weapons, and permit UN inspectors to certify the process. As Zarif put it later in a featured article in *Foreign Affairs*, Rouhani's Iran desired to move away from a "clash of civilizations" with the United States and toward "constructive engagement."[68]

Yet by early 2014, Team Obama was spending less time on a potential breakthrough with Iran than on the deteriorating situation in Syria, where three years of civil war between the brutally repressive government of President Bashar al-Assad and a kaleidoscopic array of rebel groups had created an opening for ISIS, whose leader seemed to be itching for civilizational warfare. Arguably the most ferocious jihadist organization in the world, ISIS had first emerged as al-Qaeda in Iraq (AQI), Osama Bin Laden's franchise in Baghdad, during the anti-American insurgency that exploded after the U.S. invasion in 2003. That organization would morph into ISIS thanks to the leadership of Abu Bakr al-Baghdadi, a Sunni cleric-turned-insurgent who, after completing a four-year sentence in an American-run prison just outside Baghdad in 2009, would glare at his captors and snarl: "See you guys in New York."[69] Over the following few years, American intelligence would catch sight of him now and again in the no-man's-land along Iraq's ill-defined border with Syria, where ISIS was planting its black banner and vowing to create a new caliphate. Even after al-Baghdadi rebranded his organization as "the Islamic State" in January 2014, top U.S. officials tended to dismiss ISIS as al-Qaeda's second-string affiliate in Syria. "The analogy we use around here sometimes . . . is if a jayvee team puts on Lakers uniforms that doesn't make them Kobe Bryant," Obama explained. "I think there is a distinction between the capacity and reach of a bin Laden and a network that is actively planning major terrorist plots against the homeland versus jihadists [in Syria] who are engaged in various local power struggles and disputes."[70]

During testimony before the Senate Intelligence Committee on 29 January, however, James Clapper, Obama's director of national intelligence, worried that Islamic extremists might soon be playing the equivalent of NBA basketball in "ungoverned spaces" like Libya, Yemen, and Syria. Although "the threat complex, sophisticated and large-scale attacks from core al-Qa'ida against the US Homeland, is significantly degraded," Clapper cautioned that "instability in the Middle East and North Africa has accelerated the decentralization of the movement, which is increasingly influenced by local and regional issues." Without mentioning ISIS by name, he emphasized that "Syria has become a huge magnet for extremists," with "some 1600 different groups" creating a pool of 26,000 potential Syrian jihadis. To make matters worse, the CIA estimated that there were also 7,000 foreign jihadis from fifty different countries in Syria.[71]

Despite Clapper's misgivings, Obama refused to use the deepening crisis in Syria as a pretext for launching a new crusade against radical Islam. The complex situation in the Middle East required something more sophisticated than a binary us-versus-them framework dating from the dawn of the Cold War, he told a reporter in January 2014. "I don't really even need George Kennan right now."[72] Four months later he delivered the commencement address at the U.S. Military Academy at West Point, where he spelled out what he did need—patience, persistence, and hope. Praising the thirteen hundred cadets for their courage and their commitment, he reminded those headed for the Middle East that "the landscape has changed" there, thanks to America's withdrawal from Iraq, its impending departure from Afghanistan, and the decimation of al-Qaeda's upper echelon. Sadly, "a new century has brought no end to tyranny," and "violent upheavals in parts of the Arab World" made it "easy to be cynical." Yet although turmoil in Syria and elsewhere in the region meant that Americans must "see the world as it is, with all its danger and uncertainty," the president urged the graduates also "to see the world as it should be . . . where hopes and not just fears govern."[73]

One place governed more by fear than hope was the Holy Land, where despite vehement protests from Palestinian leaders, Israeli prime minister Netanyahu pressed ahead with more settlements on the West Bank as part of his master plan to create secure borders for the Jewish state. Not long after Obama's hopeful remarks at West Point, Islamic militants aligned with Hamas began lobbing small rockets from Gaza into southern Israel, inflicting little physical damage but much psychological harm. In early July, Netanyahu struck back hard, first with air strikes and eventually with Israeli ground forces to decapitate Hamas and root out the terrorist infrastructure in Gaza. By the time Washington managed to broker a cease-fire on 26 August 2014, Operation Protective Edge had claimed the lives of more than two thousand Palestinians, many of them children. Noting that Netanyahu's retaliatory raids seemed to lack proportionality, the White House placed most of the blame for the demise of a "two-state solution" squarely on Israel. "How will it have peace if it is unwilling to delineate a border, end the occupation, and allow for Palestinian sovereignty, security, and dignity?" Philip Gordon, Obama's chief Middle East troubleshooter, wondered. "It cannot maintain military control of another people indefinitely. Doing so is not only wrong but a recipe for resentment and recurring instability."[74] Netanyahu was not amused. Nor were American supporters like talk-radio big shot Michael Savage, who blasted Obama as "a crackpot charlatan" and accused the White House of kowtowing to Muslim "vermin." Reminding his listeners that "Israel was on the front lines of the war against radical Islam," Savage castigated the Obama administration for lounging on the sidelines and enabling ISIS to wreak havoc from Damascus to Baghdad.[75]

While Israel was busy pulverizing Gaza during the summer of 2014, ISIS convoys roared out of the Islamic State's home base in eastern Syria and conquered vast swaths of northern Iraq. In early June, ISIS hoisted its black banner over Mosul, Iraq's second-largest city, and proceeded to execute hundreds of prisoners of war, burying them in mass graves. At the end of the month, Abu Bakr al-Baghdadi proclaimed himself caliph of the expanding Islamic State and launched *Dabiq*, a slick online English-language magazine, to spread the word among Muslims in Britain and the United States. Then in mid-August, "Jihadi John," an English-speaking ISIS executioner clad in black, made his Internet debut, beheading James Foley, an American journalist taken hostage two years earlier as he covered the civil war in Syria. Shortly afterward, ISIS posted a grisly high-definition video on YouTube. Several more beheadings followed in quick succession, prompting President Obama to brand the Islamic State "a terrorist organization, pure and simple," and to send 475 American military advisers back to Baghdad to help the Iraqi government turn the tide. "America will lead a broad coalition to roll back this terrorist threat," Obama told a national television audience on 10 September 2014. "We will degrade, and ultimately destroy, ISIL through a comprehensive and sustained counterterrorism strategy."[76]

For many Americans schooled in the catechism of us versus them, this sudden call for rollback was a classic case of too little, too late. Among Obama's most prominent detractors was Robert Kagan, a rock star neoconservative supporter of the global war on terror who was busy reinventing himself as a "liberal interventionist" from his perch at the Brookings Institution. A founding father of the Project for a New American Century and a former protégé of Norman Podhoretz, the editor of *Commentary* magazine whose best-selling *World War IV* had made "Islamofascism" one of Dubya's favorite buzzwords, Kagan insisted that America must remain what he claimed it had always been, a City upon a Hill. Although Kagan's own history of American foreign policy before 1914, *Dangerous Nation*, had mentioned King Philip's War and Nat Turner, two of his biggest heroes were Andrew Jackson and Theodore Roosevelt.[77]

In February 2012, Kagan's "Not Fade Away: The Myth of American Decline" appeared in the *New Republic* and caught the attention of almost everyone inside the Beltway, including Barack Obama. After issuing a stealth mea culpa acknowledging that recent U.S. actions, particularly "the widely condemned invasion of Iraq," had "tarnished the American 'brand' and put a dent in America's 'soft power,'" Kagan proceeded to dismiss half a century of setbacks from the Korean and Vietnam wars through the energy crisis and the Iranian revolution as mere background noise that should not distract attention from larger diplomatic successes. "Foreign policy is like hitting a baseball," he explained, "if you fail 70 percent of the time, you go to the Hall of Fame." What was Kagan's take-away message? Decline was "not an inevitable fate" but rather a choice that Uncle Sam simply must not make. "Preserving the present world order requires constant American leadership," he concluded, "and constant American commitment."[78]

Batting .300 was no more acceptable for Barack Obama than it had been for his predecessor, however, because despite Kagan's glib comparison with baseball, foreign policy was really more like football, where failing 70 percent of the time means that your team misses the playoffs and your coach gets fired. Kagan updated his arguments in May 2014 in another cover story in the *New Republic* titled "Superpowers Don't Get to Retire," which evoked another round of oohs and ahs from the usual suspects. Glossing over neoconservative responsibility for the debacles in Iraq and Afghanistan, he claimed that the biggest problem facing the United States twenty-five years after the Cold War was the absence of a grand strategy to replace containment: "The unanticipated fall of the Soviet empire and the collapse of international communism after 1989 inevitably raised anew the question of how to define America's purpose and its interests in the absence of an obvious threat." Fondly recalling Dean Acheson's famous quip that the United States was destined to be "the locomotive at the head of mankind" while everyone else would have to travel in "the caboose," Kagan reminded readers that for more than forty years, "fear of communism, combined with fear of the Soviet Union as a geopolitical threat allowed a majority of Americans and American policy makers to view practically any policy directed against communist forces, or even against suspected communist forces, anywhere in the world as directly serving the nation's vital interests." To be sure, "justifying everything in terms of the anticommunist struggle may have been, to borrow Acheson's phrase, 'clearer than the truth,' but it worked," he concluded, "and the results were extraordinary." Kagan did not identify a new them that might unite us, nor did he mention radical Islam or Israel, but he did provide a clue on the final page of his article, where he noted that "in the Middle East, nations worried about Iran," which they feared might soon "acquire a nuclear weapon."[79]

Among Kagan's most avid listeners was Hillary Clinton, who had invited him to join a bipartisan group of unofficial advisers while she was secretary of state during Obama's first term. Now, as she prepared to run for president, Clinton revealed a "realist" view of the world predicated on projecting American power and protecting American friends in the Middle East that closely resembled Kagan's. "While there are few problems in today's world that the United States can solve alone, there are even fewer that can be solved without the United States," she intoned. "Everything that I have done and seen has convinced me that America remains the 'indispensable nation.'"[80] During the course of a long interview with the *Atlantic*'s Jeffrey Goldberg in August 2014, Clinton spelled out just what she meant. When Goldberg asked her, "Did you learn more about the possibilities of American power or the limitations of American power" during four years at Foggy Bottom, she replied: "Both." While Clinton reaffirmed her belief in "American values that also happen to be universal values," she also confessed that "we've learned about the limits of our power to spread freedom and democracy." Did this mean, Goldberg wondered, that "the lesson for you, like it is for President Obama, [is] 'Don't do stupid shit'?" Clinton nodded, but added that "it's more complicated than that." In retrospect, it was stupid to invade Iraq but it was smart to intervene in Libya. "Great nations need organizing principles," she explained, "and 'Don't do stupid stuff' is not an organizing principle."

Clinton's organizing principle came into sharper focus when the conversation turned to the Muslim world. "One of the reasons why I worry about what's happening in the Middle East right now is because of the breakout capacity of jihadist groups," she told Goldberg. "Jihadist groups are governing territory. They will never stay there, though. They are driven to expand. Their raison d'être is to be against the West, against the Crusaders, against the fill-in-the-blank—and we all fit into one of these categories." The big question was: "How do we try to contain that?" Echoing Kagan, she continued: "I'm thinking a lot about containment, deterrence, and defeat. You know, we did a good job in containing the Soviet Union, but we made a lot of mistakes, we supported really nasty guys, we did some things that we are not particularly proud of, from Latin America to Southeast Asia, but we did have a kind of overarching framework about what we were trying to do that did lead to the defeat of the Soviet Union and the collapse of Communism." The Iron Curtain came down suddenly after 1989, proving that containment worked, but "the big mistake was thinking that, okay, the end of history has come upon us, after the fall of the Soviet Union." Unfortunately, "that was never true, history never stops and nationalisms were going to assert themselves, and then other variations on ideologies were going to claim their space." Connecting the dots between the Cold War and the war on terror was easy for Clinton: "Obviously, jihadi Islam is the prime example."[81]

The possibility that the United States was rushing into a post-Obama world where the Cold War Red Threat would be supplanted by the Green Threat of jihadi Islam made some Americans very nervous. Nick Gillespie, the editor of *Reason* magazine and one of the gurus of the budding libertarian movement, probably put it best when he took a poke at Islamophobia, American-style, in August 2014: "We don't have to pretend anymore that radical Islam is an existential threat to the West," he told a *New York Times* reporter. "It's herpes, but it's not AIDS. It's a chronic condition, but it won't kill us. Just keep the attacks to a minimum."[82] Six weeks later the Islamic advocacy group CAIR launched a new website, Islamophobia.org, "to monitor and challenge the growing anti-Muslim bigotry in American society" and to counter right-wing "hate entities" like Jihad Watch.[83] One of the few bright spots for Obama and the Democrats during off-year elections that saw the GOP gain control of both houses of Congress in November 2014 was the reelection of the Minnesota representative Keith Ellison, whose Republican challenger had hoped to make the only Muslim on Capitol Hill a whipping boy for ISIS.

Throughout the autumn of 2014 and into the winter of 2015, the Obama administration was hard pressed to determine whether containment or rollback constituted the best way to handle the threat posed by Islamic extremism. In early August, for example, a reporter had asked the president point-blank: "Is your goal there to contain ISIS or to destroy it?" Obama fudged his answer. "We can conduct airstrikes," he explained, "but ultimately there's not going to be an American military solution to this problem."[84] In an op-ed piece that appeared in the *Boston Globe* in late September, Secretary of State Kerry echoed his boss and hedged his bets. "The Islamic State controls more territory than Al Qaeda ever has," Kerry wrote, "which means it has access to money on an unprecedented scale to finance its mayhem." As grave as the threat was, however, American involvement would be limited to air strikes against ISIS and "US ground troops will not engage in combat roles." Acting together with America's allies in NATO and the Persian Gulf, "we can protect the innocent," Kerry concluded, and "contain the danger."[85]

In his cover letter for the national security strategy update that the White House issued in February 2015, President Obama sounded a little less ambivalent and lot more like John Winthrop or Harry Truman: "American exceptionalism is not rooted solely in the strength of our arms or economy," he observed, but was also "the product of our founding values, including the rule of law and universal rights." Applied to the Middle East, this meant not only continuing "to draw a stark contrast between what we stand for and the heinous deeds" of ISIS but also redoubling efforts "to dismantle terrorist networks that threaten our people" and pledging once again to "confront external aggression against our allies and partners" like Saudi Arabia and Israel. Two months later, when Thomas Friedman of the *New York Times* pressed him to summarize his approach to the world, the president responded this way: "You asked about an Obama doctrine. The doctrine is: We will engage, but we will preserve our capabilities." This suggested that contagement was alive and well. What were the implications for the Middle East? "At this point, the U.S.'s core interests in the region are not oil, are not territorial," came the reply. "Our core interests are that everybody is living in peace, that it is orderly." Put most simply, Obama concluded, his administration was committed to "really just making sure that the region is working. And if it's working well, then we'll do fine."[86]

Not surprisingly, few on the Republican side of the aisle believed that the Middle East was working well or that America was doing fine. Determined to block what many of Israel's supporters regarded as a bad deal that would lift U.S. sanctions on Iran without forcing the Iranians to suspend all of their nuclear research, Speaker of the House John Boehner invited Bibi Netanyahu to address a joint session of Congress on 3 March 2015. The Israeli prime minister did not disappoint. Implying that the Obama administration's rapprochement with Tehran was nothing less than appeasement, Netan-yahu evoked thunderous applause from Republicans by declaring that "Iran and ISIS are competing for the crown of militant Islam."[87]

Meanwhile, the leading contenders for the GOP presidential nomination one year down the road were taking turns bashing Obama's foreign policy. Team Obama had "forgotten that when America fails to lead, global chaos inevitably follows," Florida's Marco Rubio observed on 13 April, "so they appease our enemies, betray our allies and weaken our military." Insisting that a change of course was clearly in order, the junior senator from the Sunshine State trumpeted that "the time has come for our generation to lead the way toward a new American Century."[88] Two weeks later, Florida's former governor Jeb Bush, Dubya's younger brother, questioned whether Obama and the Democrats were up to the task of defeating groups like al-Qaeda or ISIS, "who have an ideology that wants to destroy Western civilization and they're barbarians." Echoing Egyptian strong man Abdel Fattah al-Sisi, the younger Bush said "it's our responsibility to confront rad-ical Islam."[89] Wisconsin governor Scott Walker was even more direct, how-ever, when he responded to a question about ISIS at the GOP's Freedom Summit in Greenville, South Carolina, on 9 May 2015 by saying: "I want a leader who is willing to take the fight to them before they take the fight to us."[90] After New York City real estate mogul Donald Trump jumped into the Republican race for the White House a month later, he too resorted to the language of us versus them to explain how he would defeat the Islamic State. "ISIS has to be dealt with firmly and strongly," Trump told CNN's Anderson Cooper on 8 July, and "I would do things that would be so tough that I don't even know if they would be around to come to the table." When Anderson pressed for details, the bombastic Trump growled: "Bomb them."[91]

Barack Obama was never a fan of us-versus-them thinking, and when he sought guidance on foreign policy, he was far less likely to turn to Jeb Bush, Marco Rubio, or Donald Trump than to John Quincy Adams or Reinhold Niebuhr. Having served as one of James Madison's most trusted diplo-mats, Adams would utter his most famous words not as president but as James Monroe's secretary of state, remarking on 4 July 1821 that America "goes not abroad in search of monsters to destroy." Once Adams moved into the White House, he had little time for Andrew Jackson or the metaphys-ics of Indian-hating, and no time at all for the "peculiar institution" or the expansion of slavery. All this helped make Adams one of Senator Obama's heroes in *The Audacity of Hope*. Indeed, one can imagine Obama recalling JQA's words of caution while he watched a pivotal scene in *Pirates of the*

Caribbean, a Hollywood blockbuster that premiered in July 2003, just three months after the U.S. invasion of Iraq. "You're off the edge of the map, mate," Geoffrey Rush's Captain Hector Barbossa tells Johnny Depp's Jack Sparrow. "Here there be monsters."[92]

Yet after Obama settled into the White House six years later, he seemed to rely less on the words of JQA or Hector Barbossa and more on the wisdom of his "favorite philosopher," Reinhold Niebuhr. A Lutheran theologian born just west of St. Louis, Niebuhr had emerged during the late 1940s as a hesitant Cold Warrior, a "Christian realist" who saw the world as divided between good and evil, between us and them. Niebuhr respected and admired Truman and Kennan, but he also worried that the fierce ideological battle brewing with the Kremlin would corrode the values that Madison and JQA held dear. He spelled out his worries in *The Irony of American History*, a meditation on the limits of American power that appeared in 1952. The key ingredients for a responsible foreign policy in an atomic age were "a sense of modesty about the virtue, wisdom and power available to us" and "a sense of contrition about the common human frailties and foibles which lie at the foundation of both the enemy's demonry and our vanities." Americans must be courageous but they must also be patient. Most important, they must retain the capacity to see themselves as others saw them.

Niebuhr detected parallels between America's contemporary confrontation with Soviet Russia and Europe's confrontation with the Muslim caliphate nine hundred years earlier. "The rise of communism in our world is comparable to the rise of Islam and its challenge of Christian civilization in the high Middle Ages," he observed. "The Islamic power finally waned. It was destroyed not so much by its foes as by its own inner corruptions." So too would "the power impulses of a Russian state" driven by "the Messianic illusions of an ostensibly world-wide political religion," provided that Americans were able to "acquire the necessary patience to wait out the long run of history while we take such measures as are necessary to combat the more immediate perils." Sixty years ago, Niebuhr urged U.S. leaders to forego international crusades and resist "the temptation to become impatient and defiant of the slow and sometimes contradictory processes of history." Should Americans become "too secure in both our sense of power and our sense of virtue," he cautioned, "we could bring calamity upon ourselves and the world by forgetting that even the most powerful nations and even the wisest planners of the future remain themselves creatures as well as creators of the historical process."

Looking back on the checkered record of American involvement in the Muslim world since 1989, Niebuhr's words seem more relevant than ever. "Great disproportions of power are as certainly moral hazards to justice and community as they are foundations of minimal order," he warned Americans at the dawn of the Cold War. "They are hazards to community both because they arouse resentments and fears among those who have less power; and because they tempt the strong to wield their power without too much consideration of the interests and views of those upon whom it impinges." In a world viewed through the prism of us versus them and ruled by the iron law of mutual demonization, American Islamophobia and Muslim anti-Americanism can easily become deadly reciprocal self-fulfilling prophecies. The final lines of *The Irony of American History* are well worth remembering today. "If we should perish, the ruthlessness of the foe would be only the secondary cause of the disaster," Niebuhr confessed. "The primary cause would be that the strength of a giant nation was directed by eyes too blind to see all the hazards of the struggle; and the blindness would be induced not by some accident of nature or history but by hatred and vainglory."[93]

Shortly after authorizing a fresh round of U.S. airstrikes against ISIS insurgents who seemed poised to wipe out thousands of Yazidi Kurds stranded on Mount Sinjar in northern Iraq, President Obama sat down with *New York Times* pundit Thomas Friedman on 8 August 2014 to discuss America's problems in the Middle East. "We are the sole superpower in the world. We remain the one indispensable nation," he told Friedman. "There's no issue in which our leadership is not critical." Yet from Libya to Kurdistan and beyond, Obama was finding it nearly impossible to lead because most Americans, like most of their friends and foes abroad, viewed politics and diplomacy as an endless battle between us and them. "The biggest impediment to American leadership is not external," Obama explained. "The thing that's gonna hold us back is gonna be us." The truth was that "our politics are dysfunctional," he sighed, and "societies don't work if factions take maximalist positions." Neither did the international system. Although he still believed that "if we make good decisions, then we will continue to be not only the dominant power but a benevolent force around the world," Obama did not sound confident.[94]

Beyond Us versus Them?

Confidence has been in short supply for a long time among Americans familiar with the Middle East. In November 2001, just nine weeks after the

9/11 attacks, I found myself on the road in Israel. Highway One curves south-east from Tel Aviv into the Judean foothills along the path of an old Ottoman thoroughfare that ran from the Mediterranean to the Dead Sea. My driver Avigdor was a veteran of Israel's war for independence who made sure that I noticed the wrecked half-track dating from 1948 scarcely visible through the roadside underbrush as our van started its climb toward Jerusalem. I spent much of the day in the Old City, walking to the Wailing Wall and the Dome of the Rock, wandering through an Arab souk, and pausing to listen to the Muslim call to prayer. Because Avigdor was not a patient man, we bypassed the rush-hour traffic on Highway One and drove back to Tel Aviv through the West Bank on Route 443, which sweeps around Palestinian villages and towns that are centuries old. As the Mediterranean began to glimmer in the twilight twenty miles ahead, I looked left and caught a glimpse of what seemed to be an enormous hilltop shopping plaza surrounded by dozens of sleek new condominiums. "That's the Israeli settlement of Modi'in," Avigdor beamed. "It's not tents in the desert."

That evening I had dinner at a beachfront restaurant in downtown Tel Aviv with my hosts, Nehama and her husband, Yigal, a college president. After chatting for a while about al-Qaeda, Hamas, and radical Islam, Yigal suggested that there might be parallels between America's newly launched global war on terror and his own country's Sisyphean struggle against Palestinian extremism. I replied that the stark contrast between the tired old Arab towns that Avigdor and I had driven past earlier that day on the West Bank and Modi'in, that shining Israeli settlement on a hill, might be responsible for some of the anger and despair expressed by so many Muslims throughout the region, who blamed Israel and the United States for their predicament. "Yes, we and the Arabs are separated by a rapidly widening political, economic, and cultural gap," Yigal sighed. "Sadly, they are very different from us." When I mentioned that Princeton University's Bernard Lewis, one of America's leading experts on the Muslim world, was about to make a similar case in his soon-to-be-published book *What Went Wrong? The Clash between Islam and Modernity in the Middle East*, Yigal replied: "Precisely."[95]

American academics and Israeli college presidents held no monopoly on us-versus-them thinking, of course, nor did George W. Bush and Ariel Sharon. In *Orientalism*, his pathbreaking account of how the West demonized Islam as backward and decadent during the nineteenth and twentieth centuries, Columbia University's Edward Said demonstrated that over the years, British, French, and American policy makers consistently relied on arguments like those put forward by Lewis to justify empire-building and military intervention in the Muslim world.[96] Yet demonization is a two-way street. In early 2002, the Anglo-Dutch writer Ian Buruma and the Israeli philosopher Avishai Margalit coined the term "occidentalism" to explain the escalating xenophobia of Muslim extremists. Their primary example was Osama Bin Laden, whose rhetoric sounded like orientalism in reverse and on steroids. "Every grown up Muslim hates Americans, Jews, and Christians. It is our belief and religion," the al-Qaeda leader told an interviewer for al-Jazeera television three years before 9/11. "Since I was a boy I have been harboring hatred towards the Americans."[97] Today, four years after Bin Laden's death, al-Qaeda franchises in Syria, Yemen, and Libya preach the same kind of violent anti-Americanism.

How might one break this vicious cycle of mutual demonization? Because the us-versus-them paradigm was so central to the Red Scare that fueled the U.S. confrontation with the Soviet Union after 1945, understanding why the Cold War ended with a whimper rather than a bang forty-four years later may provide some clues about how to cope with the contemporary "Green Scare." The first and most important lesson from 1989 is that containment proved a far more effective strategy for resolving half a century of Soviet-American conflict peaceably than rollback, saber rattling, or military intervention. After a brief flirtation with rolling back communism during Project Solarium in 1953, Dwight Eisenhower had chosen to contain the Kremlin, setting the tone for his successors. Six decades later, Barack Obama was as reluctant as Ike to place U.S. troops in harm's way and ignored shrill calls from the GOP to do more to combat radical Islam. Although he seldom used the word "containment" in the same sentence as ISIS, Obama's message was clear. The Islamic State had been successful in attracting support from abroad, Obama told reporters at the G-7 Summit in Krun, Germany, on 8 June 2015. "They're nimble, and they're aggressive, and they're opportunistic," but the most judicious and effective response was to "cut off some of that foreign fighter flow and then . . . isolate and wear out [the] ISIL forces that are already there."[98] This was in keeping with the advice of many survivors of George W. Bush's disastrous war in Iraq, which had spawned ISIS. "Maybe an incomplete and imperfect effort to contain the Islamic State is as good as it gets," General Daniel Bolger, who served in Baghdad from 2006 to 2010, wrote in an op-ed piece in the *New York Times*. "Perhaps the best we can or should do is to keep it busy, 'degrade' its forces, harry them or kill them, and seek the long game at the lowest possible cost."[99]

Beyond the value of containment, the second lesson worth remembering from the final years of the Cold War is that leaders on both sides of the us-versus-them divide must be willing to transcend ideological stereotypes, defy conventional wisdom, and take risks for peace. During his first term, Ronald Reagan trotted out all the anticommunist shibboleths, beefed up the Pentagon budget, and branded the Soviet Union an evil empire yet accomplished very little. Not until the late 1980s, when Mikhail Gorbachev, a pragmatic reformer determined to improve relations with the United States, climbed into the driver's seat in Moscow and a more flexible and temperate Reagan toned down his Kremlin-bashing and slid into the passenger seat alongside him, did the Cold War end. George H. W. Bush sealed the deal in November 1989 by ruling that there would be no dancing on the Berlin Wall. Twenty-six years later, Barack Obama faces a similar situation with Iran, a pariah state locked in a seemingly unbreakable cycle of mutual demonization with America that has been exacerbated by ugly stereotypes propagated by both sides. Should Obama and Iranian president Hassan Rouhani manage to overcome long odds and strike a deal lifting U.S. economic sanctions in exchange for Iran suspending its nuclear weapons program, Washington and Tehran would take a major step beyond us versus them.

In addition to heeding these lessons from the end of the Cold War, American leaders and the American public must be willing to reconsider some of the rules of the road that have produced such a rough ride in the Muslim world since 1989. For too long, too many U.S. policy makers have adhered to the ancient maxim: "The enemy of my enemy of is my friend." In too many cases, this sort of thinking has led the United States to align itself with friendly tyrants like Egypt's Abdel Fatah el-Sisi or reactionary regimes like the House of Saud, while signaling to those seeking political reform and social justice in the Middle East that America remains wedded to the status quo. In addition, American officials must take greater care to ensure that their high-tech way of war displays a sense of proportionality and does not inflict significant collateral damage or kill innocent civilians in places like Afghanistan, Pakistan, and Yemen. As the distinguished Israeli international historian Avi Shlaim has reminded us, there is always great temptation in the Middle East "to extract an eye for an eyelash," but at the end of the day this approach merely leaves one's adversaries blind and angry.[100] Finally, America's religious zealots must keep their crusader impulses in check and recognize that Islamophobia only plays into the hands of Muslim extremists like al-Qaeda and ISIS. When someone like General Jerry Boykin, who oversaw U.S. counterterrorist operations from Mogadishu to Baghdad between

1993 and 2003, informs a Muslim prisoner that "my God was a real God, and his was an idol," he only invites Islamic radicals to return the favor.[101]

In short, improving America's tattered relationship with the Muslim world will be neither quick nor easy. As Reinhold Niebuhr pointed out at the dawn of the Cold War, containment requires patience and bold leadership requires faith. Distinguishing accurately between friends and enemies, resisting the temptation to fight fire with ever greater fire, and throttling self-righteous religious sentiments will require Americans to work harder to understand the appeal of radical Islam than in the recent past. There are no simple solutions in the world of us versus them. Yet if we take the trouble to treat them with greater empathy and respect, then perhaps they would reciprocate with us.

Notes

Abbreviations

BNA   British National Archives, Kew, Surrey, England
FRUS   U.S. Department of State, *Foreign Relations of the United States*
GHWBL   George H. W. Bush Presidential Library, College Station, Tex.
JCL   Jimmy Carter Presidential Library, Atlanta, Ga.
NYT   *New York Times*
PPP   *Public Papers of the Presidents*
RRL   Ronald Reagan Presidential Library, Simi Valley, Calif.
WP   *Washington Post*

Introduction

1. Pew Research Center, "How Americans Feel about Religious Groups."
2. Pew Research Center, "Global Attitudes and Trends: Chapter One—Attitudes toward the United States."
3. College of Urban and Public Affairs, Portland State University, Portland, Oregon, "Gallup Metadata.".

Chapter One

1. Bush, "Address to the Nation," 20 September 2001, *PPP Bush 2001*, 2:1141–42.
2. Truman quoted in Turner Catledge, "Our Policy Stated: Welles Says Defeat of Hitler Conquest Plans Is Greatest Task," *NYT*, 24 June 1941.
3. Hoover testimony before HUAC, 26 March 1947, reprinted in U.S. Congress, Senate, *Menace of Communism*, 4, 11.
4. Kennan to Byrnes, tel. 22 February 1946, *FRUS 1946*, 6:707. For a provocative account of other sources for Kennan's "us versus them" thinking, see Costigliola, "Unceasing Pressure for Penetration."
5. "X" [George F. Kennan], "Sources of Soviet Conduct."
6. Acheson, *Present at the Creation*, 196–98.
7. "Draft Notes on Meeting to Present and Explain British Notes to Congressional Delegation," 27 February 1947, in *The Truman Doctrine and the Beginning of the Cold War*, 7.
8. Vandenberg quoted in Goldman, *The Crucial Decade*, 59.
9. Truman, "Address to Joint Session of Congress," 12 March 1947, *PPP Truman 1947*, 176–80.

10. Vandenberg quoted in James Reston, "Vandenberg Says West Pact is 'Greatest War Deterrent,'" *NYT*, 23 March 1949.

11. NSC-68, "United States Objectives and Programs for National Security," 14 April 1950, *FRUS 1950*, 4:235–92.

12. "President Truman's conversation with George M. Elsey," 26 June 1950, "Korea," Box 71, Elsey Papers, Harry S. Truman Presidential Library, Independence, Mo.

13. Little, "Cold War and Covert Action," 54–58.

14. "Discussion Meeting Report: The Moslem World," 9 May 1949, Records of Groups, vol. 28, Council on Foreign Relations Archives.

15. Acheson, *Present at the Creation*, 376.

16. Berle diary entry for 13 August 1952, in Berle and Jacobs, *Navigating the Rapids*, 607.

17. Lockman, *Contending Visions of the Middle East*, 129–33.

18. NSC adviser Robert Cutler, "Solarium Project," 9 May 1953, *FRUS 1952–54*, 2:323–26. For more on Solarium, see Pickett, *George F. Kennan and the Origins of Eisenhower's New Look*, 5–13.

19. "Summaries Prepared by the NSC Staff of Project Solarium Presentations and Written Reports," n.d., attached to James Lay to NSC, 22 July 1953, *FRUS 1952–54*, 2:416–17, 434.

20. Goodpaster quoted in Pickett, *Kennan and the Origins of Eisenhower's New Look*, 23.

21. Eisenhower, diary entry for 8 October 1953, "DDE Diary, October-December1953," DDE Diaries Series, Box 4, Dwight D. Eisenhower Presidential Library, Abilene, Kans.

22. Eden to Macmillan, 25 September 1956, Lloyd Papers, vol. 740, BNA.

23. Eisenhower to Dulles, 12 December 1956, *FRUS 1955–57*, 16:1297.

24. Eisenhower quoted in Yaqub, *Containing Arab Nationalism*, 103.

25. Lerner, *Passing of Traditional Society*, 44–45, 78–79.

26. Halpern, *Politics of Social Change in the Middle East and North Africa*, 51–78, 134–55.

27. Komer, "Our Policy in Iran," 20 October 1962, and Komer to McGeorge Bundy, n.d. [5 November 1962], *FRUS 1961–63*, 18:189–95, 202n2.

28. William Brubeck (DOS) to Bundy, 21 January 1963, *FRUS 1961–63*, 18:311–14; Komer, Oral History Interview, 31 October 1964, John F. Kennedy Presidential Library, Boston, Mass.

29. Talbot to Dean Rusk, 6 June 1963, and DOS circular telegram, 14 June 1963, *FRUS 1961–63*, 18:570–71.

30. Victor Krulak to Maxwell Taylor, "Subversive Insurgency in Iran," 13 June 1963; Shah quoted in Stuart Rockwell to DOS, tel. 24 June 1963, both items in *FRUS 1961–63*, 18:583–86, 601–3.

31. Rostow to LBJ, 17 May 1967, *FRUS 1964–68*, 22:368–70.

32. CIA, "Arab-Israeli Situation Report," 14 June 1967, 8:00 A.M., "Middle East Crisis, Vol. 11, Appendix Q (IV)," National Security File, National Security Council History Series, Box 21, Lyndon B. Johnson Presidential Library, Austin, Tex.

33. Rusk to Embassy Tehran, tel. 26 August 1967, *FRUS 1964–68*, 22:428–29; Walt Rostow to LBJ, "Visit of the Shah of Iran," 22 August 1967, "Rostow Vol. 39, 8/18–8/31/67 (2 of 2)," Memos to the President, Box 21, National Security File, Lyndon B. Johnson Presidential Library, Austin, Tex.

34. Acting FBI Director L. Patrick Gray to Attorney General Richard Kleindienst, 21 September 1972, "Operation Boulder," http://www.intelwire.com.

35. Kelley to Kissinger, 13 April 1974, and F. S. Putnam to W. R. Wannall, 6 March 1975, "Operation Boulder," http://www.intelwire.com.

36. On Qutb, see Wright, *The Looming Tower*, 7–31. On Kishk, see Ajami, *The Arab Predicament*, 52–62. On Musa al-Sadr, see Ajami, *The Vanished Imam*, 85–122.

37. George C. Denney, "The Roots of Arab Resistance to Modernization," 12 September 1969, RNA-41, "POL 2 Arab," U.S. Department of State, Alpha-Numerical File 1963-72, Record Group 59, U.S. National Archives, College Park, Md.

38. Little, "To the Shores of Tripoli," 80–83.

39. CIA, Directorate of Intelligence, "Libya: Qadhafi, Religious Revolutionary," 11 May 1973, RDP85T00875R001500050018–8; and "Libya: Arms Procurement," 25 May 1973, RDP85T00875R001500050019–7, Central Intelligence Agency, CIA Records Search Tool, National Archives, U.S. National Archives, College Park, Md.

40. Nixon-MacArthur-Haig tape transcript, 8 April 1971, *FRUS 1969–76*, E-4, document 122. For a superb account of the Nixon Doctrine in the Western Hemisphere, see Rabe, *The Killing Zone*, 119–49.

41. Nixon-Shah memcon, 31 May 1972, *FRUS 1969–76*, E-4, document 201.

42. Helms to DOS, tel. 26 June 1974, U.S. Department of State, Electronic Reading Room, "Other FOIA Released Documents." http://foia.state.gov/documents/foiadocs/2790.pdf.

43. Kissinger to Ford, "Meeting with Iranian Ambassador Ardeshir Zahedi," 21 August 1974, "Iran (1)," National Security Adviser's Country File, "Middle East-South Asia," Box 12, Gerald R. Ford Presidential Library, Ann Arbor, Mich.

44. Ford-Kissinger-Zahedi memcon, 4 March 1975, National Security Adviser's Memoranda of Conversations File, Box 9, Gerald R. Ford Presidential Library, Ann Arbor, Mich.

45. TDFIR Intelligence Information Cable, 8 May 1975, *FRUS 1969–76*, 27: 344–45.

46. "Address at Notre Dame University," 22 May 1977, *PPP Carter 1977*, 1:954–62.

47. Odom, "Cold War Origins of the U.S. Central Command," 57–59.

48. Diary entry for 7 June 1977, in Carter, *White House Diary*, 62.

49. Diary entries for 19 July and 24 September 1977, in Carter, *White House Diary*, 71, 107.

50. Vance to Carter, "Study Papers for the Camp David Talks," n.d. [late August 1978], and handwritten comment by Carter, item 535155, *Declassified Documents Reference System* (hereafter *DDRS*).

51. Brzezinski to Carter, "Strategy for Camp David," n.d. [early September 1978], item 466153, *DDRS* (emphasis in the original).

52. Diary entry for 7 September 1978, in Carter, *White House Diary*, 223–24, 226–27.

53. Diary entry for 16 September 1978, in Carter, *White House Diary*, 239–41.

54. Diary entry for 19 September1978, in Carter, *White House Diary*, 246–47.

55. Brzezinski to Carter, 9 November 1978, Brzezinski Papers, Box 42, "Weekly Reports to the President, 9/78–12/78," JCL.

56. Carter, "Toast at State Dinner in Tehran," 31 December 1977, *PPP Carter 1977*, 2:2220–22.

57. Carter to Brezhnev, enclosed in Carter to Prime Minister James Callaghan, 24 November 1978, "Political Situation in Iran—Future of Shah, Part 2," PREM 16, vol. 1720, BNA.

58. Parsons to FCO, tel. 31 October 1978, "Political Situation in Iran—Future of Shah, Part 1," PREM 16, vol. 1719, BNA.

59. Sullivan to DOS, tel. 9 November 1978, Digital National Security Archive, *Iran Revolution*, item IR01711, http://nsarchive.chadwyck.com.

60. Diary entries for 23 December and 25–31 December 1978, and 4 January 1979, in Carter, *White House Diary*, 268, 272.

61. Sick, *All Fall Down*, 142 (emphasis in the original).

62. Brzezinski to Carter, 2 February 1979, Brzezinski Papers, Box 42, "Weekly Reports to the President, 12/78–3/79," JCL.

63. INR, "The New Islamic Fundamentalism," n.d. [late February 1979], "Islamic Revival 1979," FCO 93, vol. 1827, BNA. (The U.S. embassy passed along a copy of this report to the British Foreign Office on 28 February 1979.)

64. Laingen to DOS, tel. 13 August 1979, 79TEHRAN 0890, Wikileaks, "Secret US Embassy Cables," http://wikileaks.org/cablegate.html.

65. Diary entry for 6 November 1979, in Carter, *White House Diary*, 368.

66. Diary entry for 28 December 1979, in Carter, *White House Diary*, 382.

67. Brzezinski to Carter, "Strategic Reaction to the Afghanistan Problem," 3 January 1980, *DDRS 1997*, microfiche edition, item 1672.

68. Carter, "Address to the Nation," 4 January, 1980, *PPP Carter 1980–81*, 1:22–23.

69. Diary entry for 4 January 1980, in Carter, *White House Diary*, 388.

70. Thornton to Brzezinski, 14 January 1980, "Meetings SCC 250," Box 31, Brzezinski Papers, JCL.

71. Diary entry for 14 January 1980, in Carter, *White House Diary*, 392.

72. Carter, "State of the Union Address," 22 January 1980, *PPP Carter 1980–81*, 1:197.

73. Reagan remarks at press conference, 29 January 1981, *PPP Reagan 1981*, 57.

74. Sterling, *The Terror Network*, 292–93. On Sterling's influence among Reagan administration insiders, see Naftali, *Blind Spot*, 123–24, and Law, *Terrorism: A History*, 276.

75. McMahon and Casey quoted in Persico, *Casey: From the OSS to the CIA*, 286–87.

76. Haig-Carrington memcon, 10 April 1981, "UK-USA Relations 1979–1982, Part 1," PREM 19, vol. 944, BNA.

77. Begin to Reagan, 13 April 1981, "Menachem Begin," Box 16, NSC Executive Secretariat, Heads of State Files, RRL.

78. Ambassador Samuel Lewis to DOS, tel. 3 June 1981, U.S. Department of State, Electronic Reading Room, "Other FOIA Documents," http://foia.state.gov/documents/foiadocs/6c6c.pdf.

79. Feith to Allen, 9 June 1981, and Allen to Reagan, n.d. [15 June 1981], "Iraq Israeli Strike," Box 37, NSC Executive Secretariat, Country Files, RRL.

80. Reagan remarks at press conference, 16 June 1981, *PPP Reagan 1981*, 520.

81. Draper quoted in Boykin, *Cursed Is the Peacemaker*, 49–50.

82. Haig to Begin, tel. 6 February 1982, U.S. Department of State, Electronic Reading Room, "Other FOIA Documents," http://foia.state.gov/documents/foiadocs/643a.pdf.

83. Haig and Sharon quoted in Boykin, *Cursed Is the Peacemaker*, 54–55.

84. Reagan-Begin memcon, 21 June 1982, *DDRS*, item 477205.

85. NSDD-75, "U.S. Relations with the USSR," 17 January 1983, NSC Executive Secretariat, National Security Decision Directives, RRL.

86. Reagan address, 8 March 1983, *PPP Reagan 1983*, 1:363–64.

87. Reagan radio remarks, 11 August 1984, http://www.youtube.com/watch?v=Zv13ZnkpWos.

88. CIA, "Resurgent Islamic Nationalism in the Middle East," March 1981, RDP06T00412R000200170001–0, Central Intelligence Agency, CIA Records Search Tool, National Archives.

89. CIA, "The Islamic Jihad," 25 September 1984, *DDRS*, item 251009.

90. NSDD-75, "U.S. Relations with the USSR," 17 January 1983, NSC Executive Secretariat, National Security Decision Directives, RRL.

91. Geoffrey Kemp and Philip Dur to William Clark, 26 April 1983, "Middle East Briefings (1 of 2)," Box 90585, NSC Executive Secretariat, Near East South Asia Affairs, RRL.

92. SNIE 11/37–2-85L, "Soviet Problems, Prospects, & Options in Afghanistan," March 1985, CIA, FOIA Electronic Reading Room.

93. Rashid, *Jihad: The Rise of Militant Islam in Central Asia*, 42–44.

94. Gorbachev quoted in "Diary of Anatoly Chernyaev: First Installment," 17 October 1985, National Security Archive, http://www2.gwu.edu/~nsarchiv/NSAEBB/NSAEBB 192. (Chernyaev was one of Gorbachev's most trusted political advisers.)

95. Diary entry for 6 March 1987, in Reagan, *Reagan Diaries*, 381.

96. Wright, *Looming Tower*, 131–33.

97. Zinni, *The Battle for Peace*, 112.

Chapter Two

1. Bush quoted in David Broder, "Cold War 'Not Over,' Bush Warns; Slackening Buildup Called a Mistake," *WP*, June 30, 1988.

2. Bush and Scowcroft, *A World Transformed*, 12–14.

3. National Security Review (NSR)-3, "Comprehensive Review of US-Soviet Relations," 15 February 1989, "National Security Reviews," http://bushlibrary.tamu.edu/research/pdfs/nsr/nsr3.pdf.

4. NSR-12, "Review of National Defense Strategy," 3 March 1989, "National Security Reviews," http://bushlibrary.tamu.edu/research/pdfs/nsr/nsr12.pdf.

5. Bush and Scowcroft, *A World Transformed*, 40.

6. For more on "status quo plus," see Beschloss and Talbott, *At the Highest Levels*, 44–45. For horseshoes, see Klein, "Where's George?," 24–25.

7. Condoleezza Rice interview, 6 November 1990, quoted in Oberdorfer, *The Turn*, 347. See also Bumiller, *Condoleezza Rice*, 96–97.

8. Bush and Scowcroft, *A World Transformed*, 42

9. Bush, "Address at Texas A and M University," 12 May 1989, *PPP Bush 1989*, 1:540–42.

10. George Bush interview, 1 June 1989, quoted in Oberdorfer, *The Turn*, 351–52. See also Beschloss and Talbott, *At the Highest Levels*, 81–82.

11. NSD-23, "United States Relations with the Soviet Union," 22 September 1989, "National Security Directives," http://bushlibrary.tamu.edu/research/pdfs/nsd/nsd23.pdf.

12. Gerasimov quoted in Bill Keller, "Gorbachev, in Finland, Disavows Any Right of Regional Intervention," *NYT*, 26 October 1989. See also "From Brezhnev Doctrine to Sinatra Doctrine."

13. Bush quoted in Beschloss and Talbott, *At the Highest Levels*, 132.

14. Bush-Kohl telcon, 10 November 1989, "Memcons and Telcons," http://bush41library.tamu.edu/archives/memcons-telcons.

15. Baker to Bush, 29 November 1989, National Security Archive, Electronic Briefing Book 298, "Bush and Gorbachev at Malta," http://www2.gwu.edu/~nsarchiv/NSAEBB/NSAEBB298.

16. Bush quoted in Baker, *The Politics of Diplomacy*, 170.

17. Gorbachev quoted in Beschloss and Talbott, *At the Highest Levels*, 162–63.

18. Soviet Transcript of Malta Summit, 2–3 December 1989, National Security Archive, Electronic Briefing Book 298, "Bush and Gorbachev at Malta," http://www2.gwu.edu/~nsarchiv/ NSAEBB/NSAEBB298.

19. Gorbachev-Bush telcon, 31 January 1990, "Memcons and Telcons," http://bush41library.tamu.edu/archives/memcons-telcons.

20. NIE 11-4-89, "Soviet Policy toward the West: The Gorbachev Challenge," April 1989, CIA FOIA Electronic Reading Room.

21. Douglas Mulholland (INR) to Baker, "Regional Issues at Malta," 17 November 1989, National Security Archive, Electronic Briefing Book 298, "Bush and Gorbachev at Malta," http://www2.gwu.edu/~nsarchiv/NSAEBB/NSAEBB298.

22. Bush-Saleh memcon, 24 January 1990, "Memcons and Telcons," http://bush41library.tamu.edu/archives/memcons-telcons.

23. Shamir quoted in Brinkley, "The Stubborn Strength of Yitzhak Shamir," 29.

24. Bush-Shamir memcon, 6 April 1989, "Memcons and Telcons," http://bush41library.tamu.edu/archives/memcons-telcons. On the AIPAC speech, see Thomas Friedman, "Baker, in a Middle East Blueprint, Asks Israel to Reach Out to Arabs"; and "Excerpts from Baker's Mideast Talk," *NYT*, 23 May 1989.

25. Bush-Thatcher memcon, 14 July 1989, "Memcons and Telcons," http://bush 41library.tamu.edu/archives/memcons-telcons.

26. Bush-Shamir telcon, 9 August 1989, "Memcons and Telcons," http://bush 41library.tamu.edu/archives/memcons-telcons.

27. Rubinstein quoted in Haass, *War of Necessity, War of Choice*, 40.

28. For the 16–17 October 1989 confrontation, see Baker, *Politics of Diplomacy*, 125. For the "little shit" reference, see Miller, *The Much Too Promised Land*, 210–11.

29. Bush-Shamir, two memcons, both 15 November 1989, "Memcons and Telcons," http://bush41library.tamu.edu/archives/memcons-telcons.

30. Scowcroft-Rabin memcon, 17 January 1990, "Memcons and Telcons," http://bush41library.tamu.edu/archives/memcons-telcons.

31. Bush quoted in Yossi Melman and Dan Raviv, *Friends in Deed*, 415–16.

32. Newton to DOS, tel. 21 November 1985, 85BAGHDAD3988, http://wikileaks.org/cablegate.html.

33. Hussein to Reagan, 18 November 1986, "Iraq—President Hussein," Box 16, NSC Executive Secretariat, Heads of State Files, RRL.

34. Ambassador April Glaspie to DOS, tel. 24 August 1988, 88BAGHDAD4620, http://wikileaks.org/cablegate.html.

35. DOS, "Overview of U.S.-Iraqi Relations and Potential Pressure Points," 9 September 1988, Digital National Security Archive, "Iraq-Gate," item 0632, http://nsarchive.chadwyck.com.

36. DOS, "Guidelines for U.S.-Iraq Policy," n.d. [January 1989], Digital National Security Archive, "Iraq-Gate," item 0761, http://nsarchive.chadwyck.com.

37. NSD-26, "U.S. Policy toward the Persian Gulf," 2 October 1989, "National Security Directives," http://bushlibrary.tamu.edu/research/pdfs/nsd/nsd26.pdf.

38. Haass, *War of Necessity, War of Choice*, 46–47.

39. DOS to Embassy Baghdad, tel. 13 October 1989, U.S. Department of State, Electronic Reading Room, "Other FOIA Documents," http://foia.state.gov/documents/foiadocs/2624.pdf; Baker, *Politics of Diplomacy*, 265–67.

40. Pollack, *The Threatening Storm*, 29–30.

41. Cheney, *In My Time*, 181.

42. Haass, *War of Necessity, War of Choice*, 50–51.

43. Glaspie to DOS, tel. 9 April 1990, 90BAGHDAD2098, http://wikileaks.org/cablegate.html.

44. Haass, *War of Necessity, War of Choice*, 52–54.

45. Glaspie to DOS, tel. 18 July 1990, Digital National Security Archive, "Iraq-Gate," item 1461, http://nsarchive.chadwyck.com.

46. DOS circular tel., 19 July 1990, "Working Files Iraq Pre-8/2/90 (1)," Haass Papers, GHWBL.

47. Glaspie to DOS, tel. 25 July 1990, 90BAGHDAD4237, http://wikileaks.org/cablegate.html.

48. Haass, *War of Necessity, War of Choice*, 56–57.

49. DOS to Glaspie, tel. 28 July 1990, "Working Files Iraq Pre-8/2/90 (3)," Haass Papers, GHWBL.

50. Bush and Scowcroft, *A World Transformed*, 302; Haass, *War of Necessity, War of Choice*, 3.

51. Bush diary entry for 2 August 1990, in Bush, *All the Best: My Life in Letters and Other Writings*, 476.

52. Powell quoted in Woodward, *The Commanders*, 229.

53. Bush and Scowcroft, *A World Transformed*, 315.

54. Ibid., 317–18.

55. Cheney, *In My Time*, 184, 186.

56. Haass memo, 2 August 1990, quoted in Bush and Scowcroft, *A World Transformed*, 321–22.

57. Minutes of the NSC meeting, 3 August 1990, "Working Files Iraq-August 2, 1990-December 1990 (8)," Haass Papers, GHWBL.

58. For the pipsqueak remark, see Beschloss and Talbott, *At the Highest Levels*, 249. Eagleburger's other comments are from minutes of the NSC meeting, 3 August 1990, "Working Files Iraq-August 2, 1990-December 1990 (8)," Haass Papers, GHWBL.

59. Minutes of the NSC meeting, 3 August 1990, "Working Files Iraq-August 2, 1990-December 1990 (8)," Haass Papers, GHWBL.

60. Minutes of the NSC meeting, 4 August 1990, "Working Files Iraq-August 2, 1990-December 1990 (8)," Haass Papers, GHWBL.

61. Bush and Scowcroft, *A World Transformed*, 375.

62. Fahd quoted in Bush-Toshiki Kaifu telcon, 3 August 1990, "Memcons and Telcons," http://bush41library.tamu.edu/archives/memcons-telcons.

63. Bush-Ozal telcon, 3 August 1990, "Working Files Iraq-August 2, 1990-December 1990 (3)," Haass Papers, GHWBL.

64. Haass handwritten notes, "KBT Lunch," 16 August 1990, "Working Files Iraq-August 2, 1990-December 1990 (3)," Haass Papers, GHWBL.

65. Unsigned handwritten notes (probably by Scowcroft), "P/Hussein 1 on 1," 16 August 1990, "Working Files Iraq-August 2, 1990-December 1990 (3)," Haass Papers, GHWBL.

66. Haass handwritten notes, "KBT Lunch," 16 August 1990, and Haass handwritten notecards, "KBT Lunch," 16 August 1990, "Working Files Iraq-August 2, 1990-December 1990 (3)," Haass Papers, GHWBL.

67. Bush quoted in Shlaim, *Lion of Jordan*, 494–95.

68. Unsigned handwritten notes (probably by Scowcroft), "P/Hussein 1 on 1," 16 August 1990, "Working Files Iraq-August 2, 1990-December 1990 (3)," Haass Papers, GHWBL.

69. Haass handwritten notes, "KBT 8/16/90," 16 August 1990, "Working Files Iraq-August 2, 1990-December 1990 (3)," Haass Papers, GHWBL.

70. Cheney, *In My Time*, 189.

71. Haass, "Additional Intervention for Gen. Scowcroft," n.d., attached to Haass to Scowcroft, 18 August 1990, "Working Files Iraq-August 2, 1990-December 1990 (1)," Haass Papers, GHWBL.

72. Scowcroft and Bush quoted in Beschloss and Talbott, *At the Highest Levels*, 252–53, 255.

73. Bush address to Joint Session of Congress, 11 September 1990, *PPP Bush 1990*, 2:1256.

74. Primakov and Bush quoted in Beschloss and Talbott, *At the Highest Levels*, 276.

75. Baker, *Politics of Diplomacy*, 312.

76. Beschloss and Talbott, *At the Highest Levels*, 281–82.

77. Baker, *Politics of Diplomacy*, 312.

78. Beschloss and Talbott, *At the Highest Levels*, 281–82.

79. Baker to Bush, "London Meetings," and Baker to Bush, "Paris Meetings," both 10 November 1990, "Working Files Iraq-November 1990 (2)," Haass Papers, GHWBL.

80. Baker, *Politics of Diplomacy*, 325–26.

81. Bush to Law, 22 January 1991, in Bush, *All the Best*, 505–6.

82. Haass, *War of Necessity, War of Choice*, 115.

83. Baker, *Politics of Diplomacy*, 364–65.

84. Cheney to Arens, 17 August 1990, "Working Files Iraq-November 1990 (8)," Haass Papers, GHWBL.

85. Ross quoted in Beschloss and Talbott, *At the Highest Levels*, 275–76.

86. Bush and Scowcroft, *A World Transformed*, 424–25.

87. Cheney, *In My Time*, 207, 217.

88. Baker, *Politics of Diplomacy*, 387–90.

89. Baker, *Politics of Diplomacy*, 417–25, 444–45. For the "dead cat" saying, see Miller, *Much Too Promised Land*, 197.

90. Baker, *Politics of Diplomacy*, 446.

91. Miller, *Much Too Promised Land*, 219.

92. Melman and Raviv, *Friends in Deed*, 420–21.

93. Bush remarks at Press Conference, *PPP Bush 1991*, 2:1139–40, 1141–42.

94. Bush-Shamir memcon, 30 October 1991, "Memcons and Telcons," http:// bush41library.tamu.edu/archives/memcons-telcons.

95. Bush-Shamir memcon, 22 November 1991, "Memcons and Telcons," http:// bush41library.tamu.edu/archives/memcons-telcons.

96. Scowcroft-Rabin memcon, 4 December 1991, "Memcons and Telcons," http:// bush41library.tamu.edu/archives/memcons-telcons.

97. Ross quoted in Melman and Raviv, *Friends in Deed*, 437.

98. Bush to George Klein, 19 March 1992, in Bush, *All the Best*, 552–54.

99. Dine quoted in Melman and Raviv, *Friends in Deed*, 438.

100. Lewis quoted in Melman and Raviv, *Friends in Deed*, 459–60.

101. Amitay quoted in Melman and Raviv, *Friends in Deed*, 442–43.

102. Bush quoted in Miller, *Much Too Promised Land*, 224–25.

103. Fukuyama, "The End of History?."

104. Bush-Saleh memcon, 24 January 1990, "Memcons and Telcons," http://bush 41library.tamu.edu/archives/memcons-telcons.

105. Baker to Bush, tel. 20 March 1990, U.S. Department of State, Electronic Reading Room, "Other FOIA Released Documents."

106. Wilcox to DOS, tel. 23 September 1988, 88JERUSALEM3168, http://wikil eaks.org/cablegate.html. For an inside account of the rise of Hamas, see Tamimi, *Hamas*, 52–61.

107. Brown to DOS, tel. 23 September 1989, 89TELAVIV14032, and Wilcox to DOS, 25 September 1990, 90JERUSALEM3430, http://wikileaks.org/cablegate.html.

108. Lewis, "Roots of Muslim Rage."

109. Baker, *Politics of Diplomacy*, 437.

110. Ibid., 582.

111. NSD-75, "American Policy toward Sub-Saharan Africa in the 1990s," 23 December 1992, "National Security Directives," http://bushlibrary.tamu.edu/research/pdfs/nsd/nsd75.pdf.

112. Ambassador Donald Petterson (Khartoum) to DOS, tel. 23 September 1992, 92KHARTOUM7039, http://wikileaks.org/cablegate.html.

113. Djerejian, "The U.S. and the Middle East in a Changing World." For more on the "Meridian House" speech, see Djerejian, *Danger and Opportunity*, 17–24.

114. Fukuyama, *The End of History and the Last Man*, 43–46, 235–37, 347.

115. Clarke, *Against All Enemies*, 59–60.

Chapter Three

1. Clinton, "A New Covenant for American Security."

2. Clinton comments, 11 October 1992, Commission on Presidential Debates, http://www.debates.org /index.php?page=october-11–1992-first-half-debate-transcript.

3. Michael Kelly, "The 1992 Campaign: The Democrats—Clinton and Bush Compete to Be Champion of Change; Democrat Fights Perceptions of Bush Gain," *WP*, 13 October 1992.

4. Halberstam, *War in a Time of Peace*, 175.

5. Holbrooke, *To End a War*, 52–53 (emphasis in the original).

6. Drew, *On the Edge: The Clinton Presidency*, 143–44, 157–58; Kaplan, *Balkan Ghosts*, xxiii, 286–87.

7. Lake, "From Containment to Enlargement."

8. CIA, "Somalia: Lessons Learned from What Hasn't Worked," 24 September 1992, CIA, FOIA Electronic Reading Room, http://www.foia.cia.gov/special_collections.

9. Ambassador Donald Petterson (Khartoum) to DOS, tel. 7 December 1992, 92KHARTOUM8788, http://wikileaks.org/cablegate.html.

10. Oakley quoted in Halberstam, *War in a Time of Peace*, 252.

11. Lake quoted in Drew, *On the Edge*, 319–20.

12. CIA, Office of African and Latin American Analysis, "Somalia: Dealing with Aideed," 12 July 1993, CIA FOIA Electronic Reading Room, http://www.foia.cia.gov/special_collections.

13. Aspin and Holbrooke quoted in Halberstam, *War in a Time of Peace*, 260, 265.

14. Clinton quoted in Drew, *On the Edge*, 317.

15. Clinton quoted in Clarke, *Against All Enemies*, 87.

16. Finnegan, "Letter from Mogadishu," 71.

17. Albright, *Madam Secretary*, 157.

18. White House, *A National Security Strategy of Engagement and Enlargement*.

19. Clinton, *My Life*, 554.

20. David Steiner-Haim Katz telcon, 22 October 1992, in "The Complete Unexpurgated AIPAC Tape," *Washington Report on Middle East Affairs Special Report* (December 1992/January 1993): 13–16, http://www.wrmea.org/wrmea-archives/144-washington-report-archives-1988–1993/decemberjanuary-1992–93/7066-the-complete-unexpurgated-aipac-tape.html.

21. Martin Indyk and Robert Satloff, "Issues Paper: Middle East Peace Talks," n.d. [December 1992], United States Institute of Peace, *The Peace Puzzle: Appendices and Resources*, "Transition Paper: Bush to Clinton," http://www.usip.org/publications/the-peace-puzzle.

22. Kurtzer et al., *The Peace Puzzle*, 280n63.

23. Miller, *The Much Too Promised Land*, 243.

24. Indyk, *Innocent Abroad*, 16–20.

25. Arafat quoted ibid., 73.

26. Rabin quoted in Clinton, *My Life*, 545.

27. Ross, *The Missing Peace*, 126.

28. Clinton, *My Life*, 678–79.

29. Clinton quoted in Miller, *Much Too Promised Land*, 250–52.

30. Ross, *The Missing Peace*, 236.

31. Clinton, *My Life*, 714.

32. Netanyahu, *Fighting Terrorism*, 102–4, 119.

33. Schmemann, "Outside In," 59.

34. Netanyahu quoted in Remnick, "The Outsider," 84.

35. "The President's News Conference with Prime Minister Netanyahu," 9 July 1996, *PPP Clinton 1996*, 2:1088–89. For Clinton's private remarks, see Miller, *Much Too Promised Land*, 270.

36. Ayalon quoted in Tyler, *Fortress Israel*, 396.

37. Albright, *Madam Secretary*, 292, 295.

38. Ibid., 315–16.

39. Clinton, "Press Conference with Prime Minister Netanyahu," 13 December 1998, *PPP Clinton 1998*, 2:2164.

40. Clinton, "Remarks to the Palestine National Council," 14 December 1998, *PPP Clinton 1998*, 2:2175, 2178.

41. Clinton-Hussein telcon, 17 December 1998, "Digital Declassified Records: Iraq," http://clintonlibrary.gov/assets/Declassified/2009–1292-M.pdf.

42. Indyk, *Innocent Abroad*, 31n†.

43. Ibid., 36–39.

44. Ibid., 39–41.

45. Pipes, "Interview with Martin Indyk."

46. Lake, "Confronting Backlash States," 45–55.

47. Indyk, *Innocent Abroad*, 153–58. For more on this episode, see Pollack, *The Threatening Storm*, 70.

48. Indyk, *Innocent Abroad*, 156–57.

49. Ibid., 181.

50. Charles Krauthammer, "Iran: Orchestrator of Disorder," *WP*, 1 January 1993.

51. Nixon, *Beyond Peace*, 145–46.

52. Pelletreau (Riyadh) to DOS, tel. 8 February 1995, 95RIYADH712, http://wikileaks.org/ cablegate.html.

53. Indyk, *Innocent Abroad*, 170–71.

54. DOS circular telegram, 17 November 1996, 96STATE237931, http://wikileaks.org/cablegate.html.

55. Berger quoted in Walsh, "Louis Freeh's Last Case," 71.

56. Pearce to DOS, tel. 21 May 1997, 97ABUDHABI3777, http://wikileaks.org/cablegate.html.

57. Albright, *Madam Secretary*, 320–21.

58. Talbott, *The Russia Hand*, 257–58.

59. Albright, *Madam Secretary*, 325.

60. Clinton and Gore quoted in Indyk, *Innocent Abroad*, 195–98.

61. "Summary of Conclusions for NSC Principals Meeting," 20 November 1998, "Digital Declassified Records: Iraq," http://clintonlibrary.gov/assets/Declassified/2009–1292-M.pdf.

62. Clinton-Mubarak telcon, 17 December 1998, "Digital Declassified Records: Iraq," http://clintonlibrary.gov/assets/Declassified/2009–1292-M.pdf. See also Clinton-Chirac, telcon, 17 December 1998, and Clinton-Blair telcon, 18 December 1998, both "Digital Declassified Records: Iraq," http://clintonlibrary.gov/assets/Declassified/2009–1292-M.pdf. Not everyone was happy, of course. Upset that he had not been consulted in advance, Russia's Boris Yeltsin warned Clinton on 30 December that another round of American unilateralism could damage relations with the Kremlin. "I don't want further military action," Clinton assured Yeltsin, adding that "we can't let Saddam undermine the U.S.-Russian relationship." Nevertheless, the Iraqis must realize that "if they keep shooting missiles at our planes, this could lead to a very serious confrontation." See Clinton-Yeltsin telcon, 30 December 1998, "Digital Declassified Records: Iraq," http://clintonlibrary.gov/assets/Declassified/2009–1292-M.pdf.

63. Indyk interview, 4 March 2004, quoted in Parsi, *A Single Roll of the Dice*, 24.

64. Ross, *Missing Peace*, 490–93. The Abbas quote is on 492.

65. Ibid., 509–11.

66. Clinton quoted in Indyk, *Innocent Abroad*, 336–37.

67. Miller, *Much Too Promised Land*, 284.

68. Arafat quoted in Ross, *Missing Peace*, 627.

69. Branch, *The Clinton Tapes*, 604, 607.

70. Ross-Qurei memcon, 26 June 2000, "Palestine Papers," http://www.aljazeera.com/palestinepapers.

71. Qurei quoted in Deborah Sontag, "And Yet So Far: The Quest for Middle East Peace; How and Why It Failed," *NYT*, 26 July 2001.

72. Barak quoted in Indyk, *Innocent Abroad*, 288–89.

73. Clinton, *My Life*, 913.

74. Clinton quoted in Indyk, *Innocent Abroad*, 320–21.

75. Berger quoted in Harris, *The Survivor*, 417–18.

76. Arafat quoted in Sontag, "And Yet So Far."

77. Ben Ami quoted in Shavit, "End of a Journey."

78. Albright, *Madam Secretary*, 493.

79. Indyk, *Innocent Abroad*, 336–37.

80. Berger interview, 7 July 2010, quoted in Kurtzer et al., *The Peace Puzzle*, 125, 143.

81. Abu Ala quoted in Sontag, "And Yet So Far."

82. Miller, *Much Too Promised Land*, 243, 307.

83. Zilberstein and Ben Ami both quoted in Beinart, *Crisis of Zionism*, 67, 72.

84. Clinton quoted in Miller, *Much Too Promised Land*, 303.

85. PLO memcon, 23 December 2000, "Palestine Papers," http://www.aljazeera.com/palestinepapers.

86. Ross, *Missing Peace*, 21–13.

87. Clinton quoted in Indyk, *Innocent Abroad*, 14.

88. Lake quoted in Drew, *On the Edge*, 144.

89. U.S. Department of State, *Patterns of Global Terrorism*.

90. For the broad thesis and the specifics of an "us versus them relation," see Huntington, "Coming Clash of Civilizations," 22–29. For "blood and belief," see Huntington, "If Not Civilizations, What?" 194.

91. Huntington, *Clash of Civilizations and the Remaking of World Order*, 256–58.

92. Mahbubani, "The Dangers of Decadence," 10–12.

93. Barry to DOS, tel. 16 August 1993, JAKARTA8764, http://wikileaks.org/cablegate.html.

94. Lake, "From Containment to Enlargement."

95. Christopher, "The Private Sector: Engine for Growth in the Middle East," and Christopher, "Turning Peace into Prosperity."

96. Albright, *Madam Secretary*, 327.

97. Clinton address to the Jordanian parliament, 26 October 1994, *PPP Clinton 1994*, 2:1880–81.

98. Pelletreau remarks, 26 May 1994, in "Symposium," 1–21.

99. Pelletreau, "Not Every Fundamentalist Is a Terrorist."

100. Clinton, *My Life*, 797.

101. Clarke, *Against All Enemies*, 87–88.

102. Benjamin and Simon, *The Age of Sacred Terror*, 247.

103. DOS, "INR Weekly Report," 18 July 1996, "Other FOIA," State Department FOIA Electronic Reading Room, http://foia.state.gov/Search/Collections.aspx.

104. Simons (Embassy Islamabad) to DOS, tel. 19 September 1996, 96ISLAMA-BAD8055, http://wikileaks.org/cablegate.html.

105. See the fifteen redacted reports from 1997 in National Security Archive, Electronic Briefing Book 381, "The CIA's 9/11 File."

106. Bin Laden, "Al-Qaeda's Declaration of War against the Americans," 23 February 1998, in Ibrahim, *The Al Qaeda Reader*, 11–14.

107. DOS circular telegram, 26 February 1998, 98STATE34310, http://wikileaks.org/cablegate.html.

108. Clinton quoted in Clarke, *Against All Enemies*, 190.

109. Embassy Islamabad to DOS, tel. 27 October 1998, 98ISLAMABAD8066, http://wikileaks.org/ cablegate.html.

110. Benjamin and Simon, *Age of Sacred Terror*, 284 (emphasis in the original).

111. National Commission on Terrorist Attacks upon the United States, *The 9/11 Commission Report*, 174–77. The quote is on 175.

112. Berger quoted in Clarke, *Against All Enemies*, 211–12.

113. NSC memo, "The Millennium Terrorist Alert—Next Steps," n.d. [3 January 2000], in National Commission, *The 9/11 Commission Report*, 179, 501n34 (emphasis in the original).

114. Lake, *Six Nightmares*, 222.

115. Bonk quoted in Eichenwald, *Five Hundred Days*, 1–2.

116. Sheehan quoted in Clarke, *Against All Enemies*, 223–24.

117. Benjamin and Simon, *Age of Sacred Terror*, 328.

Chapter Four

1. Bush Inaugural Address, 20 January 2001, *PPP Bush 2001*, 1:1–3.

2. Bush, *Decision Points*, 14–15.

3. Ibid., 22.

4. Bush speech at Iowa Western Community College, 21 January 2000, quoted in Miller, *The Bush Dyslexicon*, 207–8.

5. GOP Debate, 16 February 2000, *Online NewsHour*, http://www.pbs.org/newshour/bb/politics/jan-june00/se_debate 2–16.html.

6. Bush comments, 3 October 2000, Commission on Presidential Debates, "The First Gore-Bush Presidential Debate," http://www.debates.org/index.php?page=october-3-2000-transcript.

7. Rice quoted in Bumiller, *Condoleezza Rice*, 121–22.

8. Rice, "Promoting the National Interest," 46–47.

9. Project for the New American Century, "Statement of Principles."

10. Kristol quoted in Barry Gewen, "Irving Kristol, Godfather of Modern Conservatism, Dies at 89," *NYT*, 9 September 2009.

11. Hartmann, *Palace Politics*, 283.

12. Nixon-Haldeman conversation 9 March 1971, Miller Center, "Presidential Recordings Project: Nixon."

13. Bush remarks at the Citadel, 23 September 1999, http://www3.citadel.edu/pao/addresses/pres_bush.html.

14. Bush, "Remarks at Press Conference," 22 February 2001, *PPP Bush 2001*, 1:116.

15. "The President's News Conference with President Vladimir Putin of Russia," 16 June 2001, *PPP Bush 2001*, 1:688–89.

16. Rumsfeld, *Known and Unknown*, 307.

17. Rumsfeld, "Discussions with Russia," 12 July 2001, "Endnotes: Chap 23—Bears in the Woods," Rumsfeld Papers, http://papers.rumsfeld.com.

18. Linton Wells, "Thoughts for the 2001 Quadrennial Defense Review," n.d., attached to Rumsfeld to Bush et al., 12 April 2001, Rumsfeld Papers, "Document Library," www.rumsfeld.com/doclib/sp/2382/2001-04-12.

19. Rumsfeld memorandum, 31 May 2001, "Endnotes: Chap 21—Here We Go Again," Rumsfeld Papers, http://papers.rumsfeld.com.

20. Rice quoted in Bumiller, *Condoleezza Rice*, 138.

21. The account of the 30 January 2001 NSC meeting comes from Ron Suskind, *The Price of Loyalty*, 170–72.

22. Paul Wolfowitz, "Rebuilding the Anti-Saddam Coalition," *Wall Street Journal*, 18 November 1997.

23. Wolfowitz statement before the House National Security Committee, 16 September 1998, http://www.newamericancentury.org/iraqsep1898.htm.

24. Pollack, *The Threatening Storm*, 105.

25. Feith, *War and Decision*, 198.

26. Clarke, *Against All Enemies*, 233–34.

27. Cheney quoted in Lemann, "The Quiet Man," 59–60.

28. See Dark Winter, "The Final Script," and Dark Winter, "Slide Show."

29. Feith, *War and Decision*, 216–18.

30. Mylroie, *A Study of Revenge*. For the Wolfowitz quotes, see Isikoff and Corn, *Hubris*, 75.

31. Feith, *War and Decision*, 206–8.

32. Rumsfeld to Rice, 27 July 2001, "Endnotes: Chap 30—Out of the Box," Rumsfeld Papers, http://papers.rumsfeld.com.

33. Rice quoted in Bumiller, *Condoleezza Rice*, 140.

34. Tenet to Clinton, 18 December 2000, quoted in Tenet, *At the Center of the Storm*, 128–29.

35. Clinton quoted in National Commission, *The 9/11 Commission Report*, 199.

36. Berger quoted in Benjamin and Simon, *Age of Sacred Terror*, 328.

37. Sheridan quoted in Benjamin and Simon, *Age of Sacred Terror*, 328–29.

38. Clarke to Rice, 25 January 2001, National Security Archive, "Electronic Briefing Book 147," http://www2.gwu.edu/~nsarchiv/NSAEBB/NSAEBB147/clarke%20memo.pdf.

39. Clarke, *Against All Enemies*, 231–32.

40. Kerrick quoted in Benjamin and Simon, *Age of Sacred Terror*, 336.

41. Tenet, *At the Center of the Storm*, 145–46.

42. Clarke, *Against All Enemies*, 234.

43. Bush quoted in National Commission, *The 9/11 Commission Report*, 202. According to footnote 185 on page 510, Clarke said Bush made the quip in March, but Rice remembered it coming in May.

44. Tenet quoted in National Commission, *The 9/11 Commission Report*, 259.

45. Tenet, *At the Center of the Storm*, 150–53.

46. Ibid., 158.

47. CIA, "Bin Ladin Determined to Strike in US," National Security Archive, Electronic Briefing Book 343, "The Osama Bin Laden File," http://www2.gwu.edu/~nsarchiv/NSAEBB/ NSAEBB343/ osama_bin_laden_file02.pdf.

48. Bush, *Decision Points*, 135; Rice testimony before the 9/11 Commission, 13 May 2004, http://www.cnn.com/2004/ALLPOLITICS/04/08/rice.transcript.

49. Clarke to Rice, 4 September 2001, quoted in National Commission, *The 9/11 Commission Report*, 212–13.

50. Bush, *Decision Points*, 128, 134, 137.

51. Bush, "Address to the Nation," 11 September 2001, *PPP Bush 2001*, 2:1099–1100.

52. Bush quoted in Eichenwald, *Five Hundred Days: Secrets and Lies in the Terror Wars*, 50–51. Eichenwald's source appears to be "contemporaneous notes" taken by an unnamed participant in the NSC meeting.

53. Bush quoted in Woodward, *Bush at War*, 37.

54. Bush, *Decision Points*, 142.

55. Bush remarks at the World Trade Center Site, 14 September 2001, *PPP Bush 2001*, 2:1110.

56. Bush quoted in Eichenwald, *Five Hundred Days: Secrets and Lies in the Terror Wars*, 71–72.

57. Bush, "Address before Joint Session of Congress," 20 September 2001, *PPP Bush 2001*, 2:1141–42.

58. Feith, *War and Decision*, 7–8.

59. Rumsfeld quoted in Stephen Cambone (DoD), "Notes," 11 September 2001, 2:40 P.M., attached to DoD to Thad Anderson, 6 February 2006, FOIA Request 05-F-2077, TomFlocco.com, http://www.tomflocco.com/Docs/Dsn/DodStaffNotes.htm.

60. Feith, *War and Decision*, 49–51.

61. Rumsfeld to Bush, 19 September 2001, "Endnotes: Chap 26—War President," Rumsfeld Papers, http://papers.rumsfeld.com.

62. Rumsfeld to Shelton, 19 September 2001, quoted in Feith, *War and Decision*, 55–57.

63. Rumsfeld, "Vocabulary," 23 September 2001, "Endnotes: Chap 26—War President," Rumsfeld Papers, http://papers.rumsfeld.com.

64. Wolfowitz to Rumsfeld, 23 September 2001, "Endnotes: Chap 26—War President," Rumsfeld Papers, http://papers.rumsfeld.com.

65. Feith, *War and Decision*, 71 (emphasis in the original).

66. Rumsfeld to Bush, 30 September 2001, "Endnotes: Chap 27—Special Operations," Rumsfeld Papers, http://papers.rumsfeld.com.

67. Cheney, *In My Time*, 384–86. For the 20 September Dark Winter briefing, see Jane Mayer, *The Dark Side*, 3–4.

68. Bush, *Decision Points*, 157–59.

69. Rice, *No Higher Honor*, 99–101.

70. Edelman interview with the author, 27 June 2009.

71. Cheney and Tenet quoted in Suskind, *The One Percent Doctrine*, 61–63, 68–69.

72. Mayer, "Hidden Power," 44–55. The Cheney quote is on 49.

73. Institute for Advanced Strategic and Political Studies, "A Clean Break."

74. Isikoff and Corn, *Hubris*, 110–11 (emphasis in the original). On Wurmser's role at the Pentagon, see Feith, *War and Decision*, 117–18. The acronyms stand for the Popular Front for the Liberation of Palestine (PFLP), Palestinian Islamic Jihad (PIJ), the Abu Nidal Organization (ANO), and the Palestine Liberation Front (PLF). None of these groups was affiliated with or controlled by Yasser Arafat and the PLO. Neither was Hamas nor Ansar al-Islam.

75. Bush, *Decision Points*, 145.

76. Cheney, *In My Time*, 373.

77. Bush, "Address to Joint Session of Congress," 29 January 2002, *PPP Bush 2002*, 1:131–32.

78. Coleman quoted in Mayer, *The Dark Side*, 117–18.

79. Feith, *War and Decision*, 177–78.

80. Bush, "Commencement Address at West Point," 1 June 2002, *PPP Bush 2002*, 1:919.

81. Wolfowitz testimony, 26 June 2002, in U.S. Congress, Senate, Committee on Foreign Relations, *Afghanistan: Building Stability, Avoiding Chaos*.

82. OSD Policy Paper, "Sovereignty and Anticipatory Self-Defense," 24 August 2002, "Endnotes: Chap 30—Out of the Box," Rumsfeld Papers, http://papers.rumsfeld.com.

83. Cheney, *In My Time*, 388.

84. Rice, *No Higher Honor*, 152–53 (emphasis in the original). For more on the origins of NSC-2002 from the man who drafted it, see Zelikow, "U.S. Strategic Planning in 2001–2," 96–116, 210–15.

85. White House, *The National Security Strategy of the United States 2002*, 13–14.

86. Rice, *No Higher Honor*, 154.

87. White House, *National Security Strategy of the United States 2002*, 15.

88. Rice, *No Higher Honor*, 155.

89. Rumsfeld, *Known and Unknown*, 459.

90. Bush, *Decision Points*, 228.

91. Clarke, *Against All Enemies*, 30–31.

92. Gordon-Hagerty interview, in MSNBC, *Hubris: Selling the Iraq War*.

93. Bush quoted in Eichenwald, *Five Hundred Days: Secrets and Lies in the Terror Wars*, 71–72.

94. Bush, *Decision Points*, 189.

95. Rice, *No Higher Honor*, 86–87.

96. Bush, *Decision Points*, 189–90.

97. National Energy Development Policy Group, *Reliable, Affordable, and Environmentally Sound Energy for America's Future*, 85.

98. Rumsfeld Talking Points, 27 November 2001, National Security Archive, Electronic Briefing Book 418, "The Iraq War Ten Years After," http://www2.gwu.edu/~nsarchiv/NSAEBB/NSAEBB418.

99. Frum, "The Speechwriter."

100. Rumsfeld and Chalabi quoted in "Iraq's Oil," *60 Minutes*, 15 December 2002.

101. Ari Fleischer remarks, 20 March and 1 April 2003, http://www.youtube.com/watch?v=GoSBqs6y8uM; Immerman, *Empire for Liberty*, 224.

102. Brooke quoted in Cassidy, "Beneath the Sand," 73.

103. Cheney, *In My Time*, 368–69.

104. Wolfowitz quoted in Bowden, "Wolfowitz," 122.

105. Bush, *Decision Points*, 229.

106. Isikoff and Corn, *Hubris*, 6–11. The Maguire quote is on 8.

107. Bush quoted in Isikoff and Corn, *Hubris*, 2–3. Their source is Adam Levine, one of Fleischer's deputies, who witnessed Dubya's profane eruption.

108. Haass, *War of Necessity, War of Choice*, 5–6.

109. Matthew Rycroft, "Iraq: Prime Minister's Meeting, 23 July 2002," National Security Archive, Electronic Briefing Book 328, "Iraq War: Part II—Was There Even a Decision," http://nsarchive.gwu.edu/NSAEBB/NSAEBB328.

110. Haass, *War of Necessity, War of Choice*, 216.

111. Powell and Bush quoted in Woodward, *Plan of Attack*, 149–52.

112. Bush, "Remarks at U.N. General Assembly," 12 September 2002, *PPP Bush 2002*, 2:1576.

113. Bush private remarks, 20 September 2002, quoted in McClellan, *What Happened*, 139–41.

114. Bush and Makiya quoted in Draper, *Dead Certain*, 187.

115. Linda Feldmann, "The Impact of Bush Linking 9/11 and Iraq," *Christian Science Monitor*, 14 March 2003, http://www.csmonitor.com/2003/0314/p02s01-woiq.html.

116. Bush quoted in Draper, *Dead Certain*, 189.

117. White remarks, 26 June 2006, in "Warnings Went Unheeded," *MEI Publications*, www.mideasti.org/articles/doc535 (emphasis in the original). Portions of White's still-classified report dated 26 February 2003 were quoted in "Showdown with Iraq: Democracy Domino Theory Not Credible," *Los Angeles Times*, 14 March 2003.

118. Packer, *The Assassins' Gate*, 124–35. Hughes is quoted on 133.

119. Bush, "Address from the U.S.S. Abraham Lincoln," 1 May 2003, *PPP Bush 2003*, 1:410–13.

120. Feith quoted in Fred Kaplan, "Who Disbanded the Iraqi Army?" 7 September 2007, *Slate*, http://www.slate.com/articles/news_and_politics/war_stories/2007/09/who_disbanded_the_iraqi_army.html.

121. Hughes quoted in Rudd, *Reconstructing Iraq*, 332–33.

122. Zinni quoted in Ricks, *Fiasco*, 87.

123. Franks quoted in Woodward, *Plan of Attack*, 281.

124. Arcangeli quoted in Ricks, *Fiasco*, 17.

125. Ahmed and Foley quoted in Chandrasekaran, *Imperial Life in the Emerald City*, 26, 142–43.

126. Rumsfeld remarks, 18 June 2003, http://www.defense.gov/Transcripts/Transcript.aspx? TranscriptID=2758; Bush remarks, 2 July 2003, *PPP Bush, 2003*, 2:816.

127. Carney quoted in Chandrasekaran, *Imperial Life in the Emerald City*, 40.

128. Toolan quoted in Ricks, *Fiasco*, 345.

129. Gfoeller quoted in Bremer, *My Year in Iraq*, 129.

130. Bolton quoted in Scoblic, *U.S. vs. Them*, 157–60, 229.

131. Agresto quoted in Chandrasekaran, *Imperial Life in the Emerald City*, 5–6, 325.

132. Unnamed CPA aide quoted in Chandrasekaran, *Imperial Life in the Emerald City*, 314.

133. Bush, Inaugural Address, 20 January 2005, *PPP Bush 2005*, 1:16–19.

134. Bush, *Decision Points*, 232.

135. Rice, "Remarks at the American University in Cairo," 20 June 2005, http://2001–2009.state.gov/secretary/rm/2005/48328.htm.

136. Zelikow to Rice, 26 September 2005, quoted in Woodward, *State of Denial*, 412–14.

137. Rice and unnamed DoD official both quoted in Rose, "The Gaza Bombshell."

138. Hamdan quoted in Wright, *Dreams and Shadows*, 53.

139. Bush quoted in Woodward, *State of Denial*, 447.

140. Hadley to Bush, 8 November 2006, in "Text of U.S. Security Adviser's Iraq Memo," *NYT*, 29 November 2008.

141. Baloch quoted in Dalrymple, "Days of Rage," 27.

142. Bolton quoted in Steven Lee Myers, "Former Bush Loyalist Faults Administration Policy on Iran, North Korea and Israel," *NYT*, 9 November 2007.

143. Ambassador Jon Purnell to DOS, tel. 11 August 2006, 06TASHKENT1562, http://wikileaks.org/cablegate.html.

144. C. J. Chivers. "U.S. Courting a Somewhat Skittish Friend in Central Asia," *NYT*, 21 June 2007.

145. Ambassador Francis Ricciardone to DOS, tel. 17 July 2007, 07CAIRO2280, http://wikileaks.org/cablegate.html.

146. Powell quoted in David Samuels, "Grand Illusions," 52.

147. Zinni, *The Battle for Peace*, 89.

Chapter Five

1. Obama, "Inaugural Address," 20 January 2009, *PPP Obama 2009*, 1:2–3.

2. Obama, *Dreams from My Father*, 45.

3. Ibid., 85.

4. Obama, *Audacity of Hope*, 280, 282–84, 292–93.

5. Barack Obama, "Against Going to War with Iraq," 2 October 2002, *Common Dreams*, 28 February 2008, https://www.commondreams.org/archive/2008/02/28/7343.

6. Obama, *The Audacity of Hope*, 302–3.

7. Ibid., 303–11. The Ho Chi Minh quote is on 304.

8. Obama quoted in Alter, *The Promise*, 90.

9. Liu quoted in Nathan and Scobell, "How China Sees America," 39–40.

10. Johnny Lin, "Xi's Trip Intended to Allay US Misgivings about China," *Want China Times*, 20 February 2012, http://www.wantchinatimes.com/news-subclass-cnt.aspx?id=20120220000100&cid=1501.

11. An, "The Principle of Non-Interference."

12. Obama-Melhem interview, 26 January 2009, http://www.politico.com/news/stories/0109/18023.html.

13. Obama remarks in Ankara, 6 April 2009, *PPP Obama 2009*, 1:455.

14. Obama address to the Turkish Parliament, 6 April 2009, *PPP Obama 2009*, 1:454.

15. Obama address at Cairo University, 4 June 2009, *PPP Obama 2009*, 1:760–68.

16. Pew Research Global Attitudes Project, "Confidence in Obama Lifts U.S. Image around the World."

17. Obama quoted in Alter, *The Promise*, 351.

18. Reese e-mail to General Raymond Odierno, "It's Time to Declare Victory and Go Home," n.d. [early July 2009], in Michael Gordon, "U.S. Adviser's Blunt Memo on Iraq: Time 'to Go Home,'" *NYT*, 30 July 2009.

19. Obama quoted in Woodward, *Obama's Wars*, 34.

20. Jones quoted in Woodward, *Obama's Wars*, 127.

21. Biden and Obama quoted in Woodward, *Obama's Wars*, 167.

22. Obama quoted in Woodward, *Obama's Wars*, 189–90.

23. Holbrooke quoted in Woodward, *Obama's Wars*. 231.

24. Goldstein, *Lessons in Disaster*, 19–26, 229–48. On the Obama administration's required reading, see Mann, *The Obamians*, 131.

25. Gates to Obama, 13 October 2009, quoted in Gates, *Duty*, 373–75.

26. Gates quoted in Mann, *The Obamians*, 240.

27. Gates, *Duty*, 496.

28. Obama quoted in Woodward, *Obama's Wars*, 329–30.

29. Obama and McChrystal quoted in Woodward, *Obama's Wars*, 350–51.

30. Jones quoted in Traub, "A Civic War," 26.

31. Hastings, "The Runaway General."

32. Obama quoted in Alter, *The Promise*, 71.

33. Abunimah, "How Barack Obama Learned to Love Israel."

34. Radio Pacific debate between Ali Abunimah and Malcolm Hoenlein, 22 August 2001, *Electronic Intifada*, http://electronicintifada.net/content/debate-between-ali-abunimah-and-malcolm-hoenlein-kpfk/9321. On Abunimah's background, see Zeveloff, "Lightning Rod of the Boycott Israel Movement."

35. Obama and Netanyahu remarks, 18 May 2009, *PPP Obama 2009*, 1:667, 670, 672.

36. Abbas and Obama quoted in Saab Erekat, "NSU Minutes," 2 June 2009, *Palestine Papers*, http://www.aljazeera.com/palestinepapers.

37. Erekat-Hale memcon, 17 September 2009, *Palestine Papers*, http://www.aljazeera.com/ palestinepapers.

38. Erekat-Mitchell-Clinton memcon, 20 October 2009, *Palestine Papers*, http://www.aljazeera.com/palestinepapers.

39. Biden quoted in Ethan Bronner, "As Biden Visits, Israel Unveils Plan for New Settlements," *NYT*, 9 March 2010.

40. Clinton and Axelrod quoted in Daniel Nasaw, "Obama Aide Calls Israeli Settlement Announcement an 'Insult' to the US," *Guardian*, 14 March 2010, http://www.guardian.co.uk/ world/2010/mar/14/israel-palestinian-territories.

41. Saban quoted in Bruck, "The Influencer," 66.

42. "Netanyahu's Brother-in-Law: 'Obama Is an Anti-Semite,'" *Haaretz*, 17 March 2010.

43. NSU, "Prospects for Peace in the Middle East during President Obama's Administration: A Palestinian Perspective," 26 April 2010, *Palestine Papers*, http://www.aljazeera.com/palestinepapers.

44. Obama television interview with Yonit Lavi, 7 July 2010, http://www.white house.gov.

45. Obama address to UN General Assembly, 23 September 2010, http://www.whitehouse.gov.

46. Cantor quoted in Laura Rosen, "Before Clinton Meeting, Cantor's One-on-One with Bibi," *Politico*, 11 November 2010, http://www.politico.com/blogs/laurarozen/1110.

47. Dan Ephron interview with Lieberman, *Newsweek*, 27 December 2010–3 January 2011, 40–41.

48. "Explanation of Vote by Ambassador Susan E. Rice," 18 February 2011, http://usun.state.gov/ briefing/statements/2011/156816.htm.

49. Obama, "Remarks on the Middle East and North Africa," 19 May 2011, http://www.whitehouse.gov.

50. Huma Khan, "Netanyahu Office Tweets Disapproving Response," 19 May 2011, http://abcnews.go.com/blogs/politics/2011/05/netanyahus-office-tweets-disapproving-response-to-president-obamas-speech.

51. Obama's aide and Netanyahu quoted in Beinart, *Crisis of Zionism*, 151–52.

52. Obama remarks to AIPAC Annual Policy Conference, 22 May 2011, http://www.whitehouse.gov.

53. Netanhyahu address to Joint Session of Congress, 24 May 2011, http://www.cfr.org/israel/ netanyahus-address-us-congress-may-2011/p25073; Malley quoted in Helene Cooper and Ethan Bronner, "Netanyahu Gives No Ground in Congress Speech," *NYT*, 24 May 2011.

54. Cantor quoted in Jennifer Steinhauer and Steven Lee Myers, "House Republicans Discover a Growing Bond with Netanyahu," *NYT*, 20 September 2011.

55. Sarkozy and Obama quoted in Yann Le Guernigou, "Sarkozy Tells Obama Netanyahu Is a 'Liar,'" *Reuters*, 8 November 2011, http://www.reuters.com.

56. Steinberg quoted in Mann, *The Obamians*, 205.

57. GOP Debate at St. Anselm's College, Manchester, New Hampshire, 17 January 2012, http://2012.republican-candidates.org/Romney/Iran.php.

58. Romney remarks at private fund-raiser, 17 May 2012, "Rethinking National Security: 2012 Candidate Quotes on Foreign Policy and Defense," *Rethinking National Security*, http://cipnationalsecurity.wordpress.com/ resources/candidate-quotes.

59. Benn quoted in Remnick, "The Vegetarian," 26.

60. Obama remarks, 19 March 2009, http://www.youtube.com/watch?v= 6MDklneATBI.

61. Khamenei remarks, 25 March 2009, http://www.youtube.com/watch?v=t_ oAHcsYqIs. See also Parsi, *Single Roll of the Dice*, 66–67.

62. Obama address at Cairo University, 4 June 2009, *PPP Obama 2009*, 1:760–68.

63. Ramin Asgard (Dubai) to DOS, tel. 13 June 2009, 09RPODUBAI247, http://wikileaks.org/cablegate.html.

64. Obama, "Opening Remarks on Iran," 23 June 2009, http://www.whitehouse.gov.

65. Timothy Richardson (Dubai) to DOS, 20 August 2009, 09RPODUBAI316, http://wikileaks.org/cablegate.html.

66. Lizza, "The Consequentialist," 50–51. The text of PSD-11 remains classified, but Lizza has seen a copy and quotes the document extensively.

67. Chargé d'Affaires Christopher Henzel (Manama) to DOS, tel. 13 March 2009, 09MANAMA151, http://wikileaks.org/cablegate.html.

68. Ambassador Ford Fraker (Riyadh) to DOS, tel. 31 March 2009, 09RIYADH496, http://wikileaks.org/cablegate.html.

69. Ambassador Stephen Seche (Sana'a) to DOS, tel. 15 September 2009, 09SANAA1669, http://wikileaks.org/cablegate.html.

70. Ambassador Stephen Beecroft (Amman) to DOS, tel. 25 November 2009, 09AMMAN2576; and Beecroft to DOS, 3 February 2010, 10AMMAN308, http://wikileaks.org/ cablegate.html.

71. Abdullah-Stewart interview, 23 September 2010, http://www.thedailyshow.com/watch/thu-september-23–2010/king-abdullah-ii-of-jordan; and extended Abdullah-Stewart interview, 23 September 2010, http://www.thedailyshow.com/watch/thu-september-23–2010/exclusive-king-abdullah-ii-of-jordan-extended-interview.

72. Ambassador Samuel Kaplan (Rabat) to DOS, tel. 3 February 2010, 10RABAT87, http://wikileaks.org/cablegate.html.

73. Ambassador Gene Cretz (Tripoli) to DOS, tel. 29 January 2009, 09TRIPOLI68, http://wikileaks.org/cablegate.html.

74. Scobey to DOS, tel. 19 May 2009, 09CAIRO874, http://wikileaks.org/cablegate.html.

75. Scobey to DOS, tel. 9 February 2010, 10CAIRO181, http://wikileaks.org/cablegate.html.

76. Godec to DOS, tel. 23 June 2008, 08TUNIS679, http://wikileaks.org/cablegate.html.

77. Gray to DOS, tel. 5 November 2009, 09TUNIS813, http://wikileaks.org/cablegate.html.

78. Gray to DOS, tel. 3 February 2010, 10TUNIS87, http://wikileaks.org/cablegate.html.

79. De Soto, "The Real Mohamed Bouazizi."

80. Donilon press briefing, 14 January 2011, http://www.whitehouse.gov.

81. Power quoted in Mann, *The Obamians*, 258.

82. Steinberg quoted in Mann, *The Obamians*, 260.

83. Clinton quoted in Ghattas, *The Secretary*, 225–26.

84. Al-Aswany, *Yacoubian Building*, 84–85.

85. Obama quoted in Sanger, *Confront and Conceal*, 297.

86. Mubarak quoted in Lizza, "The Consequentialist," 52–53.

87. Obama quoted in Mann, *The Obamians*, 263–64.

88. Obama, "Remarks on the Situation in Egypt," 1 February 2011, http://www.whitehouse.gov.

89. Obama quoted in Sanger, *Confront and Conceal*, 295.

90. Cook, *The Struggle for Egypt*, 303.

91. Clinton, *Hard Choices*, 341.

92. Qassim quoted in *Report of the Bahrain Independent Commission of Inquiry*, 67.

93. Briefing by Press Secretary Jay Carney, 16 March 2011, http://www.whitehouse.gov.

94. Karen DeYoung, "Top White House Aide Delivers Obama Letter to Saudi King," *WP*, 12 April 2011.

95. Obama quoted in Sanger, *Confront and Conceal*, 343–45.

96. Lizza, "The Consequentialist," 55.

97. Steavenson, "Roads to Freedom," 32.

98. Chargé d'Affaires Charles Hunter to DOS, tel. 24 February 2010, 10DAMASCUS159, http://wikileaks.org/cablegate.html.

99. Clinton quoted in Goldberg, "Danger: Falling Tyrants," 54.

100. Ghattas, *The Secretary*, 277.

101. Panetta, *Worthy Fights*, 301.

102. Obama remarks at State Department, 19 May 2011, http://www.whitehouse.gov.

103. Clinton quoted in Goldberg, "Danger: Falling Tyrants," 54.

104. "The Second McCain-Obama Presidential Debate," 7 October 2008, Commission on Presidential Debates, http://www.debates.org/index.php?page=october-7-2008-debate-transcript.

105. Kayani quoted in Gul, *The Most Dangerous Place*, 218.

106. Obama quoted in Woodward, *Obama's Wars*, 302–3.

107. Brennan quoted in Baker, "Obama's War over Terror," 33.

108. Obama quoted in Woodward, *Obama's Wars*, 123.

109. Bin Laden, "Open Letter to the American People," n.d. [early 2010], Office of the Director of National Intelligence, "Bin Laden's Bookshelf," http://www.dni.gov/index.php/resources/bin-laden-bookshelf?start=1.

110. Leiter and Obama quoted in *Confront and Conceal*, 93.

111. Obama quoted in Schmidle, "Getting Bin Laden," 45.

112. Leiter quoted in Sanger, *Confront and Conceal*, 102.

113. Awlaki quoted in Scott Shane and Souad Mekhennet, "From Condemning Terror to Preaching Jihad," *NYT*, 9 May 2010.

114. Mark Mazzetti, Charlie Savage, and Scott Shane, "A U.S. Citizen in America's Cross Hairs," *NYT*, 9 March 2013.

115. Obama quoted in Jo Becker and Scott Shane, "Secret 'Kill List' Proves a Test of Obama's Principles and Will," *NYT*, 29 May 2012.

116. Obama and Koh quoted in Becker and Shane, "Secret 'Kill List' Proves a Test of Obama's Principles and Will," *NYT*, 29 May 2012.

117. For an eye-opening account of drones and domestic law enforcement, see Paumgarten, "Here's Looking at You," 46–59.

118. Shahzad quoted in Becker and Shane, "Secret 'Kill List' Proves a Test of Obama's Principles and Will," *NYT*, 29 May 2012.

119. Obama quoted in Cole, "Obama and Terror," 34.

120. "Mitt Romney's Anti-Terrorism, Pro-America Ad," April 2010, http://www.youtube.com/watch?v=v-dejS5JPPk.

121. Michelle Boorstein et al., "Origins of Controversial Anti-Muslim Video Remain a Mystery," *WP*, 13 September 2012; Marantz, "'Innocence of Muslims.'"

122. Gillian Flaccus, "Steve Klein and 'Innocence of Muslims': Film Promoter Remains Outspoken on Islam," 13 September 2012, *Huffington Post*, http://www.huffingtonpost.com/2012/09/13/steve-klein-innocence-of-muslims-producer_n_1882595.html.

123. White House e-mail, 14 September 2012, "The White House's Benghazi E-Mails," *NYT*, 15 May 2013, http://www.nytimes.com/interactive/2013/05/16/us/politics/16benghazi-emails.html?_r=0.

124. On U.S. casualties, see "Operation Enduring Freedom," http://icasualties.org/oef. On drone warfare, see "US Drone Strikes in Afghanistan Rose Sharply Last Year, UN Reports," *Guardian*, 19 February 2013.

125. Rashid, *Pakistan on the Brink*, 160–86.

126. Tim Arango and Sebnem Arsu, "Suicide Blast Kills U.S. Embassy Guard in Turkey," *NYT*, 1 February 2013.

127. Tsarnaev's note quoted in Eric Levenson, "Here's the Note Dzhokhar Tsarnaev Wrote inside the Boat Where He Was Captured," *Boston Globe*, 15 March 2015.

128. On al-Qaeda in the Islamic Maghreb, see Hammer, "When Jihad Came to Mali," 12–14; Anderson, "State of Terror," 36–47; and Dreazen, "New Terrorist Training Ground," 60–70.

Chapter Six

1. Although most Westerners refer to ISIS or the Islamic State, Obama and his national security team prefer the acronym ISIL (the Islamic State in Iraq and the Levant).

2. Obama interview with Goldberg, 19 May 2015, http://www.theatlantic.com/international/archive/2015/05/obama-interview-iran-isis-israel/393782.

3. Pew Research Center, "Republicans Want GOP Leaders to Challenge Obama More Often."

4. Glenn Greenwald and Murtaza Hussain, "Under Surveillance: Meet the Muslim-American Leaders the FBI and NSA Have Been Spying On," *The Intercept*, 9 July 2014, https://firstlook.org/theintercept/article/2014/07/09/under-surveillance.

5. Faludi, *The Terror Dream*, 200–216.

6. Drinnon, *Facing West*, 578–613; Melville, *Confidence-Man*, 163–71.

7. Lepore, *The Name of War*, xi.

8. Walker quoted in Lepore, *The Name of War*, 113.

9. Jackson quoted in Remini, *Andrew Jackson and His Indian Wars*, 85 (emphasis in the original).

10. McCarthy, *Blood Meridian; or, the Evening Redness in the West*, 34.

11. Brown quoted in Hunt, *Haiti's Influence on Antebellum America*, 100.

12. "Will the Contrabands Fight," *Weekly Anglo-African*, 15 February 1862, quoted in Clavin, "American Toussaints," 100.

13. Hayes quoted in Bridges, "The Betrayal of the Freedmen? Rutherford B. Hayes and the End of Reconstruction."

14. Hayes quoted in Miller, *The Unwelcome Immigrant*, 190.

15. Roosevelt quoted in LaFeber, *The Clash*, 80.

16. Roosevelt to Cecil Spring Rice, 1 July 1907, in Morison, *The Letters of Theodore Roosevelt*, 5:698–99.

17. Ledyard quoted in Oren, *Power, Faith, and Fantasy*, 48–49.

18. Smith quoted in Makdisi, *Artillery of Heaven*, 146.

19. Twain, *The Innocents Abroad*, 374–75, 423–24. On the popular reception of Twain's travelogue, see Oren, *Power Faith, and Fantasy*, 243–45.

20. Stoddard, *The New World of Islam*, 23–24, 41, 75–78, 98, 112, 208.

21. Lybyer, "Review of the New World of Islam by Lothrop Stoddard," 324; Harding quoted in Yellin, *Racism in the Nation's Service*, 182.

22. On Muslim immigration to the United States before 1945 and the rise of the Nation of Islam, see Abdo, *Mecca and Main Street*, 70–77.

23. OSS Coordinator of Information, "Axis Propaganda in the Moslem World," 23 December 1941, in *O.S.S. Research Reports*, part 12: *Middle East 1950–1961*, reel 1, item 2.

24. On the leaflets, see Oren, *Power, Faith, and Fantasy*, 251.

25. Ike to Mamie, 27 November 1942, in Eisenhower, *Letters to Mamie*, 66.

26. Shaheen, *Reel Bad Arabs*, 42–43, 162, 367–68.

27. Kennan, *Memoirs, 1925–1950*, 184, 380.

28. OSS, Research and Analysis Branch, "Communist and Pro-Russian Trends in the Near East," 23 May 1944, in *O.S.S. Research Reports*, part 12: *Middle East 1950–1961*, reel 1, item 11.

29. Annex 2, "Replies of the President," attached to Henderson to Byrnes, 10 November 1945, *FRUS 1945*, 8:15–16.

30. "Islam: A Threat to World Stability," 24, 34.

31. CIA, "The Resurgence of Islam," 1 March 1979, Brzezinski Papers, JCL.

32. Powell, handwritten meeting notes, 29 July 1988, "George Shultz—3 of 3," Box 3 (92477), White House Staff Offices: Colin Powell, RRL.

33. King, "Opening Statement," 10 March 2011, http://homeland.house.gov/ hearing/hearing-%E2%80%9C-extent-radicalization-american-muslim-community-and-communitys-response%E2%80%9D.

34. Ellison testimony quoted in Elise Foley, "Ellison Tears Up on Hearing about Muslim American 'Radicalization,'" *Huffington Post*, 10 March 2011, http://www. huffingtonpost.com/ 2011/03/10/keith-ellison-tears-up-muslim-hearings_n_833981. html.

35. Emerson, *American Jihad*; Emerson, *Jihad Incorporated*; and *The Grand Deception*.

36. Horowitz, *Unholy Alliance*, 183, 201.

37. "This Is War," 12 September 2001, reprinted in Coulter, *How to Talk to a Liberal (If You Must)*, 26–28.

38. Coulter, *Godless*, 131.

39. CTV News Staff, "Coulter Speech Cancelled Over Fears of Violence," 23 March 2010, http://www.ctvnews.ca/coulter-speech-cancelled-over-fears-of-violence-1.494773.

40. Other slogans include "No Sharia Law" and "Mosque Terrorist Hunter." For a full list, see http://www.cafepress.com/+islam+bumper-stickers.

41. Limbaugh transcript, 4 May 2010, http://www.rushlimbaugh.com/ daily/2010/05/04/ for_every_problem_a_villain_except_for_muslim_terrorists.

42. Jack Mirkinson, "Glenn Beck: Ten Percent of Muslims Are Terrorists," *Huffington Post*, 6 December 2010, http://www.huffingtonpost.com/2010/12/06/glenn-beck-ten-percent-muslims-terrorists_n_792726.html.

43. Frank Rich, "We'll Win This War on '24,'" *NYT*, 9 January 2005.

44. Episode 10, "Broken Hearts," and Episode 12, "The Choice," *Homeland: Season 2*, http://www.sho.com/sho/homeland/season/2#/index.

45. DeMille, *Night Fall*, 112.

46. Clancy, *Against All Enemies*; Charlie Savage and Scott Shane, "U.S. Accuses Iranians of Plotting to Kill Saudi Envoy," *NYT*, 12 October 2011.

47. Portnow quoted in *Extra Credits*, Season Three, Episode 12, "Propaganda Games," 12 October 2011, http://www.maker.tv/video/DRf4Tpgdo93h/series/ extracreditz. For more on Portnow, see "The Many Roles of James Portnow," *Digipen*, 19 March 2013, http://news.digipen.edu/academics/the-many-roles-of-james-portnow/#.VWy1eEbm44I.

48. Saleem and Anderson, "Arabs as Terrorists," 93, 97.

49. Statistics compiled from "FBI Uniform Crime Reports, Hate Crimes," http:// www.fbi.gov/ about-us/cjis/ucr/hate-crime.

50. Eggers, *Zeitoun*, 307–9.

51. Andrea Elliott, "The Man Behind the Anti-Shariah Movement," *NYT*, 31 July 2011; Matthew Brown, "North Carolina Becomes Seventh State to Ban Muslim Sharia Law," *Deseret News*, 28 August 2013.

52. ADL, "Backgrounder: Stop Islamization of America," 11 March 2011, http:// archive.adl.org/ main_extremism/sioa-a.html#.U87E8tJOV_9.

53. Gohmert speech, 16 June 2011, http://www.texastribune.org/2011/06/21/video-ac360-calls-out-gohmert-57-states-remark.

54. Limbaugh transcript, "Obama Regime Denied Requests for Help from CIA Heroes during Benghazi Attack," 26 October 2012, http://www.rushlimbaugh.com/daily/2012/10/26.

55. Limbaugh transcript, "Petraeus Changes His Benghazi Story," 16 November 2012, http://www.rushlimbaugh.com/daily/2012/11/16.

56. Nickel quoted in Fitzpatrick, "The Evangelical Crackup," 66.

57. Pew Research Religion and Public Life Project, "Little Voter Discomfort with Romney's Mormon Religion."

58. Hank Williams Jr., quoted in the *Des Moines Register*, 18 August 2012, http://desmoines. metromix.com/music/blog.

59. "Madonna—Second Night Speech—MDNA Tour—Washington DC," 24 September 2012, http://www.youtube.com/watch?v=i7R78LOpyM8&feature=player_embedded; Sally Quinn, "Madonna's 'Black Muslim in the White House' Quip Should Give Candidates Pause," *WP*, 27 September 2012.

60. Excerpt from *Savage Nation*, 2 August 2013, https://www.youtube.com/watch?v=Uei1u9qk-dc.

61. Gingrich, "America at Risk."

62. Limbaugh transcript, "The President Decides He Can Kill US Citizens without Making a Case to a Judge," 5 February 2013, http://www.rushlimbaugh.com/daily/2013/02/05.

63. Greg Richter, "Ann Coulter: Allow Fewer Muslims into the Country," 24 April 2014, http://www.newsmax.com/US/Coulter-Muslims-jihad-immigrate/2014/04/24/id/567645.

64. Obama address at the National Defense University, 23 May 2013, http://www.whitehouse.gov.

65. Obama comments, 3 July and 15 August 2013, http://www.whitehouse.gov.

66. Ellis, "Sleep-Away Camp for Postmodern Cowboys," 35–36.

67. Thom Shanker, "Hagel Lifts Veil on Major Military Center in Qatar," *NYT*, 11 December 2013.

68. Zarif, "What Iran Really Wants," 50–51. For more on Zarif, see Robin Wright, "The Adversary," 40–49.

69. Al-Baghdadi quoted in Michael Daly, "ISIS Leader: 'See You in New York,'" *Daily Beast*, 14 June 2014.

70. Obama quoted in Remnick, "Going the Distance," 57.

71. Clapper, "Statement for the Record: Worldwide Threat Assessment," Senate Select Committee on Intelligence, 29 January 2014, *WP*, http://apps.washingtonpost.com/g/documents/ world/us-intelligence-communitys-2014-threat-assessment/763.

72. Obama quoted in Remnick, "Going the Distance," 56.

73. Obama, address at West Point, 28 May 2014, http://www.whitehouse.gov.

74. Gordon quoted in Bruck, "Friends of Israel," 50.

75. Excerpt from *Savage Nation*, 21 July 2014, https://www.youtube.com/watch?v=Iu86eb8hjSE.

76. Obama, address to the nation, 10 September 2014, http://www.whitehouse. gov.

77. Kagan, *Dangerous Nation*, 11, 136–38, 184, 294–99.

78. Kagan, "Fade Not Away." On Kagan's background, see Vlahos, "The World Robert Kagan Made."

79. Kagan, "Superpowers Don't Get to Retire." On the reaction to Kagan's ideas, see Jason Horowitz, "Robert Kagan Strikes a Nerve with Article on Obama Policy," *NYT*, 15 June 2014.

80. Clinton, *Hard Choices*, xii.

81. Jeffrey Goldberg, "Hillary Clinton: 'Failure' to Help Syrian Rebels Led to the Rise of ISIS," *Atlantic*, 9 August 2014, http://www.theatlantic.com/international/ archive/2014/08/hillary-clinton-failure-to-help-syrian-rebels-led-to-the-rise-of- isis/375832.

82. Gillespie quoted in Draper, "Freedom Rocks," 28.

83. "CAIR Launches Website Exposing America's 'Islamophobia Network,'" 15 October 2014, http://www.cair.com/press-center/press-releases/12688-cair-launch- es-website-exposing-americas-islamophobia-network.html.

84. Obama, statement on Iraq, 9 August 2014, http://www.whitehouse.gov.

85. Kerry, "Under US Leadership, World Will Defeat ISIS," *Boston Globe*, 26 September 2014.

86. Obama interview with Friedman, *NYT*, 5 April 2015.

87. "The Complete Transcript of Netanyahu's Address to Congress," *WP*, 3 March 2015, http://www.washingtonpost.com/blogs/post-politics/wp/2015/03/03/full-text- netanyahus-address-to-congress.

88. Rubio, campaign launch, 13 April 2015, http://time.com/3820475/ transcript-read-full-text-of-sen-marco-rubios-campaign-launch.

89. Jeb Bush interview with Richard Lowry, 30 April 2015, http://www.c-span.org/ video/?325690–1/national-review-institute-2015-ideas-summit.

90. Walker quoted in Nick Corasaniti, "Republican Hopefuls Push a Muscular Foreign Policy," *NYT*, 10 May 2015.

91. Trump interview with Cooper, 8 July 2015, http://www.cnn.com/TRAN- SCRIPTS/ 1507/08/acd.01.html.

92. On Obama and JQA, see Obama, *The Audacity of Hope*, 280. For Hector Barbossa's words of caution, see Internet Movie Database, "Pirates of the Caribbean: The Curse of the Black Pearl," http://www.imdb.com/title/tt0325980/quotes.

93. Niebuhr, *The Irony of American History*, 134–35, 174. On Niebuhr as Obama's favorite philosopher, see David Brooks, "Obama's Christian Realism," *NYT*, 14 December 2009.

94. Obama interview with Friedman, *NYT*, 8 August 2014.

95. Lewis, *What Went Wrong?*, 96–116, 151–60.

96. Said, *Orientalism*, 284–328.

97. Bin Laden quoted in Buruma and Margalit, "Occidentalism," *New York Review of Books*, 17 January 2002, 5.

98. "Remarks by President Obama in Press Conference after G7 Summit," 8 June 2015, http://www.whitehouse.gov.

99. Daniel Bolger, "Why We Lost," *NYT*, 10 November 2014.

100. Shlaim, *Lion of Jordan*, 110.

101. Boykin quoted in William Arkin, "The Pentagon Unleashes a Holy Warrior," *Los Angeles Times*, 16 October 2003.

Bibliography

Primary Sources

UNPUBLISHED DOCUMENTS

British National Archives, Kew, Surrey, England
    FCO 93, Records of the Foreign and Commonwealth Department
    PREM 16, Records of the Prime Minister's Office 1975–1979
    PREM 19, Records of the Prime Minister's Office 1979–1990
    Selwyn Lloyd Papers
George H. W. Bush Presidential Library, College Station, Tex.
    Richard Haass Papers
    George H. W Bush Papers, Memcons and Telcons, http://bush41library.tamu.
        edu/archives/memcons-telcons
Jimmy Carter Presidential Library, Atlanta, Ga.
    Zbigniew Brzezinski Papers
William J. Clinton Presidential Library, Little Rock, Ark.
    Digital Declassified Records: Iraq http://clintonlibrary.gov/assets/
        Declassified/2009-1292-M.pdf. 28 February 2013
Council on Foreign Relations Archives, Pratt House, New York, N.Y.
    Records of Groups
Dwight D. Eisenhower Presidential Library, Abilene, Kans.
    Dwight D. Eisenhower Papers, DDE Diaries Series
Gerald R. Ford Presidential Library, Ann Arbor, Mich.
    National Security Adviser's Country File
    National Security Adviser's Memoranda of Conversations
Lyndon B. Johnson Presidential Library, Austin, Tex.
    Memos to the President File—Walt Rostow
    National Security File, National Security Council History Series
John F. Kennedy Presidential Library, Boston, Mass.
    Robert Komer Oral History Interview, 31 October 1964
Ronald Reagan Presidential Library, Simi Valley, Calif.
    NSC Executive Secretariat, Country Files
    NSC Executive Secretariat, Heads of State Files
    NSC Executive Secretariat, National Security Decision Directives
    NSC Executive Secretariat, Near East South Asia Affairs
    White House Staff Offices: Colin Powell
Harry S. Truman Presidential Library, Independence, Mo.
    George M. Elsey Papers

U.S. National Archives, College Park, Md.
  Central Intelligence Agency, CIA Records Search Tool, National Archives
  Department of State, Alpha-Numerical File 1963-72, Record Group 59

PUBLISHED GOVERNMENT DOCUMENTS

Declassified Documents Reference System. Washington, D.C.: Carrollton Press,
  1975–1997. Microfiche, various years.
The Middle East 1950–1961 Supplement. Part 12 of *O.S.S./State Department Intelligence
  and Research Reports*. Washington, D.C.: University Publications of America, 1980.
National Energy Development Policy Group. *Reliable, Affordable, and
  Environmentally Sound Energy for America's Future*, Washington, D.C.:
  Government Printing Office, 2001.
Public Papers of the Presidents. Washington, D.C.: Government Printing Office,
  1947–2014.
Report of the Bahrain Independent Commission of Inquiry. Manama, Bahrain:
  Bahrain Independent Commission of Inquiry, 2011. http://www.bici.org.bh/
  BICIreportEN.pdf.
The Truman Doctrine and the Beginning of the Cold War. Vol. 8 of *The Documentary
  History of the Truman Presidency*. Edited by Dennis Merrill. Bethesda, Md.:
  University Publications of America 1997.
U.S. Congress. Senate. 80th Congress, 1st Session, Document 26. *Menace of
  Communism: A Statement of J. Edgar Hoover Relative to Menace of Communism*.
  Washington, D.C.: Government Printing Office, 1947.
U.S. Congress. Senate, Committee on Foreign Relations. *Afghanistan: Building
  Stability, Avoiding Chaos*. Washington, D.C.: Government Printing Office, 2002.
  http://www.access.gpo.gov/congress/senate.
U.S. Department of State. *Foreign Relations of the United States*. Washington, D.C.:
  Government Printing Office, 1969–2015.
U.S. Department of State, *Patterns of Global Terrorism: 1993*. Washington, D.C.:
  Government Printing Office, 1994.
White House. *A National Security Strategy of Engagement and Enlargement*.
  Washington, D.C.: Government Printing Office, 1994.
———. *The National Security Strategy of the United States 2002*. Washington, D.C.:
  Government Printing Office, 2002.

PUBLISHED MEMOIRS, DIARIES, AND LETTERS

Acheson, Dean. *Present at the Creation: My Years at the State Department*. New York:
  W. W. Norton, 1969.
Albright, Madeleine. *Madam Secretary: A Memoir*. New York: Miramax Books, 2003.
Baker, James A. *The Politics of Diplomacy: Revolution, War, and Peace, 1989–1992*.
  New York: Putnam, 1995.
Berle, Beatrice Bishop, and Travis Beal Jacobs, eds. *Navigating the Rapids: From the
  Papers of Adolf A. Berle*. New York: Harcourt Brace Jovanovich, 1973.

Bremer III, L. Paul. *My Year in Iraq: The Struggle to Build a Future of Hope.* New York: Simon and Schuster, 2006,

Bush, George H. W. *All the Best: My Life in Letters and Other Writings.* New York: Charles Scribner, 1999.

Bush, George [H. W.], and Brent Scowcroft. *A World Transformed.* New York: Alfred A. Knopf, 1998.

Bush, George W. *Decision Points.* New York: Crown Publishers, 2010.

Carter, Jimmy. *White House Diary.* New York: Farrar, Straus and Giroux, 2010.

Cheney, Dick, with Liz Cheney. *In My Time: A Personal and Political Memoir.* New York: Threshold Editions, 2011.

Clarke, Richard. *Against All Enemies: Inside America's War on Terror.* New York: Free Press, 2004.

Clinton, Bill. *My Life.* New York: Alfred A. Knopf, 2004.

Clinton, Hillary. *Hard Choices.* New York: Simon and Schuster, 2014.

Djerejian, Edward P. *Danger and Opportunity: An American Ambassador's Journey through the Middle East.* New York: Threshold Editions, 2008.

Eisenhower, John S. D., ed.. *Letters to Mamie.* Garden City, N.Y.: Doubleday, 1978.

Feith, Douglas J. *War and Decision: Inside the Pentagon at the Dawn of the War on Terrorism.* New York: Harper, 2008.

Gates, Robert. *Duty: Memoirs of a Secretary of War.* New York: Alfred A. Knopf, 2014.

Haass, Richard N. *War of Necessity, War of Choice: A Memoir of Two Iraq Wars.* New York: Simon and Schuster, 2009.

Hartmann, Robert. *Palace Politics.* New York: McGraw Hill, 1980.

Holbrooke, Richard. *To End a War.* Revised ed. New York: Modern Library, 1999.

Indyk, Martin. *Innocent Abroad: An Intimate Account of American Peace Diplomacy in the Middle East.* New York: Simon and Schuster, 2009.

Kennan, George F. *Memoirs, 1925–1950.* Boston: Little, Brown, 1967.

Lake, Anthony. *Six Nightmares: Real Threats in a Dangerous World and How America Can Meet Them.* New York: Little, Brown, 2000.

McClellan, Scott. *What Happened: Inside the Bush White House and Washington's Culture of Deception.* New York: Public Affairs, 2008.

Miller, Aaron David. *The Much Too Promised Land: America's Elusive Search for Arab-Israeli Peace.* New York: Bantam Books, 2008.

Morison, Elting B., ed. *The Letters of Theodore Roosevelt.* 8 vols. Cambridge, Mass.: Harvard University Press, 1952–1955.

Netanyahu, Benjamin. *Fighting Terrorism: How Democracies Can Defeat the International Terrorist Network.* New York: Farrar, Straus and Giroux, 1995.

Niebuhr, Reinhold. *The Irony of American History.* New York, Charles Scribner, 1952.

Nixon, Richard. *Beyond Peace.* New York: Random House, 1994.

Obama, Barack. *The Audacity of Hope: Thoughts on Reclaiming the American Dream.* New York: Three Rivers Press, 2006.

———. *Dreams from My Father: A Story of Race and Inheritance.* 1995. New York: Three Rivers Press, 2004.

Panetta, Leon. *Worthy Fights: A Memoir of Leadership in War and Peace*. New York: Penguin Books, 2014.

Reagan, Ronald. *The Reagan Diaries*. Edited by Douglas Brinkley. New York: HarperCollins, 2007.

Rice, Condoleezza. *No Higher Honor: A Memoir of My Years in Washington*. New York: Crown Publishers, 2011.

Ross, Dennis. *The Missing Peace: The Inside Story of the Fight for Middle East Peace*. New York: Farrar, Straus and Giroux, 2004.

Rumsfeld, Donald. *Known and Unknown: A Memoir*. New York: Sentinel, 2011.

Sick, Gary. *All Fall Down: America's Tragic Encounter with Iran*. New York: Random House, 1985.

Talbott, Strobe. *The Russia Hand: A Memoir of Presidential Diplomacy*. New York: Random House, 2002.

Tenet, George. *At the Center of the Storm: My Years at the CIA*. New York: HarperCollins, 2007.

Zinni, Tony, and Tony Klotz, *The Battle for Peace: A Frontline Vision of America's Power and Purpose*. New York: Palgrave Macmillan, 2006.

Secondary Sources

BOOKS

Abdo, Geneive. *Mecca and Main Street: Muslim Life in America after 9/11*. New York: Oxford University Press, 2006.

Alter, Jonathan. *The Promise: President Obama, Year One*. New York: Simon and Schuster, 2010.

Ajami, Fouad. *The Arab Predicament: Arab Political Thought and Practice since 1967*. New York: Cambridge University Press, 1981.

———. *The Vanished Imam: Musa al Sadr and the Shia of Lebanon*. Ithaca: Cornell University Press, 1986.

al-Aswany, Alaa. *The Yacoubian Building*. New York: Harper Perennial, 2006.

Beinart, Peter. *The Crisis of Zionism*. New York: Times Books, 2012.

Benjamin, Daniel, and Steven Simon. *The Age of Sacred Terror: Radical Islam's War against America*. New York: Random House, 2003.

Beschloss, Michael R., and Strobe Talbott. *At the Highest Levels: The Inside Story of the End of the Cold War*. New York: Little, Brown, 1993.

Boykin, John. *Cursed Is the Peacemaker: The American Diplomat versus the Israeli General, Beirut 1982*. Belmont, Calif.: Applegate Press, 2002.

Branch, Taylor. *The Clinton Tapes: Wrestling History with the President*. New York: Simon and Schuster, 2009.

Bumiller, Elizabeth. *Condoleezza Rice: An American Life*. New York: Random House, 2007.

Chandrasekaran, Rajiv. *Imperial Life in the Emerald City*. New York: Vintage Books, 2007.

Clancy, Tom. *Against All Enemies*. New York: Putnam, 2011.

Cook, Steven A. *The Struggle for Egypt: From Nasser to Tahrir Square*. New York: Oxford University Press, 2012.

Coulter, Ann. *Godless: The Church of Liberalism*. New York: Crown Forum, 2006.

———. *How to Talk to a Liberal (If You Must): The World According to Ann Coulter*. New York: Crown Forum, 2004.

DeMille, Nelson. *Night Fall*. New York: Time Warner Books, 2005.

Draper, Robert. *Dead Certain: The Presidency of George W. Bush*. New York: Free Press, 2007.

Drew, Elizabeth. *On the Edge: The Clinton Presidency*. New York: Simon and Schuster, 1994.

Drinnon, Richard. *Facing West: The Metaphysics of Indian-Hating and Empire-Building*. Minneapolis: University of Minnesota Press, 1980.

Eggers, Dave. *Zeitoun*. San Francisco: McSweeney's Books, 2009.

Eichenwald, Kurt. *Five Hundred Days: Secrets and Lies in the Terror Wars*. New York: Simon and Schuster, 2012.

Emerson, Steven. *American Jihad: The Terrorists Living among Us*. New York: Free Press, 2002.

———. *Jihad Incorporated: A Guide to Militant Islam in the US*. New York: Prometheus Books, 2006.

Faludi, Susan. *The Terror Dream: Fear and Fantasy in Post-9/11 America*. New York: Metropolitan Books, 2007.

Fukuyama, Francis. *The End of History and the Last Man*. New York: Free Press, 1992.

Ghattas, Kim. *The Secretary: A Journey with Hillary Clinton from Beirut to the Heart of American Power*. New York: Times Books, 2013.

Goldman, Eric F. *The Crucial Decade: America, 1945–1955*. New York: Alfred A. Knopf, 1956.

Goldstein, Gordon. *Lessons in Disaster: McGeorge Bundy and the Path to War in Vietnam*. New York: Times Books, 2008.

Gul, Imtiaz. *The Most Dangerous Place: Pakistan's Lawless Frontier*. New York: Viking, 2010.

Halberstam, David. *War in a Time of Peace: Bush, Clinton, and the Generals*. New York: Charles Scribner, 2001.

Halpern, Manfred. *The Politics of Social Change in the Middle East and North Africa*. Princeton: Princeton University Press, 1963.

Harris, John. *The Survivor: Bill Clinton in the White House*. New York: Random House, 2005.

Horowitz, David. *Unholy Alliance: Radical Islam and the American Left*. Washington, D.C.: Regnery, 2004.

Hunt, Alfred N. *Haiti's Influence on Antebellum America: Slumbering Volcano in the Caribbean*. Baton Rouge: Louisiana State University Press, 1988.

Huntington, Samuel P. *The Clash of Civilizations and the Remaking of World Order*. New York: Simon and Schuster, 1996.

Ibrahim, Raymond, ed. *The Al Qaeda Reader.* New York: Doubleday, 2007.

Immerman, Richard H. *Empire for Liberty: A History of American Imperialism from Benjamin Franklin to Paul Wolfowitz.* Princeton: Princeton University Press, 2010.

Isikoff, Michael, and David Corn. *Hubris: The Inside Story of Spin, Scandal, and the Selling of the Iraq War.* New York: Crown Publishers, 2006.

Kagan, Robert. *Dangerous Nation: America's Foreign Policy from Its Earliest Days to the Dawn of the Twentieth Century.* New York: Alfred. Knopf, 2006.

Kaplan, Robert. *Balkan Ghosts: A Journey through History.* New York: St. Martin's Press, 1993.

Kristol, Irving. *Reflections of a Neoconservative: Looking Back, Looking Ahead.* New York: Basic Books, 1983.

Kurtzer, Daniel, Scott B. Lasensky, William B. Quandt, Steven L. Spiegel, and Shibley Z. Telhami. *The Peace Puzzle: America's Quest for Arab-Israeli Peace, 1989–2011.* Ithaca: Cornell University Press, 2013.

LaFeber, Walter. *The Clash: A History of U.S.-Japan Relations.* New York: W. W. Norton, 1997.

Law, Randall. *Terrorism: A History.* Boston: Polity Press, 2009.

Lepore, Jill. *The Name of War: King Philip's War and the Origins of American Identity.* New York: Alfred A. Knopf, 1998.

Lerner, Daniel. *The Passing of Traditional Society: Modernizing the Middle East.* Glencoe, Ill.: Free Press, 1958.

Lewis, Bernard. *What Went Wrong? The Clash between Islam and Modernity in the Middle East.* New York: Oxford University Press, 2002.

Lockman, Zachary A. *Contending Visions of the Middle East: The History and Politics of Orientalism.* New York: Cambridge University Press, 2004.

Makdisi, Ussama. *Artillery of Heaven: American Missionaries and the Failed Conversion of the Middle East.* Ithaca: Cornell University Press, 2008.

Mann, James. *The Obamians: The Struggle inside the White House to Redefine American Power.* New York: Viking Press, 2012.

Mayer, Jane. *The Dark Side: The Inside Story on How the War on Terror Turned into a War on American Ideals.* 2nd ed. New York: Anchor Books, 2008.

McCarthy, Cormac. *Blood Meridian; or, The Evening Redness in the West.* 1985. New York: Random House, 1992.

Melman, Yossi, and Dan Raviv. *Friends in Deed: Inside the U.S.-Israel Alliance.* New York: Hyperion, 1994.

Melville, Herman. *The Confidence-Man: His Masquerade.* Edited by Elizabeth S. Foster. New York: Hendricks House, 1954.

Miller, Mark Crispin. *The Bush Dyslexicon: Observations on a National Disorder.* New York: W. W. Norton, 2002.

Miller, Stuart Creighton. *The Unwelcome Immigrant: The American Image of the Chinese, 1785–1882.* Berkeley: University of California Press, 1969.

Mylroie, Laurie. *A Study of Revenge: Saddam Hussein's Unfinished War against America.* Washington, D.C.: AEI Press, 2000.

Naftali, Timothy. *Blind Spot: The Secret History of American Counterterrorism*. New York: Basic Books, 2005.

National Commission on Terrorist Attacks upon the United States. *The 9/11 Commission Report: Authorized Edition*. New York: W. W. Norton, 2004.

Packer, George. *The Assassins' Gate: America in Iraq*. New York: Farrar, Straus and Giroux, 2005.

Parsi, Trita. *A Single Roll of the Dice: Obama's Diplomacy with Iran*. New Haven: Yale University Press, 2012.

Persico, Joseph E. *Casey: From the OSS to the CIA*. New York: Viking Press, 1990.

Pickett, William B., ed. *George F. Kennan and the Origins of Eisenhower's New Look: An Oral History of Project Solarium*. Princeton, N.J.: Princeton Institute for International and Regional Studies, 2004.

Pollack, Kenneth M. *The Threatening Storm: The Case for Invading Iraq*. New York: Random House, 2002.

Oberdorfer, Don. *The Turn: From the Cold War to a New Era: The United States and the Soviet Union, 1983–1990*. New York: Poseidon Press, 1991.

Oren, Michael. *Power, Faith, and Fantasy: America in the Middle East, 1776 to the Present*. New York: W. W. Norton, 2007.

Rabe, Stephen G. *The Killing Zone: The United States Wages Cold War in Latin America*. 2nd ed. New York: Oxford University Press, 2015.

Rashid, Ahmed. *Jihad: The Rise of Militant Islam in Central Asia*. New Haven: Yale University Press, 2002.

———. *Pakistan on the Brink*. New York: Viking Press, 2012.

Remini, Robert V. *Andrew Jackson and His Indian Wars*. New York: Viking Press, 2001.

Ricks, Thomas E. *Fiasco: The American Military Adventure in Iraq*. New York: Penguin Books, 2006.

Rudd, Gordon. *Reconstructing Iraq: Regime Change, Jay Garner, and the ORHA Story*. Lawrence: University of Kansas Press, 2011.

Said, Edward. *Orientalism*. New York: Pantheon Books, 1978.

Sanger, David E. *Confront and Conceal: Obama's Secret Wars and Surprising Use of Power*. New York: Crown Publishers, 2012.

Scoblic, J. Peter. *U.S. vs. Them: Conservatism in the Age of Nuclear Terror*. New York: Viking Press, 2008.

Shaheen, Jack. *Reel Bad Arabs: How Hollywood Vilifies a People*. New York: Olive Branch Press, 2001.

Shlaim, Avi. *The Lion of Jordan: The Life of King Hussein in War and Peace*. New York: Alfred A. Knopf, 2008.

Sterling, Claire. *The Terror Network: The Secret War of International Terrorism*. New York: Holt, Rinehart and Winston, 1981.

Stoddard, Lothrop. *The New World of Islam*. New York: Charles Scribner's Sons, 1921.

Suskind, Ron. *The One Percent Doctrine: Deep Inside America's Pursuit of Its Enemies since 9/11*. New York: Simon and Schuster, 2006.

———. *The Price of Loyalty: George W. Bush, the White House, and the Education of Paul O'Neill*. New York: Simon and Schuster, 2004.

Tamimi, Azzam. *Hamas: A History from Within*. Northampton, Mass.: Olive Branch Press, 2007.

Twain, Mark. *The Innocents Abroad. Roughing It*. New York: Viking Press, 1984.

Tyler, Patrick. *Fortress Israel: The Inside Story of the Military Elite Who Run the Country—And Why They Can't Make Peace*. New York: Farrar, Straus and Giroux, 2012.

Woodward, Bob. *Bush at War*. New York: Simon and Schuster, 2002.

———. *The Commanders*. New York: Simon and Schuster, 1991.

———. *Obama's Wars*. New York: Simon and Schuster, 2010.

———. *Plan of Attack*. New York: Simon and Schuster, 2004.

———. *State of Denial: Bush at War, Part III*. New York: Simon and Schuster, 2006.

Wright, Lawrence. *The Looming Tower: Al-Qaeda and the Road to 9/11*. New York: Alfred A. Knopf, 2006.

Wright, Robin. *Dreams and Shadows: The Future of the Middle East*. New York: Penguin Books, 2008.

Yaqub, Salim. *Containing Arab Nationalism: The Eisenhower Doctrine and the Middle East*. Chapel Hill: University of North Carolina Press, 2004.

Yellin, Eric. *Racism in the Nation's Service: Government Workers and the Color Line in Woodrow Wilson's America*. Chapel Hill: University of North Carolina Press, 2013.

ARTICLES, BOOK CHAPTERS, SPEECHES, AND REPORTS

Abunimah, Ali Hasan. "How Barack Obama Learned to Love Israel." *Electronic Intifada*, 4 March 2007, http://electronicintifada.net/content/how-barack-obama-learned-love-israel/6786. 27 May 2013.

An, Huihou. "The Principle of Non-Interference Versus." *Chinese People's Institute of Foreign Affairs Quarterly*, no. 104 (Summer 2012), http://www.cpifa.org/en/q/listQuarterlyArticle.do?articleId=233. 12 June 2015.

Anderson, Jon Lee. "State of Terror." *New Yorker*, 1 July 2013, 36–47.

Baker, Peter. "Obama's War over Terror." *New York Times Magazine*, 17 January 2010, 30–39, 46–47.

Bowden, Mark. "Wolfowitz: The Exit Interviews." *Atlantic*, July/August 2005, 110–22.

Bridges, Roger D. "The Betrayal of the Freedmen? Rutherford B. Hayes and the End of Reconstruction." Rutherford B. Hayes Presidential Centre, http://www.rbhayes.org/hayes/scholarworks/display.asp?id=503. 10 July 2014.

Brinkley, Joel. "The Stubborn Strength of Yitzhak Shamir." *New York Times Magazine*, 21 August 1988, 26–29, 68–77.

Bruck, Connie. "Friends of Israel." *New Yorker*, 1 September 2014, 50–63.

———. "The Influencer." *New Yorker*, 10 May 2010, 54–67.

Buruma, Ian, and Avishai Margalit. "Occidentalism." *New York Review of Books*, 17 January 2002, 4–7.

Bush, George W. "Remarks at the Citadel, 23 September 1999." http://www3.citadel.
edu/pao/ addresses/ pres_bush.html. 15 June 2013.

Cassidy, John. "Beneath the Sand." *New Yorker*, 14 and 21 July 2003, 64–75.

Christopher, Warren. "The Private Sector: Engine for Growth in the Middle East."
30 October 1994, U.S. Department of State, *Dispatch*, 15 November 1994, 27.

———. "Turning Peace into Prosperity." 30 October 1994, U.S. Department of
State, *Dispatch*, 15 November 1994, 28.

Clavin, Matthew J. "American Toussaints: Symbol, Subversion, and the Black
Atlantic Tradition in the American Civil War." *Slavery and Abolition* 28, no. 1
(April 2007): 87–113.

Clinton, Bill. "A New Covenant for American Security." Remarks at Georgetown
University, 12 December 1991, http://www.ibiblio.org/pub/academic/political-
science/speeches/clinton.dir/c28.txtp. 13 June 2015.

Cole, David. "Obama and Terror: The Hovering Questions." *New York Review of
Books*, 12 July 2012, 32–34.

Costigliola, Frank. "'Unceasing Pressure for Penetration': Gender, Pathology, and
Emotion in George Kennan's Formation of the Cold War." *Journal of American
History* 83, no. 4 (March 1997): 1309–39.

Dalrymple, William. "Days of Rage." *New Yorker*, 23 July 2007, 26–35.

De Soto, Hernando. "The Real Mohamed Bouazizi." *Foreign Policy*, 16 December
2011, http://www.foreignpolicy.com/articles/2011/12/16/the_real_mohamed_
bouazizi. 28 July 2015.

Djerejian, Edward P. "The U.S. and the Middle East in a Changing World." *DISAM
Journal* (Summer 1992): 32–38, http://www.disam.dsca.mil/pubs/Vol%2014_4/
Djerejian.pdf. 21 August 2015.

Draper, Robert. "Freedom Rocks." *New York Times Magazine*, 10 August 2014, 24–31,
38, 43.

Dreazen, Yochi. "The New Terrorist Training Ground." *Atlantic*, October 2013, 60–70.

Ellis, Josh. "Sleep-Away Camp for Postmodern Cowboys." *New York Times
Magazine*, July 21, 2013, 34–41.

Finnegan, William. "Letter from Mogadishu: A World of Dust." *New Yorker*, 25
March 1995, 64–77.

Fitzpatrick, David. "The Evangelical Crackup." *New York Times Magazine*, 28
October 2007, 38–45, 60, 64–66.

"From Brezhnev Doctrine to Sinatra Doctrine: An Interview with Gennady
Gerasimov." *Demokratizatsiya*, 26 March 2005, http://www.ariasking.com/files/
DemGerasimov.pdf. 5 February 2013.

Frum, David. "The Speechwriter: The Rhetoric of the Iraq War." *Newsweek OnLine*,
19 March 2013, http://www.thedailybeast.com/newsweek/2013/03/18/the-
speechwriter-inside-the-bush-administration-during-the-iraq-war.html. 4 May
2013.

Fukuyama, Francis. "The End of History?" *National Interest*, no. 16 (Summer 1989):
3–18.

Gingrich, Newt. "America at Risk: Camus, National Security, and Afghanistan."
    American Enterprise Institute, 29 July 2010, http://www.aei.org/events/america-
    at-risk-camus-national-security-and-afghanistan. 12 June 2015.
Goldberg, Jeffrey. "Danger: Falling Tyrants." *Atlantic*, June 2011, 46–54.
Hammer, Joshua. "When Jihad Came to Mali." *New York Review of Books*, 21 March
    2013, 12–14.
Hastings, Michael. "The Runaway General." *Rolling Stone*, 22 June 2010, http://www.
    rollingstone.com/politics/news/the-runaway-general-20100622. 28 July 2015.
Huntington, Samuel P. "The Coming Clash of Civilizations." *Foreign Affairs* 72, no. 3
    (Summer 1993): 22–49.
———. "If Not Civilizations, What? Paradigms of the Post–Cold War World."
    Foreign Affairs, 72, no. 5 (November/December 1993): 186–94.
Institute for Advanced Strategic and Political Studies. "A Clean Break," June 1996,
    https://web.archive.org/web/20140125123844/http://www.iasps.org/strat1.htm.
    13 June 2015.
"Islam: A Threat to World Stability." *Intelligence Review* 1 (14 February 1946),
    https://fas.org/irp/agency/army/intelreview1.pdf. 21 August 2015.
Kagan, Robert. "Fade Not Away: The Myth of American Decline." *New Republic*, 11
    January 2012, http://www.newrepublic.com/article/politics/magazine/99521/
    america-world-power-declinism. 12 June 2015.
———. "Superpowers Don't Get to Retire: What Our Tired Country Still
    Owes the World." *New Republic*, 26 May 2014, http://www.newrepublic.com/
    article/117859/allure-normalcy-what-america-still-owes-world. 12 June 2015 .
[Kennan, George F.] "X." "The Sources of Soviet Conduct." *Foreign Affairs* 25, no. 4
    (July 1947): 566–82.
Klein, Joe. "Where's George?" *New York Magazine*, 24 April 1989, 24–25.
Lake, Anthony. "Confronting Backlash States." *Foreign Affairs* 73, no. 2 (March/April
    1994): 45–55.
———. "From Containment to Enlargement." Paper presented at the Johns Hopkins
    University School of Advanced International Studies, Washington, D.C., 21
    September 1993, http://www.fas.org/news/usa/1993/usa-930921.htm. 1 March 2013.
Lemann, Nicholas. "The Quiet Man." *New Yorker*, 7 May 2001, 56–71.
Lewis, Bernard. "The Roots of Muslim Rage." *Atlantic Monthly*, September 1990, 47–60.
Little, Douglas. "Cold War and Covert Action: The United States and Syria,
    1945–1958." *Middle East Journal* 44, no. 1 (Winter 1990): 51–75.
———. "To the Shores of Tripoli: America, Qaddafi, and the Libyan Revolution,
    1969–89." *International History Review* 35, no. 1 (2013): 70–99.
Lizza, Ryan. "The Consequentialist." *New Yorker*, 2 May 2011, 44–55.
Lybyer, Albert Howe. "Review of the New World of Islam by Lothrop Stoddard."
    American Historical Review 27, no. 2 (January 1922): 322–24.
Mahbubani, Kishore. "The Dangers of Decadence." *Foreign Affairs* 72, no. 4
    (September/October 1993): 10–12.

Marantz, Andrew. "'Innocence of Muslims': Viral Video Gone Wrong." *New Yorker*, 14 September 2012, http://www.newyorker.com/news/news-desk/innocence-of-muslims-viral-video-gone-wrong. 21 August 2015.

Mayer, Jane. "The Hidden Power." *New Yorker*, 3 July 2006, 44–55.

Nathan, Andrew J., and Andrew Scobell, "How China Sees America." *Foreign Affairs* 91, no. 5 (September/October 2012): 32–47.

Odom, William E. "The Cold War Origins of the U.S. Central Command." *Journal of Cold War Studies* 8, no. 2 (Spring 2006): 52–82.

Paumgarten, Nick. "Here's Looking at You." *New Yorker*, 14 May 2012, 46–59.

Pelletreau, Jr., Robert H. "Not Every Fundamentalist Is a Terrorist." *Middle East Quarterly* 2, no. 3 (September 1995): 69–76.

Pipes, Daniel. "Interview with Martin Indyk: Perspective from the White House." *Middle East Quarterly* 1, no. 1 (March 1994), http://www.meforum.org/pipes/6302/perspectives-from-the-white-house. 21 August 2015.

Remnick, David. "Going the Distance." *New Yorker*, 27 January 2014, 40–61.

———. "The Outsider." *New Yorker*, 25 May 1998, 80–95.

———. "The Vegetarian." *New Yorker*, 3 September 2012, 22–28.

Rice, Condoleeza. "Promoting the National Interest." *Foreign Affairs* 79, no. 1 (January/February 2000): 45–62.

Rose, David. "The Gaza Bombshell." *Vanity Fair*, April 2008, http://www.vanityfair.com/ news/2008/04/gaza200804. 21 August 2015.

Saleem, Muniba, and Craig A. Anderson. "Arabs as Terrorists: Effects of Stereotypes within Violent Contexts on Attitudes, Perceptions, and Affect." *Psychology of Violence* 3, no. 1 (2013): 84–99.

Samuels, David. "Grand Illusions." *Atlantic Monthly*, June 2007, 46–76.

Schmemann, Serge. "Outside In." *New York Times Magazine*, 23 November 1997, 55–50, 74–77.

Schmidle, Nicholas. "Getting Bin Laden." *New Yorker*, 8 August 2011, 34–45.

Shavit, Ari. "End of a Journey." *Haaretz*, 13 September 2001, http://www.haaretz.com/end-of-a-journey-1.288142. 13 June 2015.

Steavenson, Wendell. "Roads to Freedom." *New Yorker*, 29 August 2011, 26–32.

"Symposium: Resurgent Islam in the Middle East." *Middle East Policy* 3, no. 2 (June 1994): 1–21.

Traub, James. "A Civic War." *New York Times Magazine*, 20 June 2010, 24–29.

Vlahos, Kelly. "The World Robert Kagan Made." *American Conservative*, 16 March 2012, http://www.theamericanconservative.com/the-world-robert-kagan-made. 2 August 2015.

Walsh, Elsa. "Louis Freeh's Last Case." *New Yorker*, 14 May 2001, 68–79.

Wolfowitz, Paul. "Statement before the House National Security Committee, 16 Sept. 1998." http://fas.org/spp/starwars/congress/1998_h/98-09-16wolfowitz.htm. 21 August 2015.

Wright, Robin. "The Adversary." *New Yorker*, May 26, 2014, 40–49.

Zarif, Mohammad Javad. "What Iran Really Wants: Iranian Foreign Policy in the Rouhani Era." *Foreign Affairs* 93, no. 3 (May/June 2014): 49–59.

Zelikow, Philip. "U.S. Strategic Planning in 2001–02." In *In Uncertain Times: American Foreign Policy after the Berlin Wall and 9/11*, edited by Melvyn Leffler and Jeffrey W. Legro, 96–116. Ithaca: Cornell University Press, 2011.

Zeveloff, Naomi. "Lightning Rod of the Boycott Israel Movement." *Forward*, 16 March 2012, http://forward.com/news/israel/152716/lightning-rod-of-the-boycott-israel-movement. 12 June 2015.

Newspapers, Periodicals, and News Websites

Atlantic. http://www.theatlantic.com/international/archive/.

Boston Globe. https://www.bostonglobe.com/.

Christian Science Monitor. http://www.csmonitor.com/.

Daily Beast. http://www.thedailybeast.com.

Des Moines Register. http://www.desmoinesregister.com/.

Deseret News. http://www.deseretnews.com/.

Digipen. http://news.digipen.edu.

Guardian. http://www.theguardian.com/us.

Haaretz. http://www.haaretz.com.

Huffington Post. www.huffingtonpost.com.

Intercept. https://firstlook.org/theintercept.

Los Angeles Times. http://www.latimes.com.

Newsweek. http://www.newsweek.com/.

New York Times. http://www.nytimes.com/.

Politco. http://www.politico.com.

Reuters. http://www.reuters.com.

Slate. http://www.slate.com.

Texas Tribune. http://www.texastribune.org.

Time. http://time.com.

Wall Street Journal. http://www.wsj.com/.

Want China Times. http://www.wantchinatimes.com.

Washington Post. https://www.washingtonpost.com/.

Washington Report on Middle East Affairs Special Report. http://www.wrmea.org/

Film, Television, and Video

Extra Credits. Season 3, Episode 12: *Propaganda Games.* 12 October 2011, http://www.maker.tv/video/DRf4Tpgd093h/series/extracreditz. 2 June 2015.

The Grand Deception. http://www.granddeception.com/#sthash.DLUt9mFg.dpbs. 12 June 2015.

Homeland. Season 2. http://www.sho.com/sho/homeland/season/2#/index. 12 June 2015

Hubris: Selling the Iraq War. First aired on MSNBC, 18 February 2013. http://www. youtube.com/watch?v=B5FaMbnINwc. 12 June 2015.

60 Minutes. "Iraq's Oil." 15 December 2002.

Websites

ABC News. http://abcnews.go.com/blogs. 11 June 2015.

Anti-Defamation League. http://archive.adl.org. 2 August 2014.

Café Press. http://www.cafepress.com. 2 August 2014.

Central Intelligence Agency, FOIA Electronic Reading Room. http://www.foia.cia. gov-docs. 21 June 2013.

———. Special Collections. http://www.foia.cia.gov/ special_collections. 21 June 2013.

CNN. http://www.cnn.com.2 August 2015.

College of Urban and Public Affairs, Portland State University, Portland, Oregon. "Gallup Metadata: The Great Fear—McCarthyism and the Gallup Polls." http:// www.upa.pdx.edu/IMS/ currentprojects/ TAHv3/.../Gallup_McCarthy.xls. 29 May 2015.

Commission on Presidential Debates. "The First Clinton-Bush-Perot Debate." http:// www.debates.org/index.php?page=october-11-1992-first-half-debate-transcript. 21 August 2015.

———. "The First Gore-Bush Presidential Debate." http://www.debates.org/index. php?page=october-3-2000-transcript. 1 June 2013.

———. "The Second McCain-Obama Debate." http://www.debates.org/index. php?page=october-7-2008-debate-transcript.

Common Dreams. https://www.commondreams.org/archive. 24 April 2013.

Council on American-Islamic Relations (CAIR). http://www.cair.com/press-center/press-releases. 2 June 2015.

Council on Foreign Relations. http://www.cfr.org. 11 June 2015.

C-Span. http://www.c-span.org/video. 10 June 2015.

CTV News. http://www.ctvnews.ca. 27 May 2015.

The Daily Show. http://www.thedailyshow.com. 2 May 2015.

Dark Winter. "The Final Script." http://www.upmchealthsecurity.org/website/ events/2001_darkwinter/finding. 1 July 2013.

———. "Slide Show." http://www.upmc-biosecurity.org/website/ events/2001_ darkwinter/dark_winter_slideshow.html. 11 June 2015.

Declassified Documents Reference System. http://gdc.gale.com/products/declassified-documents-reference-system. 24 June 2010.

Digital National Security Archive. http://nsarchive.chadwyck.com. 3 June 2015.

Donald Rumsfeld Papers. "Document Library." http:// www.rumsfeld.com/library. 21 August 2015.

———. "Endnotes." http://papers.rumsfeld.com/endnotes/. 21 August 2015.

Electronic Intifada. http://electronicintifada.net. 11 June 2015.

Federal Bureau of Investigation. http://www.fbi.gov. 21 August 2014.

Intelwire. "Operation Boulder." http://www.intelwire.com. 27 July 2013.

Internet Movie Database (IMDb). http://www.imdb.com. 12 June 2015.

Middle East Institute Publications. "Warnings Went Unheeded." http://www.mideasti.org/articles/doc535. 15 June 2013.

Miller Center. "Presidential Recordings Project: Nixon." http://whitehousetapes.net/clips/ rmn_rumsfeld.html. 11 June 2015.

MSNBC. http://www.msnbc.com. 11 June 2015.

National Security Archive. Electronic Briefing Book 147, "Bush Administration's First Memo on al-Qaeda Declassified." http://www2.gwu.edu/~nsarchiv/NSAEBB/NSAEBB147. 11 June 2015.

———. Electronic Briefing Book 192, "The Diary of Anatoly Chernyaev: First Installment." http://www2.gwu.edu/~nsarchiv/NSAEBB/NSAEBB192. 9 June 2015.

———. Electronic Briefing Book 298, "Bush and Gorbachev at Malta." http://www2.gwu.edu/~nsarchiv/NSAEBB/NSAEBB298. 29 January 2013.

———. Electronic Briefing Book 328, "Iraq War: Part II—Was There Even a Decision." http://nsarchive.gwu.edu/NSAEBB/NSAEBB328. 11 June 2015.

———. Electronic Briefing Book 343, "The Osama Bin Laden File." http://www2.gwu.edu/~nsarchiv/NSAEBB/NSAEBB343. 11 June 2015.

———. Electronic Briefing Book 381, "The CIA's 9/11 File." http://www.gwu.edu/~nsarchiv/NSAEBB/NSAEBB381. 19 March 2013.

———. Electronic Briefing Book 418, "The Iraq War Ten Years After." http://www2.gwu.edu/~nsarchiv/NSAEBB/NSAEBB418. 11 June 2015.

Newsmax. http://www.newsmax.com. 27 May 2015.

Office of the Director of National Intelligence. "Bin Laden's Bookshelf." http://www.dni.gov/index.php/resources/bin-laden-bookshelf?start=1. 2 June 2015.

Online NewsHour. http://www.pbs.org/newshour/bb/politics/jan-june00/se_debate 2-16.html. 14 June 2013.

The Palestine Papers. http://www.aljazeera.com/palestinepapers. 4 May 2015.

Pew Research Center. "Global Attitudes and Trends: Chapter One—Attitudes toward the United States." 18 July 2013, http://www.pewglobal.org/2013/07/18/chapter-1-attitudes-toward-the-united-states. 29 May 2015.

———. "How Americans Feel about Religious Groups." 16 July 2014, http://www.pewforum.org/files/2014/07/Views-of-Religious-Groups-09-22-final.pdf. 29 May 2015.

———. "Republicans Want GOP Leaders to Challenge Obama More Often." 21 May 2015, http://www.people-press.org/files/2015/05/05-21-2015-Congress-release.pdf. 22 May 2015.

Pew Research Global Attitudes Project. "Confidence in Obama Lifts U.S. Image around the World." 23 July 2009, http://www.pewglobal.org/2009/07/23/confidence-in-obama-lifts-us-image-around-the-world. 20 April 2013.

Pew Research Religion and Public Life Project. "Little Voter Discomfort with Romney's Mormon Religion." 26 July 2012, http://www.pewforum.org/2012/07/26/2012-romney-mormonism-obamas-religion. 17 August 2013.

Project for the New American Century. "Statement of Principles." 3 June 1997, http://www.newamericancentury.org. 8 May 2013.

Rethinking National Security. http://cipnationalsecurity.wordpress.com. 10 May 2013.

Rush Limbaugh Show. http://www.rushlimbaugh.com/daily. 2 August 2014.

Tom Flocco. http://www.tomflocco.com. 15 June 2015.

2012 Republican Candidates. http://2012.republican-candidates.org. 11 June 2015.

U.S. Congress, House, Committee on Homeland Security. http://homeland.house. gov. 12 June 2015.

U.S. Department of Defense. http://www.defense.gov. 11 June 2015.

U.S. Department of State. http://www.state.gov. 11 June 2015.

U.S. Department of State, Electronic Reading Room. "Other FOIA Released Documents." http://foia.state.gov/documents/foiadocs. 26 May 2010.

U.S. Institute for Peace. *The Peace Puzzle: Appendices and Resources*. http://www. usip.org/publications/the-peace-puzzle. 3 July 2014.

White House. http://www.whitehouse.gov. 11 June 2015.

Wikileaks. "Secret U.S. Embassy Cables." http://wikileaks.org/cablegate.html. 11 June 2015.

YouTube. http://www.youtube.com. 11 June 2015.

A Note on Further Reading and Historical Sources

The endnotes for *Us versus Them* provide specific citations for every quotation in the text, but to avoid overwhelming general readers, I have mostly refrained from including historiographical material that might have distracted those who are not specialists on the Middle East or U.S. foreign policy. To understand the broader social and cultural context of America's recent encounter with radical Islam, readers should begin with Karen Armstrong's brief and brilliant *Islam: A Short History* (Modern Library, 2002), which captures the religious complexity of the Muslim world from the age of Mohammed to the present day. Eugene Rogan's *The Fall of the Ottomans: The Great War in the Middle East* (Basic Books, 2015) chronicles the collapse of the caliphate in Istanbul and its implications for Islam, while Taner Akçam's *A Shameful Act: The Armenian Genocide and the Question of Turkish Responsibility* (Picador, 2007) details the gruesome retribution that the Turks inflicted on non-Muslims.

Two books by John Esposito—*Islam and Politics* (Syracuse University Press, 1998) and *The Islamic Threat* (Oxford University Press, 1999)—explain the intricate relationship between mosque and state and the remarkable religious fluidity that spawned political Islam during the twentieth century, decades before Osama Bin Laden became an avatar of evil. In *The Dream Palace of the Arabs: A Generation's Odyssey* (Random House, 1997), Fouad Ajami tells the story of the battle royal between revolutionary nationalism and religious revivalism through the eyes of Arab poets and public intellectuals. Gilles Kepel traces radical Islam from Egypt and Iran during the 1940s and 1950s through the surge of Islamic extremism from Algeria to Afghanistan at the end of the Cold War in *Jihad: The Trail of Political Islam* (Harvard University Press, 2002).

During the fifteen years since the 9/11 attacks, books on Osama Bin Laden and al-Qaeda have sprouted like wild mushrooms. *Ghost Wars* (Penguin, 2004), Steve Coll's riveting account of al-Qaeda's emergence during the anti-Soviet jihad in Afghanistan and its expansion under the Taliban, remains unsurpassed. Ahmed Rashid's *Taliban* (Yale University Press, 2000) provides the most thorough analysis of Bin Laden's Afghan hosts and their brand of radical Islam. Peter Bergen's trilogy—*Holy War, Inc.: Inside the Secret World of Osama Bin Laden* (Free Press, 2001), *The Longest War: The Enduring Conflict between America and Al-Qaeda* (Free Press, 2011), and *Manhunt: The Ten-Year Search for Bin Laden* (Crown Publishers, 2012)—follows the world's most wanted terrorist from Peshawar in 1988 to Abbottabad in 2011. Steve Coll's *The Bin Ladens: An Arabian Family in the American Century* shows that Wordsworth's adage that "the child is father to the man" applies to Arab schoolboys as well as to English ones.

Although the proliferation of al-Qaeda "franchises" elsewhere in the Arab world has presented enormous problems for U.S. policy makers, it has been a bonanza for academic experts on Islam and journalists covering the Middle East. In *The Far Enemy: Why Jihad Went Global* (Cambridge University Press, 2005), Fawaz Gerges unravels the strange logic that led al-Qaeda to shift its focus away from "the near enemy"—corrupt and supposedly apostate Muslim regimes like those in Egypt and Saudi Arabia—to more distant targets like the United States. Dexter Filkins's *The Forever War* (Random House, 2008) provides a heartbreaking eyewitness account of how the Islamic backlash against the U.S. invasion of Iraq in 2003 sparked bloody sectarian warfare and spawned al-Qaeda in Iraq. Gregory Johnsen's *The Last Refuge: Yemen, Al-Qaeda, and America's War in Arabia* (Norton, 2014) examines the rapid spread of radical Islam after 9/11 in the Bin Laden clan's ancient homeland. For a harrowing account of the rise of Islamic extremism in post-Qaddafi Libya, see Jon Lee Anderson, "The Unravelling," published in the *New Yorker* (February 23 and March 2, 2015). Of the many instant books on ISIS that have appeared in the past twelve months, the best is *ISIS: The State of Terror* (HarperCollins, 2015) by Jessica Stern and J. M. Berger, who trace the origins of the Islamic State back to the anti-American insurgency in post-Saddam Iraq and provide a sobering account of how Twitter and other social media have served as "force multipliers" for international terrorism.

Revolutionary Shiism has provided an important counterpoint to the Sunni extremism preached by groups such as al-Qaeda and ISIS. Vali Nasr's *The Shia Revival: How Conflicts within Islam Will Shape the Future* (Norton, 2006) provides a concise overview of "the Other Islam" and the ideological challenge that the Islamic Republic of Iran poses for the Sunni monarchies on the opposite side of the Persian Gulf. In *Guardians of the Revolution*, Ray Takeyh explores Iranian foreign policy under Khomeini and Khamenei and highlights the role of the revolutionary guards in exporting radical Shiism. Augustus Richard Norton's splendid little book *Hezbollah: A Short History* (Princeton University Press, 2007) blends anthropology with diplomatic history to profile Iran's irrepressible Shia clients in Lebanon. William Beeman's *The Great Satan and the Mad Mullahs: How the United States and Iran Demonize Each Other* (Praeger 2005) reveals the reciprocal connection between "orientalism" in Washington and "occidentalism" in Tehran. In *Engaging the Muslim World* (Palgrave Macmillan, 2009), Juan Cole highlights the Shia-Sunni fault line. Like Beeman, however, Cole deems the biggest challenge facing the United States in the Middle East to be "Islam Anxiety" among Americans, which has generated "America Anxiety" among the world's Muslims, a central theme of his remarkable, long-running blog *Informed Comment* (http://www.juancole.com/).

Shifting from the Middle East to the global arena, readers will encounter a vast historical literature on containment and the Cold War. The best and most readable overview of the Soviet-American confrontation remains Walter LaFeber, *America, Russia, and the Cold War, 1945-2006* (McGraw Hill, 2008), now in its tenth edition, which carries the story into the Putin era. In *Strategies of Containment: A Critical Appraisal of American National Security Policy during the Cold War* (Oxford University

Press, 1993), John Lewis Gaddis analyzes the evolution and oscillation of U.S. strategic doctrine from the Truman through the Reagan administrations, an ambitious undertaking that has shaped my own thinking about the post-1989 era. For a rousing account of the impact of McCarthyism on American popular culture, see Richard M. Fried, *The Russians Are Coming! The Russians Are Coming! Pageantry and Patriotism in Cold War America* (Oxford University Press, 1998).

Many excellent books incorporating the Soviet side of the story have recently appeared. Vladislav Zubok's *A Failed Empire: The Soviet Union in the Cold War from Stalin to Gorbachev* (University of North Carolina Press, 2007) makes superb use of Kremlin archives to confirm what George Kennan, writing as "Mr. X," asserted as early as 1947—Soviet expansionism was as much the product of traditional Russian empire-building as revolutionary Marxism-Leninism. Yevgeny Primakov, one of the Kremlin's most experienced Middle East hands, provides an inside account of the Soviet Union's dealings with radical regimes from Cairo to Baghdad and with nationalist groups like the PLO in *Russia and the Arabs* (Perseus Books, 2007). *The Global Cold War: Third World Interventions and the Making of Our Times* (Cambridge University Press, 2005), Odd Arne Westad's multiarchival masterwork, confirms that Soviet and American meddling in Asia, Africa, the Middle East, and Latin America destabilized the southern half of the globe and paved the way for Muslim extremists like the Taliban in Afghanistan. Melvyn Leffler's *For the Soul of Mankind: The United States, the Soviet Union, and the Cold War* (Hill and Wang, 2007) shows how ideology and geopolitics straitjacketed American and Russian policy makers in the Middle East and elsewhere and why transformational leadership on both sides proved essential for a peaceful resolution of the conflict.

Although I have cited most of the key scholarship on U.S. foreign policy in the Middle East since 1989 in the endnotes for *Us versus Them*, readers may want to have a look at several additional items. Bruce Jentleson's *With Friends Like These: Reagan, Bush, and Saddam* (Norton, 1994) examines the economic, ideological, and geopolitical roots of the First Gulf War and provides an exquisite road map for further research. Lawrence Freedman and Efraim Karsh provide a magnificent overview of George H. W. Bush's showdown with Saddam in *The Gulf Conflict 1990–1991: Diplomacy and War in the New World Order* (Princeton University Press, 1993). A pair of page-turners written by journalists—Mark Bowden's *Blackhawk Down: A Story of Modern War* (Atlantic, 1999) and Clayton Swisher's *The Truth about Camp David: The Untold Story about the Collapse of the Middle East Peace Process* (Nation Books, 2004)—shed much light on two of the low points from the Clinton era.

Say what you will about George W. Bush, he has almost singlehandedly made diplomatic history relevant again. James Mann's *The Rise of the Vulcans: A History of Bush's War Cabinet* (Viking, 2004) shows how a group of old Cold Warriors joined forces with an arrogant band of neoconservative action intellectuals to launch the global war on terror after 9/11. Two recent books—Terry Anderson's *Bush's Wars* (Oxford University Press, 2011) and Peter Hahn's *Missions Accomplished?: The United States and Iraq since World War I* (Oxford University Press, 2011)—reveal the price that Americans, especially the men and women who took part in Operation Iraqi Freedom, have paid for Dubya's war of choice. In *Night Draws Near: Iraq's People in the Shadow of America's War* (Henry Holt, 2004), the late Anthony Shadid shows that Iraqis paid an even higher price. *Iraq and the Lessons of Vietnam* (New Press, 2007), a superb collection of essays edited by Lloyd Gardner and Marilyn Young, suggests that the Bush administration learned nothing from the past. Seth Jones makes the same point in his personal account of recent U.S. military intervention in Central Asia, *In the Graveyard of Empires: America's War in Afghanistan* (Norton, 2010), where we learn that, at least in Kabul, history does seem to repeat itself with great regularity.

Writing good history requires access to archival sources, of course, and we are fortunate that with each passing year the documentary record of recent U.S. diplomacy in the Muslim world becomes richer. The voluminous national security files at the Nixon, Ford, and Carter presidential libraries are essential for tracing the evolution of containment in the Middle East during the 1970s. The steady declassification of materials from the Reagan era—particularly NSC documents on Iran, Iraq, Israel, Lebanon, and Libya—makes it possible to track the emerging shift from the Red Threat to the Green Threat during the 1980s while gazing out at the high chaparral surrounding my candidate for the most scenically located presidential library. The pace of declassification from the George H. W. Bush and Clinton years has been much slower, but many documentary gems are available online. Currently, the only archival records from the George W. Bush and Obama administrations are to be found on the Wikileaks website, which contains thousands of State Department cables from almost every Middle Eastern capital.

Rather than making a trip to the archives, however, readers seeking a more visceral glimpse of America's encounter with radical Islam should place three books on their wish list at Amazon.com. Item number one should be Kai Bird's *The Good Spy: The Life and Death of Robert Ames* (Crown, 2014), a tragic tale of the CIA's leading expert on the Middle East, an Arabic-speaking Philadelphian who fell in love with the Muslim world only to be killed by the Hezbollah truck bomb that destroyed the U.S. embassy in Beirut, Lebanon, in April 1983. Second on the list should be Kevin Powers's *The Yellow Birds* (Little, Brown, 2012), a short but powerful novel set squarely in Iraq's heart of darkness circa 2004, where three American GI's learn an essential truth often attributed to the Greek philosopher Plato: "Only the dead have seen the end of war." The final book should be Anand Gopal's *No Good Men among the Living: America, the Taliban, and the War through Afghan Eyes* (Metropolitan Books, 2014), which shows why the United States remains so unpopular today throughout much of the Middle East and Central Asia. After more than thirty years of nonstop fighting against the Red Army, Muslim rivals, and Uncle Sam, the Afghan peasants whom Gopal interviewed placed democracy near the bottom of their list of goals. At the top was merely to survive.

Index

107–9, 113, 128; and Hamas, 109, 110,
169; and Hezbollah, 48, 65, 109, 110;
and Iran-Contra Affair, 48–49, 65;
and Iran-Iraq War, 61, 64, 65, 66, 67;
and Islamic Revolution (1979), 7,
10, 16, 32–33, 36–39, 41, 44, 221, 235;
as New Comintern, 110; and Nixon
Doctrine, 28–29, 31–32; and Obama
administration, 174, 175, 180, 188,
191–94, 210, 232; and overthrow of
Mossadegh, 24–25; and radical Islam,
23, 42, 62, 64, 65, 66, 86, 87, 89, 98, 120,
123, 141, 190, 194, 222; Red Threat in,
20, 22; and Shia Muslims, 10, 86, 166,
194, 294; White Revolution in, 26–28;
and WMD, 110, 111, 132, 160, 186, 191,
211, 232, 236, 238–39, 244.
See also Khomeini, Ayatollah
Ruhollah; Pahlavi, Shah Reza
Mohammed; Persia
Iran-Contra Affair, 48–49; and Saddam
Hussein, 65, 68
Irangate. *See* Iran-Contra Affair
Iran-Iraq War, 48, 61, 64, 65, 66, 67
Iran Regional Presence Office
in Dubai, 193
Iraq, 9, 12, 16, 28, 46, 55, 87, 121, 132, 184,
208, 220, 245, 295–96; and Axis of
Evil, 152; and Clinton administration,
112–13, 258 (n. 62); and Dual
Containment, 92, 107, 108–9, 128; and
George H. W. Bush administration,
64–69; and George W. Bush
administration, 12, 129–31, 135, 137,
138–40, 141, 145, 146, 148, 155–71, 172,
182, 222, 235; and Hillary Clinton,
236; and invasion of Kuwait, 11, 54,
69–78, 79, 81, 90; and Iran-Iraq War,
48, 61, 64, 65, 66, 67; and ISIS, 10, 13,
211, 232–33, 234, 241, 243; and Obama
administration, 13, 173, 174, 177,
178, 170–81, 183, 210, 213, 230; oil of,
157–59; and Operation Dark Winter,

141; and Osirak reactor, 45, 191; and
radical Islam, 143, 146, 150, 151, 170,
172, 195, 224; and Shia Muslims, 10,
86; and Soviet Union, 32, 45; and U.S.
Occupation, 163–68, 169, 201, 294;
and WMD, 45, 66–67, 70, 71, 112, 113,
128, 129, 140, 145, 148, 152, 155, 158, 159,
160, 161, 162, 163, 168, 172
Iraq Liberation Act, 112
Irony of American History, The
(Niebuhr), 229, 240, 241
ISIL. *See* Islamic State in Iraq and Syria
Islam, 17, 23, 293; American attitudes
toward, 5–6; and Cold War, 9–11; rise
of, 7–8. *See also* radical Islam; Shia
Muslims; Sunni Muslims
Islamic Fundamentalism.
See radical Islam
Islamic Jihad, 152; in Egypt, 120, 146;
in Palestine, 47, 87
Islamic Salvation Front (Algeria), 87
Islamic State in Iraq and Syria (ISIS), 10,
13, 211, 229, 232–33, 234, 237, 238, 239,
241, 243, 244, 294; map of, 3
Islamofascism, 89, 146, 235.
See also Fascism
Islamophobia, 13, 121, 212–13, 217,
223–28, 231, 237, 241, 244; and film,
220; and popular fiction, 225; and
talk radio, 212, 224, 227, 228, 234; and
television, 224–25; and video games,
225–26
Ismail (Shah of Persia), 8
Israel, 16, 42, 56, 66, 95, 122, 139, 165, 195,
221, 238; and Al-Qaeda, 125, 130, 144;
and Camp David Summit (2000),
115–18; and Carter administration,
34–35; and Clinton administration,
104–6, 113–15, 120–21, 128; and
George H. W. Bush administration,
61–64, 78–83, 88–89; and George
W. Bush administration, 130, 138,
162, 172; and Hamas, 85, 103–4, 120,